STATIONS
AND
CALLINGS

STATIONS
AND
CALLINGS

MAKING IT THROUGH THE SCHOOL SYSTEM

John Porter   Marion Porter   Bernard R. Blishen
with
Maria Barrados Sid Gilbert Hugh A. McRoberts Susan Russell

Ⓝ METHUEN

Toronto   New York   London   Sydney   Auckland

Canadian Cataloguing in Publication Data

Porter, John, 1921-1979.
  Stations and callings

Bibliography: p.
Includes index.
ISBN 0-458-95300-8 (bound).—ISBN 0-458-95270-2
(pbk.)

1. Student aspirations—Ontario.   2. Students—
Ontario—Socioeconomic status.   3. Motivation in
education.   4. Educational surveys—Ontario.
5. Education—Ontario.   I. Porter, Marion R., 1922-
II. Blishen, Bernard R., 1919-   III. Title.

LA418.06P67   370.19′34′09713   C82-094066-6

This book has been published with the help of a grant
from the Social Science Federation of Canada, using
funds provided by the Social Sciences and Humanities
Research Council of Canada.

Printed and bound in Canada

1 2 3 4 5   82   87 86 85 84 83

To the Memory of John Porter

Contents

Preface, xi

1/Equality and Educational Opportunity, 1

The Idea of Equality, 1/Equality of Condition and
Equality of Opportunity, 4/Education as a Means to
Equality of Opportunity, 6

2/Equality in Upper Canada and Ontario, 12

The Ontario Value System, 21

3/Theoretical Framework and Model-Building, 25

Some Guidelines from General Sociological Theory,
25/Towards a Model for the Analysis of Educational
Aspirations, 28/The Variable Sets, 29/Decomposing
the Variable Sets, 33

4/The Ontario Survey, 39

The Research Design, 39/The Students'
Questionnaire, 42/Operationalizing the Variables,
42/The Parental Interview Schedule, 50

5/The Making of Educational Aspirations, 54

Sex Differences, 55/Aspirations, Sex and Class
Structure, 57/Mental Ability and Aspirations,
61/Aspirations in Urban and Rural Settings,
64/Religion and Educational Aspirations, 69/The
Children of Immigrants, 79/Ethnic Origin,
82/Number of Children and Birth Order, 84/School-
Related Variables, 84/School Programs, 84/School
Performance, 87/Self-Concept of Ability and
Aspirations, 88/Cultural Enrichment and Parental
Education, 88

6/Tinker Tailor . . . Teacher, Typist, 94

Two Dimensions of Occupational Ambition,
95/Educational and Occupational Ambitions,
99/High Hopes and Low Expectations,
100/Ambition and Social Class, 104

7/Self-Concept of Ability, 116

Self-Concept and Learning, 118/Self-Concept and
Aspirations, 121

8/The Influence of Others on Educational Plans and
    Aspirations, 137

Who Influences the Student? 137/Social Class
Influence, 138/Degree of Influence,
142/Encouragement and Assistance from the
Family, 149/Parental Hopes and Student
Aspirations, 153/Quality of Family Life: Effects on
Student Aspirations, 154/Parental Background and
Mother's Educational Aspirations for Her Child, 154

9/School Performance, 156

Sex and School Performance, 162/Mental Ability
and School Performance, 163/Background
Characteristics and School Performance,
167/Attitudinal Variables, 176/Parents and School
Performance, 178

10/Programs, 182

Program Streaming in Ontario, 182/Reorganized
Program, 183/Who's Where, 185/Sex, 187/Age,
189/Mental Ability, 189/Family Background,
190/Getting Into High School, 195/The Sources of
Guidance, 198/The Process of Program Selection,
200

11/Sex, 210

The Development of Educational Aspirations:
Gender-Related Factors, 211/Mother's Occupation
and the Effect of a Working Mother, 216/Mother's
Level of Education, 218/Family Size, 219/Parental
Educational Aspirations, 220/Parental Attitude
Towards the Role of Women, 223/Individual

Factors, 224/Self-Concept of Ability, 225/Attitude to
Schoolwork and School Performance, 227/Attitude
Towards the Adult Female Role, 228

12/The Deviant Cases, 236

Structural Proximity to the Middle Class: The
Upper-Lowers, 240/The "Sunken" Middle Class,
242/The "Skidding" Father, 243/The Working
Lower-Class Mother, 244/The Better-Educated
Lower-Class Parent, 246/The More Affluent Lower
Class, 248/Family Friends, 249/Family Cultural
Activities, 253/Membership in Voluntary
Organizations, 253/The Lower-Class Student and
High Achievement, 254

13/The Franco-Ontarians, 258

Profile of the Franco-Ontarian Students,
260/Educational Aspirations by Social Class,
267/Francophone and Anglophone Aspirations:
Other Studies, 267/Educational Attainment of
Anglophone and Francophone Students, 270

14/The Follow-up of Grade 8 and Grade 12 Students, 274

The Grade 8 Student Cohort, 275/The Grade 12
Follow-up Study, 285

15/The Formation of Aspirations: A Multivariate Analysis, 292

Defining the Variables, 294/Ordering the Variables,
294/Background Exogenous Variables,
296/Intervening (Endogenous) Variables,
296/Estimating the Effects: The Basic Model,
297/The Basic Model: A Comparison of Grades,
300/The Grade 8 Model, 307

16/Inequality of Opportunity, 311

Future Action, 315/Further Research, 318

Bibliography, 321

Index, 327

In those establishments nearly nine thousand students and pupils receive mental training of that kind most befitting their respective stations and prospective callings.

—S.P. Day, a visitor from England to Upper Canada, 1863 (quoted in J.G. Hodgins, *Documentary History of Education in Upper Canada*, Vol. XVIII, p. 100).

Preface

In the late 1960s, when this study was conceived, there was in the Western world great enthusiasm for education and for the expansion of educational opportunity. Educational expenditures were seen as investments in human capital that would lead to increased economic productivity and, hence, economic growth. It was argued that the difference in per capita income between the United States and Canada was caused by the difference in educational attainment levels in the two countries.[1] At the same time those who believed in a more just society argued that equality of educational opportunity would permit children, whatever their social origin, to compete for the rewards of the society. In the United States this concern led to the massive study *Equality of Educational Opportunity*[2] commissioned under the Civil Rights Act of 1964 and headed by James Coleman. Also, many studies were conducted, particularly at the University of Wisconsin, to try to determine the factors that were associated with young people's aspirations and attainments.[3]

In Canada, in general, and in Ontario, in particular, educational policy went beyond equality of opportunity based on the meritocratic principle which could imply tough competition based on high levels of academic achievement. The goal was universal accessibility to assure that post-secondary education would be available for all who wanted it, provided they could meet minimum standards.[4]

Although this latter principle seems eminently fair, studies have shown that not all who could benefit from post-secondary education want it, and the desire for it is not randomly distributed through the population, but is associated with such factors as social class, ethnicity and sex. This has three undesirable consequences; firstly, the individual who does not realize his or her potential faces the possibility that the opportunity for a satisfying life, both in material and intellectual terms, will be restricted. Secondly, the society cannot make use of all the human resources that exist in the sectors that for one reason or another lack ambition. And thirdly, since higher education is a resource heavily subsidized by governments, i.e., by all tax payers, it is unfair that some sectors should benefit disproportionately from it. It becomes important, then, to understand the process of aspiration formation and to analyse the factors that contribute to it.

The first major study in Canada was initiated in 1965 with the co-operation of the Federal Department of Labour and the provincial departments of education. It resulted in 1972 in Raymond Breton's report, *Social and Academic Factors in the Career Decisions of Canadian Youth.*[5] This was a very ambitious Canada-wide study in which 145,817 students and 7,884 teachers in all ten provinces participated.

The survey of the educational aspirations of approximately 9,000 Ontario students and 3,000 of their parents on which this report is based was initiated by Bernard Blishen and the late John Porter in the fall of 1970 with the financial support of the Canada Council. A preliminary analysis of the data was published as *Does Money Matter?* by the Institute of Behavioural Research at York University in 1973, and a revised edition was published in the Canadian Library series in 1979.[6] Two follow-up studies were conducted of Grade 12 students in 1973 and Grade 8 students in 1976 to find out whether, in fact, they were able to have the post-secondary future that in 1971 they said they wanted to have.

In Quebec a similar study was conducted by Pierre Belanger and Guy Rocher in 1972.[7] Their survey included 6,204 students who attended French-language schools and 2,568 who attended English-language schools. A major interest of their study was to compare the aspirations of Francophone and Anglophone students in Quebec and in Ontario.

Ten years later the enthusiasm for education has waned. Education is no longer seen as a stimulus to economic growth and to a just society. In fact, many think that the enthusiasm of the sixties was misguided. A crisis in education has arisen as a result of a number of factors, including inflation, rapidly increasing costs for education, unemployment and lack of opportunity for young people and declining enrolments. In addition, there is a growing belief that many young people are "over-educated" in terms of the jobs that they get. As R.W.B. Jackson in his report *Implications of Declining Enrolments for the Schools of Ontario* put it, "Most would do jobs as well, or as poorly, with little more or less formal education." The consequence has been that "education is and has been throughout the seventies facing increasing competition from other areas such as health."[8]

So, along with the problems of a sluggish economy and budget deficits there is a loss of faith in the ability of education to solve society's problems, competing demands from other sectors for funds, and rising education costs caused in part by the high proportion of older faculty members who were recruited during the great expansion of the sixties. The consequence has been that governments, in particular the government of Ontario, have sought to constrain educational costs by under-funding the universities; for several years operating funds have been increased at less than the inflation rate. Among the ten provinces, in terms of operating income per full-time student,

Ontario ranked eighth in 1978-79, leading the Ontario Council on University Affairs to warn that the system stood at "the brink of serious trouble."[9] The Committee on the Future Role of Universities in Ontario, in its report issued in August 1981, calls on the Ontario government either to give its universities enough money to survive as first-class institutions of learning and research or to close down some of the institutions and to restrict the programs in others.[10] The Committee's concern is quality of education, arguing that continuous under-funding would result in mediocre institutions and that, rather than having that happen, it would be better to concentrate the resources and emphasize quality rather than quantity.

The concern of this study is accessibility. Its future depends very much on the fate of the universities. Reducing the number of universities would mean greater travel and living expenses for students forced to attend schools farther from home. Unless government student aid were increased, many students would be prevented for fincancial reasons from attending. On the other hand, if neither of the Committee's recommendations is implemented tuition fees would have to increase drastically, and again unless student aid were increased concomitantly needy students would be barred.

The Ontario Student Assistance Plan (OSAP) is one of the more enlightened ones in Canada with, in 1981, the first portion of student assistance based on need forming a non-repayable grant. However, it is necessary to be aware of events south of the border since, so often in educational matters, policies in Canada have followed those in the United States, though usually with a time lag. The Reagan administration has made the financial aid program for students a prime target for budget cuts, for philosophical reasons as well as financial ones, because as one official stated, "We believe it is the primary responsibility of students and parents to pay for post-secondary education expenses." Cuts are planned in both the loan and grant program with, according to the *New York Times*, most of the cuts to be borne by students at public colleges rather than the expensive private institutions.[11]

We are convinced that accessibility is still an important goal since, in this credentialled society, certificates are necessary to achieve occupational status, and because no one should be denied the opportunity to fulfill his or her potential because of his or her social class background. For this reason the central problem examined in the following pages, which concerns the social and cultural milieux in which educational aspirations and expectations are limited, is important.

Although there have been changes in both the occupational world and the educational world in the ten years since this survey was undertaken, the underlying social structure that conditions the outcomes of schooling has changed little. The educational changes have been in the direction of providing more freedom and flexibility for students but, we would argue, have not attacked the problems that we address. For example, the change which had begun at the time of our survey from four- and five-year programs to credits in general and advanced courses is now complete; but, as we argue in the text, it is still necessary to take courses at the advanced level as a prerequisite for Grade 13 courses. And the semester system which has been introduced in some schools may make the learning experience more satisfying for some students, but it is unlikely to affect very much students' attitudes to school and to further schooling.

We think, then, that the analysis contained in the following chapters should help us to understand the difficulties involved in formulating appropriate policies. In the first two chapters we review the historical development of the idea of equality and the distinction between equality of condition and equality of opportunity—and the manner in which Upper Canada and Ontario have responded to these ideas. In Chapters 3 and 4 we provide a theoretical framework for our subsequent analysis and a description of the ways in which the variables were operationalized. Chapter 5 contains some of our most important findings. Through cross-tabular analysis we show how many of the variables discussed in Chapter 3 affect the level of educational aspirations of Ontario high school students. We demonstrate that there is a great variation in levels of educational aspiration, and that many of our variables combine to increase or decrease these levels. Chapter 6 shows the importance of a range of social and psychological variables in the formation of occupational expectations. In each of Chapters 7 to 11 one of the variables which contributes to the variation in educational aspirations and occupational expectations is examined. These include self-concept of ability, the influence of significant others, school performance, school programs and sex. Chapter 12 contains an analysis of deviant cases—students whose aspirations differed from those of other students in the same social class. Not all upper-middle-class students aspired to go to university; nor did all working-class students not have these aspirations. In this chapter we analyse the reasons for this deviant pattern. Chapter 13 is a brief analysis of French-speaking students in Ontario. The small number of these students made a more detailed analysis impossible. Chapter 14 summarizes the result of the two follow-up studies: the one of the Grade 8 students who were contacted five years after the 1971 survey; the other of the Grade 12 students who were contacted one year after the original survey. The analysis of the Grade 8 cohort shows the effect of some of our important variables on the realization of educational goals. The analysis of the Grade 12 cohort indicates the extent to which the educational hopes of these students were realized and the factors associated with entry into the labour market.

Using path analytic techniques, Chapter 15 sorts out the relative effects of the most important variables—social class, mental ability, school program, school performance, the influence of significant others and self-concept of ability—in determining the level of educational aspirations when they are all considered together. In the final chapter we draw some conclusions from the study and make some suggestions for future research and for policy.

The Survey of Ontario Students' Aspirations (SOSA) could not have been conducted without the co-operation of a large number of people and the combination of a variety of skills. Douglas Dale of the Mathematics Department of Carleton University designed the sample. The administration of the questionnaires and the mental ability tests in the sampled schools across the province, and the interviews with parents, were conducted by the Survey Research Centre of the Institute for Behavioural Research at York University. The Centre also did the coding and punching of data cards.

Further data processing, file building and transformations were done with the co-operation of the Computing Centre of Carleton University. In this difficult and technical task, W.J. Bradley, Sidney Gilbert and Hugh McRoberts were indispensable. Maria Barrados and Susan Russell also assisted in this stage of the SOSA project.

The study was undertaken with a grant from the Canada Council. This book has been published with the help of a grant from the Social Science Federation of Canada, using funds provided by the Social Sciences and Humanities Research Council of Canada. We are pleased to acknowledge this support.

Notes

1. Economic Council of Canada, *First Annual Review* (Ottawa: Queen's Printer, September 1964), p.164.
2. James S. Coleman, *et al.*, *Equality of Educational Opportunity* (Washington: U.S. Government Printing Office, 1966).
3. The chief investigater of the Wisconsin studies has been William H. Sewell. Many of his publications are listed in the bibliography.
4. For an extensive discussion of this issue see M.R. Porter, J. Porter and B.R. Blishen, *Does Money Matter?* (Toronto: Macmillan, 1979, Carleton Library No. 110), pp.3-7.
5. Raymond Breton, *Social and Academic Factors in the Career Decisions of Canadian Youth* (Ottawa: Queen's Printer, 1972).
6. Porter, Porter and Blishen, *op. cit.*
7. Aspirations Scolaires et Orientations Professionelles des Etudiantes (ASOPE) *Analyse descriptive des données de la première cueillette* (Faculté des sciences d'education, Université de Laval, Département de sociologie, Université de Montréal, 1976).
8. R.W.B. Jackson, *Implications of Declining Enrolments for the Schools of Ontario* (Ministry of Education, Ontario, 1978).
9. Ontario Council of University Affairs, *Seventh Annual Report*, 1980-81, published by OCUA, 700 Bay St., Toronto, Ontario, M5G 1Z6.
10. *Report of the Committee on the Future Role of the Universities in Ontario* (Ministry of Colleges and Universities, Ontario, 1981).
11. *New York Times*, August 23, 1981. The reason for the fact that public colleges bear the brunt of the cuts is that financial assistance is related to the costs so that more assistance is available for students at expensive institutions.

1
Equality and Educational Opportunity

This study had its origins in the issues of equality that emerged in the 1960s. Although it is limited to the examination of equality in education in one Canadian province, Ontario, we wish to frame it within the wider context of the core values of North American and Western democracy. We propose briefly to review the history of the idea of equality and its contrary, inequality, and then to examine their application to education. We then turn in Chapter 2 to Ontario and seek to discover the extent to which ideas of equality have informed the development of educational policy since Egerton Ryerson's innovations in the 1840s when he became Assistant and later Chief Superintendent of Schools for Upper Canada. By taking this route into a major sociological report we hope to provide it with both an ethical and historical perspective.

The Idea of Equality

Although inequality rather than equality has been throughout history characteristic of human societies, the contrary view, that men are equal, has also been expressed in these unequal social structures. Aristotle identified justice with equality and distinguished between arithmetic or numerical equality—by which he meant that all should be treated alike—and proportionate equality— the share of what is good that a person has should be proportional to his merits.[1] But his views about equality applied only to free men. In his view, "the male is by nature superior, and the female inferior; and the one rules and the other is ruled." This principle (of superiority and inferiority) extends to all mankind, so that "it is clear then, that some men are by nature free, and others slaves, and that for these latter slavery is both expedient and right."[2]

Christianity, too, by emphasizing the Fatherhood of God, asserted the brotherhood of man. The position of women has been ambiguous. Men, at least, were seen as equal in the eyes of God and equally eligible for redemption.[3]

It was the development of liberalism in the eighteenth century that introduced the idea of equality to the modern world. The first political statement that all are equal is in the Declaration of Independence, a document that was deeply influenced by Locke, Rousseau and other liberal writers of the Enlightenment. It was followed within a few years by a more explicit statement in the Declaration of the Rights of Man and the Citizen adopted in 1789 by the Constituent Assembly in Paris: "The law is an expression of the will of the community and all being equal in its sight are equally eligible to all honours, places and employments according to their different abilities, without any other distinction than that created by their virtues and talents."[4]

The idea of equality was basic to the liberal mind. As Locke said, "Men being as has been said, by nature all free, equal and independent, no one can be put out of this estate and subjected to the political power of another without his own consent."[5]

But for the liberal, even more basic, as the name implies, was liberty. In the field of economics this logic of "possessive individualism" led to the doctrine of *laissez-faire*.[6] As Adam Smith expressed it, "Every man as long as he does not violate the laws of justice, is left perfectly free to pursue his own interest in his own way, and to bring both his industry and capital into competition with those of any other man, or order of men."[7]

Liberty seems to have been a more powerful drive, at least in the Western democratic tradition, than equality, but Tocqueville saw the development from political liberty to equality as "an irresistible revolution which has advanced for centuries in spite of every obstacle."[8] As an aristocrat he was not in sympathy with it, but since he regarded it as inevitable he thought it necessary to learn how to adapt to conditions of equality. That is why he made his famous journey to the United States in 1831–32 to see what the future would be like.

> The gradual development of equality of conditions is therefore a Providential fact, and it has all the chief characteristics of such a fact: it is universal, it is durable, it constantly eludes all human interference, and all events as well as all men to contribute to its progress. . . . Can it be believed that the democracy which has overthrown the feudal system and vanquished kings will retreat before the tradesmen and the capitalists?[9]

In the century and a half since Tocqueville wrote, we can see the working out of his prediction in the Western democracies: with classical bourgeois liberalism, developed in the United States after the American Revolution; in France after the revolution of 1830; and in Britain after the Reform Bill of 1832. Men were free and equal in the sense that they had equal civil rights, all were equal before the law, and although a property qualification kept the franchise from the working class, the first steps had been taken in the development of equal political rights. Relentless pressure caused the barriers to political participation to fall by the end of the nineteenth century. It was not until after the great struggles of the suffragettes and the spasms of World War I that the vote was extended to women. In Canada universal suffrage was not established until 1920. Playing political games with the franchise before that time suggests that political rights were longer in taking root in Canada.[10]

Wretched conditions for the masses that resulted from the untrammelled reign of the marketplace in the more advanced capitalist democracies led eventually to the idea of equality of social rights. The great contrast between the wealth and luxury of some and the misery of others caused socialists to seek an elimination of the capitalist system as the source of inequality and injustice. In its most extreme and millennial form, Marxist socialism foresaw that an epoch of freedom, dignity and equality would emerge from the ruins of the capitalist order. It was to constitute for a major segment of the world a counterpart to the liberalism of the Western democracies.

In the Western democratic capitalist societies the "welfare state," especially after World War II, attempted to extend equality to social and economic affairs. It was gradually being recognized that everyone has an equal right to nourishment, housing, health care and education. In the Universal Declaration of Human Rights adopted by the General Assembly of the United Nations in 1948 there is an unequivocal statement of these rights:

> Everyone has the right to a standard of living adequate for the health and well-being of himself and his family, including food, clothing, housing and medical care . . .

> Everyone has the right to education. Education shall be free at least in the elementary and fundamental stages. Elementary education shall be compulsory. Technical and professional education shall be made generally available and higher education shall be made equally accessible to all on the basis of merit.[11]

This brief discussion of the concept of equality, from civil rights equality before the law, to political rights equality of the ballot box, to social rights equality of social and economic conditions, might suggest that the war against inequality, while long, is being won, that the battles for civil, political and social rights, apart from a few skirmishes, are over. This, of course, is far from the case. Principles do not necessarily lead to practice. And even in the Western democracies the principle of equality of social and economic conditions is far from being widely accepted. Indeed, in the seventies the attacks on the welfare state indicate that even the modest commitment to a more equal distribution that it represents is bitterly resented by much of the more privileged sector of the society. Furthermore, new battles are continually fought as excluded groups and individuals make their claims for the rights that have been won by others. We can see the working out still of Tocqueville's prediction with the demands for equality, and indeed preferential treatment, of women, blacks, native peoples and other deprived groups to compensate for past injustices.

Equality of Condition and Equality of Opportunity

In spite of all the words poured out over the centuries on the subject, confusion still exists about what equality means. This is not surprising since it is a very complex principle. Consider again the distinction made by Aristotle between numerical equality and equality proportionate to desert. Sometimes in the interests of fairness we invoke one principle of equality, sometimes the other; sometimes there are great arguments about which is more fair.

The principle of numerical equality means that all are the same and should be treated in the same way. The principle of equality proportionate to desert means that individuals are different and their treatment should be determined by their particular qualities.

The principle of numerical equality calls for all workers to be paid at the same rate, while equality proportionate to desert justifies differential rates of pay according to the quality of work done, or the years of service (seniority), or the amount of education required for the job (certification). Collective bargaining agreements requiring that all with the same number of years of experience or the same level of accreditation should be paid the same without regard to the quality of their work are perhaps a combination of the two principles.

It is not only in considering rewards that these principles must be weighed. Should everyone who commits the same traffic offence pay the same fine, even though the penalty is much more severe for the poor person than the rich one? Or should there be differential fines based on ability to pay? And should everyone pay the same taxes, as they do in the case of the sales tax, or should taxation be proportionate to one's ability to pay?

People are treated equally in some things and unequally in others. In the polling booth and, theoretically at least, in the courts, for example, all are considered equal. Most strikingly, people are treated unequally in the amount of income they receive for the work they do, and this in turn determines the kind of houses they live in, the food they eat, the vacations they take, the clothes they wear. It is not, however, only with respect to financial rewards that people are treated differently. Not everyone receives the same amount of health care quite apart from ability to pay for it. Some wear glasses, some do not. Some enter hospitals, some do not. Injustice can arise, as Aristotle pointed out, from unequals being treated equally as well as from equals being treated unequally.

Fairness demands that there be relevant grounds for differentiation. Discrimination that is not founded on relevant differences is unjust. The question then is, What are relevant grounds for differentiation? Clearly in the case of health care it is not difficult to decide that unhealthy people should receive more than healthy people. But in the case of financial rewards for work done it is more difficult. Differential treatment has, in the past, been justified by the believed-in natural superiority and inferiority of particular groups of people. Lords were regarded as superior to peasants, men to women, and whites to blacks, and it followed logically that those who were seen as superior deserved greater rewards than those who were inferior.

The belief in the innate superiority of some groups over others is no longer acceptable. How then do we fairly distribute limited resources? It is still widely accepted that rewards should be based on merit, but that merit is unrelated to social class background, ethnicity or sex.

If there are differential rewards based on merit, then a commitment to equality necessitates a society in which each person has the opportunity to develop his talents and to strive for unequal rewards. Thus a policy of equality of opportunity can be considered to serve the principle of equality, but this will not result in a more equal society. Even if all started out the same—and, of course, the starting places are very different depending on where and to whom one is born—they would end up in different places. Many writers have pointed out that there could be true equality of opportunity only if children were taken away from their parents at birth and brought up in a common setting. Even if true equality of opportunity were possible it is by no means certain that the resulting society would be seen as a fairer or more pleasant place to live. Michael Young fantasizes in *The Rise of the Meritocracy* that a society in which advancement was based rigidly and solely on merit would result in an upper class of brilliant masters ruling over an under class of stupid drones. It is for this reason that many contemporary writers have attacked the idea of equality of opportunity and called for greater equality of condition.[12]

Trade-offs are clearly necessary between the two principles. The communist world started out with the principle "from each according to his ability, to each according to his need" with a commitment to equality of condition. More and more they have found it necessary to invoke the principle of equality of opportunity. Perhaps because of the priority that liberty has had over equality in the liberal mind, equality has been taken to mean equality of opportunity in the Western capitalist world, with the emphasis on the freedom of men to make themselves as unequal as they can manage. However, without greater equality of condition, equality of opportunity is impossible. For example, how can there ever be any real equality of opportunity when some children live crowded in squalid slums with no room of their own, no books, music or discussion in the home, while others have highly paid, well-educated parents and live in comfortable, spacious houses? As Richard Titmuss put it:

> We thus delude ourselves if we think we can equalize the social distribution of life chances by expanding education-opportunities while millions of children live in slums without baths, decent lavatories, leisure facilities, room to explore and the space to dream.[13]

Titmuss's remark brings to the fore the role that education has been expected to play in advancing equality, and also the confusion in people's minds that exists between the two principles: equality of condition and equality of opportunity.

Education has been seen as central to providing opportunity. Let us consider next the role of education and to what extent it might serve the principle of equality.

Education as a Means to Equality of Opportunity

Two basic arguments have always been advanced for expanding education. One is to develop the talents of the individual for his own benefit; the other, to produce the skills needed for the society. A statement of this view was made by the Commission on Post-Secondary Education in Ontario in 1972 in explaining the massive expansion of higher education in the 1960s:

> Higher education was praised as an ascending ladder of social and economic mobility; it was defended both as an avenue of personal self-fulfilment and as a way of enlarging society's knowledge of itself and of nature.[14]

Some writers argue that there are reasons other than the needs of the labour force and the provision of routes to the higher levels of the occupational structure for the extraordinary expansion of education during the last century. Charles Silberman, for example, argues that in the United States "the purpose of public education was to give the lower classes the habits of obedience and submission necessary for public peace, a docile labour force, and the protection of property."[15] As we shall see later, such arguments were also used in Ontario to justify the expenditure on public education in the nineteenth century.

There is no doubt some truth in this view. On the other hand, particularly since the Second World War, as implied in the Universal Declaration of Human Rights, education has been seen as the means by which the goal of equality of opportunity could be implemented. The Robbins Report in England and the Parent Commission in Quebec, for example, had as their terms of reference an examination of the educational systems in their respective jurisdictions in order to make recommendations about how equality of opportunity might be increased. Until recently the view generally held was that this objective would be achieved at the secondary level by having more and better equipped schools, better trained and paid teachers, smaller classes, and so on. James Coleman and his associates changed that view.

When their study *Equality of Educational Opportunity* was commissioned under the Civil Rights Act of 1964, the first task of the researchers was to determine what equality of opportunity meant. In doing so they defined five different types of educational inequality that might exist. Three were concerned with input, the amount of resources various communities put into schools, and two with the effect of schooling, that is, the amount that children learned.

Coleman has traced the evolution of the idea of equality of educational opportunity through four stages. The first was that all children must be exposed to the same curriculum in the same school—the ideal of the "common school" in the United States as contrasted to the dual school system that developed in England where the educational system was "designed to provide differentiated educational opportunity according to one's station in life."[16] However, with the expansion of secondary school education at the beginning of the century, it was felt to be inappropriate that all children should be subjected to the curriculum designed for college entrance when only a minority would go. And so the second stage evolved of the idea of equality of educational opportunity—that there should be a differentiated curriculum related to the different needs, capacities and interests of children and their different occupational futures. Later, of course, it could be seen that this differentiated curriculum was a source of inequality of opportunity because it trapped children into streams that cut off their options at an early age.

Coleman dates the third stage in the evolution of the idea of equality of educational opportunity from the United States Supreme Court decision of 1896, which upheld the contention of the southern states that separate schools could be equal. This, then, was a rejection of the idea of the common school with the assumption that what counted in equality of opportunity were equal resources, or inputs.

With the rejection of the 1896 decision in the Supreme Court decision of 1954, that there could not be equal opportunity with separate schools, the fourth stage began—that to have equality of opportunity the effects, what children in various school groups learn, must in some way be equal. However equal the facilities in schools were, if the schools were separate the *effects* of schooling would be different. And so there was a recognition that what counted in equality of educational opportunity was not the resources that were put into the school but the effects of the educational process. The two startling findings of the survey that Coleman directed were, first, that resources were not very different between schools and, second, that a difference in resources was not related to a difference in *effects* as measured by achievement scores. In fact he found what has now become widely known, that the average test scores of white and black students widened rather than diminished with more years of schooling, and that this was not significantly related to the resource inputs of the school.

The conclusions of the survey were shattering to many liberals who believed that all would be well if only enough money were spent on the schools. The reaction of some conservatives was to argue for abandoning the effort of making the school system do the job of equalizing opportunity. Coleman, however, argued that the shift in measurement of school effectiveness from inputs to outputs throws new responsibilities on the school to discover new methods to produce achievement, and to reduce achievement differences between groups and, to some extent, individuals. From having a passive role of providing education which it was the child's responsibility to master, it becomes the school's responsibility to create achievement.[17]

In any case, as we have seen, some inequalities have been regarded as acceptable as long as everyone has a chance to strive for the unequal rewards. The idea that the rewards are open to all also serves to legitimate the unequal distribution of rewards, since those who have more can feel that they are justified in their position because they have earned it through hard work or ability, and those who have less can feel that they deserve their fate because they have not worked hard enough. Equality of opportunity, particularly in education, creates social mobility and emphasizes meritocracy, which is supposed to bring the best to the top. It implies a tough competition for unequal rewards.

However we define and measure equality of educational opportunity, it still has as its goal making it possible for anyone, regardless of sex, race, ethnicity or social class background, to strive for the heights of the educational ladder, and from there, to aim for the high status, highly rewarded positions in the occupational world. Most writers, including many sociologists, accept the fact that some inequalities are essential because of society's need for hierarchical arrangements. Some have to give orders if jobs are to be done. Most also accept the fact that incentives are needed to induce people to undertake long years of training, or to work long hours, or to accept responsibility or to take risks. These incentives may be money, power, status, or a combination of the three, but in any case they result in inequalities. Whether the degree of unequal rewards that prevail in most industrial societies is necessary is a matter of dispute.

Increasingly, because of its consequences, the concept of equality of opportunity without moving towards equality of condition as a social goal has come under attack. "What is so generous," writes John H. Scharr, "about telling a man he can go as far as his talents will take him when his talents are meagre?"[18] He imagines a footrace of ten men in which three are forty years old, five are overweight, one has a weak ankle and the tenth is Roger Bannister, and asks whether it can be said that all have an equal opportunity.

In Canada Stephen Peitchinis expresses a typical, critical, current view of the meritocratic process. "The general subsidization of the academically gifted at the expense of the academically weak who are dispatched to the world of work at an early age to produce some of the subsidy," he writes, "is exploitative, discriminatory, and perpetuates a social bias in favour of the academic process."[19]

Sociologists diverge into roughly two opposing camps on the role of education in promoting equality. On the one side are those, following the initial study of K. Davis and W.E. Moore, influenced by Talcott Parsons and continuing in the research of the Wisconsin and Johns Hopkins sociologists, who see education as providing opportunity and generating social mobility.[20] They recognize the barriers that exist for children of culturally deprived backgrounds, but they see the system as one in which barriers can and should be overcome, and in which with the appropriate interventions there can be equality of opportunity through equality of educational opportunity.

On the other side are sociologists such as Pierre Bourdieu in France and Randall Collins in the United States who see the educational system as limiting opportunity, as maintaining rather than reducing inequalities, as perpetuating class relations.[21]

This class reproduction is the central thesis of two Marxist writers, Bowles and Gintis, in their *Schooling in Capitalist America*.[22] They see the educational process as a mirror image of the capitalist system of production, legitimated by what they call the technocratic-meritocratic ideology which holds that the task of education is to sort people out on the basis of their inherent ability and to give them a training commensurate with these abilities. They enter the work world at an appropriate level and progress upward according to the competence they demonstrate. Rewards are based on technical qualifications and merit, and since these are unequal, so is pay. Unequal rewards also exist because of the inducements believed necessary to encourage people to put up with education and take on responsibility.

Educational reformers generally have accepted the ideology because of its apparent support of equality of opportunity. However, sociologists in many countries have shown that meritocratic systems do not benefit the majority of working-class children because of the emphasis on early selection based on tests of intelligence and cognitive skills weighted in favour of middle- and upper-class children. This is so in part because the tests tested the kinds of things that middle-class children had an advantage in learning, but also because of attitudes and motivations, the dispositions to learning and other cultural elements that middle-class parents transmitted to their children.

Selection on the basis of tests which favour the middle-class child means that the middle-class child is more likely to find himself in a superior academic stream, providing an entry to higher learning and, finally, into positions of responsibility and control in the work world. As the student continues in the superior academic stream to the higher levels of the educational system, he is given more opportunity for creativity and independence. Those who leave at lower levels are more disciplined, have had less opportunity to be creative or to find personal fulfilment than those who continue, and are therefore more accommodative to the discipline expected of them at the lower levels of work. Schools and workplaces are similar in their ambiences, and so students are taught the appropriate patterns of personal behaviour which fit them into their job situations; drill, obedience, routine standardization and rewards for the right work characterize both, with the teacher as foreman and the principal as manager. Thus, as Bowles and Gintis argue, by a process of selective streaming, varying rates of retention and differential subjection to discipline, the educational system serves to reproduce from generation to generation the existing structure of inequality.

From this brief review of the historical development of the idea of equality and the contemporary discussion of it, we can see that the issues in all their complexities are still very much alive; that in the minds of leading writers the distinction between equality of condition and equality of opportunity has support in different philosophical traditions; and that the idea of meritocracy in education finds support by some, but is condemned by others for the injustices to which they feel it inevitably leads.

Notes

1. Aristotle, *Ethnica Nicomachea, Book V*, translated by W.D. Ross, in *Introduction to Aristotle*, Richard McKeon, ed. (New York: Modern Library, 1947).
2. Aristotle, *Politica*, translated by Benjamin Jowett (Oxford, 1916), Book I, ch. 5, pp.560–61.
3. Commenting on Christian ethics in *Marriage and Morals* (London, 1929), pp.52–53, Bertrand Russell wrote, "The Christian ethics inevitably, through the emphasis laid upon sexual virtue, did a great deal to degrade the position of women. Since the moralists were men, women appeared as the temptress." He quotes W.E.H. Lecky, *History of European Morals*, for the views of the early Christian Fathers about women: "Woman was represented as the door of hell, as the mother of all human ills. She should be ashamed at the very thought that she is a woman. . . . Women were even forbidden by a Provincial Council in the sixth century, on account of their impurity, to receive the Eucharist into their naked hands. Their essentially subordinate position was continually maintained."
4. *Declaration of Rights of Man and the Citizen*, reprinted in J. Salwyn Schapiro, *Liberalism: Its Meaning and History* (New York: Anvil, 1958), p.128.
5. John Locke, *Of Civil Government* (New York, 1942), reprinted in Schapiro, *op. cit.*, p.115.
6. For a discussion of the idea see C.B. Macpherson, *The Political Theory of Possessive Individualism: Hobbes to Locke* (Oxford, 1962).
7. Adam Smith, *An Inquiry into the Nature and Causes of the Wealth of Nations*, reprinted in Schapiro, *op. cit.*, p.112.
8. Alexis de Tocqueville, *Democracy in America*, R.D. Heffner, ed. (Mentor Books, 1956), p.29.

9. *Ibid.*, p.29.
10. R. MacGregor Dawson, *The Government of Canada* (Toronto: University of Toronto Press, 1948), pp.376-80.
11. *Universal Declaration of Human Rights* (United Nations) reprinted in Schapiro, *op. cit.*, p.139.
12. Michael Young, *The Rise of the Meritocracy* (Penguin Books, 1970).
13. Richard M. Titmuss, "Introduction" to R.H. Tawney, *Equality*, (London: Allan and Unwin, 1964), p.11.
14. *The Learning Society*, Report of the Commission on Post-Secondary Education in Ontario (Toronto, 1972), p.6.
15. Charles Silberman, *Crisis in the Classroom* (Random House, 1970), p.60.
16. James Coleman, "The Concept of Equality of Educational Opportunity," *Equal Educational Opportunity* (Harvard Educational Review, Winter 1968), p.18.
17. *Ibid.*, p.22.
18. John H. Scharr, "Equality of Opportunity and Beyond," in J.R. Pennock and J.W. Chapman, *Equality* (New York: Atherton Press, 1967), p.233.
19. Stephen G. Peitchinis, *Financing Post-Secondary Education in Canada.* A Report commissioned by the Council of Ministers of Education in Canada, 1970, p.324.
20. K. Davis and W.E. Moore, "Some Principles of Social Stratification," *American Sociological Review*, 10: 242-249, 1945. Parsons, Talcott, "The School as a Social System: Some of its Functions in American Society," *Harvard Educational Review*, Fall: 297-318, 1959. See also W.H. Sewell, A.O. Haller and M.A. Strauss, "Social Status and Educational and Occupational Aspirations," *American Sociological Review*, 22 (February) 82-92, 1957, and K.L. Alexander, J. Fennessey, and E.L. McDill and R.J. D'Amico, "School SES Influences—Composition or Context?" *Sociology of Education*, October 1979.
21. Pierre Bourdieu, "Cultural Reproduction and Social Reproduction," in A.H. Halsey and Jerome Karabel, eds., *Power and Ideology in Education* (Oxford: Oxford University Press, 1977). Randall Collins, *The Credential Society: An Historical Sociology of Education and Stratification* (New York: Academic Press, 1979).
22. Samuel Bowles and Herbert Gintis, *Schooling in Capitalist America* (New York: Basic Books, 1972).

2

Equality in Upper Canada and Ontario

How has Canada—and particularly Ontario, which is the location of our study—responded to these ideas of the Western liberal tradition? With few exceptions—C.B. Macpherson, for example[1]—Canada's philosophers have not contributed to the debate. In Canada there has been a "demonstration effect" in which ideas and social practices developed elsewhere have been put to use. There is scarcely an issue of social policy that does not take planners of public policy to the United States and Europe to find out what is going on. What is now established practice has, as we will see in the field of education, an interesting historical parallel.

The structure of inequality in Canada was examined extensively in an earlier work. With the development of the social sciences and the amassing of considerably more data since the publication of *The Vertical Mosaic,*[2] we find that very little has changed that would require a revision of its major findings with respect to income, ethnicity, education and immigration and the relationship of these to inequality. We have even had a poverty report, "real" or otherwise, to bury the myth that Canada is a country of the affluent middle class, a myth that was said to have been killed by the earlier work.[3]

Even though Ontario is one of the more affluent provinces with respect to economic resources, it does not follow that it leads the others with respect to equality. Inequalities in income depend basically on differential rewards for occupations, and can be offset by taxation and transfer payments which could have the effect of redistributing income. Although we tend to think of this as being the responsibility of the federal government, which imposes the progressive personal income tax, Allan M. Maslove[4] has shown in a survey of taxation in Canada in 1969 that only a little more than half of the taxation revenues were collected by the federal government. Somewhat more than one-third were collected by provincial governments, and 12 per cent by municipal governments.

Sales tax, the major source of revenue of the provincial government, can be regarded as unfair since everyone pays the same amount, regardless of his or her income. The $7 sales tax paid on a $100 coat in Ontario, for example, means something very different to a family with an average annual income of $36,695 (the average annual household income, according to the 1971 census, of families in Rockcliffe Village in the Ottawa region) and the family with an income of $6,637 (the average annual income of families in Lower Town, a neighbouring area to Rockcliffe).[5] The distribution of full income (before taxes but after transfer payments) in Ontario can be seen in Table 2.1. Two-fifths of all family units retained only one-fifth of total full income. The top 10 per cent received almost one-third. A study of taxation does not change the picture. Maslove draws this conclusion: "The extremely regressive nature of the tax system at the low end of the income scale and the lack of progressivity over the remainder is the predominant conclusion to emerge from this study." Furthermore, he states, "The most regressive incidence pattern over the lowest income levels is in Ontario."[6]

Income distributions are not the only measure of inequality of condition. There can also be inequalities in a wide range of resources, such as the provision of medical care, the kinds of houses people live in, and the amount of education they have. The latter, the prime focus of this volume, is demonstrated in Table 2.2 where the level of education in the adult population in Ontario and the United States is compared. In 1971, of the age group 45–64, which is the age group of parents of Ontario high school students, more than twice as many Americans as Canadians had university degrees.

In both countries the younger age group, 25–34, has a higher proportion than the older age group, 45–64, with university degrees, but the United States is still well ahead of Canada in educational attainment at the university level. And it is even further ahead in the proportions that have had four years of secondary school.

Evidently equality of condition does not exist in Ontario. What about equality of opportunity? To what extent does it exist? A reason for the survey about which we are reporting was to provide some answers to that question. It is interesting, however, to speculate to what extent equal opportunity has been a goal in Ontario, and how much the enormous expansion of educational facilities over the last one hundred years has been inspired by that idea. It would be surprising if equality of opportunity did not have a role since it has been so important in the United States, and since from the beginning of their histories there has been so much interaction between Ontario and the United States. Many argue that the United Empire Loyalists have given a conservative cast to the Canadian character since they rejected republicanism and fled the Revolution. However, it is interesting that it was they, accustomed as they were to an elected assembly, who demanded a representative legislature after their arrival. After the United Empire Loyalists many other Americans came in search of land, and many

Table 2.1
Distribution of Full Income*, 1969
Ontario

Full Income Class ($ per annum)	# of Family Units**	% of All Family Units	Cumulative % of All Family Units	Millions of Dollars in Full Income	As % of Total Full Income of All Classes	As Cumulative % of Total Full Income of All Classes
under $3,999	529,890	22.32	22.32	1,412	5.60	5.60
4,000-6,999	509,700	21.47	43.79	3,435	13.81	19.41
7,000-9,999	535,890	22.57	66.36	5,350	21.20	40.61
10,000-14,999	544,900	22.95	89.31	7,751	30.72	71.33
15,000 and over	253,510	10.68	100.00	7,283	28.86	100.00
Total	2,373,890	100.00		25,231	100.00	

*Full Income—measured before taxes but after transfer payments to persons. It includes non-monetary income components such as the rental value of owner-occupied dwellings, food and fuel produced on farms and imputed interest.

**Family Income—the number of families (a group of individuals sharing a common dwelling unit and related by blood, marriage or adopted); the number of unattached individuals—persons living by themselves or rooming in a household where they are not related to other household members.

Source: Allan M. Maslove, *The Pattern of Taxation in Canada* (Ottawa: Information Canada, 1973), Table 2.6, pp.26-27.

Canadians moved to the United States but maintained their links with Canada. So even before the day of mass communications American influences and ideas would have been felt in Canada.

The establishment of a system of free, compulsory, universal education is a prerequisite to any implementation of the idea of equality of opportunity. The development of education in Ontario followed fairly closely developments in the New England States.[7] The credit for this must go to Ontario's remarkable first superintendent of education, Egerton Ryerson.[8] Ryerson campaigned tirelessly for free, universal and compulsory education from the time of his appointment as Assistant Superintendent of Education in 1844 until his retirement in 1876. He became a friend of Horace Mann, the great Massachusetts educator, who has been called "an uncompromising egalitarian who never tired of insisting that the general diffusion rather than the liberal education of leaders should be the paramount concern in a republican society."[9] Ryerson was no republican and he never accepted Mann's views that education should be secular, but in other respects his views about education were very similar. In his massive report, which he produced in 1846 after investigating schools in Europe and the United States, an early example of the "demonstration effect," Ryerson urged that property should be taxed for the support of elementary schools, that teachers should be trained and that there should be a large measure of local management.[10] All his proposals now seem moderate and basic for any educational system, but at the time they aroused fierce opposition. There were those without children who objected to their tax money being spent on other people's children. Some argued that it was degrading to people to have free education provided for their children. Others protested that

Table 2.2
Minimum Years of Educational Attainment of the Population of Ontario and the United States, Aged 25-34 and 45-64, Not Attending School Full-time, Ontario 1971 and U.S. 1970

Minimum Educational Attainment	Age Group	Ontario %	U.S. %
5 to 8 years elementary school	25-34	97.51	98.06
	45-64	90.96	94.93
4 years secondary	25-34	39.45	71.49
	45-64	23.34	48.02
university degree	25-34	8.6	15.33
	45-64	4.4	8.97

Sources: 1971 Census of Canada, "Population: Out of School Population," Catalogue 92-743, Volume 1, part 5, p. 4-1, July 1974.

1970 U.S. Census of Population, Subject Reports: Educational Attainment, PC(2)-5B, pp.1-8, March 1973.

compulsory education was a denial of the rights of parents to do what they wanted with their children—for example, to have them work all day in the fields or factories. And there were cries of socialism and communism among those who believed strongly in private property and rugged individualism. The Rev. John Roaf, for example, in a letter to the editor of *The Globe* in 1852, wrote of "communism in education" which undermined property and society and pauperized the people. He denied the rights of "mechanics and labourers . . . to educate their children at the expense of their more wealthy neighbours."[11]

It took almost thirty years for Ryerson to achieve his goal. Finally in 1871 the Education Act of 1871 established free, universal and compulsory education, but it applied only to children aged 7 to 12 for four months per year. A glance at conditions at that time, however, reveals that, while the history books may record the year 1871 as a year of achievement in education, the reality was less satisfactory. Edwin Guillet describes an important address delivered to the Ontario Educational Association in 1873 by Dr. David Fotheringham, who was prominent in educational circles in the nineteenth century, in which the speaker deplored the very low attendance at school even though education was compulsory. Twenty-seven per cent of children in the province were not at school at all. Of those who were, half were at school less than fifty days. Only 15 per cent of the children in the province attended more than two hundred days in a school year, and only 3 per cent entered any kind of secondary institution. He urged more stringent attendance regulations, but admitted that this was only a partial solution to the problem of absenteeism:

> Much of the instruction given in Ontario is unattractive, vague, inaccurate and valueless. It is a shame, a disgrace, the way in which children are huddled, tortured and smothered in most of our schools even yet—dirt on floor and walls, dust on the desks, dust on the sills, on the maps, on the windows—outhouses exposed often, and often unfit to use, playground unsuitable, often muddy, uneven—exposed—no shade trees, no play-shed—nothing but dreary tiresome days, theirs at school.[12]

Still, it was an achievement to have overcome the opposition to universal education and to have put into place a structure that would eventually enable all children to become educated in, if not the gleaming palaces of our most affluent communities, at least warm, relatively pleasant surroundings. But what were the motives behind the promotion of universal education? Were the "school promoters," to use Alison Prentice's term,[13] anxious to provide equality of educational opportunity, or were they concerned to develop a docile, disciplined labour force. The traditional historical view has been that public-spirited individuals in the nineteenth century, in particular Egerton Ryerson, were moved to provide equal opportunities for all, and to this end persuaded their fellow citizens to support universal compulsory education. Revisionist historians have questioned this view.[14] Michael Katz in a study of American education has argued that by 1880 "American education had become universal, taxsupported, free, compulsory, bureaucratic, racist and class-biased."[15] Inspired by his work Canadian historians have also re-examined the educational developments in Upper Canada and the reason that they took place in an attempt to combat "the mythology (that) the movement for free public education is part of the larger struggle of the lower classes for participation in the democratic process, and the classic alignment of interests shows the 'conservatives' in opposition to public school establishment."[16]

Alison Prentice is one who has analysed the attitudes that led to the great expansion of education in the nineteenth century in Upper Canada. It seems clear from her examination that the professed intention was to provide equality of opportunity. She quotes Ryerson as saying in 1859 that the school system of Upper Canada was "an agency of universal education in which 'the poor man' had equal rights and privileges with the rich man."[17] The school promoters, Prentice writes, "offered education as an almost certain avenue to upward mobility," and "in the schools lay the hope of individual and class as well as collective advancement."[18] Prentice portrays a society in a period of transition and anxiety where the prospects for a stable prosperous community were very much in doubt. Life was hard in a new society in a harsh climate. Destitute, diseased peasants were flooding into the country, victims of the Irish potato famine. Crime and ignorance abounded. And to the south was the infinitely more vigorous and prosperous United States. In the mid-nineteenth century as in the midtwentieth century, education was seen as the panacea to cure society's ills. Improvement of the individual and of the society was the goal of educators, and they were convinced that it would result from universal education.

No doubt the educators did think that they were breaking down the old class system through universal education. Certainly Ryerson constantly spoke and wrote about the possibility of anyone, however poor and humble, aspiring to "respectability" and becoming "a gentleman" if he was prepared to work hard and, above all, become educated. For example, in his inaugural address at Victoria College he said that knowledge and skill were now "the fruit of labour and not the inheritance of descent."[19]

Prentice concludes that because of the realities of the social order, "there was beginning to develop in nineteenth-century Upper Canada an educational class system no less pervasive than the ranks and orders of the dying past."[20] It seems unlikely that Ryerson would be surprised. He clearly advocated a class society, but one based on education rather than birth. However, whether he realized it or not, in the nineteenth century as in the twentieth century, those with advantages of birth would be most able to take advantage of opportunity. His vision of an educational system as he described it in his Report in 1846 is unequivocal:

> The educational structure ... should be broad.... Its loftiest elevation should equal the highest demands of the learned professions, adapting its gradations of schools to the wants of the several classes in the community, and to their respective employments or professions, the one rising above the other ... yet each complete in itself for the degree of education it imparts.[21]

He evidently believed in a system of education that would prepare each person for his station in life. His strongest argument for universal education was that it would eliminate pauperism, a scourge of life in Upper Canada in the mid-nineteenth century. Ryerson saw education as "the most effectual preventative of pauperism and its natural companions, misery and crime ... ignorance is the fruitful source of idleness, intemperance and improvidence and these the foster parents of pauperism and crime."[22]

Ryerson was not alone in equating ignorance and crime. In her study of the origins of public education in Upper Canada, Susan Houston emphasizes the connections in the nineteenth-century mind between the two, and the importance of linking public schooling to crime prevention in order to get the support of property owners.

How did subsequent generations of educators see the role of education in Ontario? Did they see it as providing a route to equality of opportunity, and if so were they concerned about how well it served these ends? A partial answer to these questions can be found in *In the Cause of Education*,[23] a summary of the proceedings of the annual meetings of the Ontario Educational Association for every year from 1861 to 1960. The speeches and discussions give us an idea of the concerns of teachers and educators during these years. Salaries, status and superannuation have always interested them intensely.[24] The place of religion in the schools and the role of examinations received continuing attention. The training of teachers, the need for industrial or vocational schools and the problems of rural school consolidation were of regular concern. But a large number of speakers during the years also spoke of the importance of equality of opportunity. Principal Peterson of McGill University, for example, in 1904 spoke of the discovery of the supreme importance of education as one of the great achievements of the nineteenth century:

> And not least on this American continent where the watchword has ever been and will continue to be, Equality of Opportunity for All.... But now we have to think no longer of the professional classes only, but of the masses of people, in regard to whom it is our interest, as well as our duty to cast the net wide so as to get the greatest possible return from the available brain power of the whole community by bringing the benefits of a liberal education within the reach of all.[25]

Equality of opportunity is often called for in the pages of the OEA proceedings reported by Guillet, but it is unusual to find in his extracts recognition of the barriers that existed for lower-income children. The only one, apart from Peterson's oblique reference, was in the Deputy Minister's address in 1901 when he argued that high schools should be entirely free:

> ... for a workman on a small salary could hardly pay $20 to $30 per year—the usual fee—for the education of each of his children. . . . The eastern American states were far ahead in this respect. . . . Why should it be so? What right has the wealthy man to deprive the poor man of such advantages? In this age it strikes me not only as undemocratic but I think it is unChristian.[26]

Most often equality of opportunity was equated with a demand for special education for the gifted child. "A brilliant education should be provided for the brilliant child," said Principal W.I. Grant of Upper Canada College in 1928 in an eloquent defence of the meritocratic principle. "Democracy in education must mean as it did for Napoleon (a career open to the talents); society must not cramp and standardize at the expense of intellectual distinction."[27]

Speaker after speaker is at pains to point out that equality does not mean that all are equal intellectually, that equality of opportunity does not mean that the curriculum should be less demanding. As the Hon. Vincent Massey said in 1935, "A levelling down in education was a false conception of democracy. If mass education had that tendency in the United States, Canada should avoid imitating that country's methods."[28]

The general impression is that educators paid lip service to equality of opportunity, defined it as the opportunity of the brightest to realize their potential, and were constantly on guard against progressive educational ideas and practices coming from the United States.

That many of the speakers were more concerned with opportunity for the brightest rather than opportunity for all children is strikingly illustrated in the speech in 1934 of Dr. Madge Macklin of the University of Western Ontario, who thought that the age of the Common Man had been overdone and that it was time to think about the uncommon. She was worried that as a result of universal education and medical advances which prevent "the weeding out" of large numbers of "lower mental grades," the intelligence level of the school population is lowered. In a statement, reminiscent of a controversial speech of Sir Keith Joseph of the United Kingdom, she compared the average number of children in families sending students to the three provincial universities (3.5) with families sending children to institutes for the feeble-minded (over 9). She argued that much less was being spent on superior children who would be leaders of the future than on the sub-normal: "The whole trend of modern civilization is to take care of those who don't or who can't take care of themselves, at the expense of those who are intelligent, thrifty and able to contribute some worthwhile activity to the community."[29]

The first and most important condition for equality of educational opportunity is to have a system of free, compulsory education. Education is never free, of course, but it was a new and controversial idea in the nineteenth century to have it paid for by the society through taxation rather than by the parents through fees. The School Act of 1850 in Canada West, as Ontario was then called, introduced free education, though for the next half century poor facilities and indifference kept large numbers of children out of school. To give children the opportunity for education in spite of their parents, it was necessary to make it compulsory. In 1854 the legislature had refused compulsory school attendance as an "interference with parental rights." But without it there would be no universal education. Guillet quotes Chief Justice Hagarty on the subject:

> Any person acquainted with the lowest classes of our poor is aware of the extreme difficulty in inducing them to let their children attend school. They will keep them from school to gather wood for fuel, to beg from door to door—in short to do anything in preference to sending them to school to have the advantage of the free education so liberally provided.[30]

Elementary education was made free and compulsory by the Education Act of 1871, but as we have already mentioned it applied only from ages 7 to 12 for four months a year. Almost forty years later, in 1909, Inspector N.W. Campbell of Durham still found it necessary to call his address *A Compulsory Education Act*, and again he deplored the view that school attendance was an infringement on the rights of parents to do what they wanted with their children. He quoted statistics to show that only 50 per cent of those registered actually attended and argued for the appointment of truant officers.[31]

Fees were finally abolished in the secondary schools in 1921, and by the Adolescent School Attendance Act of 1919 the school leaving age was raised to 16. However, there were so many conditions for which permission might be obtained to leave school earlier that in 1950 the Royal Commission on Education in Ontario expressed alarm about the high drop-out rate and the low level of educational achievement in the province. According to the Report of the Minister of Education in 1948, of 100 children who entered school only 61 entered Grade 9 and only 21 completed Grade 12.[32]

We do not know why the drop-out rate was so high. Some must have left because they had to earn a living; but many more probably left because they did not like school and did not find what they learned there relevant to their life. Perhaps the curriculum, which has always been a lively concern of teachers, was to blame. From their beginning in 1871, the collegiate institutes, as the high schools were called, with their five forms divided into Lower, Middle and Upper School in the English fashion, have been oriented towards the requirements of the universities, even though only a very small proportion of their students would go there. Although vocational education had been introduced by the end of the last century and there were 62 vocational schools in the province by the Second World War, there was not a real attempt to broaden and diversify the curriculum of the collegiate institutes until the introduction of the Reorganized Program (the Robarts Plan) of 1962, which it was hoped would provide diversity and encourage students to stay longer in school. It was abandoned after less than ten years because of its rigidity. However, the proportions of students staying in school did increase during the 1960s. As we shall see in Chapter 5, the plans of Ontario students in 1970 to leave school and their educational aspirations after high school were very much related to the programs they were in and their socio-economic status, and so it cannot yet be said that we have in Ontario an educational system in which opportunities are unrelated to the social background of students.

The Ontario Value System

Over the one hundred years since free, universal, compulsory education was introduced into Ontario there have been, of course, enormous changes in the educational system as well as in all other aspects of life in the province. Whether this expansion of educational facilities has been strongly influenced by a concern for equality of opportunity we cannot emphatically state. Certainly, as we have seen, the educators at their annual convention often invoked it, although very often their concern was that the brightest should be able to develop their talents. The fear of a watering down of the content of education was frequently expressed. In 1952 a critic of the *Report of the Royal Commission on Education in Ontario* (1950) referred to "that hoary shibboleth, equality of opportunity" as an unsafe yardstick to apply in determining educational policy.[33] But actually the Royal Commission did not seem to regard equality of opportunity as one of the major goals of education. After discussing the nine aims of education that they regarded as important, they made a rather weak statement:

> Finally we emphasize the need for a wider provision of educational opportunity for children wherever they may be situated in the province.[34]

That statement is in striking contrast to one made by Dr. Wm. Carr, an American educator, to the Canadian Conference on Education in 1958 about the characteristics of the educational system in the United States:

> The first basic idea is opportunity. We hold that a comprehensive educational opportunity should be extended to every young person as an inalienable human right. To make sure that this opportunity is available public schools are supported everywhere at public expense. Furthermore to make sure this opportunity is used, school attendance laws are enforced within prescribed ages. Beyond the years of compulsory attendance, free education is also available in public secondary schools, vocational schools, adult classes, colleges and universities. Extensive scholarship

funds, both public and private, encourage and assist those who wish to secure advanced education.[35]

In 1958, when that statement was made, there was a striking difference in the educational attainment of the American population as compared to the Canadian population, as well as in the proportions of the age group attending post-secondary institutions in the two countries.[36] However, in the decade of the sixties there was a dramatic change in Ontario. There was a great expansion in opportunities for post-secondary education through the establishment of a system of community colleges (Colleges of Applied Arts and Technology) and the expansion of the university system to sixteen universities, two of which are bilingual. In 1972 the Commission on Post-Secondary Education in Ontario perhaps reflected the climate of opinion that then prevailed by going beyond equality of opportunity as a principle and calling for accessibility:

> The guiding principle of the Province's policy of financing post-secondary education should continue to be *universal access* to appropriate educational services for all who wish and are able to benefit from them. All financial barriers to accessibility should be progressively abolished.[37]

During the decade of the sixties there was a dramatic rise of 223 per cent in enrolment in post-secondary institutions, from 48,771 students in 1960–61 to 157,514 in 1970–71. At the same time, expenditures on post-secondary education increased seven-fold from $114.8 million to $767.8 million. In addition, the Ontario Student Awards Program (OSAP) was introduced to try to reduce the financial barriers to education.[38] It was not only a concern for equality of opportunity that drove this expansion. Equally important was the need to meet the occupational needs of a society that was becoming "post-industrialized." As the Commission on Post Secondary Education put it:

> We must have a continual broadening of skills and knowledge to enable us to live in a world where the problem of providing sufficient goods, the social strains of living closely together, and the ecological dangers of ruining our environment all threaten survival itself. When faced with the imperative need of education for survival, universal access should seem not a benevolent dream but a categorical necessity.[39]

In the economic climate of the late seventies and early eighties the implementation of these brave words of the Commission seems less likely. However, it is important to discover the extent to which equality of opportunity might be said to exist in Ontario. This volume is an attempt to do that through an analysis of the results of a survey of Ontario high school students made in 1971. We now turn to the sociological theory that guided our research.

Notes

1. C.B. Macpherson, *Democratic Theory* (Oxford University Press, 1973).
2. John Porter, *The Vertical Mosaic* (Toronto: University of Toronto Press, 1965).
3. Senate of Canada, *Report of the Special Committee on Poverty in Canada* (Ottawa, 1972), and Ian Adams, *et al.*, *The Real Poverty Report* (Edmonton: Hurtig, 1971).
4. Allan M. Maslove, *The Pattern of Taxation in Canada* (Economic Council of Canada, 1972).
5. Census of Canada, 1971, *Census Tract Bulletin, Ottawa-Hull* (Ottawa: Statistics Canada, July 1974).
6. Maslove, *op. cit.*, p.77.
7. There was free education in Massachusetts in the seventeenth century but it declined after the Revolution and was not revived until the 1830s. In 1851 a weak compulsory education act was passed similar to the Ontario one of 1871.
8. Neil Sutherland in his introduction to *Education and Social Change: Themes from Ontario's Past*, edited by Michael Katz and Paul H. Mattingly, claims that Donald Wilson, a revisionist Canadian historian, has "de-mythologized" Ryerson. What the de-mythologizing amounts to is to demonstrate that Ryerson was not unique, that his ideas were in the mainstream of the time and that he did not himself single-handedly put together the Ontario educational system. Nevertheless, Donald Wilson himself says, "Whether his educational ideas were original or imitative is of little consequence since his primary goal was to see them implemented." J. Wilson, R. Stamp and L. Audet, *Canadian Education: A History* (Scarborough, Ont.: Prentice-Hall, 1967).
9. Lawrence Gremin, *The Genius of American Education* (Boston: Vintage Books, 1966), p.126.
10. During his thirty years as Superintendent of Education (1846–76) Egerton Ryerson produced annual reports.
11. J.H. Putman, *Egerton Ryerson and Education in Upper Canada* (Toronto, 1912), p.167.
12. Edwin Guillet, *In the Cause of Education: Centennial, History of the Ontario Educational Association, 1861–1960* (Toronto: University of Toronto Press, 1960).
13. Alison Prentice, *The School Promoters: Education and Social Class in Mid-Nineteenth Century Upper Canada* (Toronto: McClelland and Stewart, 1972).
14. See Mattingly and Katz, *op. cit.*
15. Michael B. Katz, *Class, Bureaucracy and Schools: The Illusion of Educational Change in America* (New York: Praeger, 1971), p.xx.
16. Susan E. Houston, "Politics, Schools and Social Change in Upper Canada," in Mattingly and Katz, *op.cit.*
17. Prentice, *op.cit.*, p.140.
18. *Ibid.*, p.66.
19. *Ibid.*, p.90.
20. *Ibid.*, p.164.
21. Egerton Ryerson, "Report on a System of Public Elementary Instruction for Upper Canada," in J. George Hodgins, *Historical and Other Papers and Documents of the Ontario Educational System*, Vol.III (Toronto, 1912), p.142.
22. *Ibid.*, p.143.
23. Guillet, *op.cit.*
24. Not surprisingly since through most of the period teachers suffered from a low status, very little security and meagre financial rewards—a reflection of the attitude of the population to education. It was frequently pointed out that teachers were no better paid than labourers. In 1936 the President of the OSSTF (Ontario Secondary School Teachers Federation) deplored the low salaries and lack of tenure and demanded a Board of Reference to settle disputes between teachers and boards of education, but it was firmly opposed by the Minister of Education. Guillet, p.335.

25. Guillet, p.215.
26. *Ibid.*, p.203.
27. *Ibid.*, p.312.
28. *Ibid.*, p.334.
29. *Ibid.*, p.330.
30. *Ibid.*, p.12.
31. *Ibid.*, p.236.
32. *Report of the Royal Commission on Education in Ontario, 1950,* J.A. Hope, chairman (Toronto, 1950), p.101.
33. C.E. Silcox, *The Hope Report on Education* (Toronto: Ryerson Press, 1952), p.42.
34. *Report of the Royal Commission on Education in Ontario, 1950, op. cit.,* p.40.
35. W.G. Carr, "The Purpose of Education," in *Canadian Conference on Education, 1958* (Ottawa, 1958), p.37.
36. In 1960, 20 per cent of U.S. males aged 20-24 were enrolled in school. The percentage in Canada in 1961 was 12.
37. Report of the Commission on Post-Secondary Education in Ontario. *The Learning Society* (Toronto, 1972), p.147.
38. See Marion B. Porter, *et al., Does Money Matter?* (Toronto: Macmillan, 1979), for an extensive discussion of financial barriers to education.
39. *The Learning Society, op. cit.,* p.33.

3
Theoretical Framework and Model-Building

Some Guidelines from General Sociological Theory

Equality of educational opportunity can be obstructed or facilitated by the complex processes of social life. Of these processes none is more important than growing up and attending school. The child is a malleable substance in the hands of others as he continues through a series of unavoidably unequal relationships because of his physical and mental immaturity. In addition to this natural inequality of childhood, there is the social inequality between children arising from the fact that early growth takes place, in the main, in families with vastly different resources and values. Moreover, once the individual has been socialized he is pretty much the victim of his particular circumstances of birth. Even if we were able to obtain a reasonable degree of equality of condition, without which many would hold equality of educational opportunity to be fanciful,[1] there would still remain the differences in interpersonal relationships within the family and other small primary groups to which the child belongs.

Socialization begins in infancy and continues through childhood to embrace a multitude of experiences in the home, in school and in age-peer groups. In these settings the child, by interacting with others, learns "appropriate" social roles and the rules of behaviour that support them, that is, the behavioural norms of the groups in which he finds himself. These norms and values in turn reflect those of the wider social milieux—neighbourhoods, social classes and religious sub-cultures, for example—within which small primary groups such as families, cliques and play-groups are located.

Through interacting with others the child learns to conform to the behaviour that others expect of him, and reciprocally he learns to expect—through a process of exchange—to be rewarded by positive responses from others as they interact with him in corresponding or complementary roles.[2] Thus parents "learn" to be parents by interacting and adjusting their rewards to elicit appropriate behaviour from their children.[3] Similarly, as playmates, children learn the morality of their playgroups by interacting with their age peers,[4] and later as pupils by interacting with their teachers.

Successive roles of infant, child and pupil tend to be asymmetrical with those of mother, father and teacher because they all involve relations of authority and obedience. The adults are the socializers and the child the socializee. Although asymmetrical, the roles nonetheless require an exchange or reciprocity to make them work. If in school children cannot revolt, they have ways of breaking the peace. Peer group roles, on the other hand, tend to be symmetrical and to have elements of equality, and as Piaget has clearly shown, are important in the development of the moral sense. In both sets of roles the developing individual learns that conformity to rules brings rewards while non-conformity results in punishments and deprivations.

One important form of reward is the approval and esteem of others. If these are not forthcoming, or if having been granted are withdrawn, the child feels punished. In the early learning contexts of childhood there are, then, a set of companion role players who are highly significant for the child and whose approval and esteem are important in determining how he performs.[5] Thus he seeks to maximize gratification and minimize deprivation by conforming. These "significant others" are also agents of the wider community linking the micro-structure of the society. In the long run, socialization serves the total social system.

From infancy through adolescence, individuals learn not only the roles of their intimate primary groups but also those of the wider society. They are prepared for adult life where, in time, roles in the world of work, of citizenship and political participation, of males and females, of parenthood all await him or her. All these roles are integrated into the major institutional systems of the society, that is, the economy, the political system, the ideological system of religion and culture. Thus socialization in early primary group experience should achieve objectives for both the individual and society as his social character becomes moulded to his social structure.

Within the economy, for example, there exists a division of labour. In modern and particularly emerging post-industrial societies, this comprises a wide range of occupations requiring different levels of education and skill. If the economy, with its complex structure of occupations, is to operate at all effectively people must want to fill the various positions. Educational and occupational aspirations are therefore essential for the continuance of the division of labour. Aspirations, then, are the motivational prerequisites for filling a complex structure of adult roles, particularly those of the work world.

The roots of ambition are in the early socializing processes where individuals play their respective roles with parents, teachers and peers. These contexts also provide the vital elements for the development of the self and the perception of the self which become constitutive of personality. The development of the self and the concept of self arise from interaction with others. The formation of a self-concept is a gradual process and often involves "taking the role of the other," the condition where the child sees himself as others see him, that Cooley called "the looking glass self," evaluates what he sees and invests it with feeling.[6]

Thus the child's self-concept is a reflection of the evaluation which others have of him built up in the varied contexts of socialization. Self-concept is affected, too, by structural factors: the size of the family, the birth order of the child, the size of community, socio-economic status of the family, and religious and ethnic affiliations. The children of minorities, or workers in depressed single-industry towns, for example, learn to perceive themselves as they are seen by dominant majorities or middle-class professionals, including those of the educational system. The extreme case in Canada, perhaps, is that of the Indian child in school perceiving himself and his fellows as visibly different from the majority around him. The child receives "information" about himself in the form of negative or positive evaluations of others. From these he becomes aware of what is expected of him, his abilities, and what his future roles might be. Positive self-evaluations and encouragement of others are central to the development of ambition.

As every child, parent and teacher knows, the course of growing up and learning, of child rearing and teaching, is never plain sailing. Some of the anxieties and tensions are natural to growth from childhood through adolescence to near adulthood while still in school. The series of transitions require the child to perform one pattern of roles while preparing for others, involving him in a degree of ambivalence to his present roles. He must derive a sufficient level of gratification from his present roles in order to continue performing them, but at the same time he must have motivation to learn what will be required of him in the future and, at the appropriate time in adulthood, to abandon the cocoon of learner and move on to a new position. The biologically mature young person dependent upon his parents and subject to their authority and that of the school, while at the same time wanting to assert his own independence, provides the most obvious example of role tensions which make a balance between involvement in the present and preparation for the future difficult.

There are other examples less natural but no less obvious, and with great consequences for education. One is the changing role of women in the contemporary world. This, perhaps the most salient of social changes in the 1970s, makes for lack of clarity in expectations and behaviour. The present confusion surrounding the adult role of women, for the middle class at least, makes the creation of a self-concept for girls difficult and their aspirations ambivalent. How far down the class structure such confusion extends, and across what cultures, we have but slight knowledge.[7]

Other factors stemming from the social structure create tensions within the micro-worlds of socialization, making for a condition where expectations and behaviour do not fit. Mother and father, for example, in a situation which sociologists call hypergomy, may themselves have been socialized in different cultural milieus of class, ethnicity or religion so that awareness of behavioural norms are not shared by them. The husband may be a manual worker and his wife of middle-class origin, and similarly in the school the teacher may be middle class and the child from a deprived environment. In all of these and similar situations, the value of learning and aspirations for the adult world may fail to take hold so that the child does not care but reconciles the tensions by having low self-concepts and abandoning education.

In locating the roots of ambition and the desire to learn in the interaction processes of the small primary groups which socialize the individual and mediate between him and the wider society, we can see how great the inequalities of chances to exploit opportunity are, even when it comes in the form of elegant schools, streamlined curricula and qualified teachers. The successful socializing of young people to high levels of educational aspirations from families with plenty of resources, if not easier, is at least more realistic than instilling such ambition in children where families have few resources. As we will have occasion to demonstrate frequently, families with poor resources fail in large measure to create the extra amount of ambition required to overcome the irksomeness of learning and to overcome, in addition, social barriers and lack of resources. No doubt families with poor resources live by a "reality principle" which, encompassing a wide range of barriers from poverty to prejudice, becomes transmitted to the child in the formation of his self-image. It is at this point, if any degree of equality is to be achieved, that social policy intervention should change reality and perceptions of it. For some with few resources the barriers are overcome. Perhaps we might be able to throw some light on what the conditions are that make this possible.

So much for a broad and discursive theorizing on socialization and personality, sources of ambition, the disposition to learn and to achieve that we are calling educational and occupational aspirations. In the following section we become more specific by trying to translate these broad theoretical notions into more concrete terms so that we might measure them and see how together they operate to establish varying levels of aspirations.

Towards a Model for the Analysis
of Educational Aspirations

In most general terms, our objective in this research was to determine those factors which make students aspire to stay in school and to go on to various forms of post-secondary education. This objective required us to find ways of measuring those elusive subjective qualities and complex social processes which create ambition to stay in school and to learn. These motivating forces may appear "on the surface" as an impassioned desire to learn, or they may be social pressure to conform or relatively unconscious educational habits formed in those subcultures where education beyond high school is taken for granted. However they appeared, it should be possible to measure them and to associate their strengths and weaknesses with some of the factors which our broad general theory has suggested.

Educational aspirations could be very low, where the individual would want very little more education than he or she had received up to the present, or they could be very high, as when an individual hopes that he or she might carry on to professional and post-graduate training. What we were required to measure as our main outcome, or dependent variable, then, was the level or strength of a student's educational aspirations. Similarly we sought to measure occupational aspirations. We will discuss the exact form of these measures in the following chapter, but before doing so we want to formalize in a much more precise way what the factors are which make for variations in the levels of educational and occupational aspirations in a population of high school students.

One would have to be a relatively obtuse observer of the educational system and the young people in it not to realize that there are many factors affecting educational aspirations. Some would have more powerful effects than others; some would affect particular students more than other students. We had, therefore, to conceptualize a complex process where a multiplicity of factors were operating to make for variation in the level of educational aspirations. Some of these factors might operate directly on aspirations, or through other factors, or both. The factors might operate on each other.

Clearly such a multifactored or multivariate situation would require some systematic organization if the woods were not to be lost in the trees. One conventional way of providing this systematic organization is to construct a multivariate model consisting of a set of preceding factors, or independent variables, which would account for more of the variation in educational aspirations than any other set of preceding factors.[8]

Before attempting to establish the most powerful variables it was necessary to review the range of variables which contemporary social sciences had indicated as having some importance. These variables could be grouped into seven major sets, which we have designated as socio-cultural climate, demographic, significant other, attitudinal, school and occupational variables, and variables of life chance perceptions. This seven-fold classification represents a condensation of a very large number of variables.[9]

The Variable Sets
In Figure 3.1 we have attempted to show diagramatically how these sets of variables—socio-cultural, demographic and so forth—are related to each other and how together they operate on educational aspirations. Because

they are seen as the resulting outcome, or dependent variable, educational aspirations are placed at the right-hand side of the diagram. The solid lines linking the sets of variables are direct effects on education aspirations, that is, effects which are not mediated through any other set. The broken lines indicate indirect effects, that some portion of the influence on educational aspirations is through other sets of variables and becomes mixed in or shared with their direct effects. Both solid and broken lines have directional arrows indicating the flow of influence. In a few instances there are "dot-dash" lines with arrows at each end which signify that influence can go in either direction where there is, so to speak, a feedback loop.

By following the lines in Figure 3.1 we might trace out the flow of influence. For example, the solid line from the set of socio-cultural climate variables in which we include socio-economic status or social class, ethnic group affiliation and religion, among others, indicates a direct influence on educational aspirations because of such things as the family resources available for education and the cultural values which might be supportive of it. The set of demographic variables also have direct effects on educational aspirations. These would include sex differences, not in any physiological sense, but simply that in conforming to broad social norms boys may have higher aspirations than girls. Within this set, size of family and birth order, or a combination of both, will directly affect the amount of schooling desired.

School variables might have direct effects on aspirations through differences in physical resources, in programs, and in the overall level of academic achievement or performance in the school, that is, its academic climate. The set of significant other variables are those which operate in the individual's small primary groups—family, peers and the like—which we earlier called his micro-world. The perception of life chance variables are the individual's estimation of how well he feels he will do in the light of the situation in which he finds himself. They are subjective adjustments to reality (for example, when a person from a poor home realizes, in the light of family resources, that he cannot go to university or become a professional worker). Attitudinal variables are a set of subjective dispositions of the individual with respect to education and work, including the student's concept of his own abilities, which directly affect educational aspirations. Occupational variables are conditions of the work world or perceptions of them which affect occupational aspirations of the individual student and thus his educational aims.

As Figure 3.1 indicates by the solid lines, all of these sets of independent variables can affect educational aspirations directly. The remaining set of variables, "all other," is included simply to close the system so that we can say we have accounted for everything that explains variation in educational aspirations. "All other" would include variables we could not think of, could not measure or did not think worth measuring, as well as all errors in

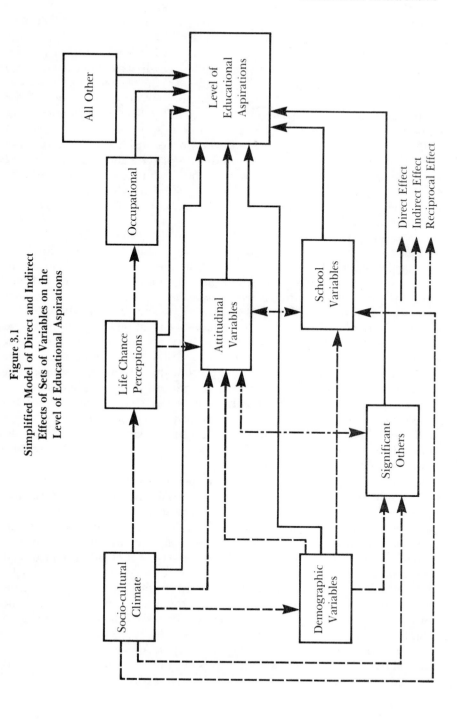

Figure 3.1
Simplified Model of Direct and Indirect Effects of Sets of Variables on the Level of Educational Aspirations

measuring and from sampling. Theoretically "all other" could explain more than the other variables in the model, either because those are not the most important ones or we have not succeeded in measuring them with sufficient accuracy, problems with which we will have to deal as we go along.

Our six sets of independent variables can also affect educational aspirations indirectly through their effect on each other, as indicated in Figure 3.1 by the broken lines. For example, socio-cultural climates will affect demographic factors such as the number of children in the family and different attitudes about, among other things, the education of boys and girls because of the different values embedded in different socio-cultural climates. Socio-cultural climates might also affect the significant other variables when, for example, the relative importance of parents, teachers or peers to the child is different in some sectors of the social structure than in others. Similarly, children from different social classes or ethnic groups, which we include in socio-cultural climates, will be differentially distributed in school programs, thereby explaining in part the relationship between school program and aspirations. The indirect influences of demographic variables are illustrated by ways in which males and females participate in different kinds of small groups and so affect the role that "significant others" play in the formation of educational aspirations of the two sexes, or the attitudes which they have about various life goals or problems. Peer groups, for example, could play quite a different role for girls than they do for boys. It is quite possible that the effects of some sets of variables in Figure 3.1 on educational aspirations would be almost entirely indirect, that is, through intervening sets. As we shall see in the analysis, those of socio-cultural climates, particularly social class, have less direct effect on educational aspirations on the surface than we expected them to have. However, their indirect effects could be very substantial through the other variables in the system.

In Figure 3.1 the direction of the arrows indicates the flow of influence and might, with some caution, be termed causal links. The spatial ordering from left to right corresponds to a rough temporal sequence of how these variables affect high school students.[10] They are born into socio-cultural climates, and none of the other variable sets can have any influence on that. That set of variables is prior to the other sets as they affect educational aspirations. School variables, on the other hand, are very close in time to the formation of aspirations—which is not to say they are more powerful in either their direct or indirect effects than the other sets. It is hoped some answers will be provided by our analysis, for which the model provides a guiding framework.

In Figure 3.1 the relation between significant others and the set of attitudinal variables is shown as reciprocal in their influence. The child is praised or highly rewarded, say, with good marks from the teacher. In response his attitude to school work is more positive, his achievement improves, and the teacher rewards him yet again. Other feedback loops are likely also between the set of school variables and attitudes.

It is important to remember that the social processes we are seeking to understand are very complex indeed. It would be quite improper for us to expect a wholly precise explanation, for that would imply a totally determinable system—a pleasant prospect for a scientific researcher, but perhaps an unhappy one for other humans.[11] The purpose of our research procedures is, then, to maximize the variation in educational aspirations that can be explained by a parsimonious selection of relevant variables. We assume that we cannot achieve the mind-boggling possibility of measuring and bringing them all into our model, nor can we explain all the variation, an achievement which would imply a wholly determined system. Our model is one which we feel can be deduced from the general theories of socialization sketched earlier.

It is also productive of hypotheses to be tested, particularly those related to the relative strengths of those sets of variables which are important early in the child's life and those sets which intervene later in adding their effects on educational aspirations. The analytical task is to determine their relationships within the school population being studied, as well as differences in their relative strengths for different sub-groups within that population, for example, males and females, different social classes and the like.

Decomposing the Variable Sets

Since the model presented in Figure 3.1 is very much simplified, it is important to break down each of the categories or sets of variables into the single variables that have been classified within them. We have done this in Figure 3.2 where twenty-six variables are listed according to the appropriate set. Variables have been arrayed from left to right to signify the same temporal ordering as in Figure 3.1. It is believed, on the basis of past findings in various countries, that all of these have some direct effect on educational aspirations.

Some variables which might have been included are not. The most obvious are a set of school-related variables, such as teachers' qualifications, educational resources, libraries, specialized teaching facilities and personnel which would give us measures of school quality. For a long time such variables were thought to affect educational achievement, that is, students do better when the resources put to their education are of high quality than when they are of low quality. We would assume that these school-related variables would affect educational aspirations through their effect on school performance. As Figure 3.2 shows, we do have a few school-related variables such as school program and academic composition of the school, that is, the proportion of students in four- and five-year programs. However, we largely

Figure 3.2
Temporal Ordering of Variables Affecting Educational Aspirations

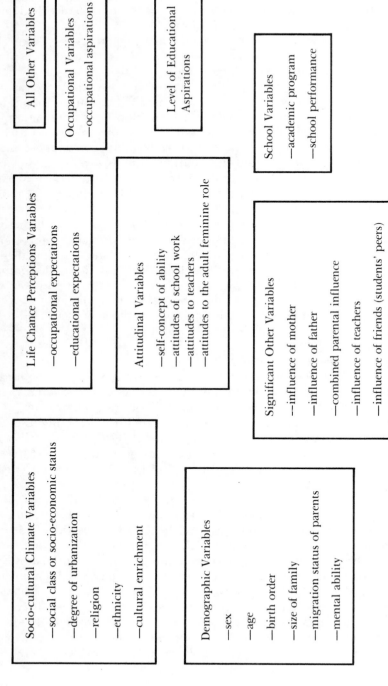

excluded school-related variables from our design for two reasons. One is that we felt Ontario high schools do not vary greatly in their resources or in the qualifications of their teachers. Secondly, as we have described in Chapter 1, the evidence from the United States was accumulating that differences in the qualities of schools had little effect on educational achievement.[12] This matter is still being debated.

Another set of school variables which we have left out are those related to the school class as a group. There was some evidence that the characteristics of a class—for example, good morale or rapport with the teacher—would affect the achievement of the members of that class, or that the social networks formed within a class were important for the educational process.[13] We left these types of variables out, because in many high schools with individual time-tabling classes do not exist as more or less permanent social units that could build up class spirit. Students are like a set of atoms which disintegrate with the end of a class period, the components of which reform into quite different sets for the next class. Moreover, as grades begin to disappear even these traditional social groupings with which students could once identify will no longer be available.

Ungraded schools with individual time-tabling may well have problems of developing intermediate structures between the student and the school mass. Some of these changes were implemented while we were doing our study, and it would have been extremely difficult to develop measures generally applicable to a variety of practices in considering these school structural variables.

Critics might raise some very pertinent questions about the selection of educational aspirations as the major dependent or outcome variable in a study concerned with equality of educational opportunity. They could argue with some validity that aspirations have an element of fantasy about the future, and real outcomes or the actual educational attainments—that is, the amount of schooling that children in time actually do receive—have much less. That is undeniable, as we know from impressions, and also from follow-up studies that demonstrate that students leave school before their earlier aspirations are realized; or it may be that their aspirations, in the light of subsequent school experience and other exposures to reality, are reduced.[14]

There are two important responses to such criticism. One is that a study of attainments would not capture the influences on those who failed to make it in the educational system. It is a deficiency in numerous studies of educational attainment based on university students or on those in the final year of high school that many of the influences have already taken their toll and such "victims" would not be picked up in the samples.[15] Thus the real influence of socio-cultural climates, for example, gets understated. The earlier in the educational system we go, at least before the legal school leaving age, the more relevant are aspirations than attainments, because all along the way the factors with which we have been dealing are at work. Thus, although we could measure the over- or under-representation of groups from particular social origins by studying the university popula- tion, or all those who have completed their education, we would not receive much insight into the process that brings such unequal representation about.

Coleman and his associates took as their major dependent variable the level of cognitive skill acquired by students as measured by special tests administered at the time of their study. Equality of educational opportunity was determined by the differing levels of cognitive skills acquired by different racial or ethnic groups in the United States. That was an imaginative and innovative shift of focus, but even the acquisition of cognitive skills at various grades in the schools does not necessarily result in educational attainments, although no doubt skill acquisition is an im- portant factor in eventual educational attainment. Whatever we might think of them, it is the credentials dispensed by the educational system in its later stages that ultimately determine access to the high status occupations.

For educational and occupational success, a necessary although not a sufficient condition is that a person must want to have it. Subjective states, aspirations, attitudes, self-concepts are all important in the achievement of status. Their strengths, weaknesses and directions will be important to the individual's grasping or neglecting the opportunities that exist in his environment. In fact, it is in the tradition of much of the literature on educational attainment that aspirations are regarded "as transmitting the influence of the prior variables—family socio-economic status, significant others' influence, mental ability and academic performance—on the de- pendent variables—educational and occupational attainment."[16] In making these observations we are not suggesting that educational attainments or the acquisition of cognitive skills are not important. We are simply asserting that aspirations are important also.

It is clear from the exposition of our model that the variables are related in such a way that their effects are assumed to be linear and additive; that is, the more "units" there are of one independent variable, there will be correspondingly greater effects on the dependent variable, and the unique effects of the several variables can be added to increase the effects on the dependent variable. We have developed a multivariate analysis of aspiration formation which appeared as an appendix in *Does Money Matter?*, the preliminary analysis of the data, and is included in this volume as Chapter 15.[17]

In our theoretical discussion we have placed great emphasis on the role of "significant others" in the development of the student's self-concept of ability and his level of aspirations. While the empirical evidence concerning the influence of teachers and peers is somewhat mixed, there is widespread confirmation that it is the significant others within the family who are the principal socializers and transmitters of societal and cultural values. Although family roles are institutionalized, and therefore have some degree of normal standards of performance—parents are supposed to support their young children, for example—role performance is not invariant.

There is reason to suppose that variations in role performance within the family, and variations in the social psychological climate arising from the interaction process, would have effects on students' aspirations. Just how they might work themselves out was never quite clear, although here and there the literature gives important clues (for example, the downwardly mobile mother encouraging the lower-class son to "recover" status).[18] Similarly, there was reason to suppose that well-integrated and happy families would provide better environments for socialization than unhappy ones for the transmission of whatever values the parents might have.

In the popular mind there has been a great deal of imagination in recent years, and no doubt also in earlier times, that children were rejecting their families for all sorts of attractions, creating in the process family tensions, some of which would be related to the role transitions of semi-adulthood of teenage high school students to which we alluded earlier. Thus family integration or solidarity was considered to be an important variable.

In the model that has been developed none of these home and family environment variables have been included, although no doubt they lie behind the formation of significant other influences, particularly that of mother and father, or both. Therefore, it would be important to expand the model to bring in these family-related variables. In our research design, which will be developed more fully in the next chapter, we obtained data about family climate variables from interviews with the parents of a sub-sample of students, and subsequently merged this parental data with that of their children.

There have been studies, of course, in which families have been intensively interviewed[19] to get a better appreciation of the subtlety of the family interaction process. Unfortunately, large surveys, for reasons of cost as well as feasibility, preclude extensive probing into family relationships of husbands and wives or parents and children. Certainly we would not have been able to obtain reliable information on this set of variables through student questionnaires.

We intend, then, further to elaborate this model by introducing such family environment variables as parent-child relationship, parental perception of child's ability, parental concern for school work and parental attitudes to education.

In decomposing the model and treating some of the important independent variables as dependent, we hope that we might understand more fully what accounts for variation in them. As it turned out, school program, school performance, the influence of significant others and self-concept of ability became important candidates for such treatment. Before proceeding with the analysis, we provide in the next chapter the design of our study and a discussion of how variables were measured.

Notes

1. See, for example, Richard Titmuss cited in Chapter 1. Equality of condition is also the major theme of Christopher Jencks, *Inequality* (New York: Basic Books, 1973).
2. George C. Homans, *The Human Group* (London: Routledge, 1951).
3. A central tenet of behaviourism. See B.F. Skinner, *Science and Human Behaviour* (New York: The Free Press, 1965).
4. Jean Piaget, *The Moral Judgment of the Child* (London: Routledge and K. Paul Ltd., 1932).
5. Within American sociology this "symbolic interactionist" approach had its beginnings in Charles H. Cooley, *Human Nature and the Social Order* (New York: Schocken Books, 1964) and was continued in George Herbert Mead, *Mind, Self, and Society* (Chicago: University of Chicago Press, 1967). See also Harry S. Sullivan, *Conceptions of Modern Psychiatry* (New York: Norton, 1953) and C. Wright Mills and H.H. Gerth, *Character and Social Structure* (New York: Harcourt, Brace, 1953).
6. These ideas relate specifically to Chapter 7, on self-concept of ability.
7. See Chapter 11 for an extensive exploration of this subject.
8. In the construction of a causal model we have been influenced by Herbert M. Blalock, *Causal Inferences in Non-Experimental Research* (Chapel Hill: University of North Carolina Press, 1964).
9. There are many individual studies which examine the influence of one or several of these variables on educational and occupational aspirations. Rather than clutter up a difficult and parsimonious argumentation with many citations, we have classified the literature into our major variable sets and included it as a bibliography at the end of the book. All of this previous research into the subject in Canada and elsewhere has had a bearing on our model-building and the operationalizing of our variables.
10. For a similar causal arrangement of variables see Robert M. Hauser, "Educational Stratification in the United States," in *Social Inquiry* (Spring 1970), pp.102–109.
11. See the observation in Peter M. Blau and Otis Dudley Duncan, *The American Occupational Structure* (New York: Wiley, 1967), p.174.
12. James S. Coleman, *et al.*, *Equality of Educational Opportunity* (Washington: U.S. Government Printing Office, 1966) and Jencks, *op. cit.*
13. Talcott Parson, "The School Class as a Social System: Some of its Functions in American Society," in *Harvard Educational Review* (Fall 1959), pp.297–318.
14. For a description of the follow-up studies see Chapter 14.
15. See an early argument on this point in John Porter, "Social Class and Education," in Michael Oliver, ed., *Social Purpose for Canada* (Toronto: University of Toronto Press, 1961), an analysis of university students based on the frequent Statistics Canada surveys of student income and expenditures. The major work in the United States, that of W.H. Sewell and his associates in Wisconsin, which greatly influenced our own research, is based on high school seniors.
16. Ruth M. Gasson, Archibald O. Haller and William H. Sewell, *Attitudes and Facilitation in the Attainment of Status* (Washington: American Sociological Association 1972), p.3.
17. Marion Porter, John Porter and Bernard Blishen, *Does Money Matter?* (Toronto: Macmillan, 1979).
18. Brian Jackson and Dennis Marsden, *Education and the Working Class* (Harmondsworth: Penguin, 1966).
19. Fred L. Strodbeck, "Family Interaction Values and Achievement," in David McClelland, *et al.*, *Talent and Society* (Princeton: Van Nostrand, 1958).

4
The Ontario Survey

To get the data needed to analyse the complex relationships outlined in the previous chapter, we chose a sample survey in which students would complete a questionnaire and in which the parents of about one-third of them would be interviewed.

The Research Design

Since we saw students' educational aspirations as the end result of the process of socialization from infancy to adolescence, we first considered the feasibility of a longitudinal study of a cohort of children before entering school, and as students during successive years as they progressed through the school system. The prototype of such a study was that of Douglas in the United Kingdom.[1] We very soon realized that we could not hope to raise the funds to support such a study, and consequently considered the possibility of studying groups of students at different stages of the educational process at the same time, a cross-sectional design. We assumed there existed particular points during this process that are especially important for decisions about the type and amount of additional education. Therefore, we decided to take samples of students in Grades 8, 10 and 12.

As we pointed out in the previous chapter, we wished to avoid a shortcoming of many studies of educational plans and aspirations, notably their being based on the final year of high school or on university years. In both cases, if observations are to be made about inequality—apart from the simple one that lower classes are under-represented in universities, a fact established with great frequency—or the effects of the social class system on aspirations and plans, to take students well advanced in the educational system is to leave out of consideration large numbers who will have already left it at earlier stages, and who are likely to come disproportionately from the lower social class levels. Consequently, the full impact of class on educational chances could not be assessed.

Some studies suggest that the impact of class begins in the cradle. No doubt it does, but we felt we could capture a good amount of these "cumulative effects of milieu" if we took students in the final year of elementary school, a middle year of high school, and what for many is the final year of high school, Grade 12—in Ontario the last year before the special pre-university year, Grade 13, which remains an anomaly in North America. There were other reasons for choosing these grades. Grade 8 was chosen because it is during his time in that grade that the student decides what kind of high school he will attend the following year, and often, too, the kind of courses he will take; Grade 10 because at the end of this grade many students reach the legal school-leaving age of sixteen, and therefore have to decide whether or not they will stay on. During their Grade 12 year, for those who are still in school, there is the decision whether to continue to Grade 13 to prepare for university, to proceed directly to non-university post-secondary education, or to go to work. Successful completion of Grade 12 provides students with their Ontario Secondary School Graduation Diploma.

Thus while we abandoned an overly ambitious longitudinal design where one cohort is followed through its school years, we have something of a "synthetic cohort" in that we have different (rather than the same) students at different points in their school history.[2] Such a design should be able to tell us something about the different times when particular effects are felt, without the too serious consequences which attach to cohort analysis based on cross-sectional designs. Moreover, we included in the questionnaire some recall questions for the later grades, asking how decisions were made at earlier levels. Recall questions, of course, have to be treated with particular caution.

As well as taking different grades across the school years, we launched the survey at the time—in the late spring—when decision-making about educational futures would be salient in the minds of students and their parents. It is at these decision-making stages that many of the factors associated with educational outcomes have their greatest impact. For example, parental or teacher encouragement to opt for the five-year rather than the four-year program which existed at the time of the survey, or the commercial or technical branches, would be particularly crucial in Grade 8.

There are times when the student comes to a branching point and selects between alternative future courses from which it would be very difficult to switch. We can conceive of these branching points, as has Boudon,[3] as having probabilistic outcomes with respect to choice of or allocation to the next stage where later branching points and outcomes make it possible to calculate subsequent probabilities of staying in or getting out. Except for a follow-up study of our Grade 8 sample, described in Chapter 14,[4] we do not have the longitudinal data to calculate the chances of children of the different social classes being on the "royal road" rather than the one leading to lesser rewards; but the logic of our selection of grades to be sampled, the branching points, is supported by Boudon's pioneering work, which became available well after we designed the present study. If the chances of children of different social classes are shown to be unequal, the loaded dice are thrown at these branching points.

As always, our sample design and size were limited by financial constraints. It was necessary, of course, for it to represent as accurately as possible the population of students in each of the selected grades in Ontario in May 1971. We had to decide whether to sample households or families, students in schools, or schools and then students. Many commercial and the one academic survey establishment had readily available household samples. If we sampled households and, say, took one child from each in the appropriate grades, we would obviously under-enumerate lower-class children, since families vary in size by social class. In addition, there would be the need to screen out households which had no children, or did not have them in the appropriate grades.

Thus, a much better strategy, and one followed in many other places, was to sample children in school. However, many Ontario school boards were adamant in their protection of the privacy of school records, particularly measured intelligence or I.Q. Any selection of willing school boards would, of course, have thrown unconscionable biases into the study. We decided, therefore, to seek the support of the Minister of Education, William Davis, who a very short while after was to become premier of the province. Davis had been responsible for the explosive development in Ontario education in the 1960s, and from our personal contact with him through university committees we were aware of his concern for equality of educational opportunity. With the understanding that we would not ask for any student's personal records and that parents would be informed of the study, he agreed to send an official letter to each of the Directors of Education in the province giving his support to the study.

With that assistance, our sampling procedures were simplified since we could draw a fully representative sample of the populations of each grade in the province. Each grade was established as a separate sampling domain from which we aimed at selecting 3,000 students. In each domain a sub-sample of 1,000 students would be drawn whose parents would be interviewed.

Since our plan was to analyse grades and language groups separately, a stratified multi-stage cluster design was employed with language (French and English) and grade (8, 10, 12) as the major strata. The result was a self-weighting (within stratum) design which can, within the limits of efficiency variations, be treated as though it were a simple random sample of each stratum.

Appropriate weights were, however, assigned to each of the grades if for any reason it was necessary to combine them. Even so, the sampling procedures were complicated since they were based on provincial enrolment statistics, and had to preserve a balance with respect to the proportions of students in the different types of programs and in large metropolitan areas, smaller cities and rural schools. A full description of the procedures followed are provided in our previous publication, *Does Money Matter?* Since the response rates were uniformly high, we are confident that our sample is representative of the school grades with which we were concerned. Details of response rates can also be found in *Does Money Matter?*[5]

The Students' Questionnaire

For Grades 10 and 12 a questionnaire of 75 items was constructed; for Grade 8 it was somewhat shorter. The questions were designed and pre-tested as measures of those variables discussed in Chapter 3. We will deal at length with these questionnaire items as variable measurements in the following chapters. We were, of course, able to draw on a large number of previous studies in designing questions. We attempted to maintain some equivalence between our questions and those of other studies for comparative purposes. We hoped, too, that we would be able to improve the design of some questions so that we might use the data obtained to construct scales that would facilitate statistical analysis.

In addition to the questionnaires students were asked to complete a mental ability test.[6] The variable of mental ability is, of course, crucial in all studies of this kind, and since we had undertaken not to use student files for private information we were required to administer a test of our own. Students completed both the questionnaire and the mental ability test grouped in a classroom under the supervision of a teacher. The field work of a survey such as this, involving over 400 schools and 9,000 students, was a substantial operation not altogether without thrills and spills.

Operationalizing the Variables

We will deal first with the student questionnaire and then with the parental interview schedule.

Dependent Variables

Our major dependent (or resulting or outcome) variable, as we have seen, is *level of educational aspirations* (LEA). To measure it, students were asked, "When would you like to leave high school?," followed by, "Then what would you like to do?" The possible responses were: go to work; go into apprenticeship or go to a private commercial, business or trade school; go to teachers' college or nursing school; go to community college; go to university but probably not graduate; graduate from university; do further studies at university after graduation from university; other, please specify; I don't know.

Community colleges in Ontario are formally called Colleges of

Applied Arts and Technology (C.A.A.T.s), but since the popular term is community college, we used it on the questionnaire.

We thought of the response categories as representing something of an ascending level of educational aspirations, although there may be some dispute about whether a teachers' college represents a higher or lower level than a community college. We felt that by graduating the response categories in this way we could obtain a better measure of aspiration than by asking the simple question of whether or not the student planned to go to college, a very common practice in studies of this kind.[7] We used these response categories as nominal or ordinal scales in cross tabular analyses, sometimes collapsing them into three categories: go to work; other post-secondary; and university. Finally, we transformed these categories into a scale of values from 1-10 which could be treated as intervals for regression and correlation statistics. To construct the scale, the responses to the two questions, "When would you like to leave high school?" and "Then what would you like to do?" were used. Responses were combined, so that one year more of education represented an increment of 1 on the scale. Thus to leave school after Grade 8 gave a value of 1 on the scale, while to complete Grade 13 and carry on through to post-graduate training gave a value of 10.

Not all educational hopes and desires can be realized. In the light of the conditions in which people find themselves, aspirations become modified by reality into expectations. Later in the questionnaire, so that it would not contaminate the aspirations question, we asked a question to determine the *level of educational expectations* (LEE). The question was, "Not everyone expects to go as far in high school as he would like. Considering your ability, marks, ambitions and family finances, how far do you actually *expect* to go after leaving high school?"

The same scales were constructed for LEE as for LEA so that they are actually parallel. As we have operationalized it, and as do many other studies, educational aspirations could involve a considerable amount of fantasy. We thought we might get some hold on this problem by including the expectations question as being more realistic. We also asked an even more realistic question about their plans for next fall, but of course the responses did not admit of scaling.

A similar attempt to distinguish between fantasy and reality was made with our other two dependent variables, *level of occupational aspirations* (LOA) and *level of occupational expectations* (LOE). First, students were asked, "If you had your choice, what sort of job or occupation would you most like to make *your life's work or career?* Think about what you would like to be doing 15 or 20 years from now." They were given places to answer "What would you like to do?" and "In what sort of place would you like to work?" To assist in the coding of these questions, examples of jobs in thirteen different categories were provided and respondents were asked to circle the category which contained the job that came closest to the one they had named. They were also given the opportunity to answer, "I have no idea what I want to do."

To distinguish expectations from aspirations, the former was worded, "Everyone does not end up doing the job he or she likes. Considering your ability, marks, ambitions, and family finances, what job do you think you will *actually end up doing?*" The responses and the examples of job titles for both occupations questions were the same.

Occupations were coded into the first two digits of the Blishen (1967) scale, which ranks census occupational titles in terms of the education and income characteristics of those in the occupations as well as prestige of the occupations derived from a national survey of the public evaluation of occupations.[8] The entire Blishen scale for census occupations ranges from 25 to 77, and thus has properties of an interval scale. Frequently, we make use of the first digit only and transform the scale into a six class level ordinal scale. Class I, the highest, includes occupations scoring 70 or more; Class II, 60–69; Class III, 50–59; and so on to Class VI, less than 29. All of the census occupations with their appropriate codes can be found in the original paper. Some examples of occupations in the various classes are:

Class I   Higher Professions: physicians, lawyers, engineers.

Class II   Other Professions and Higher Managers: actuaries, large business owners and managers, airline pilots.

Class III   Lesser Managers and Technicians: surveyors, occupational therapists, small business owners and managers.

Class IV   White Collar Clerical and Higher Crafts: bookkeepers, office appliance operators, toolmakers.

Class V   Lesser Crafts and Semi-skilled Manual and Lower White Collar: stationary engineers, sales clerks, typists, farmers.

Class VI   Unskilled: Truck drivers, longshoremen; janitors.

At times in the analysis the six occupational classes were further collapsed into Upper-middle (Classes I and II), Middle (Classes III and IV) and Lower (Classes V and VI). There would be few upper-class students in our sample, since private schools were not included. In addition to the Blishen occupational codes, all occupational responses were coded to the new 1971 CCDO census codes, mainly for future use and comparison with 1971 Census data.

Independent Variables

As presented in Chapter 3, our independent variables were grouped into six sets in terms of a temporal sequence. They were socio-cultural climates, demographic factors, life chance perceptions, attitudes, significant others and school. A description of how the independent variables were operationalized is provided below.

Socio-Cultural Climate Variables

Since one of our main concerns was structured social inequality, the most important independent variable was thought to be *socio-economic status* (SES) of the students' families. The questionnaire asked, "What is your father's job or occupation? If he works on more than one job, put down the one in which he spends the most time. If your father is unemployed or has retired put down the one he used to do." They were also asked in what sort of place their father worked. As with the occupational aspirations question, the identical list of job categories and job titles was provided to facilitate correct responses and coding. Responses were coded to the Blishen scale. At times the scale will be collapsed to a six level or three level class structure as outlined above.

Cultural climates of social origins can be measured in ways other than SES, for example, *father's education* and *mother's education*. Although father's education is a component of the Blishen scale, students were asked the educational level of both parents—"How far did your parents go in school?"—with response categories for both parents ranging from "none or some elementary school" to "did further study at university after graduation from university." Responses were collapsed into a three level ordinal scale—high, medium and low. From the responses we also constructed a new variable of *combined parental education* assigning equal weights to both parents.

For *degree of urbanization* an ordinal level scale from rural to urban was constructed by classifying students according to whether their schools were in one of four rural or urban groups: the Toronto megalopolis from Oshawa to Hamilton; other major urban centres with over 100,000 in population (London, Windsor, Ottawa and Kitchener-Waterloo); minor urban areas from 10,000 to 100,000 population, which included such towns as Thunder Bay, Sudbury, Kingston and Belleville. The fourth category, which we have called rural, includes all communities of less than 10,000. The rural category included all district high schools and district secondary schools in the sample.

For *religion* students were simply asked, "What is your religion?" and were given a list of religious denominations as response categories. They could respond "I have no religion." To try to determine *religiosity* they were asked, "How often do you attend religious services?" The response categories were: more than once a week; once a week; two or three times a month; once a month; less often; never. For Catholic students a further measure of religiosity was derived from the question, "Are you in now or have you ever gone to a separate Roman Catholic School?" An ethnic origin was obtained from the standard Canadian Census question, "To what ethnic or cultural group did you or your ancestor (on the male side) belong on coming to this continent?"

The final socio-cultural climate variable is *cultural enrichment*. As we pointed out in Chapter 3 the degree of cultural enrichment—whether students have music lessons, get taken to the theatre and so on—is so much related to social class that it may not be a genuinely "independent" variable. However, on the other hand, if children in lower social classes experience some degree of cultural enrichment, this may affect their aspirations. Students were asked three questions: "Have you ever taken lessons, *outside of school,* in art, dancing, dramatics or music?"; "About how often do you *go with your parents* to see a ballet, an opera, a play, a live performance of classical music, a museum or art gallery?"; "About how often do you *go alone or with people your own age* to see a ballet, an opera, a play, a live performance of classical music, a museum or art gallery? (Don't count the times you have gone with your school.)" For these three questions the response categories were: often; sometimes; rarely; never. For a further measure of cultural enrichment students were given a list of magazines ranging from *Reader's Digest* and *Chatelaine* to *Atlantic Monthly* and were asked which of these came into the home regularly. Values from 0 to 3 were assigned to the responses to the four questions for a total of 12 possible points in a cultural enrichment scale. (For the magazine questions up to three magazines were scored 1, four to six magazines, 2, more than six, 3.) This scale has been treated as interval and also collapsed as ordinal into low, medium and high cultural enrichment.

Demographic Variables

Sex, age, birth order and size of family were coded from straightforward questions. Migration status of parents was taken from the question, "In what part of the world were your mother and father born?" The question, "As far as you know, where did your father and mother take most of their education?" enabled us to distinguish the parents who immigrated as adults.

For studies such as this it was most important to get a measure of *mental ability,* which as we have said, we consider the "inherent ability" with which an individual was born. Apart from confidentiality there was another serious objection to using I.Q. scores. Conventional I.Q. tests which rely heavily on the meanings of words are strongly class biased, and the results show the effects of interaction between the child and his environment as much as they measure a child's basic or genetic mental ability. Verbal skills, so much a part of conventional intelligence tests, are very much related to home environment, including the language spoken in the home. In the province there were large numbers of French-speaking families, immigrant families and Native Indians who would be at a disadvantage in a conventional intelligence test. For these reasons it was decided to administer, at the time the questionnaire was completed, a "culture fair" intelligence test which used only symbolic manipulations.

Details of the tests for the various grades, the Institute of Personality and Ability Testing (IPAT) Test for "G" (Culture Fair Scale), are in the appendix to *Does Money Matter?* Raw scores were considered as interval, and the distribution of scores divided into thirds for an ordinal measure of high, medium and low were used.

As we mentioned in the last chapter, there was a relationship between mental ability and SES. The designers of the test admit that "test sophistication techniques acquired through experience of testing may be environmentally related." In addition, motivation to do well on tests, especially when there is no demonstrable reward, may be related to social class. And, of course, there is also the possibility that the society has been sufficiently meritocratic that some proportions of high mental ability people have made their way into the higher status occupations, and have passed on their superior genes to their offspring, resulting in a higher proportion of high mental ability students in the upper social classes than in the lower. However, the correlation between SES and mental ability appears to be lower with our culture fair test than with the standardized I.Q. test[9] and, hence, can be considered a truer measure of the variable with which we are concerned.

Significant Other Variables

To measure the influence of parents, teachers and peers on aspirations, students were asked, "Who helps you *most?*," first in relation to plans for next fall, then in relation to their future education. The possible answers were: father; mother; father and mother equally; teacher; school principal or vice-principal; school guidance counsellor; close friends; brothers or sisters; other; no one is helping me. From the information derived from these two questions it was possible to get a picture of the relative importance of family, friends and school personnel in helping students with their decisions about their education. As we shall see, a surprisingly large proportion of students said that no one was helping them.

To get a further measure of influence students were asked, "How much do you discuss your hopes for future education with your parents?," followed by, "How much do they help you in thinking about these hopes for your future education?" Parallel questions were asked about teachers or guidance counsellors and close friends. The response categories for each of these six questions were: not at all; some; very much.

Attitudinal Variables

As we have argued in Chapter 3, how a student perceives his own abilities is very much related to his level of aspirations. Self-concept of ability (SCA) was determined following Brookover[10] by eight questions, each comprising a five point ordinal scale, and aggregating the responses to form a scale ranging from 8 to 40. Brookover calculated Guttman scale type scores and a conventional summated score. Since there was little disparity between the two when correlated with academic achievement, the summated score was calculated and used in our analysis. The questions were, "How do you rate yourself in school ability compared with those in your class at school?," "Where do you think you rank in your class in high school?," "Do you think you have the ability to complete university?," "Where do you think you would rank in a class at university?," "In order to become a doctor, lawyer, or university professor work beyond four years of university is necessary. How likely do you think it is that you could complete such advanced work?," "Forget for a moment how others grade your work. In your own opinion how good do you think your work is?," and "What do you expect your grades to be this year?" As well as the interval scale, the scores were collapsed for low (8-18), medium (19-29) and high (30-40) self-concept of ability.

A factor analysis of the eight self-concept of ability items identified two underlying dimensions of academic self-concept. One of these related to self-concept with respect to the students' immediate school situation, school work, friends and so forth, and the other was self-concept of ability to deal with university level work. Although the original scale was no doubt intended to measure a general self-concept, at times in the analysis we will distinguish the two dimensions by *self-concept of ability school* (SCA school) and *self-concept of ability university* (SCA Univ.), as well as self-concept in general (SCA). An analysis of self-concept appears in Chapter 7.

Attitude to schoolwork was measured by three questions asking respectively whether the student found the subject matter boring, difficult and useful. For these three questions there were five response categories, ranging from very boring to very interesting, very difficult to very easy, and very useful to completely useless, and "Don't know." A scale ranging from 1-15 was constructed by combining responses to the three questions. A score of 11-15 was considered a positive response, 9-10 neutral, and 1-8 negative.

The development of the women's liberation movement and the antici-pated changing role of women led us to ask the girls in the study a set of questions to get at girls' present *attitudes to the adult feminine role*. They were given six statements about what a woman would like to do with her life. They were asked to indicate about each whether the possibility that it described meant a great deal to her, a fair amount, not very much, or nothing at all. The statements are:

1. To have a career, a long-term job that requires me to develop my skills and capacities and that would be rewarding for me personally.
2. To do community work—to help people in my community through organizations such as hospital auxiliaries, or through informal organizations such as tenants' groups, anti-pollution groups, etc.
3. To keep a good household; to be a good cook and have the other skills that go into being a good homemaker.
4. To have skills and the possibility of getting jobs that will give me

some security and allow me some independence in organizing my life as I wish.

5. To have a mutually rewarding relationship with a man.
6. To have a child, or some children, and raise and care for them.

These items were not scaled, but were to be used in an exploratory way.

School Variables

In the discussion of the theoretical model in Chapter 3, we indicated why we omitted from the study school-related variables such as teachers' qualifications, physical resources available to the school, and so on. There were, however, some school variables which are crucial, particularly in a school system which has distinct tracking or streaming as a consequence of the various programs.

At the time this survey was carried out, most schools in Ontario were following the pattern that had been introduced in 1962, the so-called Robarts Plan referred to in Chapter 2. Under this plan there were three branches of secondary education: Arts and Science; Business, Commerce and Science; and Science, Technology and Trades. Each branch was supposed to have three programs: a five-year, a four-year and a two-year program. Only the five-year program in each branch was intended to lead to university. It was hoped that the invidious distinction between academic on the one hand, and technical and commercial education on the other, would disappear. What happened instead was that the vast majority of students considering university as a possibility chose the five-year Arts and Science program. By 1969 it was clear that those who did not were being trapped in four-year or two-year programs at an early age that cut off future options. In 1969 a new credit system of courses given at an "advanced" and "general" level was introduced.[11] At the time of our survey only a few schools had adopted the system. (It was made compulsory in 1972.) Raymond Breton in his analysis[12] concluded that program was the main predictor of educational aspirations. In Ontario this was, of course, to be expected, since only those in five-year programs were eligible for university. However, program was an important intervening variable. Why students selected or how they were allocated to programs is the subject of a later chapter (Chapter 10). *School program* was measured as a dichotomous variable according to whether students were in any of the five-year programs or in the four- or two-year programs.

The marks a student gets in school are clearly a measure of how well he has mastered the subject matter of his courses, that is, his *school performance*. Unfortunately for our study, we have no standardized measure of achievement of cognitive skills because of the limits of our budget as well as the time during which the schools were available for this study. Consequently, we did not administer a standardized achievement test as distinct from the mental ability test, the former measuring how well a student performs and the latter his potential for performance.

Since the demise of any province-wide examinations administered by the Department of Education, marks are to some extent the result of subjective evaluations by teachers, as will be shown in the chapter on school performance. There may be different standards required between schools in the province, and even within schools teachers may demand varying levels of performance. Furthermore, and most importantly, marks mean something very different in the four-year program and the five-year program. Not only was the course content of subjects in the four-year program less demanding than in the five-year, but the level of mastery required of the watered-down subject matter generally was less in the four-year program. In spite of these difficulties, it clearly is important to have a measure of academic achievement in analysing educational aspirations. Students were asked to indicate what their grades were last year, whether they were: mainly 75 per cent and over (or mainly A's and B's); 66-74 (or B's and C's); 60-65 (or C's and D's); 50-59 (or D's and E's); under 50 (or F's).

We felt some uneasiness about relying on student-reported grades, and we were also constrained by our undertaking not to ask for confidential information. However, students' marks are often public information, either because they are published in some fashion or readily made available to employers, universities and the like. Accordingly, we asked the principals of the sampled schools if they could supply us with the previous year's grades of the sampled students. We received a high positive response, except in some cases where they do not in fact give letter or number grades. We were thus able to check the reliability of student-reported grades against school-reported grades. The correlations were uniformly high.

There remains the performance differences between the four- and five-year programs. We explored the possibility of some weighting mechanism, but could devise none that seemed logical. Moreover, we felt that whatever program a student was in, his level of achievement would have an effect on his aspirations, since from any program he would be able to enter a community college and other forms of post-secondary education, although not, with few exceptions, university. We saw no other way out of this problem where school program and academic achievement are variables in the same model.

The Parental Interview Schedule

Approximately 1,000 parents, primarily mothers, of students in each of the three grades were interviewed. Other studies, such as those of Coleman, Sewell and Breton, which have analysed educational aspirations and attainments, have derived family data from student questionnaire responses. Family variables collected in this manner may contain a degree of unreliability, since they are student claims and perceptions of family events and parental feelings rather than the responses parents themselves might give.

Many of the variables in the parent questionnaire are similar to those in the student questionnaire, and they were defined and measured in much the same way as the student variables; but there were important differences. Our objective was not simply to check the reliability of student responses about what things were like at home, although our data do enable us to do that, particularly reports of parental encouragement. Rather, we were seeking to supplement the student questionnaire by asking the mother directly about a range of family environment factors which might influence her child's aspirations. It was necessary to ask the mother somewhat different questions depending on whether the sampled child was in Grade 8, 10 or 12. Most of the questions relating to family interaction concerned the sample child and not any other children there might be in the family. Except in the few cases where the father was the parent interviewed, the questions relating to the father were answered by the mother.

We thought it important to distinguish the educational aspirations which the mother perceived her child as having and those which she herself had for the child. *Perceived child's aspiration* was measured by the questions, "After what grade would _____ like to leave school?," and "Then what would _____ like to do?" *Mother's own aspiration for child* were the responses to "After what grade do *you* want _____ to leave school?," followed by, "Then what do you want _____ to do?" Response formats, scoring and scaling were the same as for the student questionnaire. Our reason for asking so many similar questions was our speculation that similarities and discrepancies between parental and student aspirations and the perceptions of each of the other might have some kind of a subtle interplay, when examined against some of our other family variables, in their effect on aspirations. Within-family consistency, we thought, might have reinforcing effects on whatever level of aspirations the child had. Or high levels of aspiration on the part of the mother as reported by her might be a factor as suggested by the literature for the high aspirations of some lower-class children.[13] Moreover, at the time of the survey there was something of a conventional wisdom—to be somewhat discredited by the evidence—that young people were rejecting education and often held contradictory views to those of their parents. The expectations questions were included in the parental schedule for the same reasons, that is, to discover what gap there might be between the more realistic expectations question and the aspirations one which admits of more fantasy.

Since the parent's child was at a stage of making important educational decisions, specifically what he or she was going to do next fall, it was appropriate to ask parents what they thought the child was going to do next fall and what they would most like him or her to do.

If the sampled child was a girl, the mothers were given the same five statements about the adult feminine role that were given to their daughters. The wording of the question (38b) was somewhat different: "When you think of your daughter's future, how important do you think each of the following *ought to be to her?*" Thus we were concerned with how the mother thought about the daughter, not about how she, the mother, might think about herself with respect to the adult female role. The intention was, once again, to use these questions in an exploratory sense to discover attitudinal conjunction or disjunction between mothers and their daughters with respect to this rapidly changing aspect of modern society.

Home Environment Variables

It seemed to us that a child might be influenced by the degree of integration in his family, by his parents' attitudes to education, by whether or not his parents helped with his schoolwork, and by how well he got along with his parents. *Family integration* was operationalized by asking parental respondents, "In your family, how often do most of you do these kinds of things together?" This was followed by six areas of activity, of which five were subsequently used: hockey or football games; concerts or movies; skiing, baseball, ping-pong, card games, etc.; discuss current events or news; discuss family problems such as money, sickness, etc.; visit relatives or friends. Each of these comprised a three point ordinal scale representing "often," "sometimes," "never." The responses were aggregated to form a scale ranging from 5 to 15.

Parental attitude to education was based upon the respondent's opinion about eight statements, each comprising a five point ordinal scale. These statements were introduced as follows: "People have different opinions about certain things. I would like your opinions about each of these statements about education. After I read the statement would you tell me whether you strongly agree, agree, disagree, strongly disagree or are uncertain about it." The eight statements were: "Education determines how successful a person will be in his life's work"; "Nowadays young people are becoming over-educated"; "Experience from work and life is a better education than learning in schools and colleges"; "Education breaks up family life"; "Education is worthwhile for its own sake"; "University or college education is important in getting along socially"; "Education beyond the age of 16 is a waste of time for most students"; and "It is more important for a child to be popular in school than to get good grades."

Notes

1. James W.B. Douglas, *The Home and the School* (London: MacGibbon and Kee, 1964).
2. Aspirations Scolaires et Orientations Professionelles des Etudiants (ASOPE) is a longitudinal study conducted by Laval University and the University of Montreal.

3. Raymond Boudon, *Education, Opportunity and Social Inequality* (New York: John Wiley, 1974).

4. John Porter, Bernard Blishen and Maria Barrados, *Survival of a Grade 8 Cohort: A Study of Early School Leaving in Ontario* (Ontario Department of Education, 1977).

5. Marion Porter, John Porter, Bernard Blishen, *Does Money Matter?* (Toronto: Macmillan, 1979).

6. The mental ability test is described in *Does Money Matter?*, 1979. The Grade 10 questionnaire is reproduced in the 1973 edition of *Does Money Matter?*, Institute of Behavioural Research, York University, Toronto, or can be obtained from the Department of Sociology, Carleton University, Ottawa.

7. See, for example, Raymond Breton, *Social and Academic Factors in the Career Decisions of Canadian Youth* (Ottawa: Queen's Printer, 1972). William H. Sewell and Vimal P. Shah, "Parents' Education and Children's Educational Aspirations and Achievements," in *American Sociological Review* (Vol. 33, April 1968), pp.191–209.

8. Bernard R. Blishen, "The Construction and Use of an Occupational Class Scale," in *Canadian Society* (Toronto: Macmillan, 1961), pp.477–485.

9. Correlation coefficients of .29 for males and .32 for females were reported by Sewell, *et al.*, compared to the SOSA correlation coefficients .14 for males in Grade 12 and .16 for females in Grade 12. William H. Sewell and Vimal P. Shah, "Socio-economic Status, Intelligence, and the Attainment of Higher Education," in *Sociology of Education* (Vol. 40, Winter 1967), pp.1–23.

10. Wilbur B. Brookover, *Self-Concept of Ability and School Achievement* (Michigan: Educational Publication Services, College of Education, Michigan State University, 1962).

11. Province of Ontario, Department of Education, *Circular H.S.I.*, 1969.

12. Raymond Breton, "Academic Stratification in Secondary Schools and Educational Plans of Students," in *The Canadian Review of Sociology and Anthropology* (Vol. 7, February 1970), pp.17–34.

13. Brian Jackson and Dennis Marsden, *Education and the Working Class* (Harmondsworth: Penguin, 1966).

5

The Making of Educational Aspirations

Our task now is to determine how, independently and in combination, the many variables discussed in Chapter 3 and operationalized in Chapter 4 affect the level of aspirations of Ontario high school students. Contrary to some popular images of the mass media of the day, there was no widespread rejection of the education system on the part of the students in it.

Just over two-thirds of the Grade 8 students wanted to continue on to Grade 13. One-fifth wanted to leave at Grade 12, and only a very small proportion wanted to leave before reaching Grade 12. No doubt, as students pass through the educational system their early aspirations become modified in the light of experience. We would anticipate, therefore, that the Grade 10 sample would have aspirations somewhat lower than those in Grade 8. Grade 10 is an important school year because almost all the students are fifteen years old or older and, hence, at or near the legal school leaving age. Moreover, some of the special "industrial" or "vocational" programs end at Grade 10. The proportion of the Grade 10 students who wanted to go on to Grade 13 dropped, and the proportion who wanted to leave at Grade 12 increased considerably. These lessening aspirations continue to Grade 12, where slightly more than half wanted to go on to Grade 13.[1]

These reduced aspirations might reflect two factors. One is the lessening of aspirational horizons in an absolute sense as higher levels are achieved. The other is an increased awareness of alternatives to Grade 13 as one gets to the point of decision about going there. Only about one-third of those Grade 12 students who wanted to leave school at Grade 12 wanted to go directly to work. Over one-half of them wished to continue some form of education. More were attracted to the C.A.A.T.s than anywhere else, but private commercial and business schools were also attractive. For those who wanted to go on to Grade 13, university was the overwhelming choice for post-secondary education, with just over one-half wanting to graduate and a further tenth wanting to go on to post-graduate work. A mere 4 per cent of those who wanted to leave at Grade 13 wanted to go directly to work.

Educational aspirations were still generally high for those who had reached Grade 12, no doubt because that grade constituted something of a survival group since some proportion would have fallen out of the educational system before Grade 12.[2]

However, only 7 per cent of those in Grade 10 expressed a desire to leave before Grade 12. Of the Grade 10's who wanted to leave at Grade 10, 60 per cent wanted to go directly to work, and of those who wanted to leave at Grade 11, 46 per cent wanted to go directly to work. These two groups in Grade 10 had the lowest educational aspirations of students in the Ontario system, and it is remarkable that they constituted such a minor fraction of the students in Grade 10 in 1971. Some who wanted to leave school at Grade 10 or 11 wanted to have more education; apprenticeship, private commercial and trade schools were preferred over the publicly supported system.

Sex Differences

As we all know, the occupational world, although changing, has been very different for the two sexes. Women have not participated in the labour force to the extent that men have, and when they have they have concentrated in particular occupational categories. To the extent that the occupational world has been served by the educational system, we would expect to find considerable differences between the sexes with respect to educational aspirations and expectations. For example, we were accustomed to seeing most of the enrolment in commercial schools and programs and in nursing schools as female. Similarly, women have been drawn to teaching more than they have been to the other professional occupations. Change is taking place, however, with respect to the adult feminine role. Activities exclusive to marriage and motherhood appear to be losing some of the dominance they have had in the past, and if that is so one would expect the educational aspirations and plans of females to be undergoing change. It is for this reason we have devoted a chapter to particular aspects of educational and occupational aspirations of females in a period of social change. Here we will deal with male-female differences to the extent necessary to elucidate the influences bearing on aspirations.

As with girls, but to a lesser extent, there are for boys direct labour force links with the educational system. Boys are more likely than girls to be found in technical and trades programs at the lower end of the educational system and in the professional schools at the upper end. We would anticipate this reality to be reflected in the educational aspirations of boys.

It is probably because of the close association between their education and the occupational world that one-quarter of the girls in Grade 12 wanted to go directly to work after high school compared to one-eighth of the boys.

Table 5.1
Students' Aspirations by Sex and Grade

Aspirations	Grade 8		Grade 10		Grade 12	
	M	F	M	F	M	F
	(per cent)					
Work	20	19	16	19	13	25
Private Trade School	12	5	18	7	13	3
Teachers' College or Nursing School	2	22	2	16	1	14
Community College	7	6	14	9	16	13
University*	37	27	29	25	35	28
Post-graduate Work	7	5	6	4	8	4
Other	3	1	5	4	6	4
Don't Know	12	15	10	16	8	9
Total	100	100	100	100	100	100
N =	1,331	1,242	1,587	1,330	1,416	1,369

X^2 (7) Grade 8 = 304.6   p = .000
10 = 286.4
12 = 337.3

*Because of the very few numbers, those responding "go to university, but probably not graduate" *are included* with university in this and subsequent tables.

The desire of Grade 12 boys for some form of education beyond high school is striking. The 43 per cent of boys who at Grade 12 wanted to graduate from university seemed high in view of the then popular view of contemporary youth and their believed-in attitudes towards education. The various post-high school desires of boys and girls are presented in Table 5.1 for each of the three grades. For some boys the desire for private trade or business courses indicates once again that not all of the educational needs were provided by the public system.[3] The private trade schools seemed to compete with community colleges as the second most important post-secondary education alternative for boys. For girls at Grade 12, teachers' colleges and nursing schools competed with community colleges.[4]

The difference between the aspirations of boys and girls to go to work, which existed at Grade 12, was not as great for students in the earlier grades. It was least at Grade 8, began to diverge at Grade 10 and became quite marked by Grade 12. This shift might be interpreted as a modification by girls of their aspirations in the light of the reality they found. At Grade 8, teaching and nursing seemed desirable to girls, but that, too, was different in Grade 12. At all grades girls were less attracted to university than boys. Not unexpectedly, uncertainty about post-high school desires decreased, as indicated by the falling proportions of "Don't Knows" from Grade 8 to 12.

Aspirations, Sex and the Class Structure

Since the guiding idea of our research is equality of educational opportunity, we are concerned to discover how the social class structure of Ontario affects the educational aspirations of students. The evidence is strikingly clear. We can see from Figure 5.1 how for Grade 12 students the desire to leave school at Grade 12 rather than Grade 13 was closely related to the occupational status of the father, which we are using as our measure of social class. The relationship is monotonic, as can be seen from the gradient formed by the proportions of each class that wished to leave at Grade 12. The proportion fell at each ascending level of social class to Class I at the top, where only 24 per cent of children wanted to leave at Grade 12. The reverse gradient is found, of course, for those who wanted to leave at Grade 13.

It can also be seen from Table 5.2 how the desire to go to university after high school was related to the social class position of the family and the sex of the student. The relationship is also monotonic, as can be seen in the different proportions of students at each class level who wanted to graduate from university or do graduate work. The gradient was highest at the top social class where two-thirds of boys and three-fifths of girls wanted to attain the highest educational levels, and fell continuously through the class structure to the second lowest social class where about one-third of boys and less than one-quarter of girls wanted higher education. If there was a rejection of the educational system it was on the part of the studens from the lower social classes, not the vocal and articulate middle-class students of the early seventies. These latter, probably a minority of their social class peers, wanted to change rather than leave the schools, while a sizeable part of the lower-class young people preferred to withdraw from an educational system that served so well the middle classes.

Together, social class and sex interact to produce complex effects on educational aspirations. Generally, social class intensifies the difference between boys and girls with respect to the choice of more education or work. With the highest social class a slightly higher proportion of boys than girls wanted to go to work. Below this class, however, the differences between the sexes assumed the "normal" pattern. At the lower end of the class structure the desires of boys and girls were markedly apart, as were the desires of lower-class girls from the girls in the classes above them. At Grade 12, 38 per cent of the girls in Class VI wanted to go to work after high school compared to 13 per cent of the boys of the same class. At the top end of the class structure only one-tenth of girls in Class I and about one-eighth in Class II wanted to go directly to work. These data would suggest that it is the girls in the lower social classes for whom the relationship between the educational system and the work world was direct, and while this may seem to be efficient from the point of view of society at large it has the effect of reducing educational aspirations for these girls.

Only 22 per cent of Class VI girls wanted to go to university compared to 59 per cent of Class I girls. Although teaching and nursing education appealed to girls to some extent at all class levels, it was somewhat greater for girls at the lower end of the class structure—a fact which should raise

Figure 5.1
Grade at Which Students Would Like to Leave High School,
by Socio-economic Status

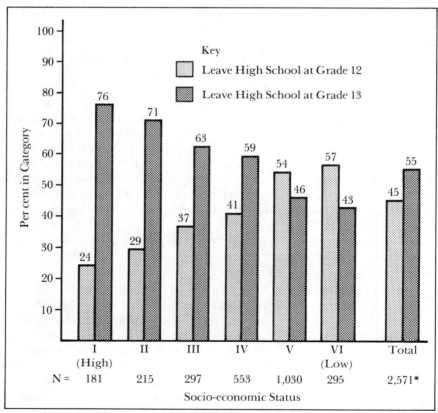

*Total will not agree with numbers in each category because of missing data.

Table 5.2
Students' Aspirations by Socio-economic Status and Sex
(Grade 12)

Aspirations	I		II		III		IV		V		VI		Total	
	M	F	M	F	M	F	M	F	M	F	M	F	M	F
						(per cent)								
Go to Work	12	10	9	14	12	19	10	16	16	32	13	38	13	25
Private Trade School	1	0	6	1	10	2	11	3	18	4	18	8	13	3
Teachers' College or Nursing School	1	8	3	7	0	11	0	14	1	15	1	14	1	13
Community College	10	10	8	10	10	14	18	15	19	14	19	10	16	13
University	54	51	40	46	44	29	40	33	26	20	31	20	35	29
Post-graduate Work	12	8	18	5	8	9	8	4	6	3	4	2	8	4
Other Plans	6	2	5	4	9	4	6	6	6	5	5	3	6	4
Don't Know	4	11	11	13	7	12	8	9	7	7	9	5	8	9
Total	100	100	100	100	100	100	100	100	100	100	100	100	100	100
N =	82	98	123	95	160	139	271	282	530	511	145	155	1,312	1,280

Socio-economic Status

$X^2 (35)$ M = 118.08   p = .000
F = 152.23

some questions about the effect on educational opportunity of raising fees for this type of education as was done in 1972.

The data of Table 5.2 reveal how the public system, the extension of which was supposed to have served a redistributive principle and expanded educational opportunity for all, served the higher classes proportionally more than the lower. For boys in Classes V and VI, about one-fifth wanted to go into private training schools, where they would pay fees or apprenticeship after Grade 12, while almost no boys in Class I did. At the other extreme, the proportion of Class I boys who wanted to go on to the more expensive post-graduate work was one-eighth, for Class II boys one-fifth, but about one-twentieth for Class V and VI boys.

Our belief that responses to the educational aspirations question— which left the student free to express his hopes and desires as he felt them to be without the constraints of his particular circumstances—would be different than responses to a question asking about educational expectations was not strikingly confirmed. It will be recalled that the expectations question specifically asked the student to take his abilities and circumstances into consideration before responding about the level of education he might really expect to attain. For all social classes fewer expected to leave at Grade 12 than would have liked to, an interesting finding since in their responses to other questions relating to further education, students wanted more than they expected to get. Neither the aspiration-education discrepancy nor the differences between the social classes in discrepancies are great. The difference is slightly greater for the top two classes and less for the bottom four, and the situation might be interpreted as the higher social classes having a greater proportion of reluctant recruits to Grade 13 than had the lower classes, a fact that should not be surprising since the former were more vocally critical and a greater proportion of them actually go there.

These minimal discrepancies between aspirations and expectations can be found also in the earlier grade samples. The correlations between aspirations and expectations, when treated as interval scales, were .899 for boys for Grade 8, .910 for Grade 10 and .914 for Grade 12, and for girls .889, .910 and .912 for Grades 8, 10 and 12 respectively. The one major conclusion is that whether they are asked about their educational futures in terms of aspirations or of expectations, their responses contain an element of fantasy, even though in the latter question they were reminded of some of the hazards ahead of them, including the limitations of their own abilities. At no time have one-third of students in any high school grade up to Grade 12 gone on to graduate from university. A follow-up of Grade 12 students two years later showed expectations, aspirations and plans all to have been unrealistic.[5]

Whatever the level of fantasy involved in prospects of educational futures, the class differences were substantial. A further difference between

Figure 5.2
Per cent Wanting to Graduate from University,
by Socio-economic Status, Mental Ability and Sex, Grade 12

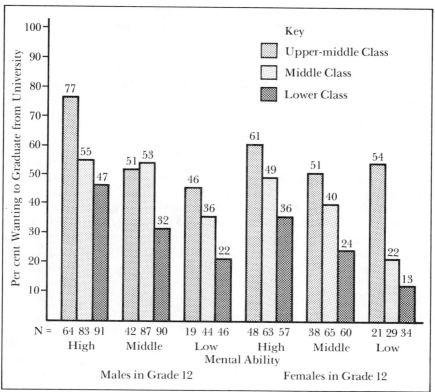

the social classes in their exploitation of the educational system was to be seen in the reasons why students chose their high school subjects. In response to the question, "Which of the following *best* describes how you choose your subjects?," 36 per cent of the Grade 10 students in Class I answered, "I need them to go into a college or university" compared to 19 per cent of Class V and 15 per cent of Class VI students. On the other hand, only 28 per cent of Class I students responded, "They will get me the sort of job I want" compared to 52 per cent of students in Class VI. About one-third of all classes took them because they liked them or found them interesting.

Mental Ability and Aspirations
One of the unfortunate consequences of the relationship between social class, sex and educational aspirations is that many able young people at the

lower levels of the class structure are unlikely to develop fully their intellectual potential. The loss is not only theirs but also that of their society. It will be recalled that to measure mental ability we employed a culture fair test, which we hoped would eliminate some of the advantages that verbal type I.Q. tests give to those from higher social classes in demonstrating inherent ability. Whatever position might be taken on the inheritability of intelligence, there is still the overwhelming fact that the lower social class structure is rich in high mental ability children.[6] Since we cannot eliminate entirely the class bias from mental ability testing, we can assume that our estimate of the loss of able students from the lower part of the class structure is conservative, an observation that is important to keep in mind in assessing the evidence we now present.

Figure 5.2 shows the percentage of students in Grade 12 who wanted to graduate from university (including those who responded to our aspiration question that they wished to go on to post-graduate work) by social class, mental ability and sex. We have reduced the six social class categories into upper-middle, middle and lower respectively. We have grouped the students into three levels of mental ability: high, middle and low. The persistence of two relationships which we have already noted is striking when we look at students of the same mental ability level. One is that the relationship between aspirations and social class holds for both males and females across all mental ability levels, and the lower aspirations of girls relative to boys holds for all mental ability levels and all social class levels with a few exceptions. The same relationships exist in Grade 10.

While 77 per cent of high mental ability boys of the upper-middle class wanted to graduate from university, only 47 per cent of the lower class did. The comparable percentages for girls were 61 and 36 for upper-middle and lower classes respectively. The one reversal in the class distribution of aspirations at the middle level of mental ability for boys is within the bounds of sampling error.

With the development of community colleges, all of the high mental ability students not going to university did not cease to be educated. Our survey data on the post-secondary expectations of high mental ability Grade 12 boys and girls show that 18 per cent of lower-class boys expected to go to community colleges, as did 17 per cent of middle-class boys. Only 2 per cent of the upper-middle-class boys did. Only about one-tenth of lower- and middle-class boys expected to go to work. By contrast one-third of lower-class girls expected to go to work, but the proportion was considerably less for middle-class girls. Clearly, it was the girls of high mental ability at the lower end of the class system who constituted the greatest loss of potentially able students from the educational stream. About one-quarter of the brightest girls from the lower class expected to go to teachers' or nursing schools or community colleges, while somewhat more of their middle-class counterparts did.

For the brightest students, one important difference between Grade 10 and Grade 12 was between boys and girls with respect to going to work. For the lower classes the proportion of boys dropped between grades and for girls it increased, suggesting that when boys did survive, the possibility of continuing some form of post-secondary education became a realistic choice, but for the brightest girls, particularly those captured in vocational programs, the work world became a more significant destination.

If we consult the theoretical model developed in Chapter 3 we can see that in discussing mental ability, sex and social class we have been dealing with factors which are early in the causal sequence in the formation of educational aspirations. Through cross-tabular analysis we have seen something of how they interplay. As with sex, we would like, ideally, to think of mental ability as something the individual "comes with," and therefore unalterable by environmental, including educational, influences. Education should have something to offer those of all mental abilities, even to the extent of redress, by which the dull might claim more than the brightest. The rational model of an educational system, however, suggests that the most talented should be steered into the most intellectually demanding forms of education, if for no other reason than that the most complex tasks in the society requiring the most education should be undertaken by the most able. But since we also value freedom, the allocation of talent to training should be voluntary, and able children should be free— if they can be regarded as mature free agents, which is questionable—to choose whatever education they want. Clearly, a society such as Canada would be in trouble if all the bright ones were to waste their talent; thus subtle forms of encouragement, which are a part of the child-rearing practices, succeed in directing some to high aspirations. But as we have seen, there are great differences between classes—so great, in fact, to suggest that the Ontario system is not "rational" in the sense just used. No doubt costs of education play some part in this irrationality, but at the same time there are important cultural differences.

To some extent individuals also "come with" their class cultures, but these are alterable through educational policy that can provide both encouragement and financial assistance. Lower social class background creates a socio-cultural climate that can be inhospitable to educational achievement and aspirations. Its effects are all the more intractable because they come early in the individual's life.

We next explore two other socio-cultural climates, not altogether unrelated to social class, which are known to have early effects on the individual's educational chances. The first is the degree of urbanization, or to take the other end of the continuum, the consequences of being brought up in small towns and rural areas. The second is religion. Both have played an important role in the history of educational policy in Ontario. In analysing our data by socio-cultural climates, we are seeking to discover where limited perspective on educational horizons exists in the Ontario social structure.

Aspirations in Urban and Rural Settings

Differences between life in the city and in the country have been discussed by observers of society as far back as Aesop with his fable of the city mouse and the country mouse. In the modern period social scientists have considered the city and the country to be the polar extremes of a continuum in which the urban milieu represents the more advanced stages of technological, industrial and cultural civilization, and the rural, the more traditional, retarded and simple. For some social theorists this urban-rural continuum is the most fundamental dimension of historical change in that more and more people have become urban dwellers earning their livelihood from industrial occupations. Industrial nations are in the vanguard of social change. But the urban-rural continuum is also a dimension of social differentiation within present societies in that, even though a country may be heavily industrialized, some portion of its population remains in rural pursuits and is believed to exhibit characteristics different from those in the city. Just what those characteristics are and what accounts for them cannot always be agreed upon, but the urban and the rural are always considered, even in the popular mind, to be distinct socio-cultural types. Urbanism as a way of life is thought to be quite different to the folk-like traditional ways of the rural society.

In Canada, the urban-rural distinction has always been fundamental both historically and in the present. The major shift from a rural-based to an industrial society gained its greatest momentum after the Second World War. This major pattern of social change, of off-farm migration, of the rapid reduction in the number of farms, and the loss of prominence of the family farm, has been accelerating over the last thirty years. As the Federal Task Force on Agriculture indicated in its Report in 1969, they are the outcomes of dynamic processes within Canadian agriculture, as well as adaptations to new economic forces outside of Canada that change Canada's position as a supplier of agricultural products.[7]

Although Ontario was the most industrialized of the provinces in 1971, one-fifth of its population lived in rural areas, some working on farms and others combining off-farm work with farming.[8] A further 6 per cent lived in towns of less than 5,000. Ontario has a high representation of that peculiar Canadian phenomenon, the one-industry town that is small, isolated and culturally impoverished as its inhabitants make a living from mills, mines and railways. How much Ontario's rural and one-industry communities constitute distinct socio-cultural milieux productive of different values, psychological dispositions, aspirations and the like may be open to question. Some differences for the one-industry town have been recently documented by Rex Lucas,[9] and for rural communities by Donald Whyte.[10]

There are, however, factors which would tend to reduce socio-cultural differences. One is that urban values and urban technology have pervaded rural areas through both productive and recreational technology as well as communications. Water, electricity and television have all been successively piped into the rural home, bringing with them lifestyles and outlooks that are predominantly urban. Many rural areas of Ontario have been overrun by the extensive urban growth, which has resulted in that massive conurbation stretching from Oshawa to Hamilton, and also by the ex-urbanite communities that are spawned by such urban expansion.

However, the rural way of life is probably not completely obliterated in present-day Ontario, particularly for communities farther from the major urban centres. Here, orientations to life can probably still be affected by the special relationship with nature, its mysteries and its rhythms, its hazards and its bounties, all of which could be the source of cultural and psychological characteristics quite different from those of the dweller in the megalopolis.

Here we are concerned with those components of culture that might affect educational aspirations. There are specific reasons why we might expect to find differences in values held about getting on in the world and being successful. For one, rural areas do not have the range of occupational differentiation that would expose rural young people to the variety of occupations offered by the urban-industrial system. Moreover, up until recently, not only has there been an occupational homogeneity within farming, but farming has not required high levels of education. The farm population has been the least educated of any segment of the society. The parental generation of present-day rural young people have low levels of education. They were brought up when the prevailing attitude was that a boy would become productive on the farm in relation to the growth of his physical strength, rather than his intellect. Thus the farmer saw schooling for his children as having limited use. We do not know, of course, the extent to which rural life continues to be less supportive of education than urban areas, nor the extent to which these rural forces of traditionalism, closeness to nature and practical pursuits have been eliminated by urban values.

With respect to equality of educational opportunity, the needs of rural youth are quite different from those of the city. If these young people are to continue in rural pursuits they need particular elements in their educational programs which emphasize the appropriate skills. Moreover, these are skills involving the new complex technology of farming as well as the management of the farming enterprise, which increasingly represents large capital investments. However, the very technological changes which are taking place greatly increase the productivity of labour in agriculture, creating in turn, because of the larger families in rural areas, a continuing stream of migrants to the city. That, in turn, means education in rural areas must give consideration to providing as much opportunity for educational and occupational mobility as exists for city youth. The major solution to the provision of educational services to rural areas in recent years has been the district elementary and secondary schools designed after the Second World War. Another factor that at times has been thought to affect educational aspirations and expectations is the distance from institutions of higher learning. In part, there is the cost of moving from rural and small-town areas and living away from home, but there is also the transmission of educational values from a nearby university or college.

It is clear from Figure 5.3 that there were differences between metropolitan students and rural ones with respect to their aspirations, with 40 per cent of boys in the former and 26 per cent of boys in the latter in Grade 10

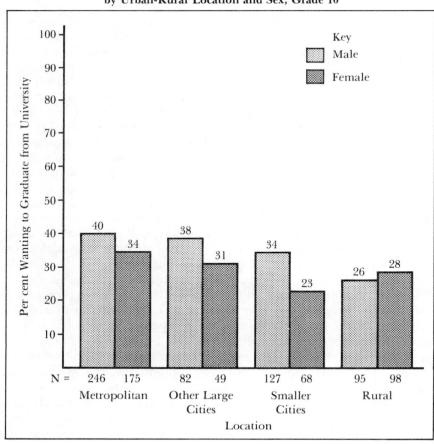

Figure 5.3
Per cent Wanting to Graduate from University,
by Urban-Rural Location and Sex, Grade 10

wanting to graduate from university. There is scarcely any difference between students in the Toronto megalopolis and other major urban centres. There is no real reason to expect that there would be since these cities can be considered in most respects to be fully urbanized. The break seems to come between the second and third category of urbanization for girls, and between the third and fourth for boys.

The differences between boys' and girls' aspirations, which we have noted previously for social class, were also striking in the urban-rural continuum, particularly at Grade 12 where fewer girls than boys in each level of urbanization wanted to go to university, and with substantial decreases in the proportions between metro and rural categories. About two-fifths of the large-city boys in Grade 10 wanted to graduate from university, while about one-quarter of rural boys did. A marginally greater proportion of rural girls than boys wanted to graduate from university in Grade 10—the only reversal we have so far come across where girls had, if not higher, at least as great aspirations as boys (Figure 5.3), all the more puzzling because it does not occur also in Grade 12. Once again, we should probably have recourse to the survival concept, that is, if rural boys did survive to Grade 12 their aspirations were substantially higher than both girls and boys in Grade 10.

When we divide our metro-rural categories into different social class levels we find that for each social class level the rural population has lower educational aspirations. That relationship is clear for all grades. To be working class and rural means a double handicap. At Grade 10, 52 per cent of upper-middle-class urban students aspired to university, while only 22 per cent of lower-class rural children did. However, at each grade, lower-class metro students were closer in aspirations to the rural lower-class children, many of whom would be children of farmers, than they were to their metro higher-class schoolmates. For example, for Grade 10 students with high educational aspirations the difference in percentage points between upper-middle and lower-class metropolitan students is 24, while between lower-class metro and lower-class rural the difference is only 6.

It is clear from our analysis that degree of urbanization is related to educational aspirations. The break between the two ends of the continuum seems to come at the point of small cities or towns where young people have, compared to their more urbanized fellows, limited educational horizons. The horizons of those from rural areas are even more limited than those from urban surroundings. The obvious question which arises is, What is there about rural life, so often viewed with nostalgia by the more severe critics of the city, which might account for the more limited perspectives of educational futures?

Earlier we theorized about how some factors such as mental ability and sex, pertaining to the individual, and others, such as values about education and school, embedded in various socio-cultural milieux, are closely associ-

Table 5.3
Percentage with Selected Characteristics by Urban-Rural Location
(Grade 12)

Selected Characteristics	Metropolitan	Other Large City	Small City	Rural
		(per cent)		
High Mental Ability	35	34	29	23
High Occupational Aspirations	46	41	35	35
In Five-Year Program	69	69	59	59
In High Social Class	22	16	13	9
Father with Some Post-secondary Education	10	12	7	5
Mother with Some Post-secondary Education	12	15	12	14
Families with Five Children or More	21	24	32	39
Positive Attitudes to Schoolwork	32	31	37	38
Positive Image of Teachers	53	54	57	48
N =	1,040	369	642	811

ated with educational aspirations. To determine whether or not these characteristics are themselves related to the degree of urbanization, we have arranged a selection of them in Table 5.3, which shows for Grade 12 the percentage of students in our four urban-rural categories having the selected characteristics.[11]

Some of these differences are striking. In Grade 12 the proportion in the top one-third of mental ability level varied monotonically from 35 per cent in the metropolitan area to 23 per cent in the rural areas. City young people had higher occupational aspirations, as indicated by the proportions aspiring to the professional and higher managerial occupations. We also find differences in the proportions in the different academic programs, ranging from seven-tenths of metropolitan youth in the five-year program down to six-tenths of those in smaller city and rural schools.

Next, we might examine from Table 5.3 a set of social structural variables for which we will also find clear differences. For the first of these—the proportion in high social class positions, that is, the top two Blishen classes—the differences were between 22 per cent for metropolitan to 9 per cent for rural, where, of course, the predominant and visible set of occupations would be those concerned with farming, and in the smaller cities, to a considerable extent, those required for the single resource-based industries. For the closely related variable of father's educational level, the same differences can be seen in the proportion of fathers who had both completed high school and had some post-secondary education. The greatest difference for Grade 12 students is between the large cities, where one-tenth of the students had such fathers, and the rural, where only one-twentieth did. For mother's education, the differences were not as marked. The educational levels of both metro and rural mothers of the present generation of high school students were more alike than for their spouses.

If, as we have seen, both social class and mental ability are related to the level of educational aspirations, then youth from small cities and rural areas are at a disadvantage because of their generally low socio-economic status and their lower scores on mental ability tests. If, as we will see later, parental education and family size are also related, the disadvantage of rural young people encompasses a range of characteristics by which they differ from their urban counterparts and which are important in the formation of aspirations. These unfavourable circumstances do not seem to depress the attitudes of rural children to school work, nor to create an unfavourable image of their teachers.

On the students' attitudes to school work, a modestly greater propor-tion (37 and 38 per cent) of small city and rural young people were positive in their attitudes to school work, compared to the 32 and 31 per cent respectively in the metro urban areas and the large cities. At Grade 10 the rural students and those from small cities were more positive in their evaluation of their teachers' competence. That relationship did not persist to Grade 12 for rural children, although it did for the small city. Thus, the one finding of rural students' evaluations of their teachers notwithstanding, it can scarcely be said that the lower educational aspirations of the small-town and rural children can be traced to poorer attitudes to school.

Religion and Educational Aspirations

There are two main reasons for examining the effect of religious affiliation on educational aspirations. The first is that religion provides the major structural division in the educational system in Ontario up to Grade 8, and on a much smaller scale to Grade 10. The second is that precisely because religions are value-loaded belief systems it could be expected that there would be different values about education and the work world, not only between Catholics, Protestants and Jews, but also between the several denominations of Protestantism.

We should address ourselves to the question of whether Catholic religious affiliation or attending a separate school makes for a different level of educational aspirations than being Protestant and attending public schools. We should also explore the effects of belonging to one of the smaller Protestant sects. Religions can be positively anti-intellectual, as when, for example, members of some sects see education as a danger and hence conform only to the very minimal requirements of the law with respect to the school attendance of their children. Some religions believe life on this earth, and hence worldly success and achievement, to be of less importance than salvation, to which formal learning, if not a direct threat, has little to contribute. With respect to such ultimate values and to conservative or liberal interpretations of religious doctrine, there is as great a difference within Protestant denominations as there might be between Protestantism and Catholicism. Such divisions have not led to a further fragmentation of the school system in Ontario, although there may be differences between denominations with respect to the importance they attach to religious teaching in the school curriculum, or the amount of religious instruction their children are given.

Historical differences between Protestantism and Catholicism with respect to the values of worldly success and the differing emphasis to be placed on sacred and secular values within the educational system have given rise to a large body of literature. There is the widely expressed view, for example, that the value of worldly asceticism that came with the Protestant Reformation, particularly Calvinism, was a precondition of capitalism.[12] According to this "Protestant ethic hypothesis," Protestantism led to accumulated savings, an emphasis on working to the greater glory of God, and to personal responsibility for achieving success in one's calling, most aptly articulated in Benjamin Franklin's advice to a young man.[13] It has also been noted that it is the predominantly Protestant societies that have been the leading capitalist ones, with the Protestant entrepreneur embodying the capitalist ethos. The Catholic value system, it has been argued, does not place such emphasis on worldly success, but it is a matter of dispute as to whether these differences represent differences in values stemming from differences in religious dogma or whether they are the result of peculiar historical conditions within varying societies.[14] For example, in Canada immigrants belonging to different ethnic groups, some of whom are Catholic, had to work their way up over generations from lower occupational levels. The fact that Catholics as a group are ethnically differentiated might lead to differences between Catholics with regard to educational values attributable to their ethnic origin and history in Canada. It would be inappropriate, for example, to attribute the low occupational status and educational attainment of the French[15] as a group in Canada wholly or even in a major part to their being Catholic, because a more important factor is that they had to emerge from being conquered. In any case, both the Protestant Reformation and the foundation of capitalism are by now sufficiently historically remote that time might well have obliterated any doctrinal incompatibility between capitalism and Catholicism, and so any social inequalities that remain are attributable to the interplay of religion and other factors peculiar to a given social structure.

Protestantism is a highly differentiated religious system, as widespread denominationalism attests. This denominationalism has been interpreted as an adaption to inequality, with the more deprived groups turning to the more evangelical forms of religion as compensation for relatively deprived status.[16] Consequently, a relationship between denominationalism and social class position has been found. Historically in Canada, there has been a relationship between Protestant fundamentalism and rural life and frontier expansion,[17] although in the modern period it is difficult to locate "bible belts" in Ontario. Thus, as value differences with respect to education and worldly success between Protestantism and Catholicism may be diminishing in the course of history, so may those between the various denominations of Protestantism. Children of all religions are now exposed much more than before to the homogenizing influence of the mass media and the modern city. Religions are not as hostile to each other as they were before the current movement towards church unity, and to some extent they have experienced the melting pot. As well, secular values have been displacing in some measure those of religion over much of social life. It is an open question, therefore, whether we should expect much difference between religious groups with respect to educational aspirations, or if we found differences, whether they could be attributed to differing value systems rather than factors of social structure, particularly social class, and history.

For the purposes of our analysis we have grouped the various religious denominations into Major Protestant, which includes United Church, Anglican and Presbyterian; Other Protestant, which includes all the other Protestant denominations; Roman Catholic; Jewish; all other religions; and no religion.

This classification is consistent with those of other investigators and represents something of a conservative-liberal continuum of religious orientations.[18] The Major Protestant denominations are those which reflect the majority values of an achievement-oriented society, while the Other Protestants include Baptists and fundamentalist and evangelical sects. We would consider those with no religion to represent more secular than sacred values. As well as the liberal-conservative dimension of religious belief, the denominations, as we have ordered them, represent the rank order of religious denominations within the class structure of the society. They would also be consistent with the rank order of the prestige of religious groups within Canada.[19] They are also similar to a rank order of the amount of education required by their clergy, thus providing some evidence of the value attached to education.

Differences in aspirational levels between the various religious denominations might, as we have said, be accounted for by their social class distribution. In Figure 5.4 we can see that Roman Catholics were very much over-represented in the lower class, with almost two-thirds of Catholic students in Grade 12 located there compared to less than half the Major Protestant group. Less than one-tenth of Catholics were in the upper-middle class compared to almost one-fifth of the Major Protestants. The somewhat lower-class status that the Other Protestants shared with Catholics is evident also in Figure 5.4, as is the high status of Jews. The small numbers for the smaller religious groups make the proportions less reliable for them.

When we look at the educational aspirations of students from the various religious groups, our data would suggest that there is really little difference in educational values between the Major Protestant group and

Figure 5.4
Religious Affiliation and Socio-economic Status,
Grade 12

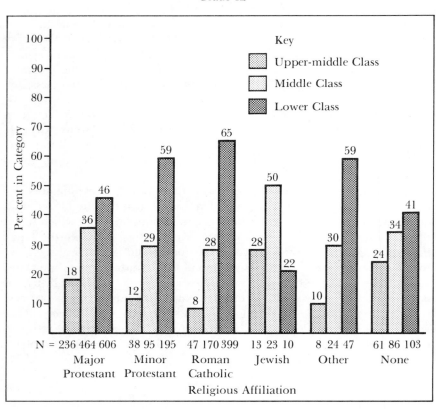

Catholics. At the Grade 8 level, for example, where religious values would probably be strongest in children's minds, there was very little difference between the two groups in the proportions who wanted to graduate from university, with over two-fifths of boys and about one-third of girls in both cases having these aspirations. For the Other Protestant group, however, only one-third of the boys and less than one-quarter of the girls were oriented to the higher levels of the educational system, and a greater portion

Figure 5.5
Aspirations for Work and University,
by Religious Affiliation and Sex, Grade 12

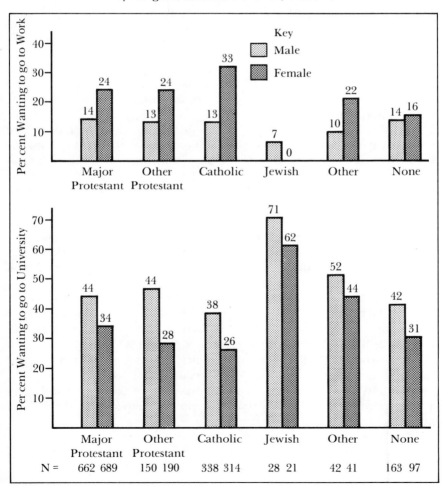

wanted to go to work than either the Major Protestant or Catholic group. Thus it may be that the combination of evangelical religious orientation and low-class position makes for lesser aspirations among the Other Protestant group. We might consider these Grade 8 students to have been at the age of maximum exposure to religious values through socialization in family and church.

In all three grades the highest of all educational aspirations were held by Jewish students. Figure 5.5 shows that in Grade 12 almost three-quarters of the boys and 62 per cent of the girls wanted to graduate from university. That, of course, is a finding quite consistent with our knowledge of the great emphasis placed by Jews on learning.

There is a divergence in aspirations between the Catholic and Major Protestant groups in Grade 12, particularly for girls, that did not appear in the earlier grades. However, we would tend to rule out the view that religious values *per se* are the source of differences in educational aspirations, and suggest alternatively that certain structural features peculiar to Ontario (such as the separate school system, the program structure, the realities of social class) have set in to modify the aspirations of Catholics by the time they reach Grade 12. It should be noted that we have excluded students in French-speaking schools from this analysis since they will be dealt with separately.

At Grade 12, unlike earlier grades, boys from the Major Protestant groups had higher aspiration levels than Catholics, with 44 per cent and 38 per cent respectively wanting to graduate from university. However, this does not mean a turning back on further education on the part of Catholic boys, but rather a shift, probably in the light of reality of their class situation and educational experience, to the community college from the university as the more desired post-secondary destination.

While Catholic girls in high school have lower aspirations than Major Protestant girls, that is not the case in elementary school (Grade 8), when children would be subject to high socialization pressures, particularly if Catholics were in separate schools. It is their experience in high school that must reduce aspirational levels for Catholic girls.

In looking at the smaller religious groups by sex, we find that Other Protestant boys have about the same aspirations as Major Protestant boys in Grade 12. These findings are scarcely consistent with the theory that religions when ranked with respect to their evangelical character will be similarly ranked with respect to the educational aspirations of their members. With respect to educational values for boys it would seem appropriate to accept the view that religions have experienced the melting pot.

So far our evidence indicates that for boys, in particular, there is little difference between Catholics and Protestants with respect to educational aspirations, and that, if anything, Catholics are more similar to the well-established Protestant groups than either group are to the Other Protestant category. We find little, that is, to substantiate the view that religious beliefs and values in themselves might be the source of differences in educational attainment and experience.

Confirmation of such findings is to be found when we analyse aspirations not simply by religious affiliation but by "religiosity." It has been frequently pointed out that a great deal of religious affiliation is nominal and, for that reason, by itself constitutes an unreliable measure of commitment to religious values. We are confining our analysis of religiosity to Catholics because we wish to find out if this major religious group experiences social disadvantage because of religious norms *per se*. If the older view that Catholic values are not as supportive of education and the work ethic as Protestant values are supposed to be is true, then individuals could be expected to have lower aspirations for education and work the more committed they were to Catholic views. We would expect, therefore, that Catholics educated in the primary grades in separate rather than public schools and Catholics who attended church more frequently would be less like Protestants, that is, have lower aspirations than their co-religionists, who were less devout by our admittedly proxy measure of devoutness.

In fact, exactly the opposite was the case. As we can see from Figure 5.6, generally the greater the frequency of church attendance for Catholics the higher were the aspirational levels. The relationship is very clear for females. While they always had lower aspirational levels than males, it was not the traditional values of the church with respect to female roles that were responsible, for quite clearly the closer females were to the church the higher were their educational aspirations. Generally the same held for males, although there were a few reversals, which might be attributed to small numbers, from the general direction of the relationship, notably for those who go to church less often than once a month in Grade 8 and for those who never go to church in Grade 12. The great majority of Catholic students reported themselves to be reasonably attached to their religion as far as church attendance was concerned. For those Catholics who were less attached or detached there is no significant increase in aspirational levels.

Our second measure of religiosity or devoutness for Catholics is whether or not they are in, or were at one time in, separate schools. Not all Catholics send their children to separate schools. Of the Catholic students in our Grade 12 sample, a little more than one-fifth had not attended separate schools. In Grade 10 about the same proportion did not attend separate schools, nor were they at that time in separate schools, as would have been possible. It seems reasonable, therefore, to consider that those Catholics who attended separate schools were closer to the church and, therefore, more likely to reflect its values than those who did not attend; and if these values are less supportive of education than are Protestant values, it could be expected that Catholics closer to the church would have lower educational aspirations than those further away from it. As with our other measure of devoutness, the contrary is the case, at least for Grades 8 and 10, where a greater proportion of those who attended separate schools wanted to graduate from university than those who did not attend separate schools. At Grade 8, 42 per cent of those who were or had attended separate schools wanted to graduate from university, compared to 34 per cent of those who were not in or who had not attended separate schools. At Grade 10 the

Figure 5.6
Per cent of Catholic Students Aspiring to University,
by Frequency of Church Attendance and Sex, Grade 12

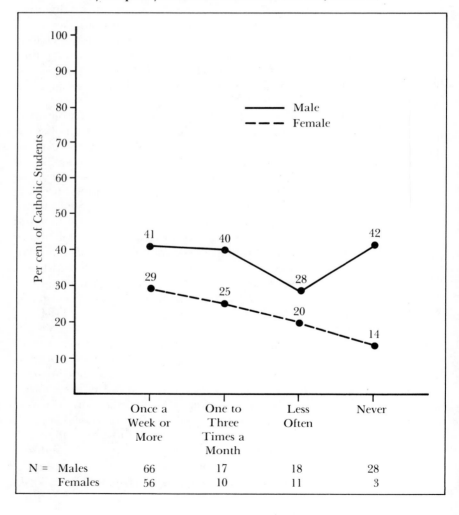

difference in proportions was even greater, with 35 and 25 per cent respectively.

However, there was a striking reversal for Grade 12. Figure 5.7 shows that of those who had attended separate schools, only 36 per cent of boys wanted to graduate from university, compared to 45 per cent of those who did not attend. It would be difficult to attribute this reversal to religious values, since it would be reasonable to expect these values to have their effect as much in the earlier grades as in the later ones.

As we have noted, often Grade 12 is a survival grade with somewhat different characteristics. It would be more reasonable to assume that it is not the effects of religious values but rather historical and structural features of

Figure 5.7
**Per cent of Catholic Students Wanting to go to Work
and University, by Separate School Attendance and Sex, Grade 12**

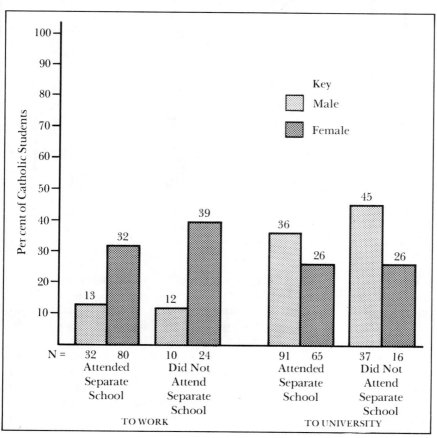

Figure 5.8
Religious Affiliation and High School Program,
Grade 12

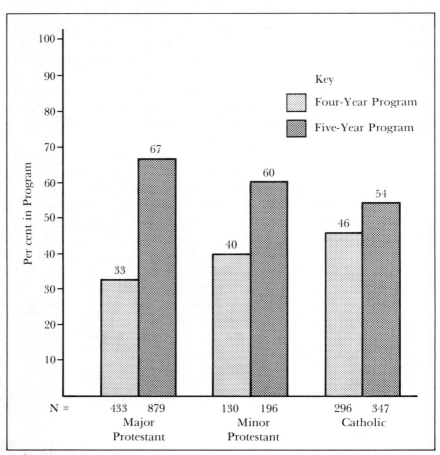

Ontario society that place Catholics at a disadvantage with respect to the occupational structure and the educational system. For example, the subcultural effects of ethnicity on the association between social class and program in school will affect the aspirations of Catholics who have survived to Grade 12.

The program assignments of Catholics were very striking in Grade 12. Almost half were in four-year programs compared to one-third of Major Protestants. Figure 5.8 shows that this over-representation in non-university stream programs did not exist for Grade 10, where the proportions of all three religious groups were about the same in both streams. It is not immediately clear why these program distributions should change between the two grades. Perhaps Catholics who withdrew from school left from five-year programs rather than four-year. Perhaps some of the separate schools and schools to which Catholics go in greater number did not have the range of programs at Grade 10. It does seem reasonable to conclude, however, that the reversal downward of the aspirational level at Grade 12 for the more devout was attributable to program incarceration as well as other social structural conditions.

In other words, as we noted earlier, the more devout Catholics were, the more by Grade 12 did they take on aspirational levels appropriate to their overall position in the social structure, whereas those who were less devout in the highest grade took on more of the aspirational levels of non-Catholics. Less devout Catholics with lower educational aspirations will have left the educational system, or have planned to, in greater proportion. However we might interpret the difference between those in Grade 12 and those in earlier grades, it would be wrong to attribute these differences to differences in values arising from religious teachings.

The general falling off of educational aspirations for Catholics between Grades 10 and 12 can be attributed to both sex and program. It can also be attributed in part to social class. Catholics are substantially over-represented in the lower class, as we saw in Figure 5.4. The data show that at Grade 10 the proportions at each class level were similar for the Catholic and the Major Protestant groups. Middle- and lower-class positions seem to have a greater influence on the Other Protestant group than on the other two. This fact reflects most likely the evangelical groups' conservative attitudes to education, even at the middle-class level and quite markedly at the lowest.

What we are arguing here is that the Major Protestant groups have long been in a superior class position, and hence have been able to transmit successfully that position through the educational system as well as through the family and the structure of educational aspirations stemming from the climate of class, and that the educational system has failed to overcome initial disadvantages for Catholics. It is the exigencies of a historically class-structured society, rather than the failure to internalize achievement values because of religious beliefs, that accounts for the continued class position of Catholics.

The Children of Immigrants

In the major cities of Ontario in the 1960s and 1970s, educators were expressing concern that the children of immigrants might constitute a deprived group with respect to educational experience. Two hundred thousand children under eighteen years of age came to Ontario from abroad between 1961 and 1970. Some of the discussion centred around the difficulty for the child who spoke his native language at home and, for him, a foreign language at school.[20] The immigrant population consisted of a socially polarized group. On the one hand, there were large numbers of unskilled workers for the large construction projects that were transforming the appearance of Canada's major cities. Low level service workers also came in large numbers. At the other extreme, Canada's approach to the post-industrial threshold required large numbers of highly qualified manpower that her own institutions of higher education were failing to provide.[21] Both the unskilled and the highly qualified moved into Canada with the capital investment of the boom years.

For some immigrants there would be both a language shock and a cultural shock mediated only by the fact that non-English-speaking immigrants tended to live close together and create their own ethnic communities.[22] One effect of such "ghettoization" could have been to perpetuate sub-cultures, or socio-economic climates that were not supportive of education, and hence children from these groups could be expected to have lower educational aspirations. If that were so, it would be a factor aiding the perpetuation of ethnic stratification—where particular ethnic groups are highly concentrated at different levels of the occupational structure—that has characterized Canadian society. Adjustment to Canadian life would require the acquisition, to some degree, of achievement values and other elements of modernity by immigrants if they did not possess them. Presumably, English-speaking immigrants and their children from Great Britain or the "white" Commonwealth would have the least problems of adaption.

While some immigrant children are likely to be seen as a disadvantaged group relative to the native-born Canadians, there is reason to think that they have one particular advantage—parents whose levels of ambition are higher than the native-born. It has long been recognized by students of migration that the driving force to migrate is the limitation of opportunities in the place of origin that frustrated ambition.[23] In addition to international migration, ambition has also been thought to be an important element in off-farm and internal migration. Of course, if children move with their families or are born after their parents migrate, it would be a matter of parents transmitting these high-achievement motives to their children, bringing pressure on them as "significant others" to do well in school and set high educational aims. As with all individuals or groups, those ambitions might well face unsuspected hazards. Perhaps it is this high motivation to learn on the part of some immigrant children that leads to their outstanding achievement, despite the language difficulties they face.

Our data tell us something about the educational aspirations of the children of immigrants. To avoid the possibility that foreign-born parents might themselves have come to Canada as children, thus raising their children in a Canadian pattern, we defined immigrant parents as those who had come to Canada after completion of their own education. However much education they might have had, they most likely would have achieved adult status before coming to Canada. A good number of immigrants take a Canadian-born spouse after arriving. We therefore have three categories of parents: both Canadian-born; one foreign-born; and both foreign-born. If we look at the educational aspirations of the children of each of the three categories of parents, it is quite clear that in general immigrant children were at no disadvantage, particularly if they were boys.

In Grade 10, where both parents were foreign-born 44 per cent of boys wanted to go to university (including 11 per cent, the highest proportion of the three groups, who wanted to go on to post-graduate work), compared to 35 per cent of boys whose both parents were Canadian. Where one parent was Canadian the proportion of boys aspiring to university was not much different from that where both parents were Canadian-born. The proportion for girls with one Canadian parent, however, was high (37 per cent), compared to the 30 per cent and 29 per cent where both parents were Canadian-born and both parents foreign-born respectively. Where both parents were Canadian-born, boys aspired somewhat more to go to work than did boys of either of the other two groups.

By Grade 12, however, an interesting pattern emerged. The "more Canadian" the children's parents (both boys and girls), the lower their aspirations. Where both parents were Canadian-born the proportion of boys wanting to go to university was 42 per cent; where one parent was Canadian-born, 46 per cent; and where both parents were foreign-born, 51 per cent. For girls the proportions were 31 per cent, 35 per cent, and 37 per cent respectively. A similar pattern existed for Grade 8.

There remains the question of the bipolar character of Canadian immigration with respect to skill level and language, two attributes which reinforce each other since the United States and Great Britain have been the major sources of highly qualified manpower for Canada. Immigrant children from these two countries would have the advantage of higher class status than the others and also that of being English-speaking. We deal here with the group that might be considered maximally disadvantaged, that is, where both parents were immigrants. Clearly, since our sample size diminishes, we have to arrange the parents in rather broad national origin groups (where they actually did most of their education). We also end up with an "Other" category that runs the gamut of all the other world cultures that have contributed to Canadian immigration.

For Grade 12 students where both parents were from Great Britain, 46 per cent wanted to graduate from university; if they were from Northwest Europe, 31 per cent; Eastern Europe, 54 per cent; Italy, 44 per cent; all other, 43 per cent. Thus, where both parents were from Northwest Europe aspirations seemed to be the lowest among the children of immigrants, but not any lower than when both parents were Canadian-born. The pattern was much the same for the earlier grades. Even the "Other" group, which would comprise a great variety of groups, had children with high aspirations. In part, this would reflect Canadian immigration policy in which those from more distant cultures, say Asian, would have to score high on education[24]; and indeed, as the census reveals, Asian immigrants from the 1960s and 1970s have been very highly educated.[25] It might be tentatively concluded that whatever else happened to them, immigrant children were not low on aspirations when compared to those whose parents were native-born.

The evidence, then, would seem to support the view that many immigrant parents transmit their own aspirations to their children. It also supports the view, made from assessments of other data on over-all educational attainment of the native-born and the immigrant labour force, that in the investment in educational resources Canada has had a generally low evaluation of education for a society so highly industrialized.[26] The data discussed here do not imply that some immigrant children, hidden by our rather broad categories, do not have learning difficulties in Ontario schools. It would take a different sampling procedure aimed particularly at immigrants to examine the social correlates of such problems.

Finally, it is interesting to note that with respect to the general theory that migration reflects or induces achievement values and aspirations, the effects seem much less positive for inter-provincial migration than for immigration from outside the country. For children born within Canada but outside of Ontario, there was no relationship for either boys or girls between being a migrant and level of aspiration. For Grade 12 there was a very modest relationship strengthening the aspirations of within-Canada migrants. Although these last observations are based on the students' birthplaces and not their parents', it would seem that the greater the distance moved with respect to geography and culture, or a combination of them, the higher the aspirations are likely to be.

Ethnic Origin

Closely linked to parental national origins in popular and official minds, but in reality quite different, is "ethnicity," or the cultures of the many nationalities of those who have come to Canada throughout its history. Although ethnicity is a very salient feature of Canadian society—the more so since the extensive examination of the bilingualism and biculturalism commission—it is difficult to categorize native-born Canadians by their ethnicity (even though the census has been doing it inappropriately for a long time). Although it is common practice in Canadian social research and official publications to include Canadian and foreign-born in the same ethnic origin categories—officialdom does not allow Canadian as an ethnicity or cultural group, hence everyone must have a non-Canadian ethnic origin—it would seem sensible to examine the effects of ethnicity to separate the foreign-born students or those with foreign-born parents from those who are Canadian-born.[27]

If for this discussion we leave the Franco-Ontarians in French-language schools aside (since they are not in our samples of English-language schools and we will be dealing with them separately), it is difficult to see how children born in Canada of Canadian-born parents, whatever their ancestry might have been, would fail to have been exposed to the prevailing cultural values of Canada in particular and North America in general. In other words, the saliency of ethnicity and personal identification, and hence cultural effects, might be strong for first generation Canadians, but it would be less so for others born in Canada of Canadian-born parents; and even if such children might have some knowledge of where their male ancestor on their fathers' side came from (the census question), their aspirations would most likely reflect the general Ontario pattern. It seems to us absurd not to recognize an Anglo-Canadian culture as a variant on general North American themes, probably, as many observers have noted, with a subdued emphasis on achievement and egalitarianism.[28] Whatever their ethnic origins in the census meaning, if Canadian-born children of Canadian-born parents share in something of a common value system, then we would expect the artificial ethnicity to have little effect on educational aspirations. Our analysis is unavoidably limited because of the fragmentation of the ethnic structure in Canada that forces us to group ethnicities within broad European categories. The data suggest that apart from those whose ethnic origin, although third-generation Canadian, was from Northwest Europe, non-British ethnic origin does not have negative effects on aspirations. Although the numbers are small and hence unreliable, those from Eastern Europe and Italy generally attained the level of the British.

The question with which we are left is, Why the lower proportion than the British for those of Northwest European origin, that is, French, German, Dutch, Norwegian, who aspired to university? Are these retentions of cultural values from an earlier age? There are other explanations. One might be that some ethnic groups, even though they have been in Canada for some generations, have failed to achieve upward mobility and have become embedded in the lower strata of the vertical mosaic. Another, and more plausible, is that most of the Northwest European category are French in English-speaking schools. At the time of our survey the improvements in educational facilities for French-speaking Ontario students were in transition. Consequently, a good number of these continued to go to English-speaking schools where, an abundance of evidence suggests, they suffered serious disabilities, not only because of language difficulties, but also because of their lower socio-economic status and location in the more remote regions of the province compared to the British. As we will show later, French-speaking students in French-language schools had higher aspiration levels than French-speaking students in English-language schools.

With the French removed, there is little in the Canadian myth of ethnic differences to explain differences in aspirational levels. In fact, a little over one-quarter of the students in Grade 12 and one-third in Grade 10 either did not know their ethnic origin or failed to respond to the question. On the other hand, the Franco-Ontarians are a distinct linguistic-cultural group of the "bilingual belt," and when they are in English-speaking schools they have the characteristics of a disadvantaged group. It must be remembered that in this discussion of ethnic effects, two generations—those born abroad and those whose parents were born abroad—are excluded. Two generations ago Ontario was more British in origin than it is now after the post-war immigration and inter-provincial migration. Until recently it did not exhibit the ethnic heterogeneity of other parts of Canada such as the prairies.

Number of Children and Birth Order

Of the demographic variables remaining in our theoretical model outlined in Chapter 3 there remain family size—the number of children in the family—and birth order, both of which have been found to have some effects on educational experience. In the case of family size it is quite obvious that whatever the social class position, the more children there are in the family the greater the costs of keeping them out of the labour force and in school or university. With birth order, particularly if families are large, two possibilities exist: one is that educational resources might be expended on educating the older children; the other is that younger children will benefit from a large number of income earners in the family. The data show that the former condition exists.

Figure 5.9 shows the proportion of Grade 10 students wanting to go to university according to the number of children in the family and social class. Around 60 per cent of upper-middle-class children in small families of one or two children had these aspirations, compared to only 43 per cent of those in large families of five children or more. For middle-class families the corresponding difference in aspirations was 55 and 34 per cent, and for the lower class it was 35 and 17 per cent.

School-Related Variables

Because of their special importance as intervening variables between socio-cultural climates and levels of occupational and educational aspirations, we are devoting a separate chapter to significant others and self-concept of ability, school performance and school program. However, we will be dealing with them summarily here to indicate their independent effects on aspiration formation.

School Programs

We have noted earlier that an accumulation of credits within the five-year program was a precondition of entering university. There may have been a few exceptions to this general rule, one obvious one being the mature matriculation provision of some universities that allowed anyone over a particular age, usually twenty-one, to enrol and try to meet first-year standards, and if successful, carry on. But these were the exceptions, and in any case, considering the low level of knowledge of the post-secondary system and its requirements, it would not have been likely that very many Ontario high school students of the time would have been aware of this delayed deviant route and taken it seriously into consideration. Although universities loosened up their entrance requirements in the early 1970s in

Figure 5.9
Per cent Wanting to go to University,
by Socio-economic Status and Number of
Children in the Family, Grade 10

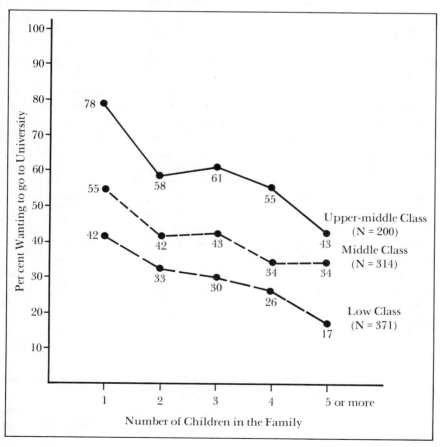

the face of falling enrolments and charges of elitism, it is unlikely that these changes, the effects of which no one has gauged in any serious fashion, would have been in the minds of the students in our survey.

The new colleges of applied arts and technology were intended to "end on" to Grade 12 to accommodate students from any of the high school programs who chose to leave at that time. Some of the courses within the C.A.A.T.s required credits in the superior five-year programs; others provided opportunity for those in the less demanding four-year programs. It was not unrealistic for those in the four-year programs to aspire to some form of post-secondary education. Although it was unrealistic for them to aspire to university, they might nevertheless set their eyes on that horizon from either ignorance or fantasy or both. Programs therefore limited opportunities as an instrument of policy, all the more so when the educational authorities at the behest of the universities insisted that the new colleges of applied arts and technology should not provide "university parallel" courses,[30] thus ruling out direct transfers with credits from the colleges to the universities. In addition, in the high schools there was a two-year program that provided "opportunity" classes for those students who, for whatever reason, were mismatched with the educational system, and for whom the school was as much a custodial as an educational institution until they reached the school leaving age.

The more prestigious academic five-year programs dominated the Ontario high school system. Just over one-half of Grade 10 students were in five-year programs or their equivalent advanced courses, then beginning to develop. By Grade 12 the proportion had increased to about two-thirds, indicating that in the years between Grades 10 and 12 the drop-outs were likely to come in greater proportion from the four-year than the five-year program. In fact, three-fifths of those in Grade 10 who wanted to leave school at that grade were in four-year programs, and a further one-fifth were in two-year programs. These proportions represented only a very small part, 7 per cent, of all Grade 10 students. Of those in Grade 10 who wanted to leave at Grade 12, three-quarters were from programs that came to an end at that time. At Grade 12, of those who wanted to leave high school, seven-tenths were in four-year programs. Conversely nine-tenths of those who wanted to stay on for Grade 13 were in five-year programs. Wanting to leave school at Grade 12 did not necessarily mean that students wanted no more of the educational system. At all grades less than one-fifth wanted to go to work. At Grade 10, of those who wanted to leave school for work, two-thirds (64 per cent) came from four-year programs, and at Grade 12 about seven-tenths did.

Programs were major channels through which students were streamed to future destinations, with one-half of those in five-year programs wanting to go to university compared to less than one-tenth in four-year programs. Those in the latter were much more heavily oriented to work than the former, and if they looked forward to post-secondary education it was to the private trade schools and community colleges. Thus, educational horizons are set early in the high school career.

Breton[31] has interpreted a similar finding with respect to the relationship between school programs and post-secondary plans as one in which the internal stratification system of the school is of greater importance than social class origins in its effect on aspirations. While we treat this argument much more extensively in a subsequent chapter, it might be pointed out here that the allocation of students to school programs was itself socially biased, and it is, therefore, necessary to look at the way in which school program is a powerful intervening factor between social class origins of the student and his hopes and desires for his future.

The logic behind the creation of the program has always been appealing, that is, to fit the intellectually less able students into less demanding and less rigorous educational experiences. Thus, if the system worked it would be anticipated that there would be an association between level of mental ability and program in which the student was enrolled. Since it would be foolish to expect a one-to-one relationship to have been achieved, it is difficult to know what distribution of mental ability by program might be considered satisfactory. Although we leave these detailed discussions until later, it might be pointed out that 14 per cent of those in four-year programs were high in mental ability while 21 per cent of those in five-year programs were low mental ability students. About an equal proportion of each program contained medium level mental ability students. Of all high mental ability students, 17 per cent were "misplaced" in four-year programs, while of all low mental ability students 44 per cent were "misplaced" in five-year programs. Although the distribution of low mental ability students was about the same for Grade 10, a considerably larger proportion, 23 per cent, of high mental ability students were in four-year programs, an arrangement which could scarcely be called satisfactory.

School Performance

One important factor influencing aspirations for and expectations about education beyond high school, which both commonsense and previous studies would lead us to anticipate, is how well students are doing in their high school work, that is, their level of academic achievement. Our concept of academic achievement and the difficulties of measuring it, and our reasons for reconceptualizing it as school performance, will be dealt with in Chapter 9. Quite clearly school performance is related to many of the factors with which we have dealt in our preceding analysis of educational aspirations. At some time girls perform better than boys, children of the higher social classes perform better than those from the lower, those with higher mental ability perform better than those with low, and so forth.

As we show in Chapter 9, school performance means something very different in the five-year and four-year programs, and since only students in the five-year program would be eligible for university we are reporting the data relating to school performance separately for the two programs. Seventy-one per cent of Grade 10 students with grades of over 75 in the five-year program wanted to go to university, while only 28 per cent of those with grades between 50 and 59 did. The relatively high proportion (24 per cent) of four-year program high achievers in Grade 10 who wanted to go to university may reflect an unwillingness to face reality. By Grade 12 reality had set in for the four-year program students, regardless of their achievement level. What is striking is the large proportion who chose other forms of post-secondary education. This always exceeds the proportions who chose to go to work. This analysis of performance levels within the two programs clearly shows how limited the educational horizons of those in the four-year program were. Many policy makers, of course, would consider such a limitation appropriate, particularly when so many are at the same time directed towards the less prestigious colleges, and not likely to make demands on university resources.

Self-Concept of Ability and Aspirations

In educational experience, as in other life activities, nothing succeeds like success. Individuals do well in school and are told they are doing well through receiving high grades, teachers' approval and parental praise. The assignment to programs and special classes for the very bright or the very dull are further signals by which the individual, from the way in which others see him or institutions place him, develops an image of himself and his capacity to do school work. From interactions with parents, teachers and peers, self-confidence is enhanced or undermined and the stage set for higher or lesser levels of achievement.

In Chapter 7 we explore the factors that contribute to a person's self-concept. Here we will merely demonstrate the relationship between self-concept of ability and educational aspiration. Sixty-five per cent of Grade 10 students with high self-concept of ability wanted to go to university, and only 6 per cent of those with low self-concept had such aspirations. And at the other extreme, only 5 per cent with high self-concept of ability wanted to go to work, compared to 34 per cent with low self-concept.

Cultural Enrichment and Parental Education

If doing well in school, developing a high self-concept of ability and wanting more education is a process of learning a culture as well as learning true instrumental and cognitive skills, then as we have suggested, early contact with that culture assists in the formation of appropriate aspirations. Since achievement and mobility values are important in maintaining status or moving up to higher occupational or social positions, the process of educational and occupational achievement involves striving for particular cultural values that might be labelled, because they are the values of the dominant class of an achievement-oriented society, the high culture of the society. To the extent that the school system, particularly in its academically oriented programs, dispenses the high culture of the society, it is for the middle-class family an adjunct to their own socialization. It is always helpful to high performance in school to have read great works or to have had them about the house, or to have some direct knowledge of great masters of the art world. Even weekly news magazines have stories of the society's high culture.

Where the school dispenses high culture to those who, because of their social class position, are already acquainted with it, there is a general compatibility between home and school. However, for lower-class children, as has often been noted, the exposure to high culture can be alienating, with all the consequences of an early rejection of it, including its achievement values.[32] Yet, as we have seen, some proportion of lower-class children do have high aspirations, a fact that we explore later in greater depth. There is some evidence from the literature that lower-class parents who have high aspirations for their children will do what they can to expose them to the high culture in the home. Often this takes the form of buying encyclopedias (the advertisements alone tell that story), subscribing to magazines, and seeing that their children have some contact with the world of the arts.

Our cultural enrichment measure tried to get at this exposure to high culture, and if it was not a measure of the extent to which children incorporate that culture in themselves, it might be taken as an indicator of parental attitudes, guidance and encouragement. As well, it might be considered an indicator of the parents' own contact with the high culture. Such contacts, of course, will be the normal expression of middle-class lifestyles, but the desire on the part of some lower-class parents to give their children the opportunity may be sufficiently widespread to play an important role in aspirations.

Since higher classes are much more likely to consume these items of cultural enrichment, it is most useful to look at the data relating aspirations to cultural enrichment controlling for social class.

The relationship between cultural enrichment and aspiration held for different levels of the class structure, as can be seen in Figure 5.10. While those of the lower class got some fillip to their aspirations from exposure to the higher culture, it was not sufficient to overcome other aspects of social class. In fact, where students of the lower class were high in cultural enrichment, they were very similar in their aspirational levels to upper-middle-class students of low cultural enrichment.

That the level of parental education should be related to the level of students' aspirations is to be expected, since the relationship implies the direct transmission of educational status and occupational opportunity. Parental education is closely associated with their social class level, since their education will already have been transformed into the appropriate standing in the occupational world, a standing which they in turn may have inherited from their parents. The transmission of educational values and class position goes with the transmission of high culture and its learning.

Table 5.4 presents the data for "combined parental education," a variable of which both the mother's and father's education are components. For both grades the relationship between wanting to go to work, wanting some non-university form of post-secondary education and wanting to go to university is clear. In Grade 10, where the combined parental educational level was high, 63 per cent wanted to go to university, compared to only 25 per cent where it was low. Thirty-seven per cent chose other non-university when their parents had least education, but only 17 per cent when they had

Figure 5.10
Per cent Wanting to go to University,
by Cultural Enrichment and Socio-economic Status,
Grade 10

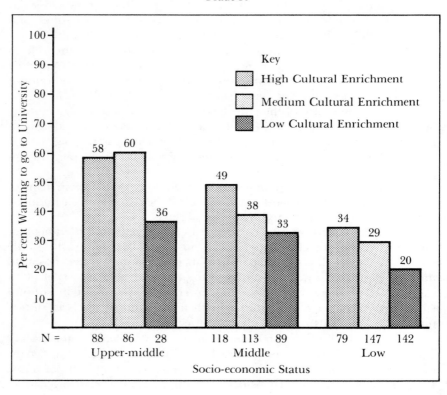

Table 5.4
Students' Aspirations by Parental Education
(Grade 10)

Aspirations	Parental Education		
	High	Medium	Low
	(per cent)		
Work	2	12	20
Other Post-secondary	17	30	37
University	63	43	25
Other	6	4	6
Don't Know	12	11	12
Total	100	100	100
N =	175	878	1,280

X^2 (8) = 171.93   p = .000

the most. For those who wanted to go to work the differences were parallel. The figures, as we have collapsed them, conceal two other important findings. Where parents were the least educated, 16 per cent of the children wanted to go to private commercial or trade schools or into apprenticeship. At the other extreme, 17 per cent of the children of highly educated parents wanted to go on to graduate work. If these aspirations were to work themselves out it would constitute an interesting "exploitation" of the public educational system.

Notes

1. Care must be taken not to treat the three samples as a single cohort proceeding through each of the grades, although it might be tempting to do so.
2. Of 100 students enrolled in Grade 9 in 1967, 91 reached Grade 10 in 1968; 73 reached Grade 12 in 1970; and 38 went on to Grade 13 in 1971. Ontario, *Report of the Minister of Education, 1971* (Toronto), Table 1.4.
3. In 1975 there were 92 private vocational schools registered in Ontario. Ontario, Ministry of Colleges and Universities, *Directory of Registered Private Vocational Schools, 1975.*
4. Since 1973 Nursing Schools have been incorporated into the system of Colleges of Applied Arts and Technology. Formerly they were linked directly to hospitals.
5. Hugh A. McRoberts, *Follow-up of Grade 12 Students from the Blishen-Porter Study of Education Aspirations.* While 45 per cent of the Grade 12 students hoped to go to university and 41 per cent expected to, in fact only 30 per cent actually did go (Carleton University), (mimeo).

6. Actually about half of all high mental ability students are in the two lowest social classes. Marion R. Porter, John Porter and Bernard R. Blishen, *Does Money Matter? Prospects for Higher Education in Ontario* (Toronto: Macmillan, 1979).

7. *Canadian Agriculture in the Seventies,* Report of the Federal Task Force on Agriculture (Ottawa: Information Canada, 1969).

8. *Census of Canada,* 1971. Catalogue 92-709. Vol.1, Part 1, Table 10.

9. Rex Lucas, *Minetown, Milltown, Railtown* (Toronto: University of Toronto Press, 1971).

10. Donald R. Whyte, "Rural Canada in Transition," in Marc-Adelard, T. Tremblay and Walton J. Anderson, eds., *Rural Canada in Transition* (Ottawa: Agricultural Economics Research Council, 1966).

11. Here we are following William H. Sewell and Archibald D. Haller, "Educational and Occupational Perspectives of Farm and Rural Youth," in Lee G. Burchinal, ed., *Rural Youth in Crisis* (Washington: U.S. Government Printing Office, 1965).

12. Max Weber, *The Protestant Ethic and the Spirit of Capitalism,* trans. Talcott Parsons (New York: Charles Scribner, 1958). See also "The Protestant Sects and the Spirit of Capitalism," in H.H. Gerth and C. Wright Mills, *From Max Weber* (London: Routledge, 1949).

13. Noted by Weber in "The Protestant Sects," *op. cit.*

14. See Bruce L. Warren, "Socioeconomic Achievement and Religion: The American Case," in *Sociological Inquiry,* Vol.40, No.2 (Spring 1970) for a review and critique of research relating to the "Protestant Ethic" hypothesis.

15. *Report of the Royal Commission on Bilingualism and Biculturalism,* Book III (Ottawa: Queen's Printer, 1969). See also John Porter, *The Vertical Mosaic* (Toronto: University of Toronto Press, 1965), pp.91ff.

16. H. Richard Niebuhr, *The Social Sources of Denominationalism* (Hamden: Conn., 1954). See also Warren, *op.cit.*

17. Samuel D. Clark, *Church and Sect in Canada* (Toronto: University of Toronto Press, 1948).

18. Warren, *op.cit.*

19. Peter C. Pineo and John Porter, "French-English Differences in the Evaluations of Occupations, Industries, Ethnicities and Religions in the Montreal Metropolitan Area," *Special Study for the Royal Commission on Bilingualism and Biculturalism.*

20. Ontario, *Report of the Minister of Education, 1971,* Table 3.61, and Edgar Wright, *Student's Background and its Relation to Class and Programme in School* (Toronto: Board of Education, 1970).

21. Bernard R. Blishen, "Social Class and Opportunity in Canada," in *Canadian Review of Sociology and Anthropology,* Vol.7, No.2, 1970; A.G. Atkinson, K.J. Barnes and Ellen Richardson, *Canada's Highly Qualified Manpower* (Ottawa: Department of Manpower and Immigration, 1970). See also John Porter, *The Vertical Mosaic,* ch.II.

22. Anthony H. Richmond, *Ethnic Residential Segregation in Metropolitan Toronto* (Toronto: Institute for Behavioural Research, York University, 1972).

23. Donald J. Bogue, *Principles of Demography* (New York: John Wiley and Sons Inc., 1969).

24. Since 1967 Canada's immigration policy was based on a point system in which educational attainment was an important component. See Freda Hawkins, *Canada and Immigration: Public Policy and Public Concern* (Montreal and Kingston: McGill-Queen's University Press, 1972).

25. Blishen, *op.cit.*

26. There are striking differences between the native-born and immigrant labour forces in Canada in educational attainment.

27. See John Porter, "Ethnic Pluralism in Canadian Perspective," in Nathan Glaser and Daniel P. Moynahan, eds., *Ethnicity: Theory and Experience* (Cambridge: Harvard University Press, 1975).

28. John Porter, "Canadian Character in the Twentieth Century," in *The Annals of the American Academy of Political and Social Sciences*, Vol.370, March 1967; Kasper D. Naegele, "Canadian Society: Some Reflections," in Bernard R. Blishen, *et al.*, *Canadian Society: Sociological Perspectives* (Toronto: Macmillan of Canada, 1961); Seymour M. Lipset, *Revolution and Counter Revolution* (New York: Anchor Books, 1970), ch.2.

29. *Report of the Royal Commission on Bilingualism and Biculturalism*, Book II, Education (Queen's Printer, 1968), pp.88ff.

30. Committee of Presidents of the Universities of Ontario, *The Community College* (Toronto: 1965).

31. Raymond Breton, "Academic Stratification in Secondary Schools and the Educational Plans of Students," in *Canadian Review of Sociology and Anthropology*, Vol.7, No.1, 1970.

32. Kurt Lewin, *Resolving Social Conflicts* (New York: Harper, 1948).

6

Tinker, Tailor . . . Teacher, Typist

Students of modern societies cannot help but be impressed by the continuing changes in the structure of occupations. As an increasingly complex technology is applied in industry, commerce and services, some occupations disappear and many new ones emerge. Increasingly, the world of work becomes based on science and technology. The advanced societies, which some call post-industrial, depend for their functioning on a sufficient number of individuals being educated and trained to fill the new types of jobs. The extent to which the supply of persons with different levels and types of skills meets the requirements of the labour market will determine the capacity of that society to be productive. As has frequently been said, Canada has failed in the past to produce the range of skills that the labour force has required, depending rather on importing highly qualified manpower.[1] It was an attempt to overcome some of these shortcomings that led to the expansion of post-secondary institutions in the 1960s.

The sifting and sorting of people into the various levels and types of jobs in the occupational structure begins some time before they get their first job. As was pointed out in Chapter 5, the individual's educational future is the result of a set of previous events and experiences that are influenced by a combination of social and psychological variables, including occupational aspirations and expectations. In this chapter, the focus is on occupational aspirations and expectations as the dependent variable, and on the manner in which they are influenced by similar social and psychological factors. It is the cumulative effect of these factors, experienced by the young person in a wide variety of situations in the home, school and in peer groups, that inclines him towards a certain occupational level or position.

Despite the advice of teachers and counsellors—if they receive any at all—few young people in elementary school or in the first year of high school have sufficient knowledge, whatever the level of their motivation, to enable them to make a realistic occupational choice. But as they approach the time when they will leave high school, say after completing Grade 10 or later, the decision must be made whether to go to work or to continue in school and prepare for some form of post-secondary education. Those who stay in school may delay a final choice of job a while longer, until Grade 12 when they can be more realistic than their younger schoolmates. They are more knowledgeable because they have learned from family, friends and school authorities about educational and occupational opportunities; they have some judgement of their capacities, of their ability to achieve academically, and they may have acquired some ambition to reach certain occupational levels that may, or may not, involve a specific choice of occupation.

When in response to a question a student specifies his occupational ambitions (or aspirations), he is not making a choice of an occupation in the same way that he will when he enters the labour force or when he chooses a particular post-secondary educational program that leads to a professional career. A student's occupational ambition is an indication of a preference rather than an actual choice. Although students were asked to specify the type of job they would like to make their life's career, in other words to indicate a specific choice, it is quite possible that the occupations that they specified were indicative of their preference for a style of life, a standard of living, a level of prestige, or a combination of all of these rather than a particular occupation. We can raise the question, although our data do not allow us to answer it, whether occupations *per se* are the salient features of ambition at this stage of the student's development. We should also keep in mind that there is a temporal aspect to a person's occupational aspirations. As Archibald Haller and Irwin Miller noted, "In any behaviour sequence which occurs over long periods, a person may anticipate that one level will be appropriate for him at one time, but that another will be appropriate at a different time."[2] Our data do not allow us to examine the difference between long-range and short-range aspirations for the same person, but we will show that differences exist in the aspirations of groups of students who are at different levels of their education.

Two Dimensions of Occupational Ambition
Our measure of occupational aspirations, or ambition, is based on responses to Question 19. The details of this question and the following one of occupational expectations can be found in Chapter 4, where we indicated that the reasons for two questions on occupational futures are similar to those for using two questions on educational futures. We theorize that there are two subjective states involved: aspirations being what students would really like to do, such wishes no doubt having a degree of fantasy, and expectations being an adjustment of realistic ambitions in the light of circumstances in which they find themselves. That the two questions, unlike those on educational aspirations, do in fact tap different subjective

dimensions was borne out by the different responses produced by each of them. Haller and Miller have shown that the differences between occupational aspirations and expectations can be regarded as differences in goal levels. They speak of idealistic occupational goal levels (which we have termed occupational aspirations) being higher than realistic occupational goal levels (which we have termed occupational expectations).

Table 6.1 shows, for the three grades, the overall levels of occupational aspirations and expectations. The occupational levels indicated are the first digit Blishen categories now familiar to readers. The highest level of aspirations is in Grade 8, where about one-third wished to have jobs, mainly professional and scientific, at the highest level. The proportion drops to about one-quarter of all students in the two high school grades, no doubt a reflection of the programs they were in and their being closer to the point of making an occupational choice. But for each grade there is a considerable downward adjustment on the part of a good proportion of students with respect to their expectations. In fact, this downward adjustment, the fantasy-reality gap, can be seen for the top two levels of occupational ambition.

In Grade 8, 41 per cent aspired to the two highest levels, but only 29 per cent expected to reach those levels, a discrepancy of 12 percentage points. The discrepancies are much the same in the other two grades. It may also be noted that students were more likely to claim that they did not know what their expectations were, rather than claim they did not know what their

Table 6.1
Level of Occupational Aspirations and Expectations
by Grade

Occupational Level	Grade 8		Grade 10		Grade 12	
	Asp.	Exp.	Asp.	Exp.	Asp.	Exp.
	(per cent)					
1	32	24	25	18	26	20
2	9	5	10	7	12	8
3	20	19	22	19	27	23
4	18	17	19	17	19	19
5	14	20	16	23	11	16
6	3	5	2	5	1	3
D.K.	4	10	6	11	4	11
Total	100	100	100	100	100	100
N =	2,722	2,722	2,964	2,964	1,114	1,114

aspirations were. The fact that more students were willing to state their aspirations than were willing to state their expectations supports the distinction between student fantasy and reality. It should also be noted that very few either wanted to be or expected to be in the unskilled occupations at the bottom, where many of them will, in fact, end up.

Table 6.1 also shows that a relatively small proportion of students aspired to Level 2 occupations, and an even smaller proportion expected to follow an occupation at this level. These small proportions in all three grades are in contrast to the proportions for the next higher and the next lower levels. Why should students prefer and expect occupations above and below Level 2? Part of the answer may be in the fact that, of the 24 occupations at Level 1, all are professional and highly visible—doctors, dentists, engineers, architects and lawyers; on the other hand, Level 2 contains predominantly high level managerial occupations. It might be

Table 6.2
Students' Occupational Aspirations
by Occupational Expectations (Grade 10)*

Level of Occupational Aspirations	Level of Occupational Expectations								
	Males (per cent)								
	1	2	3	4	5	6	Total	N	%
1	64	6	12	6	9	3	100	380	28
2	12	48	5	11	18	6	100	165	12
3	4	4	61	10	17	4	100	269	19
4	3	3	11	53	23	7	100	212	15
5	1	1	4	5	78	11	100	303	22
6	0	2	7	3	20	68	100	59	4
								1,388	100
	Females (per cent)								
1	57	3	15	14	10	1	100	314	27
2	11	38	14	22	15	0	100	89	8
3	5	4	58	12	19	2	100	325	28
4	5	2	10	59	22	2	100	299	25
5	4	1	15	16	63	1	100	142	12
6	0	0	33	0	0	67	100	3	-
								1,172	100

* "Don't Knows" are excluded.

that there is a tendency among Ontario students to aspire to, and expect to reach, professional or other non-managerial occupations. A more plausible explanation is that the occupational titles in Level 2 specify managers in specific industries ("owners and managers, paper and allied industries," for example). Even if students saw themselves as going into business, they were not likely to be so specific. Nor would coders be able so easily to assign responses to Level 2 as to the other levels. This uncertainty about Level 2 must be borne in mind.

How widely separated were students' aspirations and expectations? When faced with reality, how far and in what directions were adjustments made? Overall were there differences between males and females? More will be said on these issues later; however, Table 6.2 provides some tentative answers to these questions for Grade 10 students and highlights the problem we have been presenting: the distinction between occupational aspirations and expectations. The data are arranged in a matrix, with occupational aspirations down the side (the rows) and expectations along the top (the columns). It shows for any one level of aspiration whether the reality adjustment is up or down and the level to which adjustments are made. Reading along the diagonal, it is clear that with one exception over half of both sexes had expectations that matched their aspirations. The reason for the relatively low proportion at Level 2 may be the lack of specification of the occupational titles at that level referred to above.

For males, 64 per cent who aspired to top level jobs also expected to reach them. Downward adjustment of expectations, all there can be at the top level, are spread rather evenly among the levels, with somewhat more going to Levels 3 and 5. From Level 2 down, Level 5 is the one to which most adjustment takes place. Level 5 is also the most stable, with 78 per cent of those aspiring to it also expecting to reach it. For the few boys who aspired to Level 6, two-thirds expected to stay there, but Level 5 attracted the next largest proportion, 20 per cent. Level 5 contains a large number of skilled and semi-skilled manual occupations.

For girls in Grade 10, only 57 per cent of those who aspired to the top expected to make it, and as with males the least change is at Level 5. Since, with the exception of Level 6, perforce there are greater proportions in the upper right side of the diagonal than in the lower left, the overall expectation adjustment is downwards.

The high aspirational levels of girls in Grade 10 is striking. For those who expressed an occupational aspiration, as large a proportion (27 per cent) of girls as boys wanted top jobs. Proportions are given in the last column of Table 6.2. Almost all of these top jobs are in the higher professions in which women are greatly under-represented. School teacher just makes it into this top job level, and that, no doubt, would account for some of the high aspiring girls. Girls aspired in greater proportion than did boys to Level 3, no doubt because it contains a number of traditionally female occupations such as nursing, physiotherapy, social work, stenography, and so on. Only a small proportion of girls wanted to work at the two lowest levels, which generally are in the blue-collar world. A few may have wanted to break into it, but such sentiments were not strong.

For boys, the matrices for Grades 8 and 12 (not shown) are not substantially different. For girls in these other two grades, the pattern is much the same, except for Grade 12, where the most stable level is 4. Of those who aspired to it, 70 per cent expected to reach it. This is also a level to which adjustment is made downwards, indicating the expectation of lower white-collar occupations. Finally, zero order correlations between aspirations and expectations are fairly high: for males .71, .69 and .65 in Grades 8, 10 and 12 respectively, and for females .65, .56 and .56 in these same grades. They are not so high as the correlations between educational aspirations and expectations, which were .90, .91 and .91 for males in Grades 8, 10 and 12 respectively, and .89, .91 and .91 for females in these same grades. These data suggest that we cannot ignore the distinction between occupational aspirations and expectations. The differences in the responses to the two occupational questions bear out our feeling that there are two dimensions to occupational ambition, and that neither a straightforward aspiration question nor an expectation question alone would have revealed them.

The differences clearly leave us with the choice of aspirations or expectations as the main indicator of ambition. Having demonstrated the existence of the two dimensions, we cannot make a strong case for extending the analysis of ambition and social structure with one or the other. We have opted for expectations.

Before undertaking this analysis, we need to determine if the relationship between occupational aspirations and social structure differs markedly from the relationship between educational aspirations and our major independent variables. This we will do in summary fashion.

In some parts of the following analysis separate tables are presented for boys and girls because female occupational experience, although changing, has been very different from that of males. This will also simplify the tabular presentation.

Educational and Occupational Ambitions

We have seen in Chapter 5 the effect of a number of variables on educational aspirations. It should come as no surprise that the variables that affect the level of educational aspirations also affect the level of occupational aspirations. In this credentialled society, the amount of education attained determines to a large extent the kind of occupation that a person can enter. It is very likely the case that when a student considers the amount of education he would like to have, he first thinks of the job he would like and then considers the education he would need in order to qualify for that job. The student may not think of a specific job, but he or she very likely thinks in general terms of a professional, a clerical, a sales or a skilled occupation and picks an appropriate educational level for that job. Consequently, we find that sex, social class, mental ability, school performance, self-concept of ability and cultural enrichment are all related to the level of occupational aspirations, very much as they are to the level of educational aspirations.

High Hopes and Low Expectations

In the early part of this chapter we indicated that aspirations generally were higher than expectations, and as we saw from the size of the zero order correlation coefficients noted earlier, the difference between these two levels of occupational ambition was fairly substantial. However, although these coefficients give us some idea of the extent to which aspirations and expectations agree or disagree, they do not tell us to what extent the difference between them is in one direction or another, that is, whether aspirations are higher than expectations or vice versa. We now return to this problem.

Our measure of the direction of the difference between the two dimensions of occupational ambition is the difference between the socio-economic score, according to the Blishen scale, of the occupation to which the student aspires, and the socio-economic score of the occupation the student realistically expects.

We have categorized the differences as follows: (1) = -50 to -10; (2) = -9 to 9; (3) = 10 to 76. Since the Blishen scale consists of socio-economic scores for individual occupations ranging from 25 to 76, a minus score from -50 to -10 means that expectations are higher than aspirations, whereas a plus score 10 to 76 indicates that aspirations are higher than expectations. The score -9 to 9 means that aspirations and expectations are more or less the same. In terms of the occupational levels from 1 to 6, which we have used in our analysis, the -50 to -10 score indicates that expectations are from 1 to 5 occupational levels above aspirations; the -9 to 9 difference reflects expectations that are neither higher nor lower than aspirations but within the same or an adjacent occupational level; while the 10 to 76 score indicates aspirations that are from 1 to 6 occupational levels above expectations.

The first step in this part of our analysis is to examine the relationship between expectations and the aspirations-expectations gap. Our purpose is to discover whether the level of expectations affects the direction of the difference. Table 6.3 shows that this is the case. Nevertheless, in each grade and for each sex the lower the level of occupational expectations the higher the likelihood that aspirations will exceed expectations. In Grade 10, only 4 per cent of boys with expectations at Level 2, compared to 43 per cent with expectations at Level 6, reported aspirations that were higher than expectations. For boys, it appears that this trend became even sharper by Grade 12. The opposite is true for boys in both grades whose expectations lay at the upper levels of the occupational ladder: the higher the level of occupational expectations, the greater the likelihood that they would exceed aspirations. These two opposing trends result in another: the decrease in the proportion of boys with the same or very similar aspirations and expectations at each downward step in occupational expectations. The same trends are evident for girls. However, there is one difference between boys and girls that should be noted. In both grades, girls with expectations at Level 5 were more likely than boys with the same level of expectation to have higher aspirations than expectations. The same pattern possibly prevails for girls and boys with Level 6 expectations, but the cell frequencies for girls are much too small for us to do any more than suggest this as a possibility.

Before turning to the association between educational aspirations and the discrepancy between occupational aspirations and expectations, we will examine the size and direction of these discrepancies. The zero order correlation coefficients in Table 6.4 show that there was a fair degree of divergence between these aspirations and expectations for boys and girls in each grade and at each educational aspiration level. The coefficients ($r_{occ.\ asp. \times occ.\ exp.}$) are not high for boys or girls at any of these levels. It is interesting to note that for Grade 10 boys there is a slight increase in the size of the coefficient from .55 to .61 between the work and the university levels, but for Grade 12 boys this trend is reversed and shows a drop from .60 for those who hope to go to work to .49 for those who hope to go to university. In each grade the size of the coefficients for girls is not much different from those for boys, except for girls who hope to go to work, which are lower than the coefficients for boys at the same level of educational aspirations.

To what extent were the discrepancies between aspirations and expectations, which are evident in the size of the zero order correlation coefficients, due to aspirations being higher than expectations or the reverse? Table 6.4 provides the answer. Looking across the educational aspiration levels, it is evident that in both grades between a half to nearly three-quarters of boys and girls had matching expectations and aspirations. However, the proportion at each educational level whose aspirations exceeded their expectations was from two to ten times higher than the proportion for whom the reverse was true.

Turning now to the effect of educational aspirations on aspiration-expectation discrepancies, Table 6.4 indicates that the relationship between these two variables is evident only where aspirations are higher than expectations, when it appears that in both grades the higher the level of educational aspirations, the lower the likelihood that students' aspirations were higher than their expectations. Although the differences between them are small, it appears that by Grade 12, girls at each educational aspiration level were less likely than boys to have occupational aspirations that were higher than their expectations. It seems that in this grade girls who had post-secondary educational aspirations below the university level were more realistic in this respect than boys. In Grade 12 nearly three-quarters of the

Table 6.3
Difference Between Occupational Aspirations and Expectations
by Occupational Expectations by Sex
(Grades 10 and 12)

Occupational Expectations

Difference	Grade 10						Grade 12					
	1	2	3	4	5	6	1	2	3	4	5	6
	(per cent)						(per cent)					
Males												
1 Exp. higher (−50 to −10)	10	13	10	3	-	-	13	17	5	3	-	-
2 Exp. Asp. same (−9 to 9)	90	83	70	70	68	57	87	79	74	63	62	45
3 Asp. higher (10 to 76)	-	4	20	27	32	43	-	4	21	34	38	55
Total	100	100	100	100	100	100	100	100	100	100	100	100
N =	284	120	256	195	406	124	323	116	272	169	274	83
Females												
1 Exp. higher (−50 to −10)	18	14	8	4	-	-	24	13	7	2	-	-
2 Exp. Asp. same (−9 to 9)	82	78	74	72	48	17	76	77	83	79	40	12
3 Asp. higher (10 to 76)	-	8	18	24	52	83	-	10	11	19	60	88
Total	100	100	100	100	100	100	100	100	100	100	100	100
N =	227	64	300	299	264	18	234	100	378	353	183	8

Table 6.4
Difference Between Occupational Aspirations and Expectations and Expectations by Educational Aspirations, by Sex (Grades 10 and 12)

	Educational Aspirations					
	Grade 10			*Grade 12*		
Difference	Work	Other Post Sec.	University	Work	Other Post Sec.	University
Males			*(per cent)*			
1 Exp. higher	3	5	5	5	5	6
2 Exp. Asp. same	64	65	67	60	59	66
3 Asp. higher	33	30	28	35	36	28
Total	100	100	100	100	100	100
N =	244	559	529	184	430	592
r occ. asp. x occ. exp.	.55	.54	.61	.60	.53	.49
Females			*(per cent)*			
1 Exp. higher	4	5	7	4	6	10
2 Exp. Asp. same	56	66	65	66	71	67
3 Asp. higher	40	29	28	30	23	23
Total	100	100	100	100	100	100
N =	252	451	364	338	435	419
r occ. asp. x occ. exp.	.30	.56	.50	.33	.52	.49

girls who hoped to take post-secondary education below the university level, compared with about three-fifths of the boys with these educational aspirations, had matching occupational aspirations and expectations.

Ambition and Social Class

We have discussed the degree of agreement between occupational aspirations and expectations, and the manner in which they diverge, but as yet we have not shown how students' realistic occupational choices are affected by our major social and psychological variables.

A student's expectations for a particular job and its accompanying status develop out of a web of family, school and peer influences. While these expectations may change with time and experience, including greater knowledge of labour market conditions, a major influence, until entry into the labour force, will continue to be the family background.

The relationship between the present social class position of the boy's family and his expectations of moving higher or lower in the class structure are shown in Table 6.5. We have presented our findings in the form of a conventional mobility outflow matrix because the occupational level expected can be thought of as expected mobility. In this table the panels for each of Grades 10 and 12, when followed from left to right, indicate for each socio-economic class level (measured by the occupation of the father) the proportion of boys and girls respectively who expected to achieve the various occupational levels. The expected occupational destinations can be seen as the outputs or outflows from each level.

While overall expectations were high, the relationship to social class can be seen by reading down column 1 for each grade, which shows that as the class ladder is descended steadily decreasing proportions of students expected to achieve upper-middle occupational status. In the two grades, the proportion of girls in the top class who expected to enter the highest level was less than that for boys, indicating that proportionately fewer girls from the highest class were motivated to maintain their high class position through competition in the labour market, although it is probable that these girls would maintain their class position through marriage within their class. Even at this class level, girls may accept the realities of the sex biases built into our occupational structure and take them into account in their expectations of reaching their occupational goals. On the other hand, the proportion of girls in each grade from the lowest class who expected to get jobs at the top level was quite similar to that of boys in Grade 10, but a lower proportion than boys had these high expectations in Grade 12.

A striking feature of Table 6.5 is the proportion of girls at each class level in each grade who expected to reach the middle occupational levels. These proportions, in each case, are substantially higher than for boys. Indeed, over 50 per cent of middle- and lower-class girls and just under 50 per cent of upper-middle-class girls in both grades expected middle level

Table 6.5
Occupational Expectations by Socio-economic Status
by Sex (Grades 10 and 12)

Occupational Expectations

Socio-economic Status	Grade 10					Grade 12				
	Upper-middle	Middle	Lower	Total	N	Upper-middle	Middle	Lower	Total	N
Males (per cent)										
Upper-middle	51	32	17	100	181	56	31	13	100	186
Middle	36	33	31	100	388	36	42	22	100	389
Lower	21	33	46	100	736	28	33	39	100	607
Females (per cent)										
Upper-middle	41	47	12	100	153	42	47	10	100	173
Middle	29	53	18	100	345	29	56	15	100	394
Lower	20	51	29	100	637	21	62	17	100	634

jobs. Evidently, while proportionately fewer girls than boys expected to reach the professional and managerial levels, proportionately more girls than boys expected to have middle level jobs.

An examination of the proportion to the lower left of the diagonal in each section of this table shows that proportionately fewer girls than boys expected to get the highest jobs. In fact, when we compare the mobility expectations of lower- and upper-middle-class boys in both grades, it is clear that the latter were twice as likely as the former to expect high level jobs. On the other hand, if we read down column 3 in these grades, lower-class boys were much more likely than upper-class boys to expect low level jobs. It should be noted that expectations tended to differ between Grades 10 and 12. By the latter grade, which we have previously referred to as the survival grade, a higher proportion of both upper-middle and lower-class boys expected to get high level jobs. These increased proportions were because students with low occupational expectations would have left school at the end of Grade 10.

Upper-middle-class boys cannot, of course, move up. They are, so to speak, at the ceiling of the class structure. The proportions to the lower left of the diagonal indicate expectations to move up. For both grades it is clear that the majority of lower-class students expected to improve on the social class origins of their families, as determined by their fathers' occupations. This evidence would scarcely support the view of a working-class sub-culture of low mobility values. Having said that, however, it is striking that 46 per cent of Grade 10 and 39 per cent of Grade 12 lower-class boys expected to stay put, indicating some considerable lower-class holding power.

In each grade, lower-class girls were different from boys in the extent to which they expected to stay put or move one class up. Evidently, the lower-class holding power is not as strong for girls as it is for boys. Between Grades 10 and 12, there was little change in the proportion of girls in each class who expected to reach the top, and in each case it was lower than for boys. As we pointed out in Chapter 5, social class background affects the chances of a girl going to a university. When families face financial difficulties, parents are less willing to spend their limited educational funds on girls than on boys, and this applies particularly to lower-class girls. Knowing that they face more severe financial constraints than their lower-class brothers on the realization of their post-secondary goals, lower-class girls lowered their educational aspirations to a greater extent than boys.

While these data on expected occupational mobility show strong lower-class holding power for boys, they also indicate that by Grade 12 the majority of lower-class boys, and an even greater majority of lower-class girls, expected to improve on their fathers' occupational level. La Mar T. Empey provides similar evidence in his 1954 study of a sample of male senior public high school students in the state of Washington.[3] In addition, he showed that the absolute occupational expectations of upper-middle and middle-class male students were higher than those of lower-class males. The data in Table 6.6 show that the same pattern prevailed among our high school student sample. In this table, for each family socio-economic level we have used the average socio-economic score of occupations (according to the Blishen scale) that students expected. Keeping in mind that students with families at the highest level cannot expect to go any higher, while those from the lowest level cannot go any lower, generally speaking the higher the students' socio-economic level, the higher their occupational expectations tended to be. Nevertheless, it is clear that boys and girls at the lowest levels had higher occupational expectations, relative to their present socio-economic standing, than did students from the three highest levels. In other words, students at the three lowest levels were more inclined than those from the three highest levels to expect a job that had higher socio-economic standing than their fathers. Students at the third highest level were inclined to expect a job at about the same level as their fathers, while those at the two top levels expected a job that was somewhat below the socio-economic level of their fathers.

The presence of mobility values within the lower class bears out some observations of Ralph Turner, who suggests that all social strata accept these values but differ in the extent to which they see them as applicable to their situation. His hypothesis "rests on the assumption that there is a society-wide uniformity of values that cross-cut class lines and that apparent value contradictions between classes are largely based on mistaking differences in value relevancy for differences in the acceptance of values."[4] If this assumption is correct, it helps to explain the general acceptance by students at all class levels of relatively high occupational goals. While they are still young, and before entering the "realistic" world of work, students tend to accept the society-wide values that cross-cut class lines. Thus they generally accept the values of opportunity and success in the work world, which they translate into "unrealistic" expectations of upward social mobility.

We cannot determine the degree to which these mobility expectations were realistic without following our sample of students into the work world after they left high school or university to find out what jobs they took. This we did not do. However, while we cannot show the degree of realism of these expectations in terms of the jobs students had after completing their schooling, we can show it in terms of their family class position. We do this by measuring the correlation between occupational mobility expectation and class position. These mobility expectations are measured in terms of the difference between the socio-economic score of the occupations expected by the student (according to the Blishen scale) and the socio-economic score of the father's occupation. The zero order correlation coefficients between these occupational mobility expectations and class position ($r_{exp.\ mobility\ \times\ SES}$) are quite low: .217 and .257 for males and females respectively in Grade 10,

Table 6.6

Average SES Score, and Standard Deviation of Students' Occupational Expectations by Family Socio-economic Status, by Sex (Grades 10 and 12)

Family	SES Score	Males		Females	
		Exp.	SD	Exp.	SD
Grade 10					
1	(70-76)	62.28	14.28	50.27	13.85
2	(60-69)	55.47	15.50	54.80	13.96
3	(50-59)	53.87	16.38	52.25	13.25
4	(40-49)	50.11	16.42	51.64	12.84
5	(30-39)	46.06	15.44	48.74	13.49
6	(25-29)	46.27	15.97	46.61	11.21
Total		49.97	16.47	50.27	13.33
	N =	1310		1135	
Grade 12					
1	(70-76)	61.60	15.49	57.14	13.66
2	(60-69)	59.94	14.34	54.79	11.67
3	(50-59)	55.78	15.00	52.13	12.44
4	(40-49)	52.27	15.64	51.69	12.18
5	(30-39)	49.01	16.26	50.40	11.71
6	(25-29)	48.44	15.63	49.69	11.15
Total		52.28	16.24	51.60	12.13
	N =	1182		1201	

and .219 and .269 for boys and girls respectively in Grade 12. If social class is strongly associated with occupational expectations we could expect these correlations to be higher, although we cannot say how much higher.

In an attempt to determine if the occupational mobility experienced by the student's father was related to the student's expected occupational mobility, we computed zero order correlations between students' expected mobility, as measured above, and the fathers' mobility measured in two ways: the difference between the socio-economic score (according to the Blishen scale) of the father's first job and the grandfather's job when he was sixteen; and the difference between the socio-economic score of the father's present occupation and his first job. To do this we used data from the parental interviews. Our results show that no matter how we measure father's occupational mobility experience, there was only a small negative correlation with the student's expected mobility, the highest being a correlation of −.22 between the occupational expectations of Grade 10 boys and the occupational mobility experience of their fathers as measured by the difference between the socio-economic score of their present occupation, and the occupation they followed in their first job. These small but consistently negative correlations suggest that the occupational expectations of students from different socio-economic strata (evident in Table 6.6) are negatively related to the fathers' occupational mobility, which means that if the father is mobile the son is not as likely to have high expected mobility as if his father is not mobile.

Social class is only one, albeit an important one, among a number of social and psychological variables related to occupational expectations. If we examine the proportions of intelligent students at each class level who expect to reach the various levels of the occupational ladder, we can get some idea of the wastage of talent. Earlier we indicated that the relationship between educational and occupational aspirations and social class is consistent for boys and girls at all levels of mental ability and social class. Intelligent lower-class boys and girls were less likely than intelligent middle- or upper-middle-class boys and girls to aspire to the highest educational or occupational levels. Does the same relationship hold for occupational expectations? Figure 6.1 shows that in Grade 10 it does, with one exception. Within each class, as mental ability declines, the proportion of boys and girls expecting to reach Level 1 and 2 occupations also declines. In both grades, lower-class boys and girls of a high mental ability were much less likely than upper-middle-class boys and girls at this level of mental ability to expect to reach the highest occupational levels (Level 1 and 2). The proportion of intelligent upper-middle-class boys and girls who expected occupations at Level 1 and 2 was almost twice that of intelligent lower-class boys and girls. Girls in the middle and lower classes concentrated their expectations on middle level jobs, particularly in Grade 12, a familiar pattern in our analyses. Even the most able girls showed this tendency.

These data clearly show that a sizeable proportion of students from the largest of the three social classes, the lower class, were mentally capable of reaching high occupational levels but expected not to—an obvious wastage of talent on which we may throw some light. There can be little doubt that this is due, in part, to the relatively low educational aspirations of lower-class students, which disqualify them from the top jobs; but as we noted earlier in this chapter, both educational and occupational aspirations are strongly related not only to mental ability but to self-concept of ability as well. Such a relationship may also exist between occupational expectations and these two variables. Figure 6.2 shows that this may be the case. We

Figure 6.1
Students with High Occupational Expectations,
by Mental Ability, Socio-economic Status and Sex, Grade 10

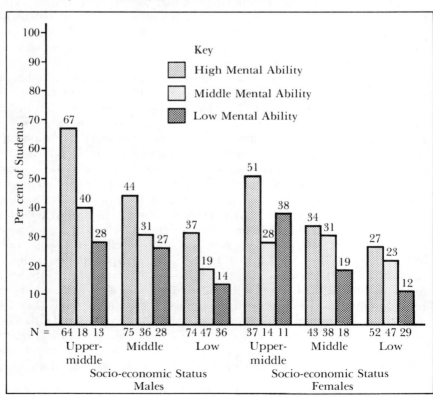

cannot be more positive because, as Figure 6.2 indicates, some proportions are based on small numbers. At each level of mental ability, as self-concept of ability declines the proportion of boys and girls who expect to reach the highest occupational level declines dramatically. In both grades boys and girls with high mental ability and a high self-concept are much more likely to expect high level jobs than boys and girls at any other level of mental ability with a medium or low level of self-concept of ability. The differences in the proportions expecting top level jobs between high and low self-concept groups at each level of mental ability is striking. For example, in Grade 10, of the boys with high mental ability and high self-concept 69 per cent expected occupations at the two highest levels. This compares with 30 per cent with the same level of mental ability and a medium self-concept.

Figure 6.2
Students with High Occupational Expectations,
by Self-concept of Ability, Mental Ability and Sex,
Grade 10

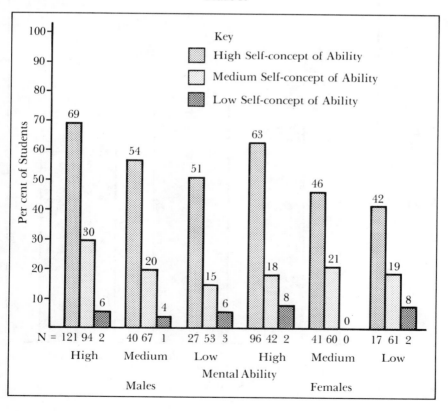

No valid comparison can be made between these two groups and boys with high mental ability and low self-concept because the percentage for the latter is based on a very small number.

To what extent is this relationship between mental ability, self-concept of ability and occupational expectations affected by social class? Unfortunately, because of the small numbers involved we cannot fully explore this relationship. However, since we are particularly interested in determining the extent to which the expectations of the most able and confident

Figure 6.3
High Occupational Expectations of Students
with High Mental Ability and High Self-concept,
by Socio-economic Status and Sex, Grade 10

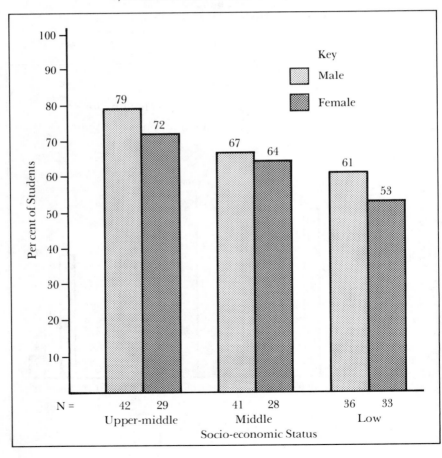

students may be thwarted, we will examine the effects of social class on the occupational expectations of high mental ability and high self-concept students. This is done in Figure 6.3, but care should be taken in making assumptions based upon the small numbers in this figure. Nevertheless, it seems clear that the occupational expectations of these talented boys and girls were affected by class background; the higher the talented student's social class the greater the likelihood that he or she expected a high level occupation. By Grade 12 the majority of these boys in each social class

Figure 6.4
High Occupational Expectations by Program,
Socio-economic Status and Sex, Grade 10

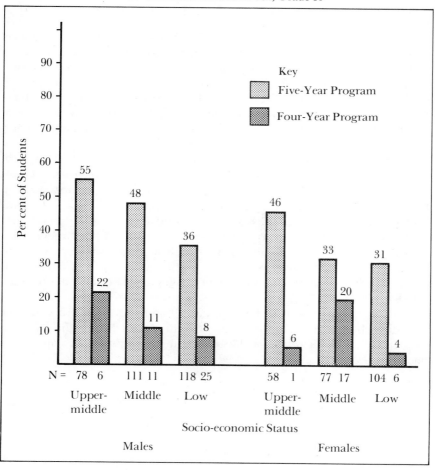

expected high level occupations, but for the talented girls the situation was somewhat different in that while the majority of those from the upper-middle class had these expectations, the majority from the lower class expected middle level occupations.

This analysis shows a strong relationship between our independent variables—social class, mental ability and self-concept of ability—and our dependent variable—occupational expectations. We now turn to another important independent variable—school program—to determine its relationship to occupational expectations.

As we have indicated in Chapter 5, at the time this study was undertaken programs were an important feature of the Ontario secondary school system. They were to some extent class biased in that middle- and upper-middle-class students tended to be streamed into the five-year program that led to entrance to university, which would eventually result in middle or higher level jobs. On the other hand, a higher proportion of lower-class than of middle- or upper-middle-class students were streamed into programs that terminated in Grade 10 or 12 and led to lower level occupations. Programs had a similar effect on occupational expectations. Although he tends to ignore the class bias in secondary school programs, Raymond Breton does recognize the importance of a student's program of study for his future career. In his analysis he shows, for example, that there is "a 35.8 per cent difference in the likelihood of expressing a preference for a high status occupation between those in the academic-university preparatory program and those in the terminal technical."[5]

Figure 6.4 shows how the class-biased school programs affected occupational expectations. At each class level, students in five-year programs were much more likely to expect a high level occupation than students in four-year programs, even though four-year programs would lead to some high occupations through the C.A.A.T.s and nursing schools; but lower-class students in five-year programs were less likely than upper-middle-class students in these programs to expect a high level occupation. In fact, as Figure 6.4 indicates, there were so few upper-middle-class boys and girls enrolled in four-year programs that percentages based on these numbers are unreliable.

As we might expect, in both Grades 10 and 12 a high proportion of girls at each class level and in each program expected to get middle level jobs. In Grade 12, regardless of class or program, at least 45 per cent of girls had these expectations.

Notes

1. John Porter, *The Vertical Mosaic* (Toronto: University of Toronto Press, 1965).

2. Archibald O. Haller and Irwin W. Miller, *The Occupational Aspiration Scale: Theory, Structure and Correlates* (East Lansing: Michigan State University, Agricultural Experimentation Station, Technical Bulletin, 1963), p.288.

3. La Mar T. Empey, "Social Class and Occupational Aspiration: A Comparison of Absolute and Relative Measurement," in *American Sociological Review* (21, 1956), pp.703–709.

4. Ralph L. Turner, *The Social Context of Ambition* (San Francisco: Chandler Publishing Company, 1964), p.80.

5. Raymond Breton, *Social and Economic Factors in the Career Decisions of Canadian Youth* (Ottawa: Queen's Printer, 1972), p.247.

7

Self-Concept of Ability

Although self-concept has been the subject of a great deal of research, there are very few instances of self-concept of ability being used as a variable in a model of aspiration formation. In most of the approximately 1,200 items of research into self-concept, the goal is to determine how self-concept or self-esteem is related to particular background characteristics such as race, religion, sex, social class, to child rearing practices, or less frequently to learning experiences.[1] In fact, in an extensive search of the literature we could find very few studies in which this variable is used in a causal model of aspiration formation. One is Chad Gordon's *Looking Ahead: Self Conception, Race and Family as Determinants of Adolescent Orientation*,[2] in which the major hypothesis is that the more favourable the student's self-conception, the higher his aspirations. Another example is in a study by Alan B. Wilson and Alejandro Portes, who try to discredit the use of self-concept as a variable in a causal model of educational aspirations.[3] However, a consideration of the theories of self-concept makes it eminently qualified as a candidate for inclusion in such a model. Whether it is possible to measure it meaningfully is a question that we will examine later.

An illustration of its importance can be found in Joseph A. Kahl's study of twenty-four "common man" boys, twelve of whom wanted to go to college and twelve of whom did not. All had I.Q. scores that indicated they would be capable of doing college level work. Kahl concluded after intensive interviews with the boys and their parents that their self-concept of ability was developed early in their school career. If they performed well in elementary school, and if their parents were not satisfied merely to "get by" but wanted to "get ahead" and praised and encouraged their sons, they developed a high self-concept of ability and continued to perform well and to see themselves as capable of going to college. One boy described the opposite situation vividly:

> I haven't got much brain for all that college stuff. . . . You know nobody
> would believe me now but I was an "A" student in grammar school. I
> dunno what happened. I just started dropping gradually.[4]

This was a boy who was not being pushed by his parents. His parents were
satisfied with their situation, and they saw no better prospect for their son.
"My folks tell me I should get out of school and get a job, any kind of job."
The fact that he was capable of doing well is apparent from his early
performance. But because his parents did not reinforce the high self-concept
of ability that he should have acquired through his superior performance,
he lost interest in trying. Then when his grades declined he felt that he
didn't have "much brain for all that college stuff."

Another example of the importance of self-concept in setting goals for
oneself is seen in the remark of another boy that Kahl says is typical of the
responses of the twelve who were not planning to go to college. He explains
how he chose among the four possible programs that he could follow in
high school, programs which all the boys could easily rank according to
increasing difficulty as trade, general, commercial and college preparatory:

> I chose commercial because it was sort of in-between the general and the
> college course. I didn't want to take the general course figuring, oh, you
> know, people would say, "Oh he must be failing." I didn't want to go to
> college. I don't have a brilliant mind.[5]

We pointed out in Chapter 3 that symbolic interaction theory has been
extremely important in designing our theoretical framework and building
our model. We believe, as we said there, that "the roots of ambition are in
the early socializing processes where individuals play their respective roles
with parents, teachers and peers." Kahl himself did not use theory to
explain his observations, but his study is an illustration of how the theory
can work out in practice.

Charles H. Cooley developed the theory that a person's idea of himself
develops through social interaction. The person derives his self-concept
from the perceptions he has of how others view him. He borrowed Ralph
Waldo Emerson's phrase "the looking glass self" and his couplet:

Each to each a looking glass
Reflects the other that doth pass.[6]

In his view there are three elements to the process. First, a person
imagines how he appears to another person; second, he imagines how the
other person judges him; and third, there is the effect of that judgement on
himself of either pride or shame. Cooley admits that the looking glass is an
inaccurate analogy to the process by which a person develops a self-concept
through his perceptions of the judgement of others since the looking glass
does not judge. However, he found it a useful image, and since it is so
frequently called on, obviously others have too. The individual's self-

concept is developed in childhood through the interactions he has with those who are close to him. Parents or others who are important to him show approval or disapproval of his behaviour by the way they communicate with him. Language, gestures and facial expressions are symbols of their feelings—thus symbolic interaction. They define him to himself. "What a clever little boy you are!" or "It's too difficult for you to do. Too bad you are not as bright as your sister." The child's self-concept is not merely a reflection of others' evaluation. He must internalize the view of himself that he imagines others have. He may not be necessarily correct in his assessment. One can imagine the stern Victorian father with very high standards of behaviour giving a son the impression that he thought his work was worthless, while in fact he might actually consider it quite good but might feel it important always to demand more.

George Herbert Mead elaborated Cooley's ideas. He theorized that a person "takes the role of the others," especially of those who are important to him, such as parents, teachers and friends, whom he called his "significant others." In doing this he tries to see himself as others see him. Mead considered that a person's self-concept at any one time provides "a frame of reference" for interpreting new experiences.[7]

It seems obvious now that the image we have of ourselves and of our capabilities is an important determinant of how we behave and what we are able to achieve, but psychologists have not always regarded this as important.

Self-concept was defined in a seminal article by V.C. Raimy in 1943:

> The self-concept is the more or less organized perceptual object resulting from present and past self observation. . . . (It is) what a person believes about himself. It is a map which each person consults in order to understand himself.[8]

The idea of a self-image and its consequences for behaviour now pervades our culture. "Black is beautiful" was adopted as a slogan to try to improve the self-image of black Americans, or Negroes as they were then called. Female consciousness raising has, as a goal, making women realize that they are equal in potentiality to men, that the reason they are not equal in the society and have not in the past believed they had equal capacities was their acceptance of the sex role into which they had been socialized. Through their interaction with their significant others, they learn to take a subordinate position and avoid the experiences that require mastering skills that are seen to be masculine. Our chapter on girls' aspirations discusses sex roles in detail and the consequence of them on girls' achievement and aspirations.

Self-Concept and Learning

W.B. Brookover, whose self-concept of ability scale we have used in this study, uses symbolic interaction theory to develop a theory of learning. He argues that it is important to have a high self-concept in order for a student to perform well, and he sees this self-concept developing through the child's perceptions of how he appears to those around him, and especially to those who are significant to him: his parents, his teachers, his friends.[9]

Brookover and Gottlieb outline a "symbolic interaction framework for understanding human learning." They state four hypotheses that they believe must be accepted if the nature of learning is to be understood:

1. People learn to behave in ways that each considers appropriate to himself.

2. Appropriateness of behaviour is defined by each person through the internalization of the expectations which others whom he considers important hold for him.

3. The functional limits of one's ability to learn are determined by his self-conception or self-image as acquired in social interaction.

4. The individual learns what he believes others who are important to him expect him to learn in a given situation.[10]

As an example, Brookover argues, "Whether or not a child is able to learn Algebra, French or any other type of behaviour is limited by his own concept of his ability to learn the particular behaviour and his perception of its appropriateness for him." His own concept of his ability to learn is "acquired in social interaction" (Hypothesis 3). "Its appropriateness for him" is defined through "the internalization of the expectations which others whom he considers important hold for him" (Hypothesis 2).

Many would think that whether or not a child is able to learn Algebra or French is limited by his intelligence. Brookover does not deny biological limits to learning, but he emphasizes other factors because he says "we cannot measure accurately innate capacities" and "few use all their capacity for learning." In any case, he points out that "this self-concept of ability is a necessary but not sufficient factor in determining the behaviour that he will learn."[11]

Brookover's goal is to change educational practices to make it possible to enhance "the achievement levels of the great majority of students to meet the demands of an increasingly complex technological society." He believes that teachers can consciously raise the self-concept of students and that this will affect their performance.[12]

An experiment that illustrates this view is described in *Pygmalion in the Classroom: Teacher Expectations and Pupils' Intellectual Development*.[13] This experiment sought to determine whether a teacher's expectation for her pupils' intellectual competence can come to serve as an educational self-fulfilling prophecy. Twenty per cent of pupils in a certain elementary school were reported to their teachers as showing unusual potential for intellectual growth. Actually the pupils were randomly drawn from the entire school population. Eight months later these pupils showed significant gains in their I.Q.s while others in the school did not. Since the gain was in the I.Q. and not in school grades, it can be assumed that the change took place in the pupils and not simply in the teachers' assessment of them. If their school grades had been higher, one might have argued that the teachers gave them higher grades because they imagined they were performing better. Presumably, the teachers treated these children as if they had special abilities and thus increased their self-concept; inevitably, according to the Brookover theory, their learning abilities improved.

A somewhat different approach, depending on perceptual theory rather than symbolic interaction theory, led A.W. Combs and D. Snygg to the same conclusion in their theory of learning, which they developed in their book *Individual Behaviour*.[14] In it they theorize that whether a person learns and what he learns depends very much on his image of whether he can learn, and whether the material that is being taught is relevant to his needs. They argue that the individual has an immense drive for self-enhancement and self-realization, and therefore there is a need for self-esteem in the learning situation. Snygg had conducted experiments with children which led him to the conclusion that "the chief motive of child behaviour and learning is their need for self-esteem and a feeling of personal adequacy." The student, to acquire a satisfactory feeling of competence and acceptance, must grow up having an experience of success. Consequently, if students are to learn, a school must provide a maximum of challenge and a minimum of threat. These theories are behind the educational changes of the fifties and sixties, in which students were to be evaluated against their own potential rather than against some objective norm or against others in their class. In fact, it was questioned that children should be evaluated at all. Learning should bring its own reward. Any evaluation might damage the child's self-esteem and reduce the likelihood that he would learn. These theories also led to the much more flexible curriculum in the high schools where students had much greater choices than in the traditional curriculum. It was felt that if students could choose subjects that interested them and that they saw as relevant to their needs, they would be more likely to learn successfully and this successful experience would enhance their self-image and, in turn, encourage them to undertake other learning experiences. Combs and Snygg assert that "it need not be feared that children in a situation where they are able to move freely toward self-enhancement will select activities that are too easy, because mastering more difficult tasks is more satisfying."[15]

A combination of the theory of learning advanced by Brookover based on symbolic interaction theory and the perceptual or phenomenological theory of Combs and Snygg seems most appealing. In both the theories, self-concept is an important factor in the learning experience, but the symbolic interaction theory postulates that an individual develops his self-concept through his interaction with significant others. An individual acquires a high or low self-concept through his perception of how others regard him. Combs and Snygg argue that a person acquires a high or low self-concept through his own experience of success or failure. What seems a likely process is that a child performs a task well, his parents praise him and, because of his successful performance, have expectations that he will continue to perform well; the child develops a high self-concept both from the successful mastery of a skill and from the recognition of that mastery that he perceives others have of it.

The mastery of a task gives satisfaction; the more difficult the task the greater the satisfaction. Failing creates feelings of humiliation and shame. One tries to maximize pleasant feelings, so one undertakes tasks that are within one's capacity. One acquires a self-concept through one's experience. If the experience is of success, one's self-concept is high. If the experience is of failure, one's self-concept is low. But how do we define our experience as successful or unsuccessful? And how do we determine whether or not a task is within our capacity? In part, it is through the responses of others, and for children, especially, their significant others, but in part it is through our knowledge of ourselves. We do not need to be told by others that we are good in mathematics when we have successfully solved a difficult problem. And having solved one difficult problem, we are prepared to undertake another. On the other hand, recognition by others of our achievement is very important for our self-esteem. And as we have seen with Joseph Kahl's "common man" boys, encouragement by significant others is essential if we are to take on difficult tasks. We are always conscious of how we appear to others and are always anxious for approval by those whose opinions we care about. Even the unrecognized genius struggling alone in his garret probably consoles himself with an image of how posterity will regard him, while at the same time searching for approval from those close to him.

Self-Concept and Aspirations

Although Brookover was not concerned with aspirations, the importance of self-concept in the development of aspirations is inherent in the preceding discussion. Consider again the socialization of girls. The result of this socialization is that they want to do what they perceive society approves for girls and women. In other words, through social interaction, they develop a concept of themselves and their capabilities which leads them to choose particular courses of action and to aim at certain goals. A girl who is brought up in the traditional female way will have a concept of herself as capable of being a wife and mother and incapable of being an executive or a political leader. Her aspiration will be to be a wife and mother, and her educational plans and aspirations will be those that are appropriate for that role. Another girl who is encouraged by her mother, or perhaps her father, to feel that she is capable of doing anything that a boy can do may reject the female role entirely. She may not see herself at all as a wife and mother, or at least not primarily, and her aspirations also will be consistent with her image of herself. Of course, this is an over-simplification of a very complex process which is confused today by the rhetoric of the women's movement, but it is surely true to say that one's image of one's capacity determines one's aspirations, that one's image of one's capacity is not necessarily correct, but it is the one that has been acquired through interacting with others.

The justification for using self-concept of ability in a model is succinctly stated by Wilson and Portes:

> A person develops and adjusts his aspirations in accordance with both the evaluations he receives from his social environment (significant others) and his own self-assessment of abilities on the basis of objective information provided by his academic performance.[16]

We introduce the quotation here because it is a clear statement of how we have used the variable in our multivariate analysis in Chapter 15. In that path model, we have hypothesized a path from school performance to significant others to self-concept of ability to educational aspirations. We have argued that the way a person performs in school contributes to the perceptions that his parents have of his capabilities. This in turn causes his parents to have particular aspirations for him, and these aspirations as perceived by the individual contribute to his self-image, which affects his own aspirations. (A person develops and adjusts his aspirations in accordance with the evaluations he receives from his significant others.) At the same time, his school performance contributes to the image he has of his

Table 7.1
Zero-order Correlations of Grade 10 Students,
Girls Above, Boys Below Line

	MA	SP	SCA	SCA-S	SCA-U
MA			.277	.147	.220
SP	.285		.594	.510	.294
SCA	.275	.553		.702	.671
SCA-S	.129	.463	.671		.035*
SCA-U	.247	.281	.677	-.014*	

MA —Mental Ability
SP —School Performance
SCA —Self-concept of Ability using eight questions
SCA-S —Questions 1, 2, 3, 7, 8, Self-concept of Ability to do schoolwork
SCA-U —Questions 4, 5, 6, Self-concept of Ability to do university level work

*Not Significant.

academic ability and thence to his educational aspirations (his self-assessment of abilities based on his academic performance).

As we explained in Chapter 4, a factor analysis of this scale revealed two dimensions of self-concept of academic ability. One of these related to schoolwork; the other consisted of questions that related to university work.

Table 7.1 shows the zero correlations of these three variables, and also of mental ability and school performance. It is interesting that SCA-S and SCA-U do not correlate with each other for either boys or girls. It seems that students do not relate their perceived ability in school to what they think they would be capable of doing at university. School performance does correlate significantly with both these measures, but the correlations are higher with SCA-S (.510, girls; .463, boys) than with SCA-U (.294, girls; .281, boys). On the other hand, mental ability, though correlations are not high, correlates more highly with SCA-U (.220, girls; .247, boys) than with SCA-S (.147, girls; .129 boys).

Of the three measures of self-concept of ability, it seems most appropriate to use SCA-U in this study, whose major dependent variable is educational aspirations.

One problem is to decide how to deal with the four- and five-year programs. Students in the four-year program were not eligible for university, and it would not be surprising if they did not have a high concept of their ability to do university level work. On the other hand, since the course content was so different in the two programs, questions asking how they ranked themselves compared with their classmates would not give comparable results for the two programs. Actually, on any of our measures of self-concept of ability, four-year-program students on the whole rated themselves lower than did five-year-program students. For example, Table 7.2 shows the percentages of Grade 10 students who considered themselves

Table 7.2
Percentage of Students Who Consider Themselves Above Average
by Program (Grade 10)

Title	Program		X^2	d.f.	p.
	Five-Year	Four-Year			
	(per cent)				
Compared to friends	30	17	54.3	4	.000
Compared to class	33	19	40.3	4	.000
Ranking in school	32	20	44.4	4	.000
N =	1,632	923			

Table 7.3
Self-concept of Ability to do University Level Work*
by Program and Sex (Grade 10)

SCA-U	Program			
	Five-Year Program		Four-Year Program	
	M	F	M	F
	(per cent)			
High 1	2	1	-	-
2	23	18	5	4
3	48	51	25	29
4	19	24	35	33
5	7	5	29	28
Low 6	1	1	6	6
Total	100	100	100	100
N =	782	777	508	352

*SCA-U

above average compared to their friends, compared to their class, and within the school. About one-third of five-year students and one-fifth of four-year students considered themselves above average.

Even though their program would not permit them to attend university, it seemed quite likely that some four-year students would consider themselves capable of doing university level work. For this reason we decided to use the SCA-U measure for both programs, but to separate the programs to gain as much understanding as possible of the factors that might affect self-concept.

Table 7.3 shows SCA-U by program and sex. The distribution of self-concept levels is, of course, quite different for the two programs, with 25 per cent of five-year boys having a high self-concept (categories 1 and 2) and only 5 per cent of four-year boys having such a high self-concept. But what is interesting is that 30 per cent of boys in the four-year program and 33 per cent of girls have an academic self-concept that falls in the top three categories. Perhaps we can learn something about the factors that contribute to a high self-concept by focussing on these three categories, which we will call high self-concept, and noticing especially the four-year program students. Seventy-three per cent of boys and 70 per cent of girls in the five-year program, and 30 per cent of boys and 33 per cent of girls in the four-year program, have a high self-concept by this definition.

It is also interesting to notice in Table 7.3 the different proportions of boys and girls in the five-year program who thought of themselves as very able. Twenty-five per cent of boys, but only 19 per cent of girls, were in the top two categories of SCA-U. In Grade 12 the comparable figures are 31 per cent of boys and 15 per cent of girls. It seems that at all ages boys are more likely to have a high self-concept than girls, and as they get older the gap between the percentages of boys and girls with a high self-concept widens.

The symbolic interaction theory that we have described postulates that a self-concept of ability arises in part from a person's performance and in part from his interactions with his significant others. We will analyse our data from these two perspectives. The measure of performance that we will use is school-reported grades. We have already demonstrated that it is related to SCA-U in the matrix of Table 7.1, but Figure 7.1 shows how the two variables are related in the two programs. In the five-year program it is

Figure 7.1
Per cent of Students with High Self-concept of Ability, SCA-U,
by School Performance, Program and Sex, Grade 10

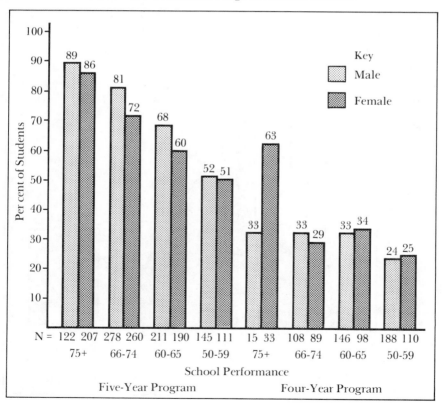

quite clear that at each higher level of school performance higher proportions had a high self-concept of ability, but in the four-year program the
relationship is not strong. In the five-year program at each level of school
performance, boys are somewhat more likely to have high self-concept than
girls, but this also is not true in the four-year program. In the four-year
program there were very few with averages over 75 per cent, and this
probably accounts for the aberrant figure of 63 per cent of girls in the four-
year program having a high self-concept.

Another possible candidate as a measure of performance is mental
ability. A bright student, whether or not he performs well in school, might
be expected to realize that he has potential and that he should be capable of

Figure 7.2
Per cent of Students with High Self-concept of Ability, SCA-U,
by Mental Ability, Program and Sex, Grade 12

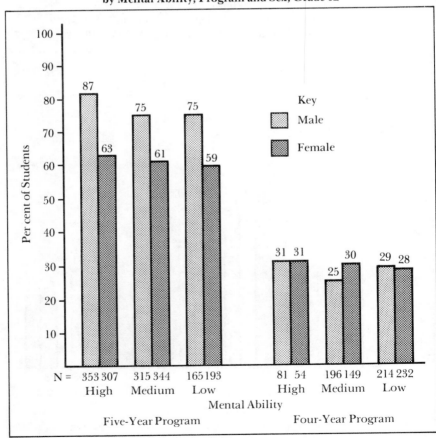

doing well. However, Figure 7.2 shows that there is very little relationship between MA and SCA-U. This figure uses the data from the Grade 12 sample, and again we see in the five-year program how many more boys than girls had a high self-concept of ability. This difference between boys and girls does not exist in the four-year program, perhaps because girls in the four-year program would be taking a commercial course and in it would acquire a feeling of competence that would at least make them as likely as boys in the four-year program to have a high self-concept of ability.

We have several measures of significant others' influence that might elucidate the formation of a self-concept of ability. With respect to parents, teachers and friends, students were asked, "How much do you discuss your hopes for future education with your parents (teachers, friends)?" and

Figure 7.3
Per cent of Students with High Self-concept of Ability, SCA-U,
by Parental Influence, Program and Sex, Grade 10

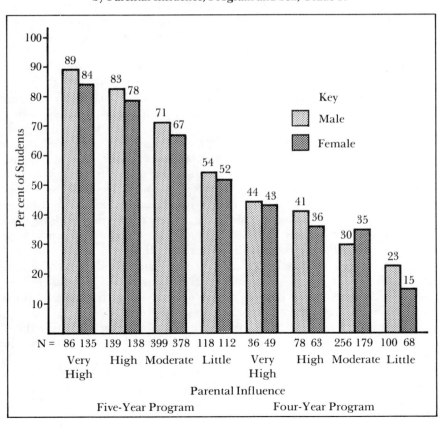

"How much do they help you in thinking about these hopes for your future education?" From these two questions, as we described in Chapter 4, we developed an interval scale which gave us the variables: parental influence, teachers' influence and friends' influence.

Self-concept of ability is strikingly related to parental influence in both the five- and four-year programs, as Figure 7.3 shows. Indeed, it is interesting to compare it with Figure 7.1, which shows how self-concept of ability is related to school performance. In both figures for the five-year program there is a monotonic relationship, ranging from almost 90 per cent with high self-concept at one extreme to a little over 50 per cent at the other. The 90 per cent is, of course, much higher and the 50 per cent is much lower than the average for the five-year program of about 70 per cent with high self-concept. Our hypothesis—that a person's self-concept arises both from his performance and from the influence of significant others—seems to be strikingly confirmed. In the four-year program, too, although the proportions are much lower, we can see that self-concept is related to parental influence, with 44 per cent of boys who reported that their parents had great influence and only 23 per cent who reported little influence having a high self-concept. There is no relationship, however, between self-concept and school performance for four-year-program boys, and that is probably because boys do not get a feeling of satisfaction from performing well in the despised four-year program. In our chapter on school performance (Chapter 9) we discuss the meaning of academic achievement in the two programs.

Teachers are supposed to be significant to children, but in very few cases was the teacher's influence very high. In both programs, for both boys and girls, less than 3 per cent acknowledged very high teacher influence. However, by combining the very high and high categories, we can get meaningful numbers. The relationship between self-concept of ability and teachers' influence, shown in Figure 7.4, is not nearly as striking as that between parental influence and self-concept of ability. Nevertheless, it does exist. For boys there is a difference of 11 percentage points in the five-year program and 14 percentage points in the four-year program of those with high self-concept between those for whom the teacher's influence is high and those for whom the teacher's influence is little.

Friends are considered to be among an individual's significant others, and many seem to think that in adolescence peers replace parents in their influence. However, our data do not show that. There is no relationship between friends' influence and self-concept of ability.

Clearly, of the significant others, parents are by far the most important. Many more students acknowledge a high influence of parents than they do of teachers or friends, and when parents do have a very high or high influence, strikingly high proportions in the five-year program and relatively high proportions in the four-year program have a high self-concept. Not many find teachers important in their influence, but when they do their self-concept is likely to be higher than if they do not. Whether friends have influence or not does not affect the student's self-concept of ability.

Another way in which parents might affect their children's self-concept of ability is in their educational aspirations for them. If parents want their child to go to university, the child is surely more likely to feel that he is capable of doing the work than if his parents felt that his destination should be to become a clerk. It is not surprising, then, to see in Figure 7.5 that when mothers are perceived to want their child to go to university 82 per cent of boys and 85 per cent of girls in the five-year program have a high self-concept of ability, and that of those whose mothers are seen to want them to leave school and go to work only 35 and 40 per cent respectively have a high self-concept.

Figure 7.4
Per cent of Students with High Self-concept
by Teachers' Influence, Program and Sex

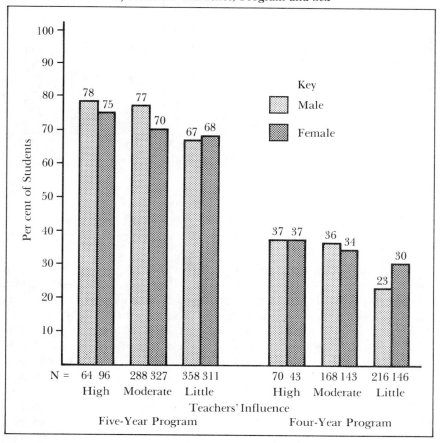

Figure 7.5
Per cent of Students with High Self-concept of Ability,
by Perceived Mothers' Aspirations, Program and Sex, Grade 10

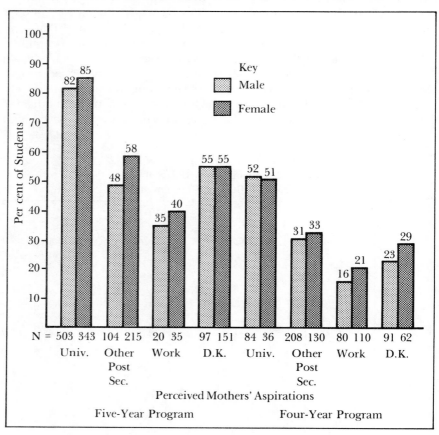

It is interesting that a considerable number of boys in the four-year program perceive their mothers as wanting them to go to university. In fact, slightly more saw them as wanting them to go to university than to work. Over half of the boys in the four-year program who thought that their mothers wanted them to go to university had a high self-concept of academic ability, and of those who thought that their fathers wanted them to go to university (Figure 7.6) 61 per cent had a high SCA. A fairly large proportion of boys and girls in both programs with respect to both their father and mother did not know what their parents wanted them to do. When that was the situation, a smaller proportion had a high self-concept than of those who thought their parents wanted them to go to university, but a higher proportion had a high self-concept than of those who thought

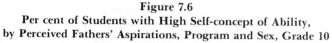

Figure 7.6
Per cent of Students with High Self-concept of Ability,
by Perceived Fathers' Aspirations, Program and Sex, Grade 10

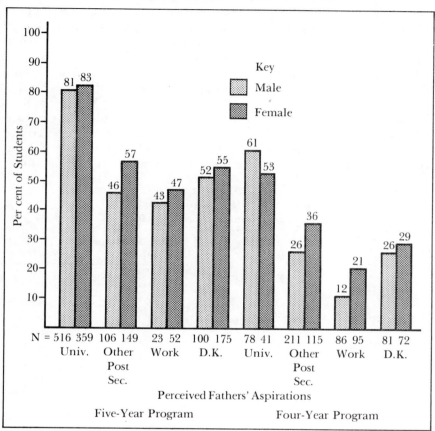

their parents wanted them to go to work. This again illustrates the importance of the parents' influence in the development of a self-concept of ability. If parents are seen to have high aspirations, children are likely to have a high self-concept of ability. If parents are seen as having low aspirations, children are likely to have a low self-concept. In the five-year program, if they do not know, they are as likely to have a high as a low self-concept.

A puzzling feature of these two figures is that in all but one category (four-year program, aspiring to university) more girls have a high self-concept than boys, while in the other figures where we have analysed self-concept of ability by school performance, by parental influence and by mental ability, in almost all cases boys were more likely to have a high self-concept than were girls. For example, of those with high mental ability in the five-year program, 82 per cent of boys and 63 per cent of girls had a high self-concept of ability (Figure 7.2). Of those whose grades in school were between 66 and 74, 81 per cent of boys and 72 per cent of girls had a high self-concept of ability (Figure 7.1). But consistently, girls are more likely to have a high self-concept than boys by each category of perceived parental aspiration, with the exception of the four-year program where if boys see either their father or their mother wanting them to go to university they are more likely than girls to have a high self-concept. What this suggests is that boys are more likely than girls to be influenced by what they see as their parents' aspirations. If they see their father or mother wanting them to go to some post-secondary institution other than university, about 57 per cent of girls but only 46 per cent of boys still see themselves as capable of doing university work. If in the five-year program they see either of their parents

Table 7.4
Students With High Self-concept of Ability
by Help from Significant Others

	Father and Mother Equally	No One
	(per cent)	
Plans for Next Fall		
5-Year Program—boys	79	72
—girls	77	62
4-Year Program—boys	30	24
—girls	38	29
Educational Aspirations		
5-Year Program—boys	78	67
—girls	73	62
4-Year Program—boys	38	26
—girls	42	26
Help in Grade 8		
5-Year Program—boys	86	67
—girls	79	62
4-Year Program—boys	36	28
—girls	44	23

wanting them to go to work, about 5 per cent more girls than boys retain a high self-concept.

Three other questions related to significant others' influence: "Who helps most in plans for next fall?," "Who helps most in your educational hopes and aspirations?" and "Who helped you most in your plans when you were in Grade 8?" Possible answers were: father, mother, father and mother equally, teacher, principal, guidance counsellor, siblings, friends, or no one. Most students answered father and mother equally, or father or mother, but almost as many answered no one. One might speculate that possibly the person who answers "no one" is independent, sure of himself and does not need help, and perhaps that is true of some; but our data show that a person is more likely to have a high self-concept if father and mother equally help most. Table 7.4 shows the difference in proportions of those with high self-concept between those who said that their mother and father were helping equally and those who said no one was helping them. In both programs and with both sexes, higher proportions had a high self-concept if their mother and father were helping them than if no one was helping them. The differences are greatest in the responses to the question about who was helping most in Grade 8. Eighty-six per cent of boys in the five-year program whose both parents helped them had a high self-concept, compared to 67 per cent of those who said no one helped them. Not all the differences are great, but all are significant.

If the answer was that father helps most or mother helps most, the results are inconsistent. If father helped most, students were likely to have a high self-concept; but in response to the question about who helped most in Grade 8, if the answer was mother, boys especially were not as likely to have a high self-concept. Sixty-five per cent of boys in the five-year program and only 19 per cent of those in the four-year program had a high self-concept if their mother helped them most when they were in Grade 8. Whether these were boys whose parents were separated, or whose father was often away, we cannot say. But our data certainly suggest that a united and concerned family is more likely to produce children with a high self-concept of ability.

We considered that the family environment might have an effect on students' educational aspirations, and we asked three questions to try to determine how democratic the family was: "How much influence do you have in family decisions affecting yourself? Do you have much influence, some or none?," "If a decision is made that you don't like, do you feel *free* to complain, do you feel a little *uneasy* about complaining, or is it *better not* to complain?" and "If you do complain, does it make any difference in your parents' decision? Does it make a lot of difference, some, or none?" In the next chapter on significant others' influence we examine the responses to these questions to see whether they are related to educational aspirations. Here, however, it is worth considering whether the student's self-concept of ability is related to the power that he feels he has in the family.

We have followed the practice in this chapter of analysing the data in each case by program, and we continue to do it here. There is a somewhat surprising difference in the way students in the two programs replied to these questions. Clearly students in the five-year program were more likely than those in the four-year program to feel that they had some power in the family. Ninety-four per cent of both boys and girls in the five-year program said that they had some or much personal influence on family decisions. In the four-year program, however, only 47 per cent of boys and 71 per cent of girls thought they had some or much influence.

Much the same was true in the responses to the question about freedom to complain. More in the four-year program felt they could not complain, and in that category the percentage with a high self-concept was low.

Figure 7.7
Per cent of Students with High Self-concept of Ability,
by Effect of Complaints, Program and Sex, Grade 10

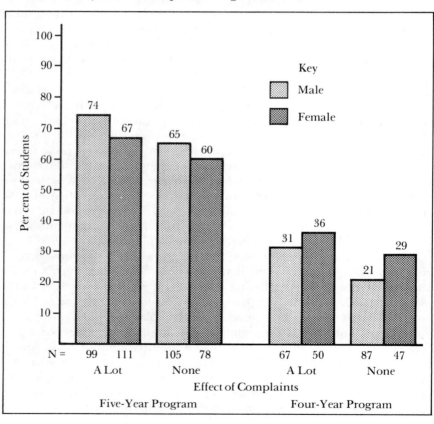

Figure 7.7 illustrates the responses to the third question on the effect of complaints. The middle category is omitted to clarify the picture. The differences in the proportions of those having a high self-concept according to whether they felt that their complaints had a lot of effect or none are not large, but they are consistent.

It seems, then, and this is quite plausible, that the person who feels that his views count in the family is more likely to have a high opinion of his own ability. The opposite relationship is also possible. A person with a high self-concept of ability has greater self-confidence than one without. His greater assurance makes him more influential in the family. This could explain why fewer four-year-program than five-year-program students felt they had some or much influence in the family.

The following chapter explores, in more detail, the importance of significant others' influence and what our data can tell us about it. In this chapter we have outlined a theory of self-concept of ability, justified using it as a variable in a model of aspiration formation, and discussed the possible ways of measuring it. We have demonstrated in an analysis of some of the data that self-concept of ability as we have measured it is related strikingly to school performance and to the amount of influence that parents have. This is consistent with the theory we formulated that self-concept of ability develops in part as a result of an individual's performance and in part through his interaction with his significant others.

Notes

1. Ruth C. Wylie, *The Self Concept; A Critical Survey of Pertinent Research Literature* (Lincoln: University of Nebraska Press, 1961). This is an exhaustive attempt to evaluate research methodology in the field of self-concept.
2. Chad Gordon, *Looking Ahead: Self-Conception, Race and Family as Determinants of Adolescent Orientation*, The Arnold and Caroline Rose Monograph Series, American Sociological Association.
3. Alan B. Wilson and Alejandro Portes, "The Educational Attainment Process," in *American Journal of Sociology* (Vol. 81, 1975), pp.343–362.
4. Joseph A. Kahl, "Educational and Occupational Aspirations of 'Common' Boys," in *Harvard Educational Review* (Vol.XXIII, No. 3, Summer 1953), p.202.
5. *Ibid.*, p.199.
6. Charles W. Cooley, *Human Nature and the Social Order* (New York: 1962), p.152.
7. George Herbert Mead, *Mind Self and Society from the Standpoint of a Social Behaviourist*, C.W. Morris, ed. (Chicago: University of Chicago Press, 1948), pp.77-78.
8. V.C. Raimy, "The Self-Concept as a Factor in Counselling and Personality Organization," Doctoral dissertation (Ohio State University, 1943). Digest published in *Consult Psychology*, 1948, 12, pp.153-163.
9. W.B. Brookover and David Gottlieb, *A Sociology of Education* (New York: American Book Co., 1964), p.471.
10. *Ibid.*, pp.34-35.
11. Wilbur B. Brookover and Edsel L. Erickson, *Society, Schools and Learning* (Boston: Alwyn & Bacon, Inc., 1969), p.105.
12. *Ibid.*, p.95.

13. Robert Rosenthal and Lenore Jacobson, *Pygmalion in the Classroom: Teacher Expectations and Pupils' Intellectual Development* (New York: Holt, Rhinehart and Winston, 1968).
14. Arthur W. Combs and Donald Snygg, *Individual Behaviour*, rev. ed. (New York: Harper, 1959), pp.369, 379.
15. *Ibid.*
16. Alan B. Wilson and Alejandro Portes, *op. cit.*

8

The Influence of Others on Educational Plans and Aspirations

In the last chapter we developed a theory of self-concept of academic ability and showed that it was related both to school performance, to the amount of parental influence and to the aspirations that students see their parents having for them.

In this chapter we continue to decompose our model and explore in greater depth the role that significant others play. In this study we have included a wide range of possible significant others. The two relevant questions were, "In making plans for next fall, who is helping you *most?*" and "Who helps you *most* in thinking about your future education?" The reason we asked the first question was, as we have said, that in selecting Grades 8, 10 and 12 for study we were purposely focussing on decision-making points in the high school student's career.

In the first part of this chapter we show the relative importance of various significant others in helping students to think about their immediate and future plans and aspirations at these important decision-making points. We then look at the degree of influence, and source of assistance with schoolwork, by social class and other background characteristics of students. This will be followed by an analysis of the relationship between student and parental aspirations, parental attitudes and their effects on the mother's aspirations for the child, and lastly, the quality of family life and its effects on student aspirations.

Who Influences the Student?
Two striking facts emerge from the data. They are, first, that where students state a source of help—and most of them do—it comes overwhelmingly from parents. Secondly, a large proportion of students receive help from no one. The simplicity of the questions and the few "don't know's" and "no answers" gives us confidence in the accuracy of this picture. It means, of

course, that the school as an institution intervenes minimally in providing encouragement or otherwise influencing students.

Social Class Influence

Now that we have established the students' views of the relative influence of various significant others in their educational plans and aspirations, we seek to determine how these findings are affected by social class and other background factors. We have grouped together some categories of significant others. Father, mother, and father and mother equally have been combined into one parent category. The category "school personnel" includes teacher, school principal or vice-principal and school guidance counsellor. Close friends and brothers and sisters are grouped as peers.

It is sometimes said that school guidance counsellors and teachers are the important educational decision-makers, directing young people through the streams and channels of the educational system towards the occupational structure. It is to be hoped they might stand as counter-influences to the family, particularly where families come from environments that are not supportive of education. We might hypothesize that for both plans and aspirations there would be a stronger influence of school personnel on those from the lower class than on those from the middle and upper-middle. One of the major tasks of the school system is to intervene between these deprived environments and the opportunity structure of the work world. Thus, school personnel may be more important to lower-class than upper-middle-class students since the former, coming from economically and culturally deprived families, are the most obvious target for information and counselling concerning educational and economic opportunities. We might also expect that the influence of school personnel on working-class students would be helping them to make plans for next fall, rather than in mapping long-range horizons implied by the second question about future education. Whatever their family educational values may be, because of their deprived background and lack of resources to enable them seriously to consider long-range post-secondary educational opportunities, lower-class students will be more interested than upper-middle-class students in the short-range economic advantages of getting a job rather than getting more education.

The predominant declining influence of parents on students' educational aspirations held for both sexes in each class and grade. This is evident in Table 8.1. In general, parental influence was more pronounced for upper-middle than for middle- and lower-class boys and girls in each grade. Peers were next to, but a great deal less influential than, parents for both sexes in all grades. In Grade 8 school personnel had marginally more influence on lower-class children than on middle and upper-middle class, but on the whole there was very little difference for both sexes in the influence of peers and school personnel in the three classes. Evidently, only a small but fairly constant minority of students in each class and grade saw school officials, including the guidance counsellor, as a source of support and advice concerning long-term educational aspirations.

The substantial decline, which we have noted in each succeeding grade, in the influence of parents on the educational aspirations of students in each class was matched, to a large extent, by increases in the percentage of students claiming no one helps them. This increase was fairly general for boys and girls in each class and grade, although less for girls than boys in the upper-middle and middle classes. In Grade 12 the proportion who said that no one was helping them was much the same in the three social classes, except for upper-middle-class girls, more of whom acknowledged help. The help that was acknowledged in all social classes continued to be predominantly from parents, but a larger proportion of middle- and lower-class boys and girls than those of the upper-middle class said that the school personnel were helping them most.

Apparently, by Grade 12, one-third of boys in each class and girls in the middle and lower classes, and about a quarter of the upper-middle-class girls, had become independent of the influence of school personnel, parents and peers, at least in thinking about their future education.

Our earlier finding—that in all grades parents are more influential for the longer run than on near plans for next fall—holds also for the three classes and both sexes, as can be seen in Table 8.1. As with aspirations, parents were more influential with respect to the plans of upper-middle-class than middle- and lower-class boys and girls in the two earlier grades, but for boys this class difference disappeared by Grade 12. Parental influence for both sexes declined sharply from Grades 8 to 12 for each class.

School personnel were more influential for short-term plans than for long-term aspirations, and this was true for both sexes in each class and grade. As far as short-term plans were concerned, the influence of school personnel was next in importance to that of parents, whereas it was the influence of peers that was second in importance to that of parents as far as aspirations were concerned. Over the three grades it appears that there was an increase in the influence of school personnel in the immediate plans of upper-middle-class boys and girls, so that by Grade 12 there was not much difference between students in each class in the extent of influence from school personnel. School personnel had most influence on the immediate plans for lower-class students in Grade 8 compared to other grades—a finding which suggests, as we would of course expect, that they had some bearing on directing about one-quarter of these students in the transition from elementary to high school.

As in the case of educational aspirations, the decline in the influence of parents on the educational plans of students in all classes was matched by increases over the three grades in the proportion of students in each class who claimed that no one helped them in short-run plans. There was one

Table 8.1
**Significant Others in Students' Educational Aspirations and Plans
by Socio-economic Status, Sex and Grade**

(per cent)

Grade 8

Significant Others	Aspirations						Plans					
	Socio-economic Status						Socio-economic Status					
	Upper-middle		Middle		Lower		Upper-middle		Middle		Lower	
	M	F	M	F	M	F	M	F	M	F	M	F
Parents	70	73	70	67	61	63	62	68	52	60	47	47
School Personnel	4	6	7	5	11	9	10	9	23	14	24	24
Peers	6	6	8	6	7	11	10	12	11	13	14	16
Others	0	0	0	1	1	2	1	0	0	1	1	1
No One	20	15	15	21	19	5	17	11	14	12	14	12
Total	100	100	100	100	100	100	100	100	100	100	100	100
N =	188	154	341	309	705	665	192	153	363	319	719	674

Grade 10

Parents	61	56	55	54	48	53	40	48	36	37	32	36
School Personnel	5	5	6	4	7	6	15	13	16	13	18	20
Peers	6	11	8	14	12	13	7	8	7	11	11	12
Others	1	1	1	2	0	1	1	0	1	1	1	1
No One	27	27	30	26	33	27	37	31	40	38	38	31
Total	100	100	100	100	100	100	100	100	100	100	100	100
N =	200	171	442	387	803	692	194	170	433	375	788	687

Grade 12

Parents	46	58	41	40	40	38	26	36	25	32	23	28
School Personnel	4	5	9	11	11	10	16	20	21	21	21	18
Peers	13	12	14	14	14	18	12	10	9	12	14	14
Others	0	1	1	2	1	1	1	2	1	1	1	2
No One	37	24	35	33	33	33	45	32	43	33	41	38
Total	100	100	100	100	100	100	100	100	100	100	100	100
N =	204	188	420	420	666	660	207	184	427	412	664	652

exception: a slight decline between Grades 10 and 12 in the proportion of middle-class girls who said that no one helped them, and also an increase between these grades in the proportion who acknowledged most help from school personnel. Help from no one was more pronounced for boys than for girls, probably indicating a slightly more independent attitude for boys. An interesting feature of Table 8.1 is that in Grade 8 both sexes show slightly more independence of the influence of others with respect to their educational aspirations than they do with respect to their educational plans, but in the two higher grades, with the exception of middle-class girls in Grade 12, the pattern was reversed. Why this pattern of greater independence in short-run decision-making than in longer-run aspirations in high school should exist is difficult to surmise. Perhaps parents do not know very much about the details that are important in immediate decision-making, and so are more able to influence their children in the less precise aspirations than in plans for next fall. In any case, by Grade 12, the immediate decisions concerning leaving school and getting a job or continuing one's education were made independently by a large proportion of students in each class. In fact, class background appears to have had little effect on this pattern. By Grade 12, social class also appears to have had little effect on the reduced role of the family on immediate decisions, which was most marked by that grade. In making these short-term decisions themselves, students, regardless of class, were making, perhaps without realizing it, long-term commitments about their education and future opportunity. Considering their general ignorance of post-secondary opportunities, they probably could have done with much more help than they received.[1] Our evidence suggests that the influence of significant others may not be as important as previously thought, or if it is, it is a much more complex process than we have yet determined.

In the remainder of this chapter our attention will be focussed on educational aspirations rather than on educational plans, since it is the former which is a major dependent variable in this study. As we have seen in Chapter 5, by Grade 10 and certainly by Grade 12 the approaching reality of post-secondary education and job requirements and possibilities have resulted in an adjustment in the students' educational aspirations. For this reason the remainder of the analysis in this chapter will concentrate on Grades 10 and 12, and the role that significant others might play at these times.

Degree of Influence

We have shown the relative importance of parents, school personnel and peers in helping the student to think about his future educational plans and aspirations, but we need to know the degree of influence coming from each source. We have already considered in Chapter 7 how the influence of parents, teachers and friends was related to self-concept of ability. Here we

Figure 8.1
Per cent of Students with High and Very High Influence
of Parents, Teachers and Peers on Thinking About Future Education
by Sex, Grades 10 and 12

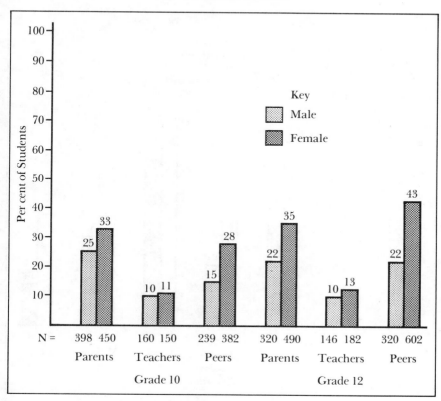

will look at these questions more carefully and in relation to educational aspirations. Figure 8.1 shows that the proportion of boys and girls who reported a very high or high degree of influence of parents remained about the same between Grades 10 and 12, while the proportion who reported a similar degree of influence of peers increased. These data confirm that what has been said already is applicable to boys; between Grades 10 and 12 there was a tendency for the influence of peers to increase and for the influence of parents to decline slightly.

The pattern for girls differs slightly from that for boys. The proportion who reported a very high or high degree of influence of parents for both grades was appreciably higher than that for boys, and was at about the same level in each. The proportion who reported the same level (i.e., very high or

Figure 8.2
Per cent of Students Aspiring to University
by High and Little Influence of Parents,
Socio-economic Status and Sex, Grade 10

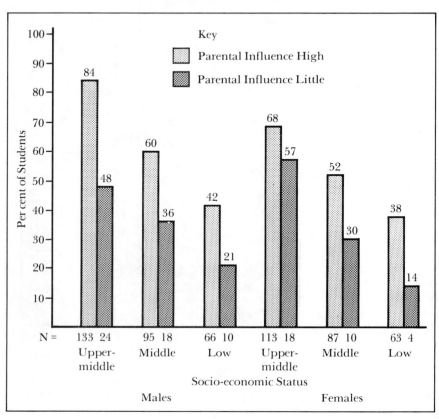

high) of influence of peers increased between the two grades, and this increase for girls was double that for boys. The difference between boys and girls is that more girls than boys reported a very high or high influence of parents and of peers, but for both sexes in both grades a very large proportion acknowledged only moderate or little influence from all three sources.

Why should girls be more influenced by both parents and peers than boys? We can only surmise that the socialization of girls in the home, and in peer groups, makes them more susceptible to the influence of these significant others. Perhaps this female socialization, based on norms of passivity and acceptance, makes girls more open to influence from these

Figure 8.3
Per cent of Students Aspiring to University by High and Little
Peer Influence, Socio-economic Status and Sex, Grade 10

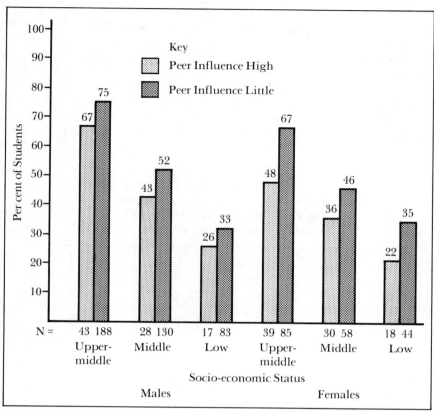

sources than boys, who are socialized to norms of activity and independence.

We might now explore what effects these reported influences of parents and friends have on educational aspirations. (In view of the low influence of school personnel, we propose to drop this from further analysis.) We first examine the percentage of students aspiring to go to university according to the influence of significant others and social class. Figures 8.2 and 8.3 show that generally the pattern of a positive relationship between parental influence and university aspirations on the one hand, and a negative relationship between peer influence and university aspirations on the other, holds when both class and sex are controlled. We see also that in both grades a high degree of influence from parents of upper-middle-class boys and girls was much more likely to be associated with university aspirations than a similar level of influence from parents of middle- or lower-class boys and girls.

What is striking is that at each class level for both boys and girls, greater proportions aspire to university when parental influence is high than when parental influence is low. And looking at Figure 8.3 we see the opposite tendency. At each class level and for both sexes more students aspire to university when peers have little influence than when they have a lot. Also, it is worth noting that a smaller proportion of girls than boys aspire to university at all levels of parental and peer influence in all classes.

Turning to the relationship between the influence of significant others and mental ability, in Figures 8.4 and 8.5 we see the reverse influence of parents and peers also holds when mental ability and sex are controlled. In

Figure 8.4
Per cent of Students Aspiring to University,
by High and Little Influence of Parents,
Mental Ability and Sex, Grade 10

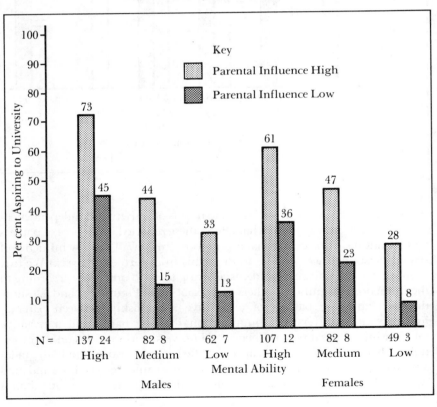

general, for boys and girls in both grades at each level of mental ability, greater proportions aspire to university when parental influence is high than when parental influence is low, and the reverse is true when peer influence is high and low.

Figures 8.6 and 8.7 show that the same relationship between parent and peer influence and educational aspirations exists when school performance is controlled.

What explanation can we give for our finding of a positive relationship between parental influence and university aspirations, and a negative relationship between peer influence and university aspirations, regardless of what controls are used? Unfortunately, our data do not provide us with an explanation. It may be that students who are caught up in school social

Figure 8.5
Per cent of Students Aspiring to University,
by High and Little Influence of Peers,
Mental Ability and Sex, Grade 10

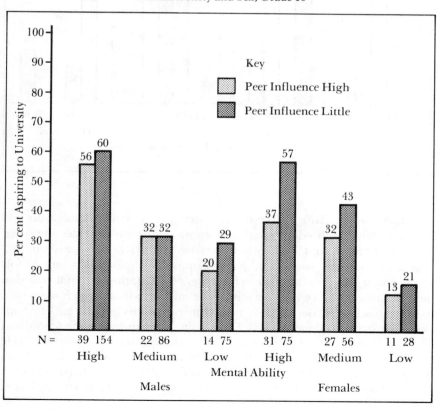

Figure 8.6
Per cent of Students Aspiring to go to University,
by High and Little Influence of Parents,
School Performance and Sex, Grade 10

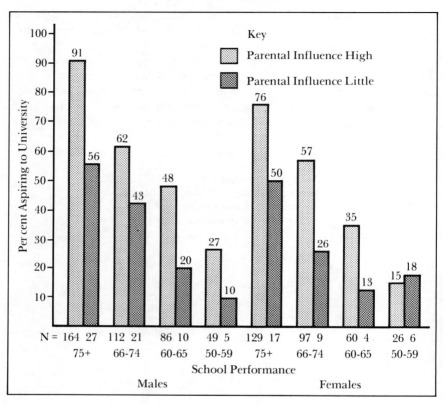

activities, or otherwise involved with peers and less with family, are less likely to have high educational aspirations. Coleman provides some evidence that this is so. He suggests that status in the school is based on non-scholastic activities such as athletics. Competitive games between schools "are almost the only means a school has of generating internal cohesion and identification, for they constitute the only activity in which the school participates as a school. ... It is a consequence of this that the athlete gains so much status in these schools. He is doing something for the school and the community in leading his team to victory, for it is a school victory!"[2] He goes on to say that the academically inclined student has great difficulty in bringing acclaim to his school because his scholarship is a personal rather than a school victory, "often at the expense of his classmates, who are forced

Figure 8.7
Per cent of Students Aspiring to go to University,
by High and Little Influence of Peers,
School Performance and Sex, Grade 10

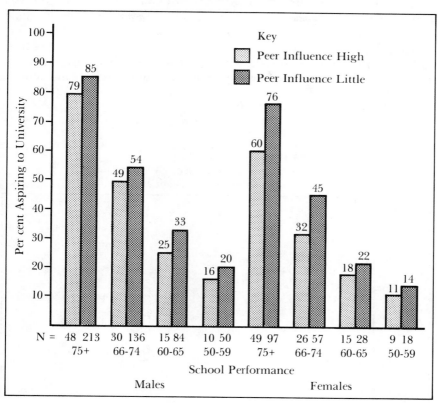

to work harder to keep up with him. Small wonder that his accomplishments gain little reward, and are often met by such ridicule as 'curve raiser' or 'grind,' terms of disapprobation having no analogues in athletics."[3]

Encouragement and Assistance from the Family

As we have seen, parental influence is paramount in educational plans and aspirations. One of the ways in which it is felt by students is through the assistance and encouragement parents give regarding schoolwork. There is much evidence that such parental involvement has positive effects on aspirations.

In order to ascertain the family member or members who assisted the student when he had problems with his schoolwork, we turn to parental interviews. We should keep in mind that over 97 per cent of respondents in our parental sample were mothers. Each was asked, "Who in your family helps *most* when _____ has problems with schoolwork (e.g. homework, understanding projects, etc.)? Is it you, your spouse, both you and your spouse, brothers and/or sisters, no one, other (specify), don't know, not applicable?" The main points that emerge from Figure 8.8, which is based on the answer to this question, are that there was very little difference between parents in the extent to which they assisted their children with their schoolwork. Upper-middle-class boys and girls were much more

Figure 8.8
Source of Student Family Assistance Within Family
by Socio-economic Status, Grade 10 Males

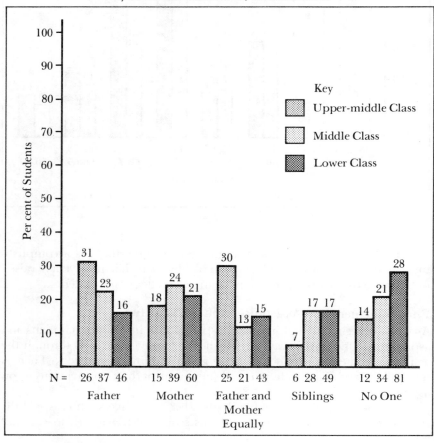

likely than lower-class boys and girls to receive the assistance and encouragement that helps them to be academically successful.

Figure 8.8 shows the relationship between social class of the family and the source of assistance with schoolwork when the student is having problems. The figure has three interesting findings. First, middle- and upper-middle-class boys were much more likely than those of the lower class to receive help from their parents. Secondly, the lower-class mother played a more important role than did the father, in contrast to the upper-middle class where the father was more likely to help. Thirdly, there was a

Figure 8.9
Source of Student Family Assistance Within Family
by Program, Grade 10 Males

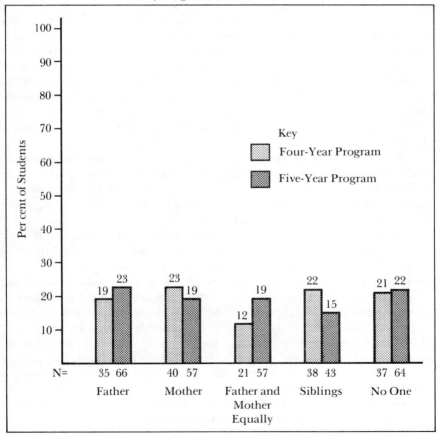

sizeable proportion of lower-class mothers who reported their children received no help from the family. The often-found greater maternal than paternal support in the lower class is quite clear in the case of Grade 12 boys (not shown). Siblings provided a considerable amount of help, except for the upper-middle class, where there were probably fewer of them.

These class differences in the proportion of parents, individually or together, who assisted children with their schoolwork are quite large. In Grade 10 there is a difference of 27 percentage points between upper-middle and lower-class boys, and of 13 percentage points between upper-middle and lower-class girls. By Grade 12 these differences rose to 34 and 41 respectively. The substantial difference between upper-middle and lower classes in this regard means that by Grade 12 many lower-class students received help from no one in the family. At least 25 per cent of lower-class boys and girls in Grade 10, which is double the percentage for upper-middle-class children, and at least 37 per cent two years later in Grade 12, which by then is at least three times the percentage for upper-middle-class children, got no help at all.

We looked at the source of assistance by mental ability and found that the assistance given to their children by father or mother separately and together did not vary a great deal between boys and girls, or between the three levels of mental ability in either Grade 10 or Grade 12. There were relatively low combined percentages for boys and girls of low mental ability in Grade 12, suggesting that parental assistance was less forthcoming for these less fortunate children. It seems also that they were the most neglected children, for the boys among them have the highest percentage indicating that no one helped them.

We also looked at the relationship between program and source of student assistance. Figure 8.9 shows that in Grade 10 fathers were more likely to assist their children in the five-year program than in the four-year program, and mothers were more likely to assist their children in the four-year program than in the five-year program.

Another indication of whether family members take an interest in their child's schoolwork can be obtained from the following question directed to mothers: "When _____ brings home his report card, who goes over the grades your child gets? Is it usually: you, your spouse, both of you, neither of you, other (specify), don't know, not applicable?" Responses to this question showed that overwhelmingly both the mother and the father went over the student's report cards. This was true for both sexes and grades. When cross-tabulated by social class, mental ability, academic achievement, program and self-concept of ability, little different or discernible pattern emerged, other than a tendency for mothers to be left with problem children. A slightly greater proportion of mothers than fathers checked by themselves the report card of children of low mental ability, low achievement, in four-year programs and with low self-concepts.

Parental Hopes and Student Aspirations

Because parents are so important as significant others, and because we know that the family is so important in the transmission of values, we would expect a close relationship between the student's educational aspirations and the mother's and father's educational aspirations for the student. This relationship can be seen in Table 8.2, where mother's educational aspirations for the student are based on her responses and student's educational aspirations are based on student responses.

Table 8.2 shows that in Grade 10 there was a high level of agreement between mother and child on the child's educational aspirations. The level of agreement was highest where the mother hoped the child would go to university; three-quarters of mothers and their children agreed on this educational destination. By Grade 12 this proportion had slightly increased, but by that time an even higher level of agreement had been attained where mothers hoped their children would go to work after school; four-fifths of mothers and their children agreed on the aim in this grade, compared with two-thirds in Grade 10. This increase in levels of agreement between parent and child might be accounted for by the fact that where there was disagreement in the earlier grade, the child likely tended to drop out of school before Grade 12. It is also possible that when disagreement on aspirations between mother and child occurred in Grade 10, if the child continued through to Grade 12 the additional two years of schooling gave mother and child more time in which to see the other's point of view and come to some agreement on educational aspirations.

Table 8.2
Students' Educational Aspirations After School
by Mothers' Educational Aspirations for Students After School
(Grade 10)

Students' Educational Aspirations	Mothers' Educational Aspirations for Students		
	Work	Other Post-Secondary	University
		(per cent)	
Work	67	27	6
Other Post-Secondary	27	62	19
University	6	11	75
	100	100	100
N =	51	282	335

Quality of Family Life:
Effects on Student Aspirations

We theorized in Chapter 3 that the parental values and attitudes that the child meets in the home, and the quality of family life, have a profound effect on the development of the child, including the development of his educational aspirations. Early socialization occurs in the context of a set of parental attitudes and a web of family relationships which channel the child's interaction with parents and siblings. It is the quality of that interaction which is associated with his level of aspiration. We have already shown in Chapter 5 that in a culturally enriched home a student was more likely to have high educational aspirations than a student from a culturally deprived home. We would also expect that harmonious family relationships would result in great consistency between mother-child aspirations, as well as higher aspirations on the student's side. Our questionnaire allows us to test these assumptions, since we asked our student and parental respondents a number of questions aimed at eliciting their perceptions of a number of characteristics of family interaction. However, nearly all of these family characteristics, family interaction, family integration, and integration with relatives bore no significant relationship to the consistency of mothers' educational aspirations for students and students' educational aspirations, nor to the level of student aspirations.

One family variable which showed a striking relationship to the level of student aspirations was his perception of his freedom to complain about parental decisions. We viewed this type of freedom as conducive to harmonious interaction between family members which could generate high aspirations. We therefore asked each student respondent a question related to the process of decision-making in the family. In Grade 10 our data showed that when students felt free to express themselves by complaining about family decisions, they were more likely to aspire to some form of post-secondary education than to hope to go to work. In fact, by Grade 12 those who felt free to complain were more likely to hope to go to university than either to other post-secondary institutions or to work.

Parental Background and Mother's
Educational Aspirations for Her Child

In our attempt to uncover the important variables associated with the mother's educational aspirations for her children, we examined a number of parental background characteristics which it seemed would affect that relationship (such as parents' satisfaction with their own schooling and mother's mobility experience, i.e., whether she married up or down), but these and other background variables showed no such association. However, when we turned to family class position and mother's aspirations a different picture emerged.

A mother's educational aspirations for her children are affected by the family class position. Not unexpectedly, by far the highest proportion of upper-middle-class mothers in both grades wanted their children to go to university, around three-quarters in each grade. This compares with about two-fifths of lower-class mothers who had these ambitions for their children. While the difference between upper-middle and lower-class mothers in this regard is large, the substantial proportion of lower-class mothers who had university aspirations for their children should be noted.

We have shown in Chapter 5 that students' educational aspirations are related to parental education. Using student responses, we showed that the higher the parents' educational levels, the higher the students' educational aspirations. Besides being related to students' educational ambition, we could expect that mothers' level of education would be related to their educational ambitions for their children. Using the parental responses, our data show that nearly 90 per cent of mothers who had sixteen years or more education, compared to around 45 per cent who had up to eleven years, wanted their children to reach the highest level of education. A similar picture was evident in both grades. Apparently, a substantial proportion of even the least-educated mothers had high educational aspirations for their children.

There can be no doubt that the influence of their significant others, particularly parents, is an important factor in a student's educational aspirations, as our analysis of the data relating to significant others has shown.

Notes

1. A preliminary analysis of the data in this survey reported that large proportions of students and their parents lacked knowledge of the post-secondary system. See Marion R. Porter, John Porter and Bernard R. Blishen, *Does Money Matter? Prospects for Higher Education* (Toronto: Macmillan, 1979).
2. James S. Coleman, *The Adolescent Society* (New York: The Free Press, 1961), pp.308–9.
3. Coleman, *op.cit.*

9
School Performance

"Achievement is no more." So might lament educators of the traditional mould who saw the process of schooling as one in which individuals were submitted to a long, continuous and competitive testing. Two essential qualities to be tested were native ability and effort to perform as well as native ability would allow. Rewards for this combination of native ability with effort were considerable: high ranking and prestige relative to fellow students; advancement up an academic ladder, with increasingly severe tests and greater rewards; higher education and a preferred position in the professional and occupational world. The rewards, or the aspirations for them, were thought to be important stimuli to effort. This meritocratic system could be considered a reflection of and a preparation for the competitive world of the marketplace.[1]

Educational policy in societies in the vanguard of industrial development strove to search out and identify native ability at an early age and to provide the facilities for the development of excellence among the intellectually superior. To make such a meritocratic system relatively free from financial burdens was thought sufficient to overcome the social and cultural handicaps of the class structure and its inequalities. Such ideas were central, for example, to the great educational reforms of 1944 in the United Kingdom.[2]

For traditionalists among educational policy makers, the meritocratic principle seemed to conform to the natural order of things. In many countries, England and continental Europe for example, education continued to be governed by the meritocratic principle, with severe testing to sort out those who were to attend the superior secondary schools leading to higher education from those who were thought to deserve less at the secondary level because of their early assignment to the labour force.[3]

The deep-rootedness of this traditional view of education in some countries is illustrated by the unending battle to establish comprehensive schools in England and to lessen the dominance of the grammar schools, whose students win out in the early stages of competition. Despite the easing of financial costs, middle-class children continue to dominate the superior secondary schools, no doubt because, as many studies have indicated, the superior home environments from which they come give them great initial advantages in the competition for academic rewards. The norms of achievement prove to be stronger in the middle class, so the meritocratic principle seems to be designed for them.

In North America, particularly in the United States, meritocracy has been less firmly entrenched. There are many reasons for this, among them the somewhat different objectives of public education, such as the egalitarianism implied by the comprehensive schools,[4] and more democratic attitudes about education as a social right or as a mechanism for Americanizing the children of immigrants. However, these more democratic American schools in the main upheld the principle of competitive academic achievement, with its rankings, promotion through consecutive grades and some separation into college preparatory streams and more vocationally oriented ones. But the American system was not as rigid as the European, and its selective elements did not limit opportunity as much. There was ample evidence, however, that children of the middle classes benefitted more from public education, particularly at the higher levels, than did those of the working or lower classes. In some jurisdictions racial segregation belied the egalitarian thrust of American education.[5]

Ontario schools—like so many aspects of social life in English Canada—were somewhere between those of England and the United States. There was a strong element of tradition, which gave support to the principle of competitive academic achievement. Students were ranked relative to each other on some supposedly objective scale of school performance duly noted on monthly report cards. They faced the hurdle of progress through grades and of being sorted into streams or programs on the basis of past performance. We have outlined in Chapter 2 how after 1962 the program structure affected the high schools. Capping this competitive achievement system, for those who survived, was (until 1968) a province-wide Grade 13 examination, the results of which determined entrance to university and access to the relatively meagre amount of scholarship funds. Although secondary education was nominally free, survival through it was very much class related, as was continuing on to the universities, where financial barriers for the less privileged who did survive were substantial.[6]

In both the United States and Ontario, public education was more exposed to change than in Europe, and by the 1960s an important change taking effect was the gradual dismantling of the system of competitive achievement. It was a move away from tradition and elitism to democratization, for if the economically less privileged lost out in the contest for marks, the contest itself was seen as a barrier to equality in education. Competitive grading on school performance, successive promotion through the grades and the guardian of academic standards, the Grade 13 examinations, were all to go. Any teacher oriented to the traditional meritocratic role of schooling might well lament the passing of competitive achievement.

The system went out with the blessing of a special committee appointed by the Ontario government to examine the educational system. The report of the Hall-Dennis committee[7] was hostile to the traditional academic values. It had great influence, particularly on lessening the role of competitive school performance. In the high schools the program system was to be gradually withdrawn, schools were to become ungraded, marking was to be left to individual teachers and standards to individual schools, children were to make their way through high school at their own pace to collect sufficient credits for a secondary school graduation diploma. Along with the changes in the high schools, which we have elaborated more fully elsewhere, there were changes taking place at the post-secondary level, reflected in the doctrine of universal accessibility which held that post-secondary education, including the universities, should be accessible to those who met a minimum standard of academic performance.[8] In addition, there was a progressive reduction in the proportion of university costs which the student was expected to pay, and more money became available for student aid to be distributed on the basis of economic need rather than academic performance.[9] The development of alternative post-secondary institutions with even less demanding entrance standards than the universities widened the range of universal accessibility. Thus the rewards for academic achievement in the school years were substantially reduced. Perhaps this break with tradition helps to account for the findings in Chapter 15 that school performance does not contribute a great deal to the explanation of variance in educational aspirations.

In Ontario in 1971, the time of our survey, it was quite possible to reach the post-secondary level with relatively low grades,[10] acquired through increasingly dubious standards of grading that lacked the common judgements imposed by the old Grade 13 examinations. What the educational effects of these changes might be is something the educational traditionalists dispute with the educational innovators. The social effect can also be disputed. If the traditional achievement system was something much more congenial to middle-class students than to those from the lower classes, then its dismantling might appear as a reform in the direction of democratization in which the less privileged have fewer barriers to surmount. On the other hand, the substitution of more subjective measures (such as teachers' evaluations, or the student being judged against some perceived ability standards of his own) for the more objective standards might penalize the lower-class student as he becomes increasingly judged by middle-class teachers. It could be argued that the bright lower-class student is done a disservice when he does not have the opportunity to prove himself by objective standards. The middle-class student, on the other hand, depends less on certification by objective standards because when he gets into the work world he has other devices acquired through middle-class norms and more sensitive information networks through which to exploit opportunities. If that is so, the reduced value of school performance and the lessening of objective standards of grading is scarcely a democratic reform as far as equality of educational opportunity is concerned.

In the literature of the sociology of learning, academic achievement, usually measured by grades obtained in school, has been considered important. Factors both within the school and stemming from the wider social structure making for academic success have been extensively explored. The development of academic self-concept was also thought to be closely and reciprocally linked to achievement in school. Studies focussed within the schools on such characteristics as libraries, equipment, teachers' qualifications, the proportion of students planning to attend university and other conditions establishing cultural climates within schools. At times, the classroom itself became the centre of interest with the exploration of inter-personal relations and sociometric networks among students and relations with the teacher.[11] However, with a system of ungraded schools, with individual student timetables and a ten minute/day home room participation, all of which were in existence in some schools at the time of our study, it is doubtful that the classroom could continue to be a miniature social system within which achievement took place. Perhaps other groups formed within the school. Perhaps, too, the break-up of the classroom as the unit of social structure within the school was a factor in the relatively unimportant role that teachers played as significant others in forming the aspirations of students, a condition which we reported in Chapter 8. There would seem, then, little left to explore concerning the relationship between school factors and achievement.

Outside of school, however, the wider social structure could continue to have important effects on how well students performed. Before the demise of traditional achievement, the effects of neighbourhood and community, of the cultural influence of social class, religion and ethnicity, were thought to be important in accounting for variations in achievement. Thus the structure of the society at large, since it is still differentiated in these and other ways, remains to be examined for its effects on achievement.

If achievement has lost any objective and uniform standards within schools, or between schools or school districts and regions, then we might have employed an objective test of achievement as part of our inquiry rather than, as we did, collecting information on student-reported grades and school-reported grades. Such a procedure, however, would not have served our needs. If, as with Coleman's massive study of equality of education in the United States, we conceived achievement as the acquisition of cognitive skills, as a form of school output—that is, given numbers of students at given achievement levels—then an objective test would have been appropriate.[12] That was not our purpose. Rather, we wished to determine the role of achievement in aspirations. Clearly, the results of an objective measure of cognitive skills would not be known or understood by students, and hence would unlikely be a factor in their aspirational levels. On the other hand, the marks they get in school have some meaning for them, and however subjective and unstandardized they might be, they could be an element in self-appraisal and in setting educational goals. Good performance in school would be, from the students' point of view, consistent with high aspirations since it could be interpreted as a capacity to cope with more advanced work. Also, high grades could spark aspirations where they did not previously exist. These reciprocal effects around achievement are a part of our model outlined in Chapter 3; that is, within the interactive framework that is our theoretical perspective, grades obtained in school are a form of teacher response to the learning behaviour of the student, who is able to assess himself in part by this indicator of how others see him. It is necessary that he receive these signals if they are to play a part in the formation of his self-concept, his aspirations for more education or for jobs. The signals come most clearly in the marks his teachers give him.

We considered, then, that the grades he obtained in school would be a signal in a way in which objectively measured cognitive skills never would be. Although a student has no way of telling whether he is in an easy or hard grading school, it is only necessary that there be some range of marks by which he can judge his performance as better or worse than others. There was, as we will see, a range and distribution of marks, at least as far as all the students in our sample are concerned. Of course, our logic in using school grades as a measure of school performance was not without weaknesses. Ideally, we should have had something like percentile standing in the class or grade because, as a result of our sampling procedures, relatively small numbers of students were selected from each school. Thus in dealing with province-wide achievement distributions, school idiosyncracies are lost. If there are lots of high (or low) grades in one school and few in another, they are likely to mean different things to students depending upon which school they are in. Perhaps it is this fault in measuring school performance that reduces its capacity to explain variance in aspirations. Perhaps, that is, performance is a school specific variable and could not be expected to explain aspirations in provincial populations.

It will be noticed that we have dropped the term academic achievement and substituted for it school performance. The reason is that achievement is ambiguous in the literature of the sociology of learning. At times it refers to the acquisition of cognitive skills, at other times it is synonymous with attainment, that is, the level of schooling reached. The terminology is all the more confusing when achievement and attainment are considered as dependent variables, because often the same range of independent variables is examined. We take school performance to be a less ambiguous term than the others.

Our survey yielded three possible measures of school performance, which we have described in Chapter 4. The first was from responses to the question, "What were most of your grades or marks last year?" The second measure of school performance, or anticipated school performance, came from the question asking students to state what grades they expected to obtain in the current year. Our third measure was from the school records for the previous year.

It can be debated which measure of school performance might be most satisfactory. Expected grades this year might contain a fantasy element, although students would have some knowledge of how well they were doing from tests during the current year. Whatever indications students had of how well they were doing, we suspected that it would be difficult for them and for the school to put these in a uniform scale. On the other hand, grades obtained last year would more likely be uniformly reported in any one school, and would be a real measure of how the students were doing. Of course, their fantasies during the current year might be more appropriate to their aspirations than their known accomplishments the previous year. As it turned out, the distribution of expected grades was very close to the distribution of grades last year. The correlations from the cross-tabulations of the two sets (gammas) were .82, .71 and .82 for Grades 8, 10 and 12 respectively.

Some differences existed between the distribution of school-reported and self-reported grades for last year. For the former there were generally fewer higher marks (top two categories) reported and more lower marks (bottom two categories) reported. Correlations (gammas) for school-reported and self-reported grades were .78, .89 and .91 for Grades 8, 10 and 12 respectively, indicating that while students tended generally to enhance their own marks, those in higher grades did it less frequently than those in lower grades. Perhaps they became more accurate in their recall. Of the three possible measures we chose school-reported grades as likely to be the most reliable. We also restrict our analysis here to Grades 10 and 12, in part because of the greater variation in methods of reporting school performance in Grade 8.

For the two high school grades it is necessary to separate students in the four- and five-year programs (or general and advanced courses). The intrinsic achievement levels of the two programs represent something quite different. The program structure is itself a selection by achievement, and in the separate programs there are different levels of instruction and expected performance. Students in both programs were well aware of the differences in achievement which the two programs represented. Students in the five-year program knew they were performing better than those in the four-year program, who for their part knew that their performance standards were lower.[13] At one time we thought of weighting the grades for the five-year program to reflect this higher standard. However, teachers did not award as great a proportion of high grades in the four-year program as they did in the five-year, suggesting that at that level they did not mark in a normal distribution because of some notion that their four-year students were not good enough for high grades. It seems they would not adjust their standards downward for the four-year program. In view of this evidence it seemed more appropriate, rather than to add weights, to separate four- and five-year programs entirely in the analysis. Moreover, it should be remembered that graduation from the five-year program was almost a requirement to fulfill high educational aspirations, and as we have seen earlier (Chapter 5) the aspirational levels of students in the two programs were quite different.

If school performance does not represent traditional achievement as we suggested at the beginning of the chapter, it does represent something. There is a distribution of marks in all classes. Some are motivated to do their homework, to complete their assignments, to study for examinations and to get high grades. Who are they? What characteristics do they have? If, with the elimination of departmental examinations, the content of courses has been watered down and the standard expected of students has been reduced, it could be expected that mental ability might not be closely related to grades in schoolwork. If a high level of intelligence is not required to master the subject matter of the courses, or to satisfy the teacher in examinations or essays that one has attained some grasp of the subject matter, then high grades would not depend on a high level of mental ability. Instead, we would expect that they would depend almost entirely on motivation, the desire to do well. This no doubt explains why, as we shall see, girls outperform boys in all grades at all mental ability levels. But though girls on the whole do better than boys, among both boys and girls some perform well and some do not. What accounts for the difference in performance?

Sex and School Performance

Uniformly girls perform better in school than do boys. This is true for both grades, both four- and five-year programs and, with one exception, all mental ability levels. For example, in Grade 10 in the five-year program 26 per cent of girls, but 16 per cent of boys, make the highest grade average of 75 per cent or more (Table 9.1). Of the brightest of these, in terms of mental ability, 36 per cent of girls, but only 23 per cent of boys, make the top grades. Girls with low mental ability perform better than do boys of the same mental ability level, 45 per cent of them, despite their lower aptitudes, achieving at levels of 66 per cent averages or more, compared to 33 per cent of boys. As can be seen from Table 9.1, the sex difference in school performance in the five-year program is similar in Grade 12.

Our finding that girls outperform boys is not a new one. The Atkinson Study on the Utilization of Student Resources, reporting on the Ontario Grade 13 students of 1955–56, showed that for each of their high school years girls in this student group achieved higher grades in greater proportion than did boys.[14] These findings are consistent with results from studies in the United States surveyed by Sarane Boocock, except that it would appear that reversals occurred in the later years of high school with boys catching up and overtaking girls.[15]

There have been many theories put forward and tested to account for this sex difference in school performance. There is no evidence that girls are inherently more able than boys in terms of "general" abilities, and in any case, as we have seen, the higher performance of girls persists when mental ability is controlled. There is some evidence, however, that when the level of performance in specific subjects is considered, say mathematics, languages and the like, there might be some difference between the sexes in intrinsic capacity to master them.[16] Our data do not allow us to pursue that line of inquiry.

It is much easier to attribute sex differences in school performance to the effects of socialization, both early child rearing and later childhood orientation to sexual roles. Girls have traditionally been brought up to be more submissive than boys, to try to please, to play the game, to follow the rules. Coleman suggested, for example, in his study of adolescent society in the United States that girls are less likely to do well in later years of high school for fear that conspicuous achievement will make them unpopular with boys.[17] That girls in Ontario have consistently done better in school than boys for all grades suggests that there could well be a significant cultural difference between Canada and the United States in the adolescent socialization process. It could be that by the 1970s women's liberation has had a sufficient impact that girls no longer feel they have to hide their abilities.

Mental Ability and School Performance

The association between mental ability (as measured by the IPAT culture fair test) and school performance is for both boys and girls only moderate. By no means do all of the brightest perform at the highest level. For both grades almost the same proportion (about one-third) of girls of high ability have averages in the range 66-74, and almost one-third have averages below 66 per cent. Similarly, about two-fifths of high mental ability boys in both grades have grade averages below 65 (Table 9.1).

Although not all students with high mental ability perform well at school, there is some association between mental ability and levels of school performance. For example, the proportions of girls in Grade 10 with grades over 66 per cent were: 69 per cent of the brightest girls; 57 per cent of those with medium mental ability; and 45 per cent of those with low mental ability. For boys, too, there is a clear relationship, with 63 per cent of high, 41 per cent of medium, and 33 per cent of low mental ability boys having grades over 66 per cent. The same pattern can be seen in Table 9.1 with the Grade 12 students, although the difference in the proportions of girls with

Table 9.1
School Performance by Mental Ability and Sex,
Five-Year Program

Grade 10

Mental Ability

School Grades	High		Medium		Low		Total	
	M	F	M	F (per cent)	M	F	M	F
75+	23	36	9	22	9	15	16	26
66-74	40	33	32	35	24	30	36	33
60-65	25	23	30	26	30	29	27	25
50-59	11	8	23	15	32	25	19	15
-50	1	0	6	2	5	1	3	1
	100	100	100	100	100	100	100	100
Ns	395	337	261	295	162	170	818	802

Boys $x^2 = 75.32$ df^8 p = .000
Conditional Gamma = .365

Girls $x^2 = 54.62$ df^8 p = .000
Conditional Gamma = .303

Grade 12

Mental Ability

School Grades	High		Medium		Low		Total	
	M	F	M (per cent) F		M	F	M	F
75+	26	34	15	28	9	15	18	27
66-74	33	35	28	38	21	36	29	36
60-65	23	24	32	24	32	33	28	26
50-59	16	6	21	10	34	14	21	10
-50	2	1	4	0	4	2	3	1
	100	100	100	100	100	100	100	100
Ns	356	305	317	338	164	194	837	837

Boys x^2 = 50.16 df^8 p = .000
Conditional Gamma = .290

Girls x^2 = 37.10 df^8 p = .000
Conditional Gamma = .227

high and with medium mental ability who had over 66 per cent is not large. One can also see the relationship between mental ability and performance, of course, by looking at the proportions of those with low grades. For example, 37 per cent of low mental ability boys in Grade 10 had grades of less than 60, but this was true of only 12 per cent of the boys with high mental ability. However, having high mental ability is not a necessary condition for performing well at school since some in the lower third of the mental ability range also get over 75 per cent.

The relationship between mental ability and school performance is even less marked in the four-year program. As we have said, the course content in the four-year program was quite different than that of the five-year program. In the four-year Business and Commerce and in the four-year Technology and Trades branches, there was an attempt to make the academic courses more practical and less abstract. Instead of learning algebra and geometry, students would take commercial arithmetic. Instead of the traditional history of revolutions and wars, they would learn something about economic history, the history of money, of the breakdown of the feudal system and the rise of industry. In addition to the academic courses, there was in the Commercial and Technical branches a fairly large segment of time devoted to the learning of job skills, the alleged purpose of the program. These included typing, shorthand, sewing, cooking, woodworking, motor mechanics. Getting a high grade in commercial arithmetic would probably be facilitated by a high level of mental ability, and so we might expect a relationship between mental ability and school performance in the academic subjects in the four-year program of the Business and Commerce and Technology and Trades branches; but performing well in typing or woodworking depends on quite different aptitudes. However, in the four-year Arts and Science course, when it was offered (and by no means was it universally offered), the aim was quite frankly to offer a less demanding version of the traditional subject matter.

Since the grades in the four-year program reflect the students' performance in both academic and practical subjects, we would not expect too much association between mental ability and school performance in the four-year program. Table 9.2 shows that this expectation is more or less borne out. The relationship is not statistically significant for boys in Grade 10 or for girls in Grade 12. However, it is statistically significant for girls in Grade 10 and boys in Grade 12. Why there should be the difference is hard to say. As we mentioned earlier, girls in the four-year program as well as the five-year outperform boys in both grades and at all mental ability levels except the low mental ability level in Grade 10. In the four-year program this superior performance of girls is not surprising, since the qualities that are most likely to lead to success are, as we suggested earlier, the qualities that girls are more likely to have. In addition, neatness, industriousness, attentiveness and docility would be rewarded in the vocationally oriented programs.

Some differences between the two programs in the relationship between mental ability and school performance might be noted. One is the different proportions with high mental ability in the five- and four-year programs, as can be seen from Tables 9.1 and 9.2. The totals show that in the five-year program more than 40 per cent of boys in Grades 10 and 12 and girls in Grade 10 had high mental ability. In Grade 12 the percentage of girls with high mental ability was 36. In contrast, the percentages in the four-year program with high mental ability were much lower. They were: in Grade 10, 25 per cent of boys and 19 per cent of girls; in Grade 12, 16 per cent of boys and 12 per cent of girls. One might think that this is a reason for the lower range of marks in the four-year program. In Grade 10 in the five-year program, 52 per cent of boys and 59 per cent of girls had grades over 66 per cent. Only 25 per cent of boys and 34 per cent of girls in the four-year program had such grades. The lower level of mental ability, however, cannot explain the lower level of marks, because we can see the same differences in marks between the programs when we control for mental ability. This is shown most strikingly for Grade 10 boys. Of those with high mental ability, 63 per cent in the five-year program, but only 28 per cent in the four-year program, had grades over 66 per cent. As we suggested above, the explanation for the lower level of marks must be either that teachers saw the course content as less demanding, and therefore not worth as much in terms of marks as in the five-year program, or that students in the four-year program did not perform as well in their less demanding courses.

Background Characteristics and School Performance

"The family characteristic that is the most powerful predictor of school performance is socio-economic status (SES): the higher the SES of the student's family, the higher his academic achievement." This conclusion was made by Boocock[18] and she goes on to discuss the many studies that show this relationship. While the relationship between socio-economic status and academic achievement is complex, in general "communication by middle class parents of a certain set of values and of an outlook on life that incorporates educational and occupational success in turn produces higher actual achievement."[19] David E. Lavin, in his 1965 review of research on *The Prediction of Academic Performance*, lists thirteen studies that report that socio-economic status, or social class, is directly related to academic performance—the higher one's social status the higher his level of performance.[20] Both Lavin and Boocock draw special attention to Rosen's 1956 article on the "achievement syndrome" in which he reported that achievement motivation is directly related to social class, and that both achievement motivation and social class are directly related to the grades of high school students.[21]

On the other hand, Boocock reports that some researchers during the sixties were beginning to cast doubt on the strength of the relationship between social class and academic values. She refers to Ralph Turner's

Table 9.2
School Performance by Mental Ability and Sex,
Four-Year Program

Grade 10

Mental Ability

School Grades	High		Medium		Low		Total	
	M	F	M	F (per cent)	M	F	M	F
75+	4	17	3	15	3	3	3	9
66-74	24	44	22	20	20	21	22	25
60-65	31	19	29	30	26	30	28	28
50-59	29	19	36	30	41	37	37	31
-50	12	1	10	5	10	9	10	6
	100	100	100	100	100	100	100	100
Ns	134	70	160	113	240	186	534	369

Boys $x^2 = 6.06$ df8 p = .640
Conditional Gamma = .08

Girls $x^2 = 40.93$ df8 p = .000
Conditional Gamma = .342

Grade 12

School Grades	Mental Ability (per cent)							
	High		Medium		Low		Total	
	M	F	M	F	M	F	M	F
75+	12	18	8	7	4	10	7	10
66-74	35	33	32	42	24	35	29	37
60-65	26	33	32	32	36	36	33	34
50-59	27	16	21	18	33	18	28	18
-50	0	0	7	1	3	1	4	1
	100	100	100	100	100	100	100	100
Ns	81	55	195	152	224	240	500	447

Boys $x^2 = 25.56$ df ^{8} p $= .001$
Conditional Gamma $= .186$

Girls $x^2 = 8.1$ df ^{8} p $= .424$
Conditional Gamma $= .07$

suggestion that either the value system or the stratification system in American society might be changing, because he found that the overall relationship between social class and performance was actually rather small when he re-analysed his data on students in California.

The role of the upper- and middle-class family in fostering occupational and educational aspirations is an important component of our model of aspiration formation, as we have indicated in our theoretical discussion and shown empirically in Chapters 5 and 6. Here, however, our data suggest that school performance is in something of an anomalous position in the aspiration and attainment sequence, at least in contemporary Ontario with its changed ideology about school grades and its open accessibility to post-secondary education. If school performance does not mean as much as it once did, then the middle-class advantage in motivation to do well should be less visible.

Whatever effects we might expect from these changed circumstances, it is still surprising to find that for many of our program/grade/sex sub-groups the relationship between social class and school performance does not exist. It is found only for Grade 10 males and Grade 12 females in the five-year program. For the former, the percentages getting more than 75 per cent range from 35 in Class I (Blishen occupational scale) to 13 in Class VI. The comparable figure for the Grade 12 girls is 38 per cent in Class I and 22 per cent in Class VI (Table 9.3). One can speculate that social class counts for boys, but not for girls, in Grade 10 in their attitude to schoolwork and to doing well because girls are all, regardless of social class, socialized to be obedient and to follow the rules; but the socialization of middle- and upper-class boys is different from lower-class boys, especially when it relates to achievement in school. In Grade 12 the reverse is true; social class counts for girls but not for boys. For boys, the change in the effects of social class is probably because those boys who have survived to Grade 12 have learned to adapt to the norms of the school, and there is no difference in behaviour and attitudes according to class background. The girls' marks are still higher than the boys' in Grade 12 at each social class level, but they are related to social class in a way that they were not in Grade 10. We will show later that the variable that has the strongest association with school performance is level of educational aspirations. Lower-class girls have much lower educational aspirations than those in higher classes, and this then affects their academic performance.

In the four-year program the association between socio-economic status and school performance is not statistically significant in any of the four sub-groups. Generally, then, findings on the relationship between social class and school performance are not striking. They are not what would be expected from previous studies, and we might therefore seek to explain it.

First of all, there is the fact that will be demonstrated in Chapter 10 that the school programs are themselves class biased, with the chances of lower-class students being in the four-year program much greater than for higher-class students. Thus we already have a major sorting out of students in terms of their past achievement and their social class origin, so that it is through the programs that the relationship between social class background and school performance can be seen. That within each program the relationship should fall away may reflect the fact that school-reported grades are not a good measure of academic achievement when standards vary from school to school and when teachers' subjective evaluations of students may vary within schools. In the four-year program, we have already argued that grades do not measure performance in cognitive skills or in the mastery of academic subject matter. In fact, in our data, performance in the four-year program is related in only a very few cases to the variables that we expect to affect academic achievement. For this reason, in the remainder of this chapter we will leave out the students in the four-year program, unless there is a significant association between their school performance and any of the variables that we will be discussing.

Other background characteristics or social structural variables that are related to social class and are generally found to be related to academic achievement are parents' education, ethnicity, religion, family size and cultural enrichment. We will discuss our data with respect to these structural variables, showing that on the whole the relationships to school performance are not strong.

To show the relationship between school performance and these background characteristics, we are presenting the data only for those students who had school-reported grades of over 75 per cent.

Table 9.3 shows the percentage of boys and girls with grades over 75 per cent in Grades 10 and 12 according to socio-economic status, religion, size of family and combined parental education. In columns after these percentages are the Chi square values for each full table (including the 65–74, etc. cells); the degrees of freedom for each full table of cross classification; the significance level; and the gamma value which measures the degree of association between two ordinal level variables.[22]

Religion shows no significant relationship with school performance, except perhaps for Grade 10 females. There is little to suggest that religion accounts very much for school performance, except that strikingly higher proportions of Jews (considered as either a religious or an ethnic category) perform at high levels, a finding that is consistent with those of other studies. It is interesting to note that Catholics have as large a proportion of high performers as Protestants, except for Grade 12 boys. Thus, as we found with aspirations, whatever effect the Protestant ethic might once have had to make for differences between the two groups, it no longer has.

We could find no relationship between ethnic origin and school performance, which is not to deny that one exists or that the achievement

Table 9.3

High Performance (75 per cent and over) by Selected Background Characteristics,
Five-Year Program, Grades 10 and 12, Males and Females, Percentages

	I	II	III	IV	V	VI	Total	X²*	d.f.	p.	gamma
							(per cent)				
Grade											
10 Males	35 (68)***	20 (83)	16 (108)	13 (160)	13 (264)	13 (105)	16 (788)	43.2	20	.002	.118
Females	39 (66)	36 (81)	30 (113)	21 (151)	24 (271)	24 (87)	27 (769)	25.2	20	.191	.115
12 Males	22 (67)	23 (97)	18 (110)	18 (162)	18 (227)	18 (74)	19 (787)	14.8	20	.785	.013
Females	38 (82)	30 (79)	34 (91)	24 (190)	24 (279)	22 (76)	27 (797)	37.9	20	.009	.103

Religion

	Major Protestant	Other Protestant	R.C.	Jewish	Other	None	Total	X²*	d.f.	p.	gamma
Grade											
10 Males	15 (373)	14 (77)	17 (259)	43 (14)	15 (20)	11 (57)	16 (799)	22.5	20	.313	**
Females	23 (402)	27 (102)	26 (222)	67 (15)	52 (21)	29 (35)	26 (797)	33.4	20	.031	
12 Males	20 (398)	23 (82)	13 (173)	25 (24)	19 (31)	17 (114)	18 (822)	23.0	20	.200	
Females	26 (447)	30 (105)	23 (163)	44 (18)	23 (26)	33 (69)	27 (828)	23.2	20	.472	

			Number of Children in Family							
	1	2	3	4	5+	Total				
Grade										
10 Males	23 (40)	19 (153)	15 (227)	19 (166)	10 (203)	16 (789)	29.0	16	.024	.079
Females	26 (27)	30 (151)	27 (219)	28 (176)	22 (210)	26 (783)	14.8	16	.537	.053
12 Males	8 (40)	18 (211)	22 (217)	19 (160)	16 (199)	18 (827)	19.0	16	.266	.034
Females	32 (37)	27 (186)	30 (235)	29 (167)	22 (203)	27 (828)	20.1	16	.213	.051

		Parental Education						
	High	Medium	Low	Total				
Grade								
10 Males	21 (71)	17 (301)	12 (319)	15 (691)	10.1	8	.255	.153
Females	43 (77)	29 (291)	20 (300)	27 (668)	29.9	8	.000	.176
12 Males	24 (75)	18 (341)	19 (319)	19 (735)	4.52	8	.808	.001
Females	42 (89)	26 (337)	24 (327)	26 (753)	11.4	8	.178	.154

*Chi square values are for full contingency table.

**Gammas omitted because the measures are nominal.

***Numbers in brackets are the column marginal totals.

Table 9.4

High Performance (75 per cent and over) by Personal Attitudes, Five-Year Program, Grades 10 and 12, Males and Females, Percentages

Educational Aspirations

Grade	University	Other post-sec.	Work	Other	D.K.	Total	X²*	d.f.	p.	gamma
					(per cent)					
10 Males	25 (426)**	4 (190)	4 (52)	11 (46)	4 (94)	16 (808)	140.8	16	.000	.376
Females	40 (315)	16 (250)	17 (59)	18 (33)	23 (130)	27 (787)	86.7	16	.000	.262
12 Males	25 (514)	5 (136)	4 (52)	14 (43)	11 (75)	19 (820)	91.2	16	.000	.292
Females	40 (377)	12 (263)	17 (72)	21 (39)	28 (78)	27 (829)	112.3	16	.000	.307

Occupational Aspirations

Grade	High	Medium	Low	Total	X²*	d.f.
10 Males	22 (418)	10 (271)	3 (154)	16 (733)	69.9	8
Females	34 (336)	20 (383)	13 (102)	26 (767)	36.1	8
12 Males	23 (473)	12 (261)	10 (132)	18 (805)	46.0	8
Females	37 (350)	18 (413)	12 (83)	27 (807)	45.6	8

Occupational Expectations

Grade	High	Medium	Low	Total	X²*	d.f.	p.	gamma
10 Males	26 (314)	10 (251)	3 (154)	15 (719)	91.1	8	.000	.423
Females	40 (245)	20 (368)	13 (102)	26 (715)	56.3	8	.000	.336
12 Males	25 (365)	14 (226)	10 (132)	19 (723)	49.7	8	.000	.316
Females	40 (276)	21 (397)	12 (83)	27 (756)	69.7	8	.000	.373

	Self-Concept of Ability									
	(high) 1	2	3	4	5 (low)	Total				
Grade										
10 Males	25 (195)	16 (373)	7 (153)	4 (52)	0 (9)	16 (782)	100.5	16	.000	.359
Females	36 (143)	32 (399)	13 (187)	7 (41)	0 (7)	27 (777)	101.4	16	.000	.329
12 Males	27 (254)	19 (356)	6 (141)	5 (42)	10 (10)	19 (803)	109.4	16	.000	.286
Females	47 (120)	27 (381)	25 (253)	4 (48)	8 (13)	28 (815)	77.4	16	.000	.305

	Attitude to Schoolwork							
	Positive	Neutral	Negative	Total				
Grade								
10 Males	23 (231)	19 (314)	13 (276)	18 (837)	21.1	12	.048	.172
Females	38 (128)	27 (394)	20 (274)	26 (802)	29.9	12	.002	.226
12 Males	23 (231)	19 (314)	13 (276)	18 (837)	21.1	12	.048	.171
Females	31 (262)	28 (344)	22 (218)	27 (837)	31.6	12	.002	.129

*Chi square values are for full contingency table.

**Numbers in brackets are the column marginal totals.

syndrome is not stronger among some ethnic sub-cultures. Whatever might be there, we could not easily detect it. For one reason, the number of students of particular ethnic groups that might be included, even in our large sample, would be too small to permit statistical analysis when broken down by sex and program. Also, any regrouping of ethnic categories would lose the particular qualities of ethnic groups which might be important. For example, if Chinese students are high achievers, that fact would not be detected by grouping Chinese with other groups such as Asian. Moreover, it would be necessary to separate ethnic groups into native and foreign-born to control for the effects of migration or assimilation. That would leave even fewer cases for analysis. We must, therefore, fall back on special studies to get at whatever relationship exists between ethnicity and school performance. These remarks do not apply to differences between Franco-Ontarians and Anglo-Ontarians, a subject to which we devote a separate chapter.

Size of family seems to have some effect on the performance of Grade 10 boys but not on the other sub-groups, and the amount of education that their parents have affects girls' performance in both Grades 10 and 12, but not boys'. For high performing girls in Grade 10 there is a large difference of about 20 percentage points between those who have highly educated parents and those with poorly educated ones. It is worth noting the performance level of girls compared to boys. In both grades there was the same percentage of high performing girls with poorly educated parents as there was of boys with well-educated ones. In all of the forty possible male-female comparisons provided by the categories of Table 9.3, girls outperform boys.

So far only sex and mental ability appear to be associated with school performance. While there is a trend in most of the rows in the SES size of family and parental education sections of Table 9.3 that conforms to our expectations, in very few of them, contrary to findings elsewhere, are there significant associations between school performance and these variables. However, we do have a set of variables that are strongly related to school performance. These are what we might call attitudinal variables.

Attitudinal Variables

Table 9.4, set up in the same way as Table 9.3, shows the relationship between school performance and educational aspirations, occupational aspirations, occupational expectations, self-concept of ability and attitude to schoolwork. In all cases there is a statistically significant association, and in many of the sub-groups a moderate association is measured by the gammas.

The first section shows a striking relationship between wanting to go to university and a high performance in school. In both Grades 10 and 12, one-quarter of the boys and 40 per cent of the girls who wanted to go to university had grades of over 75 per cent. Of those who wanted to go to work only 4 per cent of boys and 17 per cent of girls had such high grades. There was very little difference in the proportion with high grades between those who wanted to go to work and those who wanted some non-university form of post-secondary education. In fact, a higher proportion of Grade 12 girls who wanted to go to work were high achievers than of those who wanted to go to community college, teachers' college or nursing school. It is interesting that there was a high percentage with high grades among those girls who did not know what they wanted to do after leaving high school and among those who wanted to do something other than work or continue their education.

A degree of association is, of course, no indication of the direction of cause and effect. We treated level of education aspirations as the dependent variable in Chapter 5 and school performance as one of the independent variables, arguing that the way a student performed in school would have an effect on what he wanted to do after school. It seems logical enough that a student who liked school and performed well would want to continue studying at university, and that those who disliked school and had difficulty with schoolwork would want to get out of the system and into a more congenial setting. However, we recognize that the causal relationship could also be the reverse, that educational aspirations could affect the level of performance in a complex structure of reciprocal influences, and so wanting to go to university could provide the motivation to do well in school.

Wanting to achieve a high occupational level could also provide an incentive to do well, since many high level occupations require university degrees which in turn require a level of academic achievement.[23] As in the case of educational aspirations, one can argue that a high level of academic achievement encourages a young person to aspire to a high occupational level; but once again the reverse or a reciprocal relationship is also plausible: both probably exist and reinforce each other. In any case, as the second section of Table 9.4 shows, occupational aspirations are related to school performance. Very similar proportions in each category who aspire to university and who would like to have high occupations have marks of over 75 per cent. Expecting to reach a high occupational level, rather than simply aspiring to one, is even more strongly related to superior school performance. The panel of the table relating occupational expectations to school performance shows in every category a higher Chi square value (with equal degrees of freedom) than in the corresponding occupational aspirations category. Gamma values are also uniformly stronger for occupational expectations than for occupational aspirations.

As we have indicated earlier, the correlation between educational aspirations and educational expectations was very high (over .9 for both grades and sexes), suggesting that the questions meant much the same to the student. Between occupational aspirations and expectations, however, the correlation was not so high (e.g., .691 for boys, .557 for girls in Grade 10), suggesting the fantasy-reality gap. Therefore, perceptions of high level occupational futures based on realistic assessment of possibilities, a subject explored more extensively in Chapter 6, are likely to be a greater spur to superior school performance than aspirations. Fewer girls than boys have high educational aspirations and occupational expectations, but among those who do a very large proportion (40 per cent) in both grades had marks of over 75 per cent.

The relationship between school performance, educational aspirations and expectations and occupational aspirations and expectations is obviously a complex one. We have already mentioned that very high achievement levels at high school are not necessary to be admitted to university. Most universities accept students with a 60 per cent average. But this is generally true only of Arts and Science programs. Almost all professional programs are restricted, and an initial selection is made of applicants on the basis of grades. High occupational aspirations, as we have defined them, include aspirations to higher professional occupations. Perhaps what happens is that a young person thinks he would like to enter a particular profession, but to do that requires a university education in a program where admission levels are high. The student then has a reason to strive for high grades in high school. If he gets high grades he will then feel that his hopes are not unrealistic, and he can therefore legitimately expect to be admitted to a professional program at a university.

Self-concept of ability for university work also shows a strong relationship with school performance. If a young person has a high self-concept of ability, he also has confidence in his ability to perform well, and that creates a positive attitude to learning which would certainly contribute to greater success. Again, as in the case of educational aspirations, the relationship is probably reciprocal and reinforcing. A person does well in school, that gives him self-confidence and a high self-concept of ability, and that in turn makes it more likely that he will continue to perform well.

Finally, from Table 9.4 we see that attitude to schoolwork has some effect on school performance. Attitudes to Schoolwork, a scale measuring the student's opinions about whether his subjects are interesting, easy and useful, or boring, difficult and useless, is related to school performance, although only marginally for males. This finding also raises the question why some should find subjects interesting and useful when others find them boring and useless, but such feelings do not have high correlations with the background variables with which we have been dealing.

Parents and School Performance

While it seems obvious that parents must have some influence on how their children perform in school, and that the social climate of the home must contribute towards the child's attitudes to schoolwork, it is very hard to measure these family characteristics and to assess the results where they have been studied. In reviewing the research on the effect of family interrelationships, Boocock[24] describes two separate views: one, that families of high achievers are characterized by relatively greater warmth, with many shared activities and closer primary relationships than low achievers; the other, that the need to achieve arises in more reserved families in which children are not sure of their parents' love and therefore need to achieve in order to win it. We asked a sub-sample of mothers a number of questions to try to determine the effects of their attitudes and the family environment on their child's attitudes and behaviour in school. In most cases the responses were not enlightening. For example, 98 per cent responded "yes" to the statement "I am proud of him if he does well and tell him so," and 98 per cent with children in Grades 10 and 12 also said "yes" to the statement "As long as I feel he is doing his best I am satisfied."

However, to another statement, "No matter what his marks are I always urge him to do better," there was a variation in response, and this variation was related to school performance. The relationship was somewhat unexpected. The children of non-urging parents had higher grades than had children of parents who agreed with the statement. It is plausible that a nagging parent who is never satisfied could have the effect of turning off her child.

Since it seems likely that a parent's attitudes to education would have an effect on a child's attitudes, aspirations and performance, we asked the mothers whether they agreed or disagreed with seven statements about education.[25] On the whole, the attitude of the mothers was positive about education, and there was therefore no relationship between their attitudes and the students' grades. Only one statement, "Nowadays young people are becoming over-educated," with only one of the grade/sex sub-samples had a significant relationship to school performance. For Grade 12 boys whose parents were uncertain or disagreed, a considerably larger number had grades of over 75 per cent than of the boys whose parents agreed with it. However, this finding was not significant in the case of the Grade 10 boys or in either sample of girls, so it does not seem very important.

One measure of parental influence that is very strongly related to school performance is the mother's level of educational aspirations for her child. Boocock writes, "It is clear that high-achieving children tend to come from families who have high expectations for them, and who consequently are likely to 'set standards' and to make greater demands at an earlier age."[26] Kahl's analysis of "common man" boys showed that lower-class boys had high educational aspirations when their parents were not satisfied with their own achievements and urged them to do better.[27] A re-analysis of a part of the Coleman *Equality of Educational Opportunity* data by Chad Gordon[28] showed that the performance level and aspirations of students were related to their parents' aspirations controlling for socio-economic status and race.

In Ontario the overwhelming majority of parents, of boys particularly, wanted their children to go to university. In the interview sub-sample of mothers of Grade 10 boys, 79 per cent wanted their sons to go to university, and of the mothers of girls, 57 per cent had these aspirations for their daughters. The proportions in the student sample who thought that their mothers wanted them to go to university is very similar: 80 per cent of the boys and 58 per cent of the girls. Of Grade 12 boys whose mothers wanted them to go to university, 22 per cent performed at averages of 75 per cent or more, but of those who wanted them to go elsewhere or to work, the proportion of high performers is much smaller. The same pattern was true for girls: that is, lesser proportions of high performers with the lower maternal aspirations with, of course, girls always outperforming boys. The relationships are parallel in Grade 10.

We have noted frequently that friends and peers are among the important "significant others" affecting a student's educational experience. It would seem that although students may or may not be aware of it, having close friends who themselves have high educational aspirations plays some part in the student performing well in school. Strikingly higher proportions of those whose friends wanted to go to university had Grade averages over 75 per cent than of those whose friends wanted some other kind of post-secondary education or wanted to go to work.

Notes

1. Samuel Bowles and Herbert Gintis in *Schooling in Capitalist America* (New York: Basic Books, 1976) present a forceful argument that the market economy and the class structure have shaped educational systems into their becoming important factors in class reproduction. While much of our data would support such a view of the Ontario school system, the elitism of achievement seems to have fallen away as an element in the relationship between class and education.

2. Michael Young's *The Rise of the Meritocracy* (London: Penguin, 1961) is the celebrated satirical account of the consequence of the English educational changes. For an empirical account, one among many, see James W.B. Douglas, *The Home and the School: A Study of Ability and Attainment in the Primary Schools* (London: MacGibbon & Kee, 1964). See also *15 to 18*, Report of the Central Advisory Council for Education (London, England: Her Majesty's Stationery Office, 1960), and T.H. Marshall's essay, "Social Selection in the Welfare State," in his *Class, Citizenship and Social Development* (Garden City: Doubleday, 1964).

3. For France see, for example, Pierre Bourdieu and Jean-Claude Passeron, *Les Heritiers* (Paris: Editions de Minuit); for England, *15 to 18*; James W.B. Douglas, Jean M. Ross and Howard R. Simpson, *All Our Future* (London: Peter Davies, 1968).

4. The common schools of the New England colonies were an early part of the democratic ideology. Some revisionist historians have questioned the democratic purpose of the common schools. See the discussion in Chapter 2.

5. James S. Coleman, *et al.*, *Equality of Educational Opportunity* (Washington, D.C.: U.S. Department of Health, Education and Welfare, U.S. Government Printing Office, 1966). For class differences see, for example, Patricia Cayo Sexton, *Education and Income* (New

York: Viking, 1961) and *The American School* (Englewood Cliffs: Prentice-Hall, 1967). For a recent summary review see William H. Sewell, "Inequality of Opportunity for Higher Education," in *American Sociological Review* (Vol.36, No.5, Oct.1971), pp.793–809.

6. For an earlier study in Ontario see William G. Fleming, *Background and Personality Factors Associated with Educational and Occupational Plans of Ontario Grade 13 Students* (Toronto: Ontario College of Education, University of Toronto, 1957). See also John Porter, *The Vertical Mosaic* (Toronto: University of Toronto Press, 1965), ch. 6.

7. *Living and Learning*, The Report of the Provincial Committee on Aims and Objectives of Education in the Schools of Ontario (Toronto: Department of Education, 1968).

8. *The Learning Society, Report of the Commission on Post-Secondary Education in Ontario* (Toronto: Government of Ontario, 1972). See also John Porter, *et al.*, *Towards 2000* (Toronto: McClelland and Stewart, 1971).

9. For a review see Marion R. Porter, John Porter and Bernard R. Blishen, *Does Money Matter? Prospects for Higher Education in Ontario* (Toronto: Macmillan, 1979).

10. Most universities in Ontario accepted for non-professional programs students with a minimum 60 per cent average.

11. For reviews of these studies and their findings see David E. Lavin, *The Prediction of Academic Performance* (New York: Russell Sage Foundation, 1965) and Sarane S. Boocock, *An Introduction to the Sociology of Learning* (Boston: Houghton Mifflin, 1972).

12. Coleman, *et al.*, *op.cit.*

13. This is an impressionistic statement based on our acquaintance with schools and students in them.

14. Fleming, *op.cit.*, pp.19–22.

15. Boocock, *op.cit.*, p.80. The flagging performance of girls in the later years of secondary school has been noted for England in Douglas, *et al.*, *op.cit.*, pp.31ff.

16. Boocock, *op.cit.*, p.81, and Douglas, *et al.*, *op.cit.*, p.29.

17. James S. Coleman, *The Adolescent Society* (New York: The Free Press, 1961), pp.38ff.

18. Boocock, *op.cit.*, p.36.

19. *Ibid.*, p.37.

20. Lavin, *op.cit.*, p.125.

21. Bernard C. Rosen, "The Achievement Syndrome: A Psychocultural Dimension of Social Stratification," in *American Sociological Review* (Vol. 21), pp.203–211.

22. Values of gamma which might roughly be interpreted as a correlation coefficient can be from +1 a perfect positive relationship (high on one variable is high on the other) to a −1 a perfect negative relationship (high on one variable is low on the other). Zero would be no relationship.

23. See Chapters 5 and 6.

24. Boocock, *op.cit.*, p.64.

25. See Chapter 4.

26. Boocock, *op.cit.*, p.60.

27. Joseph H. Kahl, "Educational and Occupational Aspirations of 'Common Man' Boys," in *Harvard Educational Review* (Vol.23, Summer 1953), pp.186–203.

28. Boocock, *op.cit.*, p.62.

10
Programs

In previous chapters we have seen that the program of study in which a student is enrolled in high school is a consistent factor in mediating the effects of both family background and school-related factors on educational and occupational aspirations. In this chapter we will shift our focus on program from an emphasis on its role as an independent or intervening variable in the prediction of other outcomes to an emphasis on program placement as an outcome. Empirically, we will be concerned with two questions: Who is placed where in the program structure? What factors seem to be salient in program placement? Before we turn to an examination of these questions in the light of our data, we will first look at the evolution of program differentiation in the Ontario system.

Program Streaming in Ontario
The formal differentiation of secondary school offerings into distinct streams began in Ontario with the Act to Improve the Common and Grammar Schools of the Province of Ontario, passed in 1871, which introduced the distinction between high schools and collegiate institutes. The chief distinction was that the program of studies in the latter institutions included Latin and Greek, which were at that time a necessary prerequisite to university admission, while the former did not offer these languages. Thus, the collegiate institutes were regarded as offering a university preparatory course, with the high schools offering a secondary education for those who would not be going on. However, for a mixture of reasons, of which prestige and grants appear to have been the most important, the distinction became quickly blurred, with the final outcome that by the turn of the century both courses were generally offered in both types of schools. Changes since that time in the academic program, apart from an increasing number of options, were primarily the result of changes in university admission policies by the universities in Ontario, and most importantly by the University of Toronto.

Commercial education was first offered as a part of the high school program following the reforms of 1871 and by the turn of the century had developed into a program in its own right. Vocational education began somewhat later, becoming established as a regular part of secondary education following the Seath Report of 1911 and the subsequent passage of the Industrial Education Act, 1911.[1]

Thus, by the end of the First World War, the structure of the Ontario secondary school system was well on its way to crystallization into the form it had until the introduction of the 1962 reforms. There was the matriculation stream, which was for those hoping to go on to the universities, and there were the commercial and vocational programs for those who were not. There were, of course, minor changes in content, curriculum structure and length of program during that period, but the essential elements of the structure remained relatively fixed.[2]

Reorganized Program

In 1961 the Department of Labour of the federal government initiated a federal-provincial cost sharing agreement under the Technical and Vocational Training Assistance Act. The concern motivating the federal government was the discovery that Canada was not producing a sufficient number of skilled blue-collar workers to supply its manpower needs. Among other things, it was noted that 35 per cent of the skilled workers in five industries were trained outside of Canada, and further, that vocational enrolment accounted for only 15 per cent of secondary school enrolments in Canada at that time.

This situation led C.R. Ford, Director of the Technical and Vocational Training Branch of the federal Department of Labour, to comment in 1961, "The responsibility for the direction, administration and co-ordination of the arrangements for training manpower is much more important than some Department of Education people realize."[3] With respect to the situation in the province of Ontario at that time, this was a drastic understatement of the situation. Fleming devotes a whole chapter to an overview of the discussions in Ontario of the aims of education.[4] Much of this discussion took place in the fifties and early sixties, but in general the tone and content were more appropriate to Plato's Athens than to a twentieth-century industrial society. There was much concern with the values of learning and scholarship and, through them, for the development of the whole person. There is, of course, nothing really wrong with such concerns, except that in general they are the preserve of a privileged few, and further, that they appear to have both obscured and denigrated discussion of the more pressing problem of preparing the vast majority of students not destined for a life of scholarship and "high culture" for participation in the labour force.

The result of the federal thinking in this area was the Technical and

Vocational Training Assistance Act (1961), which we have mentioned above. Initially, the act appeared only to refer to capital expenditures with respect to provincial institutes of trade and technology, that is, for training at the post-secondary level. However, by the time the federal-provincial agreement took effect, "secondary school facilities would be approved if they were to be used for '. . . those courses, given as an integral part of high school education, in which at least one half of the school time is devoted to technical, commercial and other vocational subjects or courses designed to prepare students for entry into employment by developing occupational qualifications.' "[5]

According to Cameron, the province of Ontario decided to place the emphasis, in its participation in the scheme, on the secondary level rather than on the post-secondary level, as had been the original federal intent:

> Before launching this response, the Cabinet sought assurance from officials of the Department of Education that the secondary school course of study could, in fact, be revised in such a way as to make possible the channelling of a provincial programme of technical and vocational education through the secondary system. It was only after receiving that assurance that the Cabinet decided to proceed with the programme in this manner.[6]

Ontario formally entered into the agreement with the federal government on June 26, 1961. On August 28, the Department of Education announced the Reorganized Program, which became known as the Robarts Plan after the minister of education at the time. It was to begin with those entering Grade 9 in September 1962, and was the form of course organization most commonly in effect at the time of our study in May 1971.

The new plan had three basic types of course: Arts and Science (A & S); Science, Technology and Trades (ST & T); and Business and Commerce (B & C). Each of these courses was to be offered at two levels: a five-year level which would qualify the student for university admission, and a four-year level which would end at Grade 12. Additionally, there would be one- and two-year occupational programs available for those students who were unable to complete public school. "The change was made in such a way that all the components of the new course of study, save only the arts and science branches, met the standards of the federal government for inclusion in the terms of the capital grant scheme."[7]

The students' specialization began at Grade 9. In theory, the student was supposed to be able to transfer from one stream to another, but each succeeding year effectively locked the student more firmly into the stream he was in. In practice, downward mobility from five-year to four-year was easy, but upward mobility from four-year to five-year was difficult, and after Grade 9 could usually only be accomplished at the cost of an extra year. In addition, while the five-year B & C and ST & T streams led to university admission, unless the student was careful in his selection of courses and options throughout the five years of high school, he stood a good chance of finding the range of courses to which he could gain admission at the university level restricted.

Some of these limitations were eventually recognized by the Ontario Department of Education, and in 1968–69 a number of innovations were introduced on an experimental basis into six schools. These involved an abolition of the distinction between four- and five-year programs and the offering of courses, instead, on two levels: the advanced level, for those wishing to obtain Grade 13 credit in the subject; and the general level, for those whose interest or abilities did not extend to Grade 13 credit in the subject. Students were allowed to take a mixture of courses on either the advanced or general level depending on their needs, although the student who had ambitions for Grade 13 had to take at least some of his credits at the advanced level.

At the time of our study the older Robarts Plan system of branches and programs was still in effect in most schools. There were a very few who had switched over to the Advanced/General level system.

This, then, was the system into which the students in our study had to fit. We have already seen the consequences of this system in terms of its effects on students' aspirations; we will now turn to our data to see, first, who was placed where under this system, and secondly, to look at the process whereby students were placed in programs.

Who's Where

Table 10.1 presents the distribution of students' responses to the question which asked them to indicate the program in which they were enrolled in school, or, in the case of the students who were in Grade 8 at the time of the study, what program they expected to be enrolling in in high school in the fall. It is noteworthy that 12 per cent of the students in Grade 8 answered that they did not know, or did not answer at all. As we have already shown in previous chapters, the choice of the program in which a student is enrolled is a decision which vitally affects his entire educational and occupational future. We will be looking at these students and their source of assistance and guidance in a later section of this chapter called "Getting Into High School."

In looking at the data for Grades 10 and 12, the most notable thing is the relatively stable distribution of students with respect to programs. When we look at the Grade 8 students in relation to those in Grades 10 and 12, the distribution changes somewhat, with the Grade 8 students showing somewhat more preference for the five-year Business and Commerce programs than the Grade 10 and 12 students. Secondly, it will be noted that the objective of the federal-provincial grant scheme which led to the Robarts' Plan certainly had the desired effect, as enrolments and expected enrolments

Table 10.1
Major Program by Grade

Program	Grade 12	Grade 10	Grade 8
	(per cent)		
Business & Commerce, 4-year	14	13	12
Business & Commerce, 5-year	4	4	13
Science, Trades & Technology, 4-year	12	15	10
Science, Trades & Technology, 5-year	7	8	7
Arts & Science, 4-year*	9	8	10
Arts & Science, 5-year**	54	52	48
Total	100	100	100
N =	2,714	2,568	2,256
Other & Occupational	69	230	146
DK/NA	79	166	320

*Includes those taking mostly general level courses.

**Includes those taking either advanced level courses or a mixture of advanced level and general level courses.

in the vocational branches were now between 37 per cent (Grade 12) and 42 per cent (Grade 8), as opposed to the 15 per cent found in the Department of Labour study referred to earlier.

In looking at the overall effect of this plan on the student's life chances, at least as they were reflected in educational and occupational opportunity, the stream in which the student was enrolled was the most important. It determined, almost in the manner of a switch, whether or not the student would be able to go on to university. Once a student was in a four-year program, university admission in the normal course of events was a virtual impossibility. The options open to a student in such circumstances who did wish to go on would be either to return to secondary school and acquire an honours matriculation, which would require at least two years, or to enter the work force and apply some years later for admission as a mature matriculant. In addition, being in a four-year program placed some limitations on the prospects for community college admission.[8] The community colleges were designed in some measure to satisfy the post-secondary aspirations of those students graduating from the four-year programs. However, while Grade 12 is the minimum admission standard for the majority of courses of study, the enrolments of most of the premier courses are limited and admissions are on a competitive basis. The consequence is that even at this level, Grade 13 is a practical necessity to ensure a broad range of options.

It will be noted that the majority of students were in, or expected to be in, the five-year program, and as can be seen the vast majority of these students were in the five-year Arts and Science program. This program was certainly the broad channel to higher education. However, it is possible that enrolment in this program may have exacted a serious penalty on the unsuccessful student, in that it could leave him in a job market in which he had few if any saleable skills. This situation would, of course, be even more serious for the student in the four-year Arts and Science program who found that he could not obtain post-secondary education. The vocational branches, while offering more immediately marketable training, did so at the cost of limited opportunity.

We will now look at some of the characteristics of the students who were enrolled in these different programs. We would expect to find in a system which stresses universalism and achievement as strongly as the Ontario education system does that there would be few if any systematic variations with respect to background characteristics between the students in the various programs.

Sex

Table 10.2 shows the distribution of students by program, branch and sex for Grade 12 students. Since there is strong consistency between Grades 10 and 12, we will present the data for Grade 12 only. The Grade 8 students will be treated in a separate section.

This table shows that the two vocational branches are very clearly split into a girl's world (Business and Commerce) and a boy's world (Science, Trades and Technology). Over four-fifths of the students in the four-year program and over three-quarters of the students in the five-year program in the Business and Commerce branch in Grade 12 were girls. On the other hand, over 95 per cent of the Grade 12 students in both programs of the Science, Trades and Technology branch were boys.

The reasons for this sex division become clear when we note that in both the vocational branches the vast majority of students were in the four-year program, which was intended to offer vocational skills rather than to lead to post-secondary education. Two-thirds of the boys in the vocational branches and four-fifths of the girls in the vocational branches were in the four-year program. In the Business and Commerce branch, the courses in the four-year program are primarily concerned with teaching secretarial and clerical skills. In the Science, Trades and Technology branch, much of the course work is directed towards building a foundation for training as skilled labour. In 1971 secretarial and clerical work was the largest single job category for females, employing over a third of all the females in the labour force, and within that category females accounted for almost three-quarters

Table 10.2
Program by Branch and Sex
(Grade 12)

Program	Branch								
	Business & Commerce			Science, Trades & Tech.			Arts and Science		
	M	F	T	M	F	T	M	F	T
					(per cent)				
Four-year	17	83	100 (383)	95	5	100 (338)	53	47	100 (252)
Five-year	22	78	100 (100)	97	3	100 (177)	46	54	100 (1,459)
All programs	18	82	100 (483)	96	4	100 (515)	47	53	100 (1,711)
	P > .05			P > .05			P > .05		

of all employees. For males, the category of craftsmen and production workers constituted the largest single category of employment, and over 80 per cent of those so employed were males. In short, these distributions within the schools reflected quite accurately the realities and sexual typings with respect to sexual roles in the division of labour in the larger society. While the vocational branches exhibited extreme sexual typing, the Arts and Science branch showed none.

Age

In looking at the distribution of students by program and by age, one thing becomes clear. For those students who were registered in a four-year program, the median age was 18, and for those students in a five-year program the median was 17. This would suggest that there was a probability that a student who was in the four-year program had failed at least once in his educational career up to that point. For many it was highly likely that this event of failing a year was a major causal factor in their being placed in the four-year program.

Mental Ability

Table 10.3 shows the distribution of students by program and by mental ability. As we have earlier explained, the measure which we used of mental ability was the Cattell and Cattell "culture fair" test. In forming our measure we attempted to form cutting points which fell as closely as possible to the thirty-third and sixty-seventh percentiles of our distribution. Thus, high mental ability students corresponded to those who scored in the upper 30 per cent of the distribution, medium mental ability students were those who scored between the sixty-nine percentile and the thirtieth percentile, and low mental ability students scored below the thirtieth percentile. It should be noted that in some ways this tended to minimize the effects of mental ability with respect to program, as the age differential between four- and five-year programs would tend to further accentuate differentials in mental ability between streams if age standardization—a common procedure with measures of mental ability—had been carried out.

In looking at the data, a very definite relationship between mental ability and stream can be seen. This is illustrated in Figure 10.1. Here we can see that over 80 per cent of the high mental ability students were in the five-year programs, while over 50 per cent of the low mental ability students were in the four-year programs. Table 10.3 shows that regardless of branch, the distribution of students with respect to mental ability was virtually the same for the four-year programs. However, when we look at the five-year programs, some differences do emerge. The Business and Commerce five-year program had a smaller proportion of high mental ability students than the Science, Trades and Technology and the Arts and Science five-year

Table 10.3
Program by Mental Ability
(Grade 12)

| Program | Mental Ability | | | | |
	High	Medium	Low	Total	N
			(per cent)		
Business and Commerce 4-year	12	30	58	100	383
Business and Commerce 5-year	32	36	32	100	100
Science, Trades & Technology 4-year	17	41	42	100	340
Science, Trades & Technology 5-year	44	38	18	100	177
Arts and Science 4-year	15	44	41	100	252
Arts and Science 5-year	39	40	30	100	1,462
All programs	31	39	30	100	2,714

$p < .05$

programs, while the Science, Trades and Technology five-year program had the highest proportion of all.

The main differences remain those between the mental ability distributions of the four- and five-year programs. Here one is led to wonder about the direction of the relationship. In short, is low mental ability caused by the inferior teaching and perception of ability which is a result of being in a four-year program, or conversely, is being placed in a four-year program the result of a lower level of mental ability? The answer is no doubt a combination of the two effects. But when we recall some of the studies on the effects of test labelling on student performance, we must suggest that certainly the former effect deserves consideration.[9]

Family Background

There are many factors in a student's family background which the literature would have us believe are likely to be related to his program. Among these are religion, ethnicity, the size of his family, and whether the student is attending school in an urban or rural setting. In fact, none of these factors showed any relationship to the student's program. However, several status-related variables did show significant effects. They were: the student's father's occupational status, the student's mother's and father's educational attainment.

Figure 10.1
Program by Mental Ability, Grade 12

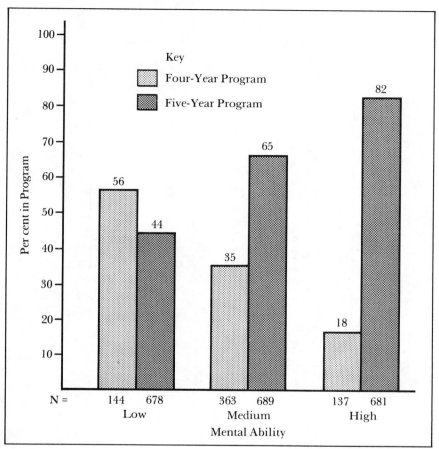

Table 10.4 shows some measure of the relationship. Only in the five-year Arts and Science program were students whose fathers had higher level occupations over-represented. They were roughly proportionally represented in the five-year Science, Trades and Technology program. In all other programs, students whose fathers had lower occupational status were clearly over-represented.

In Figure 10.2 the picture is further sharpened. As we go across the chart from the highest class to the lowest class, the proportion of students in the four-year program increases sharply from 14 per cent for the highest class to nearly 50 per cent for the lowest. Conversely, in the five-year program, we find

Table 10.4
Program by Socio-economic Status
(Grade 12)

Program	Socio-economic Status						Total	N
	I	II	III	IV	V	VI		
				(per cent)				
Business and Commerce 4-year	2	4	9	16	52	17	100	347
Business and Commerce 5-year	1	6	5	23	52	13	100	97
Science, Trades & Technology 4-year	2	3	6	18	53	18	100	315
Science, Trades & Technology 5-year	8	10	13	23	35	11	100	166
Arts and Science 4-year	4	6	12	21	43	14	100	228
Arts and Science 5-year	10	11	14	22	34	9	100	1,380
All programs	7	8	12	21	40	12	100	2533

that over 80 per cent of the students in the two highest classes are in the five-year program compared to only 50 per cent of the students in the lowest class.

As education is very closely related to one's occupational status, and further, as it is a component of the construction of the Blishen scale (our measure of occupational status), it is not surprising to find that both the student's mother's and father's level of educational attainment were linked to his program in high school. Table 10.5 presents the data on this relationship for the father. The relationship is almost the same for mother's education.

What we find in looking at these data is a distribution of students into programs in a manner which appears to be very closely linked to their social status. Indeed, it would appear that the schools were creating, using the programs which they offered, a micro-stratification system where the privileged were likely to end up in programs appropriate to their status. In

Figure 10.2
Program by Socio-economic Status, Grade 12

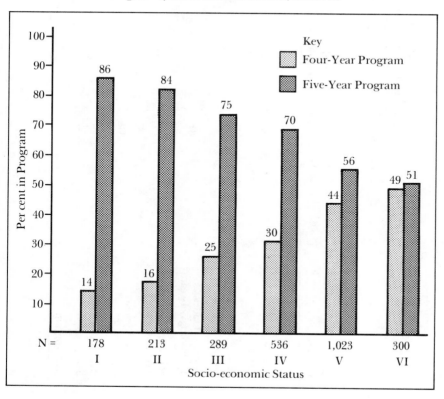

Table 10.5
Program by Father's Education
(Grade 12)

Program	Up to Some High School	Completed High School	Some Post-Secondary	University Graduation Or More	Total	N
			(per cent)			
Business and Commerce 4-year	79	12	6	3	100	334
Business and Commerce 5-year	73	19	7	1	100	93
Science, Trades & Technology, 4-year	81	10	5	4	100	288
Science, Trades & Technology, 5-year	57	18	14	11	100	166
Arts and Science 4-year	69	17	9	5	100	225
Arts and Science 5-year	57	16	9	18	100	1,330
All programs	64	15	9	12	100	2,436

$p < .05$

short, the program structure acted as a mechanism for the mediation and transmission of existing inequalities.

In general, the main thing which becomes clear from these data is that the five-year Arts and Science program was the broad channel of secondary education. Its completion could lead to university. Its students were younger and brighter, their parents had better jobs and more education, and the students thought more of themselves and were in turn better thought of than those in other programs.

Those students who were in a five-year program in a vocational branch were in general in a lower social class than those in the Arts and Science branch, but only moderately so. However, those students in a four-year program tended to be older, less bright, have lower-class parents, and to think less of themselves. In short, they had a much lower chance of success as it is defined in our society.

Table 10.6 should serve to bring home the class bias in the system. This table shows the distribution of students by their father's occupational status with respect to whether they were enrolled in the five-year Arts and Science program or not. For the upper three classes, between three-quarters and three-fifths of the students were in the five-year Arts and Science program. For the two lowest classes, less than half the students were in the five-year Arts and Science program. It might further be noted that Class V is by far the largest class, and thus the impact of this is in numerical terms even more severe than mere percentages would indicate.

Getting Into High School
As we have suggested above, and as has been shown in other chapters, the high school program in which a student was placed was a decision which

Table 10.6
Five-Year Arts and Science vs. All Other Programs
by Socio-economic Status (Grade 12)

Program	Socio-economic Status						
	I	II	III	IV	V	VI	Total
	(per cent)						
All Others	22	27	36	42	54	60	46
Five-year Arts and Science	78	73	64	58	46	40	54
Total	100	100	100	100	100	100	100
N =	178	213	289	536	1,023	300	2,539

$p < .05$

would alter the rest of his life. It would affect the educational future which he could expect in a very direct fashion. Given a specific educational future and the increasing emphasis on certification in the labour force, it would affect his whole working career and, through that, his lifestyle. In short, this is not a decision which should be made either lightly or hastily.

In the Ontario system, the decision had to be made relatively early in a student's life—at the end of Grade 8, when the student was between thirteen and fourteen years old. Most fourteen year olds would not have the wisdom or even the understanding of the consequences of such a decision to be able to make a decision of such crucial importance unaided. As a result, one would expect to find that the Grade 8 year involved a heavy round of consultation among the school, the parents and the student in order to determine what program the student should enter when he went to high school. However, as noted earlier, over 10 per cent of the Grade 8 students in our sample did not know what program they would be taking in high school, and this at a very late stage in the school year.

In this section, we will examine some aspects of the way in which students were allocated to programs of study. We will first look at and comment upon some of the criteria which were used in the assignment of students to programs. Then we will look at the issue of who was getting or not getting guidance, and from whom. Finally, we will look at the degree to which the outcome of such guidance was consistent with the educational and occupational desires of the student.

In his study of Canadian high schools, Raymond Breton asked principals to rate in order of importance a number of criteria which might be considered to be of importance in assigning a student to a program of study.[10] The result of this question can be seen in Table 10.7. The table shows that the factors fell into three groupings in order of magnitude of importance. The two factors of the first order of importance were grades and teachers' and principals' judgements. Of a second order of importance were the judgements of guidance counsellors, the interests of the students and standardized tests. Of very minor importance were interest "tests" and the wishes of the students' parents. Two points of interest come immediately from these data.

First, it will be noted that in our discussions of the program a student was in we have constantly used the student as the object of transitive verbs such as "place" or "assign" with respect to program. These data amply support such usage. The student's wishes, hopes and interests were fourth in importance in the mind of the school, and were very clearly of a second order of importance with respect to the first two school-related criteria.

The second point to be noted is the very strong emphasis which is placed on the first two items. It should be clear that these cannot really be called independent criteria, as in many ways the marks which a student receives are a reflection of the judgements of teachers and principals. This may be increasingly so as marking moves away from an emphasis on

Table 10.7
Importance of Different Criteria in Assigning Students
to Programs of Study

Criterion	Very Important (per cent)
School marks or grades	63
Judgement of teachers or principal	52
Judgement of guidance counsellor	36
Student's expressed interest in certain subjects or career	31
Intelligence or achievement test	27
Interest test	11
Parents' wishes	9

Source: Adapted from Raymond Breton, "Academic Stratification in Secondary Schools and the Educational Plans of Students," in *Canadian Review of Sociology and Anthropology*, Vol. 7, pp. 17-34.

judging the students based on "hard" evidence (examinations and independent work) and universalistic criteria for evaluation, towards an emphasis on "relativistic" criteria (i.e., how well is the student doing compared to others like him?), or even particularistic evaluation (i.e., is he doing as well as he could?). In these latter two types of evaluation, there is a tendency to shy away from the use of hard evidence and towards the use of such amorphous criteria as "attitude" and "effort."

The trend in this direction in Ontario has been especially noticeable in the elementary schools. This is a direct outcome of the "implementation" of the "Hall-Dennis" Report in the elementary system.[11] The individualistic and particularistic emphasis in the Report can be seen very clearly by quoting a few of the Report's recommendations on "evaluation of pupil progress":

73. Develop student learning profiles that reveal the individual progress and experience of each student throughout the learning continuum.

74. Abandon the use of class standing, percentage marks, and letter grades in favour of parent and pupil counselling as a method of reporting individual progress.

75. Abandon the use of formal examinations except where the experience would be of value to students planning to attend universities where formal examinations may still be in use.

78. Permit individual schools to develop their own systems of reporting pupil progress to parents and pupils.[12]

It is important to be aware of these considerations when we realize that it is the grade and evaluation that was placed on the student in elementary school which served as the primary basis for the placement of students into programs in high school. This is very much so when we consider that the more particularistic forms of evaluation with their emphasis on presentation of self are, to an even greater extent than in the case of universalistic evaluation, more likely to favour the upper- and middle-class student at the expense of the lower-class student.

Before looking at the potential outcome of the application of these criteria to our Grade 8 students, we will first examine the extent to which the students were receiving guidance from their parents and from the schools on their educational plans. This is particularly important in light of the fact that 12 per cent of these students were unable to answer the question regarding the program in which they would be located on entering high school in the fall.

The Sources of Guidance

As explained in Chapter 8, in order to determine who was helping the students in making their educational plans, they were asked two questions: "In making plans for fall, who is helping you *most?*" and "Who helps you *most* in thinking about your future education?" It was observed that in terms of making plans for the fall and for the future most students saw their parents as the most important source of assistance. However, it was noted that parents were of more importance in thinking about the longer term than in thinking about the shorter term. Members of the school staff and "Others" were of more assistance in the short run than in the longer-term considerations. We were struck that 12 per cent of the students claimed that "No One" was helping them make plans for the fall, and that 17 per cent claimed that "No One" was helping them in thinking about their future education.

When we ask whether or not this helping has had any effect on the students' knowledge of their program for the fall, we find that the differences are minimal. Over 90 per cent of those students who were receiving assistance knew which program they were entering. Of those who responded "No One," 89 per cent knew their future program. This difference between the two groups is very small and could easily be an artifact of sampling error.

An examination of students by social class who claimed that nobody was helping them again indicates very little difference. Indeed, the differences which do exist suggest that upper-middle-class students are likely to be over-represented among the group who did not know their program. However, the differences are small and one would be reluctant to place much substantive weight on them.

In sum, when we look at sources of advice and at social class with

Table 10.8
Program by Highest Grade Which Respondent Expects
to Complete in High School (Grade 8)

Program	9	10	11	12	13	Total	N
			Expected Grade				
			(per cent)				
Occupational	9	52	15	10	14	100	58
Four-year	1	4	9	62	24	100	716
Five-year	0	1	2	14	83	100	1,670
							2,444

$p < .05$

respect to the students' knowledge of their program for the fall, it seems fairly clear that neither factor had much effect. We will look now at only those students who did know their program for the fall and attempt to see whether the advice which they had (or had not) received led to an appropriate program selection in terms of their educational expectations.

Table 10.8 presents the students' program by the highest grade which the student expected to complete in high school. A student will be considered inappropriately placed if his/her educational expectations extended beyond the grade level at which the program would normally terminate. Students in the occupational stream would normally terminate at the end of Grade 10, those in the four-year stream would terminate after Grade 12, and those in the five-year stream would usually complete Grade 13. As can be seen from the table, the majority of students were correctly placed with respect to their educational expectations in high school. Nonetheless, two-fifths of those in the occupational stream and nearly a quarter of those in the four-year stream were misplaced. It may well be that their expectation was an unrealistic one, but at the very least, these students would appear to be unaware of the implications for their future education of the program into which they had been placed. It should be noted, however, that an examination of the relationship of "correct" placement versus "incorrect" placement to several variables, including social class, grades and mental ability, shows that there was no systematic variation. This in turn suggests that, on the whole, this "misplacement" with respect to expectations may well be simply the type of slippage which is bound to occur in a large bureaucratic system.

In conclusion, it would appear that the vast majority of students were getting advice on the matter of program selection and that advice resulted, on the whole, in a program assignment that was consistent with their expectations for further schooling. Further, it would appear that those who were not getting advice, or who claimed they were not, seemed to be no different from those who were with respect to background, and they seemed to fare about as well as their "advised" counterparts in their decision making.

The Process of Program Selection

We will now look at the relative importance of various factors in the process of program selection. As it is really the length of the program (five-year vs. four-year) that is crucial in the determination of future educational attainment, the focus will be on that aspect of the program structure.

One of the factors with which will be examined is social class. As indicated in our earlier profile of the program structure for those students already in high school, the distribution was strongly related to this factor. Given our concern with equality of educational opportunity, it then becomes a matter of some importance to understand the role of this factor in the assignment of students to programs. In particular we will be concerned with the effect of this factor vis-à-vis factors such as grades, mental ability, students' aspirations and their parents' aspirations for them.

Earlier in this discussion a set of factors was examined which high school principals regarded as important in the allocation of students to programs (Table 10.7). Ideally, we would wish to have a measure for each of the items on that list. We do not. However, we do have the student's grades, his/her interests as expressed through educational aspirations, a measure of the student's mental ability, and the student's report of his/her parents' aspirations for him/her.

Table 10.9 presents associations for the relationship of each of the factors already discussed to program (occupational, four-year and five-year). It is clear that the student's aspirations and those of his/her parents have

Table 10.9
Gammas for Relationship of Various Factors to Program

Factor	Gamma
Students' Educational Aspirations (work, other post-secondary, university)	.75
Students' Perceptions of Mothers' Educational Aspirations (as above)	.71
Students' Grade 7 Grades (divided into quartiles)	.62
Family Socio-economic Status (Upper-middle, Middle, Low)	.37
Mental Ability (in tertiles)	.36

stronger relationships to the program that a student will be in than do mental ability, social class or grades. This conclusion should be tempered, however, by the observation that the two items of information were not gathered independently and that it would be surprising if the aspirations of many students and of their parents were not coloured by the process of program selection and/or assignment which had been completed shortly before our questionnaire was administered. The direction of influence is, in this case, an uncertain one. In this analysis we will assume that the relationship is uni-directional. Figure 10.3 shows this relationship. When a student had aspirations for university it would appear that he or she was almost certain to be placed in a five-year program (93 per cent). Those with other post-secondary aspirations (e.g., nursing or a community college

Figure 10.3
Program by Aspirations After Leaving High School,
Grade 8

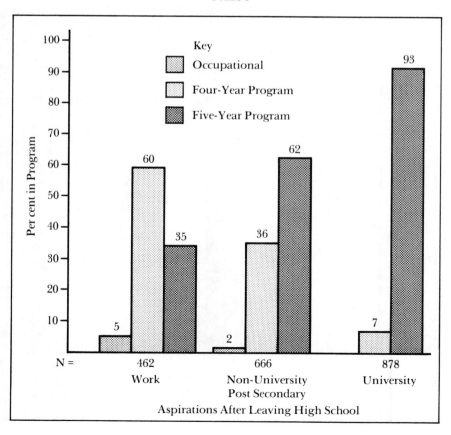

program) were more likely to be placed in a five-year program than not, but over a third of these students were in a four-year program, and a small number even ended up in an occupational stream. In the case of those students who wished to work after high school, the majority were placed in either four-year programs or in an occupational program (60 and 5 per cent respectively), and just over a third were placed in a five-year program.

The next in order of importance is grades. The fact that grades are associated with program is not in itself surprising. What is perhaps surprising is the relative weakness of the association given the high degree of importance attached to this factor by school officials. However, a look at Figure 10.4 showing the relationship between grades and program further clarifies the picture. In looking at those students above the median, the

Figure 10.4
Program by Grades in Quartiles, Grade 8

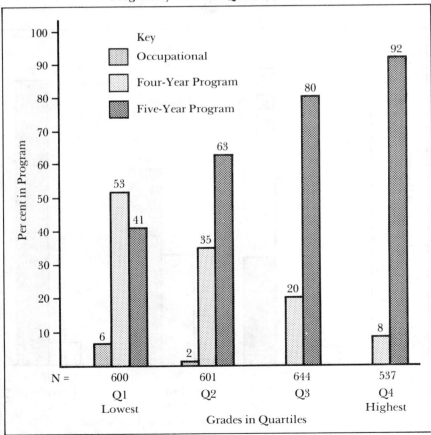

situation is relatively clear. Over 90 per cent of those in the highest quartile of the distribution were placed in a five-year stream, and 80 per cent of those in the second highest quartile were placed in a five-year stream. When we come to look at the students whose grades lie below the median, things become less clear. The same general relationship continues to hold: the higher the grades the higher the stream placement. Regardless of grades, the proportion of students in the five-year stream remains substantial (41 per cent in the first quartile and 63 per cent in the second quartile). However, the factors which would permit a differentiation between those students who scored in the two bottom quartiles, and who were variously allocated to five-year, four-year and occupational streams, are not clear from this table.

Figure 10.5 shows the relationship between the students' social class and their placement by stream. This table conforms to the distribution

Figure 10.5
Program by Socio-economic Status, Grade 8

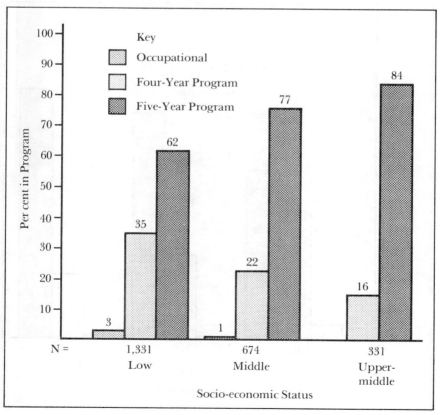

noted earlier in our examination of Grade 12 students, and confirms the findings in the literature concerning the relationship between stream and social class.[13] Over 80 per cent of the students from the upper-middle class were in the five-year stream, whereas only 60 per cent of the students from lower-class backgrounds were similarly placed.

When the relationship between stream and mental ability is looked at, a moderate relationship is found (Figure 10.6). However, as the results from our tests were not available to the schools as part of their decision making process, this factor will not be considered as part of the process in the later stages of our analysis.

Clearly, the two most important factors in the allocation of students were their grades and their aspirations. We will now look further at the

10.6
Program by Mental Ability, Grade 8

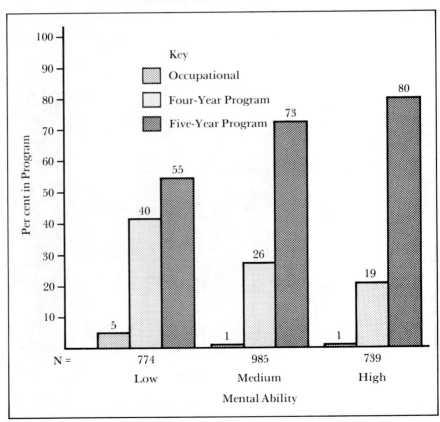

Table 10.10
Percentage in Five-Year Program
by Grades and Aspirations

	Grades	
Aspirations	Above Median	Below Median
Work	46 (52)	31 (99)
Post-secondary but not University	83 (244)	46 (158)
University	96 (541)	96 (241)

inter-relationship between these two factors and social class in the determination of stream.

Table 10.10 shows the percentage of students in five-year programs by aspirations controlling for grades. The prime determinant of program allocation would appear to involve an interaction between grades and aspirations. This interaction divides the allocations into three clear groupings. First, when the student had grades which were above the median and had university aspirations, allocation to a five-year stream would seem to have been virtually automatic. Secondly, where the student's grades were above the median and the student had post-secondary aspirations, or when the student had university aspirations but grades below the median, the chances of assignment to a five-year stream were very high. For those students in the remaining three categories, the chances of being in a five-year program were much lower.

Table 10.11
Percentage of Students in a Five-Year Program
by Aspirations, Grades and Socio-economic Status

	Aspirations		
Grades	Work	Other Post-Secondary	University
Below Median:			
Upper-middle	47 (7)	48 (11)	85 (41)
Middle	33 (21)	52 (49)	85 (69)
Lower	29 (59)	43 (88)	86 (108)
Above Median:			
Upper-middle	83 (5)	88 (23)	96 (124)
Middle	56 (14)	85 (68)	96 (171)
Lower	43 (32)	82 (147)	96 (222)

An examination of the effect of social class on stream (Table 10.11) shows that within the three most favoured categories of the aspiration-grades interaction, social class makes no difference. Of the three remaining groups in the interaction, social class seems to have an effect only when the students' aspirations are to go to work after leaving high school. Here the higher social class of the student, the more likely it is that he or she will be in a five-year program. However, even these differences are not large if we ignore the upper-middle-class cells where the numbers are too small to be considered.

It would appear that the process of getting students into programs was one which operated in a universalistic manner. Those students who had high grades and high aspirations were very likely to be in a five-year stream regardless of their origin, and those who had lower aspirations and/or lower grades were less likely to be in a five-year stream. For this latter group, social class made a slight difference, but on the whole it was a small one.

If the decision making process is a relatively universalistic one, how then do we account for the strong relationship between social class and program which can be clearly seen in Figure 10.5? The answer lies in the fact that neither grades nor aspirations are independent of social class.

Tables 10.12 and 10.13 give the distribution of grades and aspirations respectively by social class. As can be seen, both are clearly related to it. In the case of grades, almost two-thirds of the upper-middle-class students had grades above the median, while less than half of the lower-class students scored that well. Turning to aspirations, it is evident that almost three-quarters of the upper-middle-class students aspired to university, compared to just under a half of the middle-class students and just over a third of the lower-class students. While socio-economic status is clearly more strongly related to aspirations than to grades, the latter relationship is by no means negligible.

To look at the combined relationship of these three variables we have created a new variable based on the decision rules for stream allocation

Table 10.12
Grades by Socio-economic Status

Grades	Upper-middle	Middle	Lower	Total
		Socio-economic Status		
	(per cent)			
Above the median	66	52	45	50
Below the median	34	48	55	50
Total	100	100	100	100
N =	353	690	1,382	2,425

discussed earlier. This variable combines grades and aspirations into two groups: more favoured for five-year allocation (university aspirations regardless of grades, and grades above the median with aspirations to non-university post-secondary schooling); and less favoured for five-year allocation (aspirations to work after high school regardless of grades, and grades below the median combined with other post-secondary aspirations). It will be recalled from the discussion of Table 10.11 that for the former group (more favoured) the allocation to a five-year program was a virtual certainty (per cent so allocated ranges from 96 to 82), with only slight social class effects for those whose grades were above the median and who aspired to other post-secondary; and that for the latter, the likelihood of five-year allocation was much lower and, further, was weakly related to social class.

Table 10.14 illustrates the relationship between this created variable and social class. The table clearly shows the way in which this seemingly universalistic decision rule favours the socio-economically privileged and generates the distribution of status by program, which was viewed earlier. Over 80 per cent of the upper-middle-class students were in the more-favoured category compared with just over one-half of the lower social class students. Thus, most of those students who come from privileged backgrounds have no need of particularistic rules to assist them on their way, whereas almost half of those from the least well-off background fall into the less favoured decision group. Indeed, if we use this table as a prediction table for the distribution of program (five-year, other) by social class, we would find that only 9.5 per cent of the cases would be misallocated.

In sum, two conclusions about the process of program allocation can be made. First, on the surface the process is a fair one. As factors, grades and aspirations are clearly the most important, and allocation decisions are by and large congruent with them. In combination these two factors account for most of the variability in stream allocation, especially in the combina-

Table 10.13
Aspirations by Socio-economic Status

Aspirations	Upper-middle	Middle	Lower	Total
	Socio-economic Status			
	(per cent)			
Work	8	17	28	22
Other post-secondary	20	34	37	34
University	72	49	35	44
Total	100	100	100	100
N =	293	573	1,168	2,034

Table 10.14
Program Allocation Status by Socio-economic Status

Program Allocation Status	Upper-middle	Socio-economic Status Middle	Lower	Total
		(per cent)		
Most favoured	83	64	52	60
Least favoured	17	36	48	40
Total	100	100	100	100
N =	282	555	1,109	1,946

tion we have labelled the most favoured group. Once these two factors have been considered, the direct effect of other factors (mental ability, mother's aspirations, social class), either singly or in combination, is very small. Second, while the direct effect of social class on stream allocation is negligible once the impact of grades and aspirations has been controlled for, this factor has a very strong indirect effect due to the relationship of social class to both of these factors. The well-off, then, do not need special rules to favour them; the universalistic rules of the present system favour them quite well enough.[14]

To the extent that the program system served as a mechanism whereby the process of status transmission was carried on, this operation was on the whole a blind one. There is little in our data to suggest that in weighing the available evidence the officials of the system acted to favour one group at the expense of others. However, when the student was placed in a program, his or her educational future was largely determined. The fortunate students who entered a five-year program entered the broad channel leading to higher education and had the opportunity to get a university education. On the other hand, those entering a four-year or occupational program were routed off into side streams which very likely led to early termination of schooling and early entry into the labour force, or to the pool of the unemployed.

What becomes clear from these data is that if we wish to understand why, even operating in a "fair" way, the schools end up by reproducing in large measure the class structure of the previous generation, then we must look back beyond decisions about program and seek to answer two questions: Why do the most privileged consistently have the highest aspirations and the least the lowest? And why and how do the most privileged consistently and disproportionately manage to achieve the grades and other evidence of attainment that serve to make their aspirations more realistic than those of the others?

Notes

1. William G. Fleming, *Education: Ontario's Preoccupation* (Toronto: University of Toronto Press, 1972), pp.179-183.
2. See William G. Fleming, *Ontario's Educative Society*, Vol.III (Toronto: University of Toronto Press, 1971), chapters 4-6 for a much more detailed discussion of these issues.
3. David M. Cameron, *Schools for Ontario: Policy Making Administration and Finance in the 1960's* (Toronto: University of Toronto Press, 1972), p.164.
4. Fleming, 1971, *op.cit.*
5. Cameron, *op.cit.*, pp.166-68.
6. *Ibid.*, p.167.
7. *Ibid.*, p.168.
8. The Colleges of Applied Arts and Technology (CAATs), popularly called Community Colleges, were established in Ontario in 1965 as an entirely different post-secondary experience from the university. Unlike some other provinces, British Columbia, Alberta and Quebec for example, it was intended that there should be no system of transfer from them to the universities.
9. See for example, Robert Rosenthal and Lenore Jacobson, *Pygmalion in the Classroom* (New York: Holt, Rhinehart and Winston, 1968) described in Chapter 7 on self-concept of ability.
10. Raymond Breton, "Academic Stratification in Secondary Schools and the Educational Plans of Students," in *Canadian Review of Sociology and Anthropology* (Vol.7, 1970), pp.17-34; and Sidney N. Gilbert and Hugh A. McRoberts, "Academic Stratification and Educational Plans: A Reassessment," in *Canadian Review of Sociology and Anthropology* (Vol.14), pp.34-47.
11. In 1965 the Ontario government appointed a commission chaired by Justice E.M. Hall and L.A. Dennis to examine primary education in the province. In 1968 they published their controversial report entitled *Living and Learning*.
12. *Living and Learning*, p.186.
13. Breton, *op.cit.*
14. See Karl L. Alexander, Martha Cook and Edward McDill, "Curriculum Tracking and Educational Stratification: Some Further Evidence," in *American Sociological Review* (Vol.43), pp.47-66, for very similar findings based upon the American experience.

11
Sex

Social scientists have used gender as a control variable in a myriad of studies, but only recently has sex been recognized as one of the most basic and pervasive categories by which society is structured and the division of labour is maintained. This form of the social structure, as the others to which sociologists have turned their attention, has many inter-related composite aspects. Sex structure is reflected in the occupational hierarchy with its related components of income, status and power; it is revealed in the educational system, primarily with respect to educational attainment and choice of disciplines; and it is most pervasively apparent in the fundamental unit of social organization, the family. Just as is true of other categories of social structure, sex structure has a value hierarchy attached to it, as revealed both in the beliefs commonly held concerning stereotyped sex character which are positively or negatively valued, and the differing social importance attached to the conventional roles of men and women. When male-female differences become the prime focus of attention in this study, an entirely different light is shed on the data and on the social situation which they reflect. The purpose in this chapter is to examine the sex structure of this society as it is revealed in a comparison primarily of educational aspirations, but also of occupational expectations, of boys and girls.

During the past twenty years women have rediscovered some of the facts concerning their subordinate role in Western society, and are upstaging other waves of protesters in making their claims heard and their dissatisfactions felt. The correct word is "rediscover," because other eras have witnessed large movements of women taking to the streets in protest, for example, during the long and bitterly fought struggle for the vote; invading the economic sphere, particularly during the Second World War; and assuming numerically significant proportions in the graduate schools in Canada during the decade of the 1930s.[1] However, the benefits from each of these gains, the lessons learned, were at each stage lost. After the victory of winning the vote, the suffrage movement suddenly, without specifically articulated purpose, disintegrated. After the Second World War, women were convinced that they should leave their new-found occupations and return to their homes. This evacuation from the labour force was accelerated by the sudden withdrawal of government-sponsored day care centres.

However, the present wave of discovery of the unequal status of women is different in that it is inspiring a more fully articulated statement of the problem as it touches every sphere of life:[2] the occupational structure, the educational system, the political system, the family, as well as the basis of the inequality in all areas, as Kate Millett so aptly phrased the politics of personal relations between the sexes. This deluge of written material, some popularized, some academic, on the social conditions of women in the Western, primarily English-speaking countries, is providing a basis for social theory on the inequality between the sexes. Women, divided socially and psychologically by socio-economic status, ethnicity, race and the family, represent the last oppressed group in society to attain any degree of self-conscious awareness of their objective social position and social status.

Whereas before the Industrial Revolution women performed essential economic functions in the home as well as a role in the economic sector through such institutions as cottage industry, after the Industrial Revolution women were relegated primarily to the home, with only a secondary and subordinate role (which was usually a sign of deprivation) in the occupational structure of the society.[3] Since that time also, the work of the household has become increasingly less demanding and less fulfilling. The net result of this loss of function is that, in increasing proportions, particularly since the turn of the century, women have turned to the occupational structure for work. Since their roles as mothers, cooks and housekeepers were considered to be of primary importance (and men, of course, had an obvious stake in maintaining this status quo, both for their own comfort and for minimizing competition in the occupational sphere), work outside the home was always seen as peripheral. However, there is no reason at this stage, with fewer children, lighter housekeeping chores and easier food preparation, why women should be made to maintain this order of priority. For the most part, however, this division of labour has been maintained, primarily by means of individually restricting and outmoded conceptions of "masculinity" and "feminity," which are still strongly adhered to by the majority of both men and women in the society.

The Development of Educational Aspirations:
Gender-Related Factors

The position taken here is that the socialization of girls and the life expectations which girls have, as a result of both this process and a realistic appraisal of the roles which they currently see adult females performing, are inconsistent with academic success and achievement. To examine this position, two highly inter-related questions will be posed: first, what patterns of success and failure do girls exhibit in the educational system? and second, to the extent that the phenomena are understood, why do they behave in these ways?

The most general statement that can be made to characterize the pattern which males and females exhibit in elementary and high school is that girls are initially more successful in school in terms of achievement as measured by grades, and that this early success tapers off during the later years of high school; males, on the other hand, after a less promising beginning, start to excel at about this time and prove to be more successful in the educational system over the long run.[4] This general reversal in degree of, and interest in, academic success, coming as it does in the crucial last years of high school, means that girls are less likely to plan for the kinds of occupations in diverse fields of which their early all-round academic success indicates they are capable. Why do girls do well initially at school, and why do they lose interest or possibly ability in later years, which in turn discourages them from pursuing their education? Briefly, the theory is that in the early sex role socialization in the family girls are encouraged to be dependent and boys independent. The elementary school in North America is a female sphere of influence in which the same process continues.

Just as boys assert their autonomy from their mothers through negativistic and independent behaviour, so they must resist identification with the school which represents a female activity. On the other hand, the school environment which, via the teacher, values obedience, decorum and the inhibition of aggression favours the traits already internalized by girls through identification with their mothers and other female role models (most importantly, the teacher). This, plus a stronger desire for adult approval and acceptance, leads girls to perform better academically in the first years of school.

As schooling continues, changes occur in the attitudes which boys and girls have towards education. Maccoby suggests that the social pressures to do well or poorly may have a reverse time sequence for the sexes, and she further suggests that the achievement drop-off among girls as they reach maturity is linked to the adult female sex role.[5] For girls, correlations between ability and achievement are high during early school years, but later pressures are exerted on intelligent girls not to do as well as they might. The social pressures on girls to turn their attention away from academic success, and even to consciously lower their academic performance, have been explored by several writers such as Coleman,[6] Douvan and Adelson[7] and Komarovsky,[8] among others. On the other hand, a reverse situation is apparent for boys who are initially engaged in an effort to achieve autonomy and are therefore less likely to accede to the demands of female teachers and perform well at school. Two changes take place over time which lead boys to value academic success. First, there is a change in perception of the sex-typed character of the school, and indeed, the high school has more male teachers, and new subjects are introduced into the curriculum which boys feel free to identify with since they are associated with males in this culture. Second, boys, particularly middle-class boys, are under pressure in high school to succeed in order to qualify for university. For boys education becomes intrinsically linked to future occupations, to success and to personal identity. In the minds of girls, on the other hand, education is less important to future identity and success, while popularity with boys, interpersonal relationships, attractiveness and social poise become more coveted identifying features.[9] Girls, despite the fact that the typical girl graduating from high school today may expect to spend twenty-five years of her life working outside the home,[10] are loath to plan for occupations and to see themselves in terms of those occupations, because they consider their future roles as wives and mothers to be their primary goals and anything else to be, if necessary, basically undesirable.

Self-concept of ability is another important factor determining a female's educational aspirations, since a low self-concept figures prominently in the persistently low aspiration level of girls, as was demonstrated in Chapter 7. Self-concept is closely linked to future role expectations in two ways. First, because independence is not encouraged in young girls by parents, girls do not develop self-confidence in their ability to cope with their environment. Since girls also receive less encouragement from parents to continue with their education (particularly lower-class girls whose parents maintain more traditional ideas concerning sex roles), and precisely because they have been reared to be overly dependent on the opinions of others, this lack of encouragement takes a high toll in terms of low aspirations. Second, a diminished self-concept comes in part from observing the roles which women actually do play in society.

It is obvious that by the end of high school girls have experienced a different kind of "world" from boys, and that they anticipate a very different life for themselves in the future. For boys education and occupation are closely related, and boys realize their ambitions and attain their status through their occupations. Girls are taught to realize their ambitions through marriage and to accept passively the social status which their husbands bring them. The result of this different experience which girls have by way of socialization and perception of future roles is best seen in the area of higher education.

When all institutions of post-secondary education in Ontario are examined, it is found that men constitute 61 per cent of the enrolment, women 38 per cent.[11] When these figures are further broken down into undergraduate university and post-secondary non-university (community colleges, schools of teaching and nursing), it is found that girls are under-represented in the university (70 per cent of the males and 56 per cent of the females) and over-represented in non-university institutions (22 per cent of the males and 40 per cent of the females). Three per cent of the women are in graduate schools, and 7 per cent of the males.

Throughout this volume we have repeatedly indicated, with respect to the various variables we have analysed, the differences between males and females, but with only minimal attempts at explanation. The literature that we have just reviewed offers guidance for a more thorough analysis.

In Chapter 5 we demonstrated the different educational aspirations of boys and girls in the three grades surveyed, and we pointed out that though there was almost no difference in the proportions of boys and girls in Grade 8 who wanted to go to work immediately after leaving high school, in Grade 12 twelve per cent more girls than boys wanted to follow that course. We suggested that the shift might be interpreted as a modification by girls of their aspirations in the light of the reality that they found. After a consideration of the literature in this chapter, it is to be expected that the gap will increase between the educational aspirations of boys and girls over the years, primarily because both sexes are becoming more aware and more realistic about the adult role that they will soon have to assume. Boys become increasingly aware of planning for the occupation that they must have throughout their adult lives. As a result, their interests will be directed away from going out to work directly after high school, and into the various training and educational institutions, such as community colleges, business colleges and universities. Taking cue from Ginzberg's typology on the phases of occupational choice, we see the student progressing from a "fantasy" stage of choice to a "tentative" period in which personal interests, capacity and values are more realistically taken into account.[12] Ginzberg points out that up to this "tentative" phase, boys and girls exhibit much the same pattern. Although he does not make the point, the occupational choices which are made up to that stage are probably highly sex-typed. However, the stage at which Ginzberg noted the sexes differ is in the transition to the final occupational selection. Boys at this stage look forward to college to help them resolve their dilemmas concerning occupational choice. When they enter college they are considering ways and means of eventually entering the work world, and they are concerned with the type and conditions of the work. Girls, on the other hand, view the work problem as peripheral, and see the future as largely outside their control. This is probably a function both of viewing work as a stop-gap measure to keep body and soul together until marriage, and the more limited selection facing women in making an occupational choice.[13] Girls, perceiving the adult role which awaits them and which is organized around husband and children, will be less likely to plan to enter institutions for further training, and in increasing numbers will plan to go directly to work after high school. Boys are directed by guidance branches of high school, to a certain extent, and by their parents, to a greater extent, to seek further training in order to obtain a better paying, more interesting job. For girls, further training is very often seen as a waste of time and money, since it is commonly thought that they will not use their skills for long (or even at all) in the work world. As mentioned above, despite the fact that the average woman leaving school today will spend twenty-five years of her life actively participating in the labour force, women are not encouraged or expected to improve their skills in order to up-grade their work potential.

Another related reason for the different trends exhibited by boys and girls in educational aspirations pertains to the realities of the occupational structure. There are two points to be made here: one relates to actual access into the occupational structure, and the other to the traditional attitudes concerning gender specific occupations on the part of both employers and employees.[14] Large numbers of women, without much formal training, assume clerical positions directly after high school. Positions such as these have relatively low status, but they are perceived as proper and acceptable positions for women, and they do afford some job security. There are few or no corresponding positions which are seen as suitable and which are open to men directly after high school.

Because education, although generally considered to be a positive good in its own right, is instrumental in terms of future occupational choice, data will be considered at certain points in this chapter on the occupational expectations of men and women. There are many problems involved in ranking women in an occupational scale, due primarily to the fact, as noted above, that women are heavily represented in very few occupations. When a man expects to have a high status occupation, he could be thinking of a variety of different types of employment; however, a woman with high occupational aspirations would probably be planning to be a teacher in elementary or high school, a librarian or a social worker. All the professions in which women predominate (or semi-professions as these are usually termed), generally gain the position of "high status" because of the amount of education required, but they do not carry with them the same high social status or esteem as those in which men predominate (for example, law or medicine).[15]

In Chapter 6 we showed the occupational expectations for Grade 10 boys and girls. Table 6.2 showed that a lower proportion of girls expected to have high status occupations, which follows, in part, from their lower educational aspirations. Over half the girls expected to have occupations in the middle range, while the male expectations are more evenly distributed through the scale. As noted earlier, there is fairly easy access for women into middle-range occupations requiring a minimum amount of training. This is probably one important reason why girls are not encouraged as boys are to seek higher training.

Some of the factors that contribute to the probability of different levels of aspirations for boys and girls are social class and religion. Since their impact on aspirations was analysed in Chapter 5, we will not go into their effects here, other than to repeat briefly the conclusions. The aspirations of upper-middle-class girls differed very little from the aspirations of upper-middle-class boys, but in the middle and lower classes the aspirations of girls lagged far behind those of boys. This can be explained by the differences in sex role socialization by class, the greater availability of resources in the upper-middle classes and the growth of the women's movement, at present a primarily middle-class movement. When the data on educational aspirations by religion are controlled for social class, the differences for males of all social classes disappear, but for girls religion remains a significant factor. For girls of lower-class backgrounds, university aspirations vary from 19 per cent of the Catholic faith to 38 per cent of girls with "other" religious affiliations. It might be said, then, that religious affiliation makes a difference for girls in terms of educational aspirations, regardless of social class, compounding the effects of social class and sex.

Mother's Occupation and the Effect of a Working Mother

There are three main questions which arise in relation to these data when considering the effect of the mother's role in the labour force:

First, does the fact of whether or not the mother is actually working outside the home while the children are in school have an effect on the educational aspirations of the student?

Second, does the status of the mother's occupation have an effect on the educational aspirations of the children? Does it have a different effect depending on whether or not the mother is currently using her skills in the labour force?

Third, does the fact of whether or not the mother is working outside the home while the children are in school have any effect on the daughter's expectations of her future activity in the labour force?

For this part of the analysis, data will be taken from the parent interviews,* due primarily to the very large proportion of missing data on the occupations of mothers not at present working outside the home as reported by the students. Only 53 per cent of the students whose mothers were not currently working were able to report the mother's previous occupation. The problem encountered when using the data for mother's occupation from the parent interviews is the very small number of respondents reporting an occupation which is classified as high status. In the Grade 12 sample there are only 71 mothers (about 9 per cent of the sample) with high status occupations, of whom only 43 were actively employed at the time of the study.

---

*This data source will be used in all parts of this section pertaining to Family Factors, with the exception of Parents' Level of Education, Family Size, and Birth Order.

In considering the first question posed in this section, our data show that the fact of whether or not the mother was currently working had no significant effect on the educational aspirations of the children. Therefore, mothers working *per se* makes no overall difference, and the slight variations which the data indicate may be attributed as easily to the fact that mothers who were working were slightly more likely to have high status occupations than mothers who were not as to the fact of whether or not they were currently employed outside the home.

The second question pertains to the occupational status of mothers. Our data show that male university aspirations ranged from 38 to 69 per cent by mother's occupational status, while the university aspirations of daughters ranged from 19 per cent to 62 per cent. For the daughters, aspirations to work ranged from 10 per cent for those whose mothers had high status occupations, to 40 per cent for those whose mothers had low status occupations.

Related to this question was a further interest in whether or not the mother's occupational status had a different effect on the educational aspirations of the children depending on whether or not she was currently employed outside the home. Our data indicate that regardless of present participation, mother's occupational status, which is highly correlated with social class, had a significant effect on the educational aspirations of both sons and daughters, and in both cases this effect was stronger for girls than boys. Very little can be said about the effect of high status occupations of mothers, since introducing the further control diminishes the numbers to 22 or less. However, for mothers of low occupational status, it is interesting to note that if the mothers were currently employed, the daughters were more likely to aspire to university (23 per cent compared with 14 per cent) and were less likely to aspire to work (37 per cent compared with 43 per cent). This observation might be related to the fact that there would be additional money from the mother's working to be used by the family; or perhaps it is related to the fact that if a daughter perceives her future role to include employment outside the home, she may wish to upgrade her work potential in order to achieve a more interesting, more lucrative position.

The third question pertains to a daughter's expectations of labour force participation by the mother's working status. In the questionnaire, the girls were asked if they expected to work full or part time before they married, after they married when their children were young, and after their children were grown. The data correspond to the typical pattern of female labour force participation: work before marriage and after children have grown. The majority of respondents indicated that they would work before marriage regardless of their mothers' working status. However, the data show that a daughter's expectations of future labour force participation after marriage depend to some extent on the mother's current employment status. Very few expected that they would work full-time when they have young children, but 58 per cent of those whose mothers worked indicated that they would work part-time during this stage, compared with 43 per cent of those whose mothers were not currently employed. Forty-four per cent of those whose mothers were working indicated that they would work full-time after their children were grown, compared with 34 per cent of those whose mothers were not working. Thus, the role model presented by the mother does influence a girl's expectations of her future labour force participation to a certain extent.

Mother's Level of Education

The level of education attained by the parents, and particularly by the father, will be closely related to the social class status of the family. Certain researchers have argued strongly that the parental level of education is a better indicator of the educational aspirations of the children than any other variable, including social class, combined family income, and father's occupation.[16] In this section we will examine the different effect of the mother's educational level on the aspirations of male and female children.

The importance of role models has already been examined in the review of the literature, and it is assumed here, therefore, that the mother's level of education will have a greater effect on the educational aspirations of girls than of boys. In the 1968 Bureau of Statistics study, "Educational Attainment in Canada: Some Regional and Social Aspects," Lagacé examined the main characteristics of inter-generational change in educational attainment. The major conclusion drawn from that section of the study was that,

> the highest degree of inheritance (in educational attainment) occurs between university trained parents and sons or daughters. Furthermore, the strongest relationship at this level of parental attainment arises between mothers and daughters, where the index (of association) reaches a value of 5.4. In all other cases concerning university-trained parents and sons or daughters, the value of the index is about 4.0.[17]

From this conclusion, the importance of the female role model and also, probably, the high expectations on the part of a university-trained woman that her daughter will go to university can be clearly seen.

Figure 11.1 presents data showing the correlation between mother's level of education and the proportion of sons and daughters who were in Grade 12 and who aspired to university. The effect that a university-trained mother has on a daughter's educational aspirations is clearly evident from this graph. This is one of those rare situations in which the university aspirations of the female cohort are actually higher than those of the male, albeit by an extremely small margin. A similar graph depicting the educational aspirations of students and the fathers' level of education shows an even stronger correlation between university-educated fathers and the university aspirations of the sons. Since more fathers have a university education than mothers (in this study approximately three times as many), fewer girls than boys have either the role model or maternal expectations which appear so influential in encouraging them to pursue their education.

Family Size

Family size is an important variable in examining the educational aspirations, as we have suggested in Chapter 5, partly because of its close

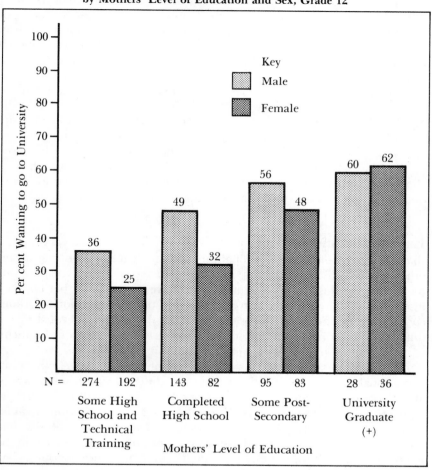

Figure 11.1
Per cent Wanting to Graduate from University,
by Mothers' Level of Education and Sex, Grade 12

association with social class. Large families tend also to be lower-class families. Parents with large families have more difficulty in maintaining children in school, both because of the expense of child rearing and because of their low incomes. In cases where a choice is even feasible, parents must decide upon which child should be sent to university to continue being educated.[18] Because of the present-day sex structure, reflected both in attitudes to the adult female role and in differing values placed on the education of males and females, the child most often chosen to go is a son. Because the role of the adult male is centred around his occupation, and that of a female around her family, the returns are obviously perceived as greater for educating a son than a daughter. Thus, family structural factors such as family size and sibling position will have a greater effect in lowering the educational aspirations of girls than of boys.

The data show that a girl has the best chance of aspiring to university if she is an only child. As the size of the family increases, a girl's chances of aspiring to university drops radically. University aspirations for males drop significantly in families in which there are five or more children, but even in that situation first-born males have relatively high aspirations relating to university.

Figure 11.2 shows the proportion of males and females aspiring to university and to work by size of family. The graph exhibits clearly the rapid and large decline in the proportion of girls aspiring to university as family size increases, and a corresponding rise in work aspirations.

These data give an indication of the different value or priority placed on the education of males and females. Girls, it would seem, have the best chance of aspiring to university if there is little or no competition from others within the family for further education.

Parental Educational Aspirations

In our chapters on self-concept of ability and on the influence of significant others we have discussed the importance of parental educational aspirations on children's educational aspirations. We have pointed out that boys are more likely than girls to have high educational aspirations without considering carefully the reasons for this. In this chapter devoted to the different educational aspirations of boys and girls and the reasons for them, we will look at some of these data again from this perspective.

Since parental attitudes are so important in the development of educational aspirations, it follows that since different values are traditionally placed on the education of boys and girls, children will in turn reflect these attitudes. Part of the socialization process is the inculcation of values from parents to offspring, and their success in the area of sex role socialization has already been documented. This, in turn, is reflected in the lower educational aspirations of female children. Since working-class

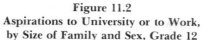

Figure 11.2
Aspirations to University or to Work,
by Size of Family and Sex, Grade 12

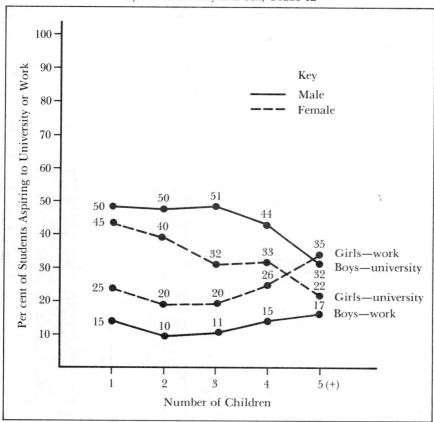

parents have a more traditional conception of the sex roles than their middle-class counterparts, it follows that their daughters will have the lowest educational aspirations. Lower-class girls have both social class and stronger sexist pressures working against high educational aspirations.

In this survey the higher classes' aspirations differ for sons and daughters only in minor proportions, although these are in the expected direction. However, there is a 20 per cent difference in university aspirations between sons and daughters in middle-class families and a 25 per cent difference for sons and daughters of lower-class families. This evidence supports the finding on the effect of social class aspirations of boys and girls that the higher the socio-economic standing the closer the educational aspirations for boys and girls. It also lends support to the more general

Figure 11.3
Correlations Between Students' Educational Aspirations
and Mothers' Educational Aspirations, by Sex, Grade 12

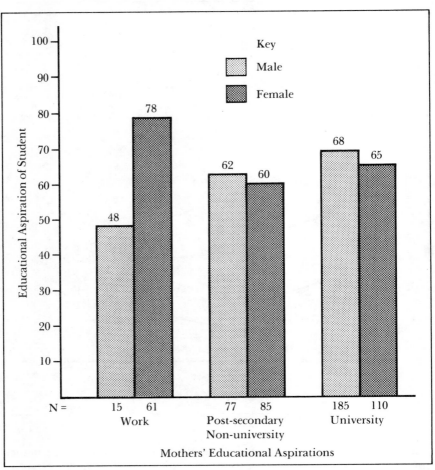

finding that lower-class families have, as a result of both belief system and necessity, more traditional ideas concerning the role of women.

Figure 11.3 indicates the correlation between mothers' educational aspirations and students' educational aspirations for the Grade 12 sample. The highest correlation is for girls aspiring to work whose mothers wanted them to go to work after high school. Seventy-eight per cent of girls whose mothers wanted them to work also wanted to do so. Less than half the boys whose mothers wanted them to work wanted to do that; and in fact, though it is not shown on this graph, of the boys whose mothers wanted them to work, 29 per cent wanted to go to a community college or a university. In this respect males show much more independence of action, as might be expected from the literature cited earlier. It also suggests that there is some other intermediary force at work for the boys between family and educational aspirations that is not influencing the girls.

Parental Attitude Towards the Role of Women

In examining the attitudes towards the role of women, it would be useful to have as a reference point a continuum which reflects traditional attitudes on the one hand and a more modern set of attitudes on the other. Komarovsky used a "feminine-modern" typology, and she saw the conflict between these two ideal types as centring around academic work, social life, vocational plans, excellence in specific fields and a number of personality traits.[19] Kammeyer employed a similar typology in his research, but restated it in terms of a "traditional-modern" continuum. Again, the conflict revolved around the orientation to the female role and beliefs about "feminine" personality traits.[20] The traditional view perceives the female role as centred about home and family, and the feminine person as nurturant, passive, unintellectual, socially poised and friendly. On the other end of the continuum, the modern woman has a more career-oriented perspective, and she is more independent, personally aggressive and more concerned with the development of her own skills and abilities.

The attitudes that parents have towards the adult female role will have a great influence on the growth and development of the children. As we explained in Chapter 4, parent respondents were asked to give their opinions on the importance of household work, volunteer work, skills, children and a "mutually rewarding relationship with a man" for the adult female. In examining the data on these five indicators of the mothers' attitudes to the adult female role, a number of problems are encountered. First, there were very few mothers who did not highly value the traditional sex role, and therefore the marginals are heavily weighted to that end of the continuum. As a result, there is very little that can be said concerning the effect of "modern" ideas on the educational aspirations of the daughters. Second, the indicator which was to tap career ambitions of mothers for their daughters, and which theoretically would have been the most important one for this paper, was omitted from the parental interview form. An attitude towards the career question was asked of the female students and will be examined later in the section in which student attitudes to the adult female role are studied. The next most relevant indicator was the importance for a girl to "have a career that would require her to develop skills and would give her independence." This question concerning skills was interpreted very broadly by the respondents and was widely held as a positive value by the mothers being questioned. It had very little relationship to high educational aspirations on the part of the daughters, since "skills" could just as easily and legitimately be interpreted to mean the skills of typing and shorthand, with which it is widely known that a girl can "always get a job," as to mean the skills of a doctor or a lawyer.

Despite the overwhelmingly traditional attitudes expressed by the mothers who were interviewed, modest relationships can be found for three of the five indicators between "modern" attitudes and university aspirations of daughters.

The average proportion of daughters aspiring to a university education ranged from 25 per cent for daughters of traditional mothers to 40 per cent for daughters of mothers with more modern attitudes towards the adult female role. Given the overwhelmingly traditional bias exhibited by the mothers, these data cannot be taken as proof of the importance of such attitudes on the educational aspirations of women.

In sum, a number of variables pertaining to the family have been examined in order to observe their relationship to the educational aspirations of girls. These data are extremely important for the light they shed on two areas of interest: first, for the indication that they give of the extremely traditional milieu in which most girls are raised; and second, for the startling effect on the educational aspirations of girls when one or more of these traditional norms are broken. That the traditional sex role standards are still espoused by the majority of parents and pervade the family atmosphere is clear from the low educational aspirations of parents for their daughters, and from the traditional sex role attitudes held by the great majority of mothers. We get a further indication of this from the effect of family size and birth order on the educational aspirations of daughters as opposed to sons. On the other hand, when certain of these norms are broken in a particular family—when, for example, a mother has an upper-status occupation, a university education or high educational aspirations for her daughter—the educational aspirations of the daughters rise significantly. However, relatively few girls are as yet affected by such "modern" home environments, all of which are highly correlated with high social class and high educational expectations of them. Because the traditional sex role structure and patterns pervade most families, girls are still far from achieving educational equality.

Individual Factors

Some of the "individual factors" that might influence educational aspirations are mental ability, school performance and self-concept of ability. The different educational aspirations of boys and girls at different mental ability levels and at different levels of school performance have been sufficiently analysed in Chapters 5 and 9. However, self-concept of ability is such an important variable in accounting for the different educational aspirations of boys and girls that, although we have already analysed in Chapter 7 the factors that might contribute to it, we will examine it again here in relation to the goal of this chapter, i.e., to explain the differences between boys and girls. Two other variables that are illuminating with respect to female educational aspirations are attitudes towards schoolwork and to the adult female role. Both of these will be considered in this section.

Self-Concept of Ability

We pointed out in our chapter on self-concept of ability that at all ages boys are more likely to have a high self-concept of ability than girls, and as they get older the gap between the proportions of girls and boys with a high self-concept widens. Here we will offer some explanations for that phenomenon. It was found in the literature review that women have a relatively lower opinion of their ability than men, and that they maintain this low opinion despite evidence to the contrary, such as high grades at school. This low self-concept is in part a result of accepting the stereotyped image of the female as less able to cope intellectually and personally, and in part a result of the subordinate roles which women see other women generally performing in the society. The truly "feminine" woman does not compete with men but takes a secondary position to them, silently acknowledging their greater ability and judgement. The process becomes self-fulfilling. Women, thinking of themselves as less able, do not prepare themselves by obtaining further education or skills, and therefore they are, in fact, less able as adults to cope in various fields.

A recent piece of research on the development of self-concept lends some support to the hypothesis that the self-concept of females declines as they mature. It was found in a study of pupils in Grades 4, 6, 8 and 10 that the self-concepts of the girls in Grade 10 were significantly lower than both their male peers and all other female groups. Other age and sex comparisons were not found to be significant. In the discussion of these findings, the researcher points out that adolescence is the period of "most intense evaluation of roles as well as the apex of sex role development,"[21] and that the adolescent girl, recognizing that the role she is expected to assume is inferior in status and prestige, accepts and incorporates this evaluation. As a result, the self-concepts of girls decline as they adapt to the adult role.

In Chapter 7 we used a scale which we called SCA-U and which consisted of responses to questions relating to the student's perception of his/her ability to do university work. Here we will look at the individual items in discussing the differences between boys and girls.

From Figure 11.4 it can be seen that on each of the indicators relating to ability to do university work, girls lagged behind boys by 8 to 10 per cent. Despite the fact that the girls were doing better in terms of school grades than boys, more boys felt that they had the ability to complete university than girls, twice as many boys as girls thought that they had the ability to rank high in their university class, and nearly twice as many boys felt that they were very capable of doing graduate work. Even in their immediate classroom situation, in which it would be clear to the actual participants that girls performed better than boys, more boys than girls ranked themselves as "high" in comparison with their classmates.

Furthermore, lending some support to the piece of research noted above on the decline of female self-concept, it is found that when the items are examined for differences between Grade 8 and Grade 12 students, male concept increased on six of the indicators, including the indicators concerning ability to complete university (the proportion of males who ranked

Figure 11.4
High Self Rate of Ability on Four Indicators,
by Sex, Grade 12

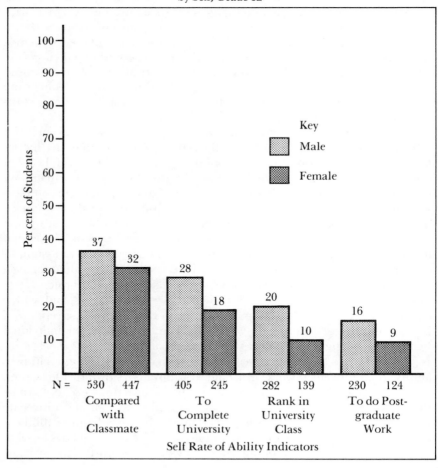

themselves as "high" rose from 15 to 28 per cent, females from 12 to 18 per cent), rank in university class (males rose from 17 to 20 per cent, while females went from 12 to 10 per cent), and ability to do post-graduate work (the self-concept of the males rose from 14 to 16 per cent, while that of the females declined from 14 to 9 per cent). Overall, in comparing the ranking on the items between Grade 8 and Grade 12 students, it is found that although the overall female self-concept of ability did not actually decline by Grade 12, it did not rise in equal proportions to that of the males. The end result is to leave the women proportionately even lower than the men on self-concept of ability by Grade 12.

Attitude to Schoolwork and School Performance

As seen in the literature review, from the beginning of school girls have a more positive attitude to school and schoolwork, they are more accepting of the demands made upon them by the school and are more eager to do well, thereby pleasing teachers and parents. It was also seen that the desire for approval which initiated the high academic achievement did not fully develop for girls into a desire for mastery of the actual subject matter as reward in itself. This was one reason for the slackening off of academic ambitions of girls towards the end of high school.

Girls in Grade 12 were proportionately more likely to have a positive attitude towards schoolwork than the boys. Thirty-nine per cent of the girls, compared with 31 per cent of the boys, had a positive attitude, while correspondingly 31 per cent of the boys had a negative attitude compared with 23 per cent of the girls.

However, while having a positive attitude towards schoolwork is correlated with university aspirations for boys, it has no such correlation for girls. From negative to positive attitude, the university aspirations of boys ranged from 36 to 45 per cent, while the university aspirations of girls, regardless of attitude towards schoolwork, remained fairly constant at about 30 per cent. Of the girls with a positive attitude towards schoolwork, equal proportions (about 30 per cent each) aspired to work, to post-secondary non-university institutions and to university. A higher proportion of girls with a positive attitude towards schoolwork aspired to work than girls with a negative attitude. It might be concluded from these data that a girl's attitude towards schoolwork has very little to do with a desire for learning or with academic ambitions. It would seem, rather, that the school environment suits older girls, just as it suits little girls, far better than it suits boys. Girls are more willing to accept instruction passively and to strive to do well in order to achieve good results. However, this would appear to have very little relation to high educational aspirations. In this respect, then, these data lend support to the information presented in the literature review on the nature of the academic success of girls in the high school.

Attitude Towards the Adult Female Role

As we mentioned earlier, girls in this survey were asked a set of six questions to try to determine their attitudes to the adult feminine role.

It is very difficult, perhaps impossible, to create a set of indicators which would be useful in determining the degree to which a young woman has a "traditional" or "modern" view of her adult role. It might be said that the traditional role of women is to marry, raise children, cook, keep house and participate in the community through volunteer work. At what point does one include in this traditional image of woman that she also has some skills which are saleable on the job market, which can be picked up, dropped and resumed relatively easily depending either on the family cycle or the need of additional money by the family? In actual fact, the completely domestic image of women as noted above has only been true for a short period of recent history and, even then, for only a small, relatively wealthy class of persons. Working outside the home has been a growing trend in the lives of all women, particularly since the turn of the century, and it is highly questionable whether this trend marks a significant change in the traditional role of women.[22]

At what point does the image become "modern"? Does the modern woman eschew all the traditional items in favour of a career? It is most unfortunate that the male respondents in the study were not asked a set of questions, complementary to those put to the female respondents, concerning their attitudes to the adult male role. How would the male respondents have weighed the various pulls between work and family life? Would a "modern" man be one who considered raising children and preparing a good meal to be as important as a career? Clearly, raising children, cooking food and removing dirt from floors are not activities which will conveniently disappear as women diversify their interests. Nor can most families afford to pay others to perform all these tasks for them. If women are in greater numbers coming to redefine their roles, then men will be obliged to do so also.

In this study, it is understandable that a large proportion of the girls endorsed fully all the items open to them as meaning "a great deal" to them. As a result, these young women in Grade 12 appear extremely traditional, positively endorsing as they do most of the traditional functions of women; and at the same time, 40 per cent felt that a long term career was very important to them. At this time of redefinition of the roles open to women, there is a great deal of confusion concerning what is suitable and proper for women. In this period of transition, individual tastes and choices are subordinated as many women, baffled by a changing image of what they should be, attempt to be everything: good homemakers, full-time mothers and career persons.

The six indicators of attitudes, which were originally four digit items, were collapsed to three digit scales since very few respondents felt that any

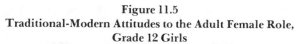

Figure 11.5
Traditional-Modern Attitudes to the Adult Female Role,
Grade 12 Girls

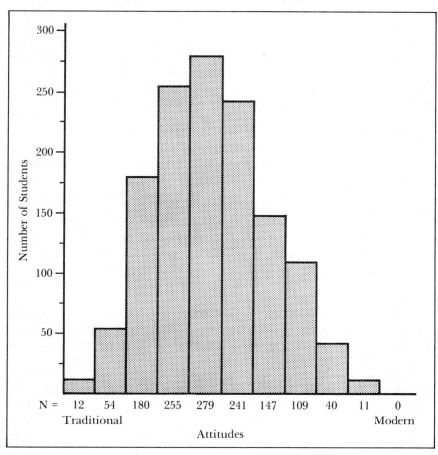

indicator meant "nothing" to them. As a result, the responses range from meaning "a great deal" to "a fair amount" to "not very much/nothing" to the respondents. Five of the items were selected for the "traditional-modern" scale used here. They were the importance of a career, community work, homemaking, job skills and children. The indicator on the importance of a man was eliminated since 95 per cent of the respondents felt that a mutually rewarding relationship with a man meant either "a great deal" (73 per cent) or "a fair amount" (22 per cent) to them.

The responses to each indicator were ordered from "traditional" to "modern" for the scale. The only indicator that might be controversial in this regard is the one dealing with job skills. A response that skills meant "a great deal" to the individual was taken as traditional. The reason for this is that the skills indicator is worded so as to suggest the picking up and dropping of occasional jobs in order to confer some sort of personal security, whereas the career indicator definitely implied a long-term commitment to some particular type of work which would involve learning and other intrinsic rewards. Proof that these indicators were interpreted in this way by the respondents is suggested by the significant correlation between the importance of a career and both high educational aspirations and high occupational expectations, and the non-significant relationship between the skills indicator and these two variables. Developing certain skills and having them at one's disposal does not necessarily involve a great deal of education nor a personal commitment to a particular occupation. It is, in fact, an "extension of traditional responsibilities, another way of nurturing the family."[23]

It should be clear, then, that "modern" on this continuum means that a career is very important and that community volunteer work, household work, job skills and children are not very important. Referring to the discussion above, it is certain that it would not be desirable if all people eschewed all these traditional functions of women. On the other hand, it is of great interest to witness the gradual transformation of attitudes of women away from the strictly traditional role that has placed a good many restrictions on their lives.

From Figure 11.5, which is a histogram of the number of girls who fall in each category of the traditional-modern continuum, it can be seen that the majority fall on the traditional side. However, it can also be seen that there is nothing like full-scale endorsement of the traditional package by these young women. Only twelve persons fall in the extreme "traditional" end of the continuum. These are the persons who completely endorsed the traditional items and indicated that a career meant "not very much" or "nothing" to them. No respondents fall in the extreme "modern" end of the continuum, which would mean that a career was very important and none of the traditional items were. The modal category (N=279) is just to the "traditional" side of the centre of the continuum.

It would be expected that girls showing a less traditional attitude towards the adult female role would have both higher educational aspirations and higher occupational goals. Table 11.1 shows that there is a significant relationship between educational aspirations and the adult female role scale. For this table, the first two categories from Figure 11.5 on the traditional side were grouped together, while the last four categories of the graph (excluding the empty cell) were collapsed in pairs. It can be seen from the table that aspirations to go to work directly after high school decline from 32 per cent to 8 per cent, while university aspirations rise in the expected direction from 23 per cent to 54 per cent. These trends show a

Table 11.1
Educational Aspirations by Scale on Attitudes to the Adult Female Role
(Grade 12 Girls)

Educational Aspirations	Attitude Scale						
	(Traditional)					(Modern)	
	1	2	3	4	5	6	7
	(per cent)						
Work	32	34	24	33	18	20	8
Post-secondary Non-university	34	34	34	30	32	28	26
University	23	23	28	27	37	36	54
Other/ Don't Know	11	9	14	10	13	16	12
Total	100	100	100	100	100	100	100
N =	65	179	248	271	240	245	50

$X^2 = 56.92$ p = .01

relatively steady progression, with the exception of the high proportion of respondents at the centre of the scale who aspire to work directly after high school (33 per cent in column 4).

Of some interest also in this table is the relatively high proportion of persons in column 6 who fall in the "Other/Don't Know" category (17 per

Table 11.2
Occupational Expectations by Scale on Attitudes to the Adult Female Role
(Grade 12 Girls)

Occupational Expectations	Attitude Scale						
	(Traditional)					(Modern)	
	1	2	3	4	5	6	7
	(per cent)						
High	25	18	25	24	30	30	54
Middle	54	63	61	60	55	55	34
Low	21	19	14	16	15	15	12
Total	100	100	100	100	100	100	100

$X^2 = 28.41$ p = .01

cent). This would suggest an atypically high degree of indecision, perhaps born out of confusion over the suitability of roles.

Table 11.2 shows the relationship between occupational expectations and the attitudinal scale. It is more difficult to perceive a correlation between the scale (and indeed, many other variables) and occupational goals for women since the vast majority of traditional female occupations fall in the middle range of the occupational scale. In the Blishen occupational scale, occupations generally defined as "female" (social worker, nurse) fall in the middle range, and at the same time, those involving steno-clerical work are also defined as middle status. The major "female" occupations which are considered high status are elementary school teacher and librarian, neither of which can be considered high status in terms of prestige or related income but achieve that position primarily due to the educational requirements. Even with these considerations in mind, there is a discernible relationship between occupational expectations and attitudes to the adult female role.

Whereas a quarter of the "traditional" respondents had high occupational expectations and a fifth had low expectations, on the "modern" end of the continuum over half the girls had high expectations and 12 per cent had low occupational expectations. Judging from the Chi square scores, the strength of this relationship is not as great as that with educational aspirations; however, this may be due as much to the problems of creating an occupational scale for women as to other factors.

When we broke down the scale to its composite items, it was clear that the main source for the strength of the relationship between educational aspirations and the attitude scale is the "career," "household" and, to a lesser extent, "children" indicators. The positive relationship between the attitudinal scale and occupational expectations stems mainly from the "career" and "household" indicators. This is important information and attests to the validity of these indicators on the adult female role. It is understandable that women who perceive a career as important to them realize that something in the traditional package will have to be relinquished, and the choice appears to be household work and, to a lesser extent, a large family.

The question of the relationship between attitudes and social class is always an important and pervasive one, and it might well be argued that the significant correlations between educational aspirations and the attitude scale, and occupational expectations and the attitude scale, are in fact another measure of social class. From Figure 11.6 it can be seen that there is a significant relationship between social class and the attitude scale. Fifty-one per cent of the upper-middle-class girls fall in the three cells on the "modern" end of the continuum as compared with 37 per cent of the lower-class girls and 44 per cent of the middle-class girls.

In order to test whether the attitudinal scale has any validity in and of

Figure 11.6
Attitude Scale on the Adult Female Role,
by Socio-economic Status, Grade 12 Girls

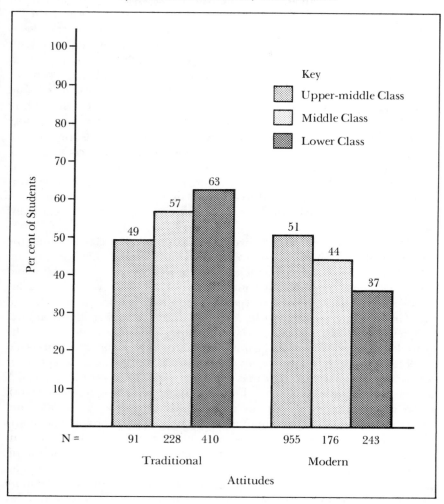

itself in relating to the educational aspirations of girls apart from social class, the original table must be controlled for socio-economic status. When this is done, it is found that the relationship is not significant statistically for either upper-middle or middle-class girls, although it is significant for lower-class girls. Even though the relationship is not statistically significant for upper-middle-class girls, the percentages still indicate a definite trend in which those with a "traditional" view of their adult role were more likely to plan to go to work after high school, while those with a "modern" view were proportionately more likely to plan to go to university. The same statement can also be made of the middle-class respondents, but the pattern is much less clear and direct. However, the relationship is very clear for lower-class girls. Forty-two per cent of those on the extreme traditional end of the continuum planned to go to work after high school compared with 17 per cent of those on the "modern" end. Similarly, the range of those who aspired to university was from 5 per cent of the "traditional" to 44 per cent of the "modern" girls. Thus, when controlled for social class, it is found that the attitude scale is most significant for lower-class girls. This finding probably reflects the fact that a post-secondary education is much more acceptable for upper-middle-class girls while it is not nearly as common for lower-class girls. Therefore, other factors must be taken into consideration when the high aspirations of lower-class girls are examined, such as the attitudes of the individual girl to her future role. Thus, social class explains much of the original relationship observed in Table 11.1, but the attitudes towards the adult female role have an independent effect on the aspirations of lower-class girls.

When the relationship between occupational expectations and the attitude scale is controlled for social class, it is found that the ensuing relationship is significant in the expected direction for both middle- and lower-class girls, and that although it is not statistically significant for upper-middle-class girls, the percentages indicate a similar pattern. It is of great interest that the relationship is maintained at a higher statistical level between the attitude scale and occupational expectations than between the attitude scale and educational aspirations. This is probably due to the fact, as noted above, that a university education is more widely accepted for women now than a life-long career and a personal investment in a career. A university-educated woman is as likely to find herself doing secretarial work upon graduation as any sort of more highly skilled work. Middle- and upper-middle-class women are more likely now to get a broad general arts education, and this sort of education is not a particularly useful one in terms of future employment. If a woman is interested in a long-term, personally demanding occupation, she must be more highly motivated than is at present necessary for a girl to aspire to university. She must be more determined to remould the traditional woman's role to suit her own needs and wants.

Notes

1. The proportion of women in graduate schools was larger in the 1930s than in the last decade. Derived from data presented on p.68 of the *Report of the Royal Commission on the Status of Women in Canada* (Ottawa, 1970).
2. See for example, Simone de Beauvoir, *The Second Sex* (New York: Drofft, 1961); Shulamith Firestone, *The Dialectic of Sex* (New York: Bantam, 1970); Vivian Gornick and Barbara K. Moran, *Women in Sexist Society* (New York: Basic Books, 1971); Anne-

Marie Henshel, *Sex Structure* (Don Mills: Longman, 1973); Kate Millett, *Sexual Politics* (New York: Doubleday, 1970).

3. Alva Myrdal and Viola Klein, *Women's Two Roles: Home and Work* (London: Routledge, 1956).

4. Eleanor E. Maccoby, "Sex Differentiation in Intellectual Functioning," in E.E. Maccoby, ed., *The Development of Sex Differences* (Stanford, 1966), p.31. However, as Chapter 9 of this book demonstrates, girls in Ontario were on the whole still getting higher grades than boys in our Grade 12 sample.

5. Eleanor E. Maccoby, "Woman's Intellect," in Seymour Morgan Farber and Roger H.L. Wilson, *The Potential of Women* (New York: McGraw-Hill, 1963), p.31.

6. James Samuel Coleman, *The Adolescent Society* (New York: Free Press of Glencoe, 1961).

7. Elizabeth Douvan and Joseph Adelson, *The Adolescent Experience* (New York: Wiley, 1966).

8. Mirra Komarovsky, *Women in the Modern World: Their Education and Their Dilemmas* (Boston: Little-Brown and Co., 1953).

9. Ralph H. Turner, "Some Aspects of Women's Ambition," in A. Theodore, ed., *The Professional Woman* (Mass., 1971), p.239.

10. Kathryn Patricia Cross, *Beyond the Open Door* (San Francisco: Jossey-Bass, 1971), p.147.

11. Lorna R. Marsden and Edward B. Harvey, "Equality of Educational Access Reconsidered: The Post-Secondary Case in Ontario," in *Interchange* (Vol. 2, No. 4, 1971), p.20.

12. Eli Ginzberg, *et al.*, *Occupational Choice: An Approach to a General Theory* (New York: Columbia University Press, 1951), pp.161-165.

13. In 1961, 70 per cent of the female work force was in twenty-five occupations. S. Ostry, *The Occupational Composition of the Canadian Labour Force* (Ottawa, 1967), p.27.

14. Bruce A. McFarlane, *National Policies and Highly Qualified Manpower in Canada* (Ottawa: Department of Sociology and Anthropology, Carleton University), ch. 1.

15. Whether women have been allowed into them because they are for various occupational-related reasons "semi-professions" or whether they are "semi-professions" because women are in them becomes a vicious circle. However, the fact remains that the two go together. For a discussion of this question, see Simpson and Simpson, "Women and Bureaucracy in the Semi-Professions" in Amitai Etzioni, ed., *The Semi-Professions and their Organization* (New York: The Free Press, 1969).

16. Marsden and Harvey, *op.cit.*

17. M.D. Lagacé, "Educational Attainment in Canada," *Special Labour Force Studies No. 7* (Ottawa: Dominion Bureau of Statistics, October 1968).

18. John Porter, *The Vertical Mosaic* (Toronto: University of Toronto Press, 1965), p.168.

19. Mirra Komarovsky, "Cultural Contradictions and Sex Roles," in *American Journal of Sociology* (Vol.52, 1964), pp.184-189.

20. Kenneth Kammeyer, "Sibling Position and the Feminine Role," in *Journal of Marriage and the Family* (Vol.29, 1967), p.494.

21. Janis S. Bohan, "Age and Sex Differences in Self-Concept," in *Adolescence* (Vol.8, No.31, Fall 1973), pp.379-384.

22. For a discussion of women's work as an extension of traditional responsibilities, see Ruth E. Hartley, "Some Implications of Current Changes in Sex Role Patterns," in Judith M. Bardwick, ed., *Readings on the Psychology of Women* (New York: Harper, 1971), pp.119-124.

23. *Ibid.*, p.117.

12
The Deviant Cases

Throughout our preceding analysis, social class origin has been shown to influence the educational and occupational aspirations of Ontario students. Family membership in the upper-middle and middle classes greatly increased the likelihood that a student would aspire to complete high school and to attend university. However, as we saw, not all students in the upper-middle and middle classes aspired to go to university, nor did all lower-class students not aspire to go to university. We will now look in greater detail at lower-class students who did aspire to university, and compare them with lower-class students who did not, to see what characteristics set the two groups apart.[1]

Lower-class students with university aspirations are not the only ones who could be singled out because they deviate from the general relationship found for the whole sample or some sub-sample. Upper-middle-class students with no university aspirations, for example, also deviate from the general trend for their class peers. Lower-class students, however, are given special attention because one of the more general social issues to which this study addresses itself is that of equality of educational opportunity in Ontario. We take it that financial and socio-cultural barriers to high aspirations are not problems for upper-middle-class students who do not wish to continue in school or go to university. Whatever reasons there might be are likely individual or idiosyncratic, rather than arising from conditions of social structure. Those conditions which we examine here are associated with lower-class status and can be detrimental to the development of high educational aspirations. This analysis focusses on the variation in aspirations to attend university within the lower class and how some of this variation can be accounted for by variables that have not been included in the broader analysis.

As we saw in Chapter 5, Grade 12 students in the upper-middle class were more than twice as likely, and in the middle class were one and a half times as likely, to have university aspirations as students in the lower class.

Yet 30 per cent of all lower-class students did have aspirations to attend university. Similar differences in the chances for high aspirations existed in the other two grades.

In anticipation of these findings of a group of lower-class students who deviate from the general pattern of lower-class student aspirations, specific questions were incorporated into the study design, particularly the parental interview schedule, to test hypotheses relating to lower-class students with high educational aspirations.

Past studies had suggested that the socio-economic status of the student's grandfathers, previous work experience of the father, the educational experience of frequent family visitors, family cultural activities and parental membership in voluntary organizations were all important factors. Some of these past studies will be briefly examined, since they provide the theoretical framework for the analysis of this chapter. Three major themes are developed in these studies: the relationship of lower-class members to other social classes, the importance of parental encouragement and the importance of high academic achievement. All of these themes are consistent with our general interactionist framework. We have already discussed in Chapter 7 in our analysis of self-concept of ability the importance of both parental encouragement and high performance in developing a high self-concept of academic ability, which is probably a prerequisite of aspiring to university.

The first theme examines the relationships between members of the lower class and members of other social classes, the argument essentially being that as the range and intensity of experiences and contact outside the lower class expands, there will be a shift away from lower-class evaluations and aspirations. Thus the lower-class family with the greatest exposure to the middle class would be the most likely to have a positive evaluation of higher education and encourage its children to go to university.

The second theme, that of parental encouragement, was initially developed by Joseph Kahl, who, as we have described in Chapter 7, found that lack of encouragement was the main distinguishing characteristic between lower-class students with university aspirations and those without.[2]

In the United Kingdom Brian Jackson and Denis Marsden came to similar conclusions.[3] Their emphasis is on lower-class students; however, this relationship also holds for members of the upper-middle and middle classes (as we have seen in our chapter on significant others' influence), although the proportion of parents providing little encouragement is higher in the lower class than in the upper-middle and middle classes.

In this chapter, hypotheses concerning parental encouragement or the role of significant others will not be re-examined; rather, the focus of the analysis is on the effect of differing lower-class relationships on the development of educational aspirations. In the last theme, the argument for the special function of high achievement in the lower class will be examined and tested.

Of the three themes, it is the first, that of the relationship of members of the lower class to the middle class, which has received most attention. Some of the former are exposed to contact with the middle class. This contact is often discussed in terms of "structural proximity" to the middle class as measured by high rank within the lower class itself, or holding a position in the "buffer zone" between the lower and middle class through regular contacts at work or with friends who are members of the middle class. Downward social mobility can also be a form of contact, as when, for example, the father has been downwardly mobile within his career, or when either parent has been inter-generationally downwardly mobile by having been middle class in terms of his or her parents' status.

Joseph Kahl and Elizabeth Cohen[4] found that sons of foremen were significantly more likely to have college aspirations than the sons of skilled and semi-skilled workers. Neither found any difference between the aspirations of skilled as compared to the sons of semi-skilled workers, such as those reported by Irving Kraus.[5] The latter found that the higher the status of the father within the lower class, the more likely his son is to have college aspirations (47 per cent of the students in his sample whose fathers were craftsmen or foremen planned to attend college in contrast to 36 per cent whose fathers were in semi-skilled, service or labouring types of jobs). Jackson and Marsden, in their study of eighty-eight successful working-class children in a northern industrial city in England, found that two-thirds of the sample came from the uppermost levels of the working class and most of the others had middle-class connections.[6]

Another form of structural proximity is through the mother's job. In a U.S. study it was found that the socio-economic status of her job, but not the fact of her working outside the home, was significantly related to a son's aspirations about college. If the mother had a white-collar job, her son was more likely to have plans to attend college than if she held a manual job.[7] In our analysis of sex differences (Chapter 11), we found that the mother's occupational status, whether or not she was at present working, had a significant effect on the educational aspirations of both sons and daughters, and that this effect was stronger for girls than for boys.

In the case of downward mobility—"the sunken middle class"[8]—the transmission of the middle-class evaluations of education is likely to be much more direct than through contact alone. Harold Wilensky and Hugh Edwards, in a factory study of downwardly mobile men or skidders, concluded that the values of the middle class retained their force despite status loss.[9] In their sample, lower-class men who had previously been in the middle class rejected identification with the working class, believed in an open class meritocracy, aspired to mobility and expected their children to achieve middle-class status. They found that 34 per cent of inter-generationally downwardly mobile workers identified with the middle or upper class, as compared with 19 per cent of non-skidders. Other researchers have found that where there has been downward mobility by a member of a lower-class family, the children are more likely to aspire to attend university than in families where neither parent has ever been in one of the higher classes.

Maternal downward mobility measured in terms of higher job status of the family of origin has been found to be significantly related to the presence of university aspirations.[10] Kraus[11] noted that in working-class families where the father had not completed high school, such factors as low occupational and income levels may limit the effect of the mother's greater education. It has been found that if either the mother's or the father's parents had high status, there is a positive influence on educational aspirations. Kraus reports findings showing the favourable influence on college aspirations if at least one grandparent had non-manual status. Fifty-six per cent of working-class students who had at least one grandparent in a non-manual occupation had college aspirations, while 41 per cent who had grandparents in manual occupations were found to have college aspirations.

Similar effects can follow from the frustrated mobility aspirations of fathers of lower-class origin. Kahl and Cohen[12] both report data showing a relationship between a father's job dissatisfaction and a greater likelihood of his son having higher educational aspirations. They argue that the father's own dissatisfaction leads him to encourage his son to get a better education in order to take advantage of the mobility opportunities that he missed, despite the implied definition of the father as somewhat of a failure. In this case, of course, we would have to explain why an immobile lower-class father had mobility aspirations. No doubt there are ways other than middle-class contacts by which such aspirations can be acquired. In the North American context, at least, where communal sentiments of class are not strong, such aspirations could be acquired from the dominant values, as these are reflected through such things as the mass media.

In summary, then, structural proximity or other contact by lower-class parents with the middle class was found to increase the likelihood of lower-class children developing university aspirations. These lower-class parents would tend to encourage aspirations that would be more like those of the middle class than the lower class. They would also be encouraging occupational and status attainment that would be higher than their own present position. As we mentioned in Chapter 7 on self-concept of ability, Kahl characterized those parents who encouraged their sons as ones who believed in "getting ahead" and usually were somewhat frustrated with their own lack of success. The lower-class parents who did not encourage their sons to do better were characterized as believing in "getting by."[13]

The main proposition that can be formulated from these studies, and that we will examine here, is that lower-class families who are near the middle class would tend to have a higher proportion of their children aspiring to attend university than other lower-class families. The various indicators of nearness to the middle class that we will use are: structural proximity to the middle class as measured by holding a job in the upper part of the lower class (occupations scoring 35-39 on the Blishen scale); middle- or upper-class status of either the maternal or paternal grandfather; downward intra-generational mobility of the father as measured by the socio-economic status of his first job; middle-class job status held by the mother in a lower-class family; greater parental educational experience than the average lower-class parent; higher household total yearly income than the average lower-class family; post-secondary school experience of frequent family visitors; family participation in cultural activities more than other lower-class families as measured on an index of cultural enrichment; and membership in voluntary organizations.

A test will also be made of the proposition that lower-class parental dissatisfaction is associated with increased proportions of lower-class youth aspiring to attend university. The indicator of parental satisfaction that is used is the mother's evaluation of her own and her husband's satisfaction with their level of education.

Throughout the analysis of this chapter, controls for the sex of the student will be introduced wherever possible in the cross-tabulations, since as was shown in Chapter 11, the depressing effect of lower-class status on the development of high educational aspirations is consistently stronger and more pronounced for girls than it is for boys. In some tabulations, particularly those using data from the parent sample, the control for sex could not be used because of the small number of cases falling into some cells.

Structural Proximity to the
Middle Class: The Upper-Lowers

It is hypothesized that with a higher position in the lower class the likelihood of university aspirations by lower-class children will be greater than if their parents hold positions in the lower part of the lower class. The occupations on the Blishen scale scoring between 35-39 are representative of the most skilled lower-class jobs, some of them overlapping with lower-middle-class jobs in prestige, income or educational requirements. Table 12.1 shows the proportions of students aspiring to attend university within two segments of the lower class.

From the table it can be seen that the findings generally support the hypothesis, with the exception of the Grade 12 girls. Family position in the top of the lower class increases the likelihood of university aspirations for boys in Grades 8, 10 and 12. For boys, the contrast within the lower class was the greatest in Grade 8, the difference in proportions aspiring to go to

Table 12.1
Percentage of Lower-class Students Aspiring to Graduate from University
by Levels of Lower-class Status, Sex and Grade

Grade	Males		Females	
	Lower* Lower	Upper* Lower	Lower Lower	Upper Lower
	(per cent)			
Grade 12	36 (374)**	42 (206)	24 (393)	25 (202)
Grade 10	29 (480)	36 (191)	21 (382)	36 (179)
Grade 8	36 (417)	47 (187)	26 (405)	38 (154)

*Lower Lower = 20-34 on the Blishen scale
 Upper Lower = 35-39 on the Blishen scale

**Numbers in brackets are those upon which percentages are based.

university between the upper lowers and the remainder of the lower class being 11 percentage points. For Grades 10 and 12 the differences were 7 per cent and 6 per cent respectively. The reduction in the difference within the lower class is most likely the result of early school leaving and shifts in aspirations by some students away from university as high school graduation approaches.

The results for the Grade 8 and 10 girls are the same as those for the boys, with upper-lower-class status marking a relative position of advantage within the lower class. The results for Grade 12 girls do not fit this overall pattern and are not in support of the hypothesis. For Grade 12 girls, the likelihood of university aspirations is low regardless of position within the lower class. The advantage of middle-class contact evident for Grades 8 and 10 appears to be off-set by other factors. We have noted in the previous chapter how girls' socialization and vocational preparation on the way to Grade 12 reduces their educational aspirations, particularly for the lower class. It would seem that not even the structural proximity to middle-class status exercises a sufficiently strong influence to offset completely these school and social factors.

However, if the proportion of lower-class Grade 12 girls not aspiring to university is decomposed, the differences within the lower class once again become evident. Of the upper-lower Grade 12 girls not aspiring to university, 55 per cent aspired to some other form of post-secondary education, while 48 per cent of their counterparts in the lower-lower class did. Thus proximity to the middle class had a modest effect.

That the upper part of the lower class, that is, the families of more skilled workers, should take on some of the values of the middle class can be viewed as part of the process of class transformation that has been called *embourgeoisement.* This process of being "like the middle class" is thought to be the result of high rates of economic growth and the generally raised living standards that followed World War II. The evidence is contradictory about how far down into the lower class these middle-class values have gone, as sociologists have sought to locate the divide between middle class and genuinely proletarian values. As far as educational aspirations of Ontario lower-class students are concerned, if we split the lower-lower class even further than we did above, that is, from 25 to 29 and from 30 to 34 on the Blishen scale, we find no evidence for Grade 10 or Grade 12 students of a systematic reduction of educational aspirations among the children of less skilled workers as was found by Kraus,[14] for example, in the United States. However, there was some reduction among the Grade 8 students. Thus, the evidence of continuing working-class values with respect to educational aspirations below the level of skilled workers' children is mixed.

The "Sunken" Middle Class

Our second measure of nearness to the middle class was the existence of grandparents of middle or higher social class. One or both of the student's own parents under these circumstances would have been downwardly mobile. It would be expected that these "sunken" parents would still have many of the middle-class values and outlooks that would encourage higher

Table 12.2

Percentage of Lower-class Students Aspiring to Graduate from University by Social Class of Grandfathers (Grades 8, 10 and 12)

	Socio-economic Status of Grandfather	
Grade	Upper-middle & Middle	Lower
	(per cent)	
Grade 12		
Father's father	39 (54)*	33 (307)
Mother's father	41 (68)	30 (319)
Grade 10		
Father's father	32 (62)	30 (314)
Mother's father	33 (63)	29 (333)
Grade 8		
Father's father	40 (55)	34 (260)
Mother's father	37 (57)	36 (283)

*Numbers in brackets are those upon which percentages are based.

education. The process of value transmission could, of course, be direct from the grandparents to the student, as well as indirect through the parents.

Our data on the students' maternal and paternal grandfathers' occupations, which were obtained from the smaller samples of parental interviews, are not ideal to test such an hypothesis. Even when we combine boys and girls, as in Table 12.2, the numbers with downwardly mobile parents are very few, a fact which is not altogether surprising considering the general trend of upward mobility with the growth of industrialization.

Of the six possible comparisons in Table 12.2 between lower and higher social class of grandparents, all are in the expected direction; that is, where grandparents come from higher or middle classes, educational aspirations of students are higher. The findings for either grandfather of Grade 12 students and for the paternal grandfather of Grade 8 students support the hypothesis that the higher status of grandparents increases the likelihood of university aspirations in lower-class youth. The findings for Grade 10 and the maternal grandfather in Grade 8, while in the hypothesised direction, show differences that are too small to be considered significant. Whatever differences there are do not appear to be related to whether it is the maternal or paternal grandfather that is being considered.

The "Skidding" Father

Wilensky and Edwards,[15] as we previously noted, found that members of the lower class whose earlier jobs had previously placed them in the middle class, those he referred to as "skidders," maintained strong links with the middle class, hoped to be mobile themselves and expected their children to achieve middle-class status. For the Ontario sample, the children of such skidders can be identified by comparing their fathers' first full-time job with their job at the time of the survey. Unfortunately, the number of fathers who moved from first jobs of middle or higher status to present jobs of low status are few, as we can see from Table 12.3, limiting our ability to make a stringent test of the hypothesis. The findings are as expected in that for all grades where the fathers are downwardly mobile within their careers, their children are more likely to have university aspirations than are the children of fathers who have maintained a status within the lower class. The finding is least striking for Grade 10 and most striking in Grade 8. No doubt the few cases in each grade account in part for the variability of these proportions. One of the reasons why middle-class values persist among those who are downwardly mobile with respect to their parents or in the course of their careers is that most mobility takes place over a short distance, so that those who "sink" or "skid" have probably remained fairly close to the middle class. Our data do not permit us to separate out lower-lowers and upper-lowers to explore this possibility.

Table 12.3
Percentage of Lower-class Students Aspiring to Graduate from University
by Occupational Status of Father's First Full-time Job
(Grades 8, 10 and 12)

| | Status of Father's First Full-time Job | |
Grade	Upper-middle	Lower
	(per cent)	
Grade 12	41 (32)*	32 (346)
Grade 10	34 (32)	30 (360)
Grade 8	54 (35)	33 (350)

*Numbers in brackets are those upon which percentages are based.

The Working Lower-Class Mother

Sociological research indicates that the lower-class mother is the centre of the home and has a greater influence on the development of the children than does the working-class father. We have discussed this in a limited way in the chapter on significant others, and in the chapter on sex differences. Here we look at two factors related to the lower-class mother: whether or not she was working at the time of the survey; and, if she had ever worked, the status level of the job she had held or was holding at the time of the survey. It could be argued that any contact outside of the home by the mother would broaden the range of lower-class experience, and this in turn might

Table 12.4
Percentage of Lower-class Students Aspiring to University
by Employment Status of Mother*, by Sex
(Grades 8, 10 and 12)

| | Employment Status of Mother | | | |
| | *Males* | | *Females* | |
Grade	Mother Working	Mother Not Working	Mother Working	Mother Not Working
	(per cent)			
Grade 12	38 (271)**	39 (293)	29 (293)	21 (308)
Grade 10	35 (298)	28 (356)	26 (258)	25 (295)
Grade 8	43 (270)	36 (317)	31 (255)	28 (296)

*As reported by the student.
**Numbers in brackets are those upon which percentages are based.

be associated with increased university aspirations. The mere fact of the mother working outside the home may or may not have such an effect. Much will depend on the kind of work the mother does and on the reasons for her working. That the mother works may increase the family income so that the family experiences *embourgeoisement* with a corresponding increase in aspirations. On the other hand, the mother may be working to bring family income to a minimal level to cover necessities, in which case we would not expect a relationship between the fact of a mother working and university aspirations of her children. If, however, experience of working involved middle-class contact because the mother held a middle-status occupation, then that experience should increase the probability of university aspirations for lower-class students.

Table 12.5
Percentage of Lower-class Students Aspiring to University
by Social Class Level of Mother's Occupation*, by Sex
(Grades 8, 10 and 12)

| | Status of Mother's Occupation | | | |
| | *Males* | | *Females* | |
Grade	Upper-middle and Middle	Lower	Upper-middle and Middle	Lower
	(per cent)			
Grade 12	50 (159)**	34 (222)	34 (169)	22 (251)
Grade 10	45 (184)	28 (257)	37 (154)	21 (228)
Grade 8	52 (137)	40 (244)	38 (148)	28 (239)

*Job ever held.
**Numbers in brackets are those upon which percentages are based.

Tables 12.4 and 12.5 present the data concerning both these factors. For Grade 8 and Grade 10 boys, the mother working outside the home increases the probability of aspirations for university, a condition which is not shown for Grade 12. For girls, it is at Grade 12 that these positive effects of the working mother are found. Overall, the support for the hypothesis is again somewhat inconclusive, since of the six possible comparisons of mothers working or not working, four show a relationship, sometimes very weak, in the expected direction. These findings, however, do not support other studies that have reported categorically that there is no relationship between the mother working outside the home and the presence of university aspirations.[16]

Table 12.5 shows the relationship between university aspirations and social class level of the job that the mother held at any time in the past, whether full-time or part-time. The findings in Table 12.4 and Table 12.5 are not directly comparable because of different levels of specificity of the two questions. The question relating to the type of work the mother did or had done was asked very generally, with no reference to job duration or recency of the job. For the purpose of analysing middle-class contacts by lower-class mothers (as defined by the father's job) the specific details of the job duration or time are not important. Rather, the fact that the child reported a particular job status of the mother indicates an identification with that status.

The findings in Table 12.5 clearly support the hypothesis that upper-middle or middle-class work experience is associated with the increased likelihood of lower-class boys and girls having university aspirations. For boys and girls of all three grades, the fact that a lower-class mother had a middle- or upper-class job positively affected the development of university aspirations. Thus it would seem that if the lower-class mother has had contact through the white-collar work world with the middle class, she brings a range of knowledge, experience and values into her home that are not found as widely in other lower-class homes.

The Better-Educated Lower-Class Parent

Because the Blishen occupational scale, by which we allocate students through the father's occupation to a position in the social class structure, has educational level as a major component, each of the class levels tends to have members relatively homogeneous with respect to educational attainment. However, each of the class levels does have some variance, and hence it is possible to divide these working-class fathers into the better and the less well educated. It would be expected that where lower-class children have better educated fathers they will have higher educational aspirations than those whose fathers were less well educated. We showed in general in Chapter 5 how educational aspirations were related to parental education. Here we look at the lower class exclusively. A better-educated working-class father could, of course, be one who has experienced downward mobility or is under-employed, which is a form of downward mobility.

To test for these relationships, we take the level of education of the parents as reported by the student and dichotomize that measure into "some high school or technical school or less," and "graduation from high school or technical school or more." As can be seen from the numbers in Table 12.6, the great majority of lower-class fathers had educational attainment which was short of high school graduation. However, for those lower-class fathers who had completed high school or better, their children did have substantially higher probabilities of having university aspirations: at least 15 percentage points higher for Grade 8 and Grade 12 boys, somewhat less for Grade 10. Although the effects for a lower-class girl of having a father

Table 12.6

Percentage of Lower-class Students Aspiring to University by Educational Level of Father and Mother, by Sex (Grades 8, 10 and 12)

Educational Level of Father

	Males		Females	
Grade	Some High School or Less	High School Graduation or More	Some High School or Less	High School Graduation or More
	(per cent)			
Grade 12	37 (421)*	53 (83)	24 (453)	25 (71)
Grade 10	31 (461)	39 (101)	24 (396)	36 (78)
Grade 8	37 (333)	52 (69)	31 (323)	35 (66)

Educational Level of Mother

	Males			Females		
Grade	Some High School	High School Graduation	More than High School Graduation	Some High School	High School Graduation	More than High School Graduation
	(per cent)					
Grade 12	36 (358)	37 (92)	51 (59)	23 (398)	27 (83)	39 (49)
Grade 10	29 (385)	34 (119)	58 (57)	22 (372)	36 (75)	47 (43)
Grade 8	33 (287)	58 (71)	60 (47)	28 (298)	35 (72)	43 (42)

*Numbers in brackets are those upon which percentages are based.

with high school completion are not as great as for lower-class boys, they are nonetheless there. The least effect for all sex and grade groups is for girls in Grade 8.

Since lower-class mothers are not allocated to their class on the basis of their occupations, as are their husbands, there is a greater variability in their educational attainment levels. Generally these women are better educated than the men. For this reason the level of education of the mother was trichotomized into "some high school or technical school or less," "graduation from high school," and "further post-secondary education after high school graduation."

The data in Table 12.6 support the hypothesis that a higher level of education of the mother within the lower class increases the likelihood of her children having university aspirations. For boys and girls in all three grades, a higher level of educational attainment by the mother is associated with an increase in the proportions of lower-class children aspiring to university.

For Grade 8 the proportion of boys with university aspirations increased at least 25 percentage points when the mother had more than some high school education, with little distinction between whether this involved high school graduation only or some post-secondary education. For boys in high school, the mother's greater educational attainment is also associated with marked increases in the proportions aspiring to university. However, for these boys high educational aspirations are not as much associated with the mother having graduated from high school as they are with the mother having some education beyond high school. Mother's educational level has similar effects for girls, except that in all categories, as we have established earlier, lower-class girls have lower aspirational levels than boys. It is clear, then, that when lower-class students have parents whose education is above the average for parents of that class, there is a positive influence on educational aspirations.

The More Affluent Lower Class

The sample of parents was asked to give an approximation of their household total yearly income, of which the father's income would be the major component (where the father is working). Since the Blishen scale uses income as one of its criteria for ranking, the father's income would be closely associated with our indicator of social class.

The measure of household income is a much broader measure in that it would include other sources of family income from the working mother, older siblings, boarders, and other jobs held by the father. In general, lower-class families with a total family income higher than the average lower-class family income would be able to afford a style of living that would more closely approximate that of the middle class. It might include an ability to incur some of the costs involved in university education. There would clearly be an exception to this generalization in the case of very large families or other circumstances such as dependent aging parents.

Table 12.7 presents data to test the hypothesis that increased family income within the lower class will increase the likelihood that lower-class boys and girls will have university aspirations. The level of household income was trichotomized into less than $4,999, $5,000-$9,999, and $10,000 or more, with the majority of the lower-class families falling into the middle category. It should be noted that there are very small cell frequencies for the proportion of lower-class students aspiring to university in the less than $4,999 income bracket, and the figures should be treated with caution. Consequently, not much can be said about this group, except that with one exception (Grade 8 girls) the level of university aspirations is the lowest of all the income groups. The larger number of cases for the two higher income groups lets us speak with more confidence about the differences between these two groups.

The most striking aspect of the findings in Table 12.7 is the difference in the association between household income and university aspirations by grade level. The hypothesized relationship between higher income and higher education is found for Grade 12 boys and Grade 12 girls. With an increase in income from $5,000-$9,999 to over $10,000, the likelihood of Grade 12 lower-class boys having university aspirations is increased by 7 percentage points, and the likelihood of Grade 12 lower-class girls having university aspirations is increased by 12 percentage points. Similarly, for Grade 10 girls an increase in income is associated with an increase in the likelihood of university aspirations, in this case an increase of 18 percentage points. However, no significant relationship between an increase in income from the middle to higher brackets and university aspirations is found for Grade 8 and 10 lower-class boys.

A higher family income is found to be positively associated with the presence of university aspirations in the senior grades, where the actual costs of higher education have to be considered directly. The direct effect of income is seen earlier in high school for girls than it is for boys. The ability of the family to contribute financially to higher education appears to be a consideration for lower-class girls and their families sooner than for lower-class boys in encouraging aspirations for university.

Family Friends

Another way in which a lower-class family may come into contact with middle-class values and lifestyles is through visitors who come into the home as friends of the parents. If, for example, these visitors have had some post-secondary school experience, they may be the source of information and encouragement associated with the development of high educational aspirations. Children in lower-class families that had such friends and visitors might be more likely to want to go to university than children of

Table 12.7
Percentage of Lower-class Students Aspiring to University by Total Family Income, by Sex (Grades 8, 10 and 12)

	Total Family Income					
	Males			Females		
Grade	Less than $4,999	$5,000-$9,999	More than $10,000	Less than $4,999	$5,000-$9,999	More than $10,000
			(per cent)			
Grade 12	28 (18)*	43 (102)	50 (70)	12 (17)	14 (99)	26 (61)
Grade 10	17 (23)	33 (121)	33 (85)	16 (19)	22 (86)	40 (62)
Grade 8	23 (13)	46 (91)	44 (50)	29 (21)	29 (104)	33 (46)

*Numbers in brackets are those upon which percentages are based.

lower-class families that had not. The parental interview contained a question to explore this hypothesis: "Apart from your spouse and children who are the three people whom you visit most or who visit you most? Did any of them attend university or college?" It should be noted that the answer would include a wide range of educational experiences, from business college to post-graduate work at university.

Because of the small number of lower-class homes with friends who had continued their education after high school (perhaps the most striking finding in these responses), it is necessary to consider boys and girls together in Table 12.8, which presents the data for both the first most important family visitor and the second most important.

The findings in Table 12.8 support the hypothesis with one exception. No relationship was found between the educational experience of the second most frequent visitor and university aspirations for Grade 8 boys and girls, although as can be seen from the table, a marked difference, in the hypothesized direction, is evident for the same relationship for the first most frequent visitor. If the most frequent visitor to a lower-class home had post-secondary experience, the likelihood of the students in that home having university aspirations increased by 7 percentage points for Grade 12, 22 percentage points for Grade 10, and 12 percentage points for Grade 8. Similarly, if the second most frequent family visitor had post-secondary experience, the likelihood of lower-class youth aspiring to university increased by 10 percentage points for Grade 12 and 13 percentage points for Grade 10, but no significant difference was found for Grade 8.

Table 12.8
Percentage of Lower-class Students Aspiring to University
by Post-Secondary Experience of Frequent Family Visitors
(Grades 8, 10 and 12)

| | Post-Secondary Experience of Frequent Family Visitors | | | |
| | *First Most Frequent Visitor* | | *Second Most Frequent Visitor* | |
Grade	Some Post-Secondary	No Post-Secondary	Some Post-Secondary	No Post-Secondary
	(per cent)			
Grade 12	39 (31)*	32 (337)	42 (36)	32 (322)
Grade 10	51 (41)	29 (357)	42 (50)	29 (343)
Grade 8	47 (40)	35 (284)	35 (40)	37 (277)

*Numbers in brackets are those upon which percentages are based.

Table 12.9

Percentage of Lower-class Students Aspiring to University by Overall Family Cultural Enrichment, by Sex and Grade

Cultural Enrichment	Overall Family Cultural Enrichment					
	Males			Females		
	High	Medium	Low	High	Medium	Low
			(per cent)			
Grade 12	56 (71)*	43 (179)	32 (300)	32 (119)	29 (214)	16 (256)
Grade 10	43 (74)	41 (202)	23 (357)	38 (108)	25 (216)	21 (210)
Grade 8	51 (71)	42 (193)	36 (292)	40 (128)	27 (193)	24 (200)

*Numbers in brackets are those upon which percentages are based.

Family Cultural Activities

In Chapter 5 we showed that the educational aspirations of students were related to the level of cultural enrichment in the home as measured by the number of magazines coming into the home, whether the respondent had ever taken lessons outside of school in art, dancing, dramatics or music, and whether the student had attended ballets, opera, plays, performances of classical music, museums or art galleries. Cultural enrichment is related to social class, but when we controlled the data for social class we found that within each class educational aspirations were related to the level of cultural enrichment. When the data for lower-class boys and girls are separated, as they are in Table 12.9, the relationship is even more striking. Fifty-six per cent of Grade 12 boys with a high level of cultural enrichment wanted to go to university compared to 32 per cent of those with a low score. As we have repeatedly pointed out, fewer lower-class girls had university aspirations, but for them, too, the relationship is striking, with twice as many Grade 12 girls scoring high on cultural enrichment having university aspirations as those scoring low. The relationship is very similar for Grade 8 boys and girls and less striking but still present in Grade 10.

Membership in Voluntary Organizations

James Curtis has found that members of the lower class participate less than those above them in voluntary organizations.[17] However, there is some overlap in participation rates between the upper part of the lower class and the lower part of the middle class. The reduced lower-class participation is thought to reflect a lack of identification with the goals of voluntary organizations—most frequently those related to the community and the

Table 12.10
Percentage of Lower-class Students Aspiring to University
by Parental Participation in Voluntary Organizations, by Sex
(Grades 8, 10 and 12)

	Parental Participation in Voluntary Organizations			
	Males		*Females*	
Grade	One or More	None	One or More	None
	(per cent)			
Grade 12	47 (104)*	42 (106)	21 (102)	16 (91)
Grade 10	38 (130)	26 (110)	33 (93)	21 (85)
Grade 8	45 (101)	38 (68)	31 (103)	26 (77)

*Numbers in brackets are those upon which percentages are based.

school—and feelings of discomfort in the social relationships that emerge from participation in voluntary organizations. Participation in community and school-related associations would be expected to be related to an identification with middle-class interests and the development of university aspirations. It is hypothesized that where lower-class participation in voluntary organizations is high, children would be more likely to have university aspirations than in the lower-class homes where there is a low level of participation in voluntary organizations.

Table 12.10 presents the cross-tabulation of participation in voluntary organizations and university aspirations for lower-class boys and girls. Parents were asked to identify adult family participation in parent-teacher associations, young people's groups, church groups, political parties or neighbourhood associations. We divide the respondents into those who participate in one or more of these organizations and those who participate in none. The findings in Table 12.10 support the hypothesis that participation in voluntary organizations increases the likelihood that lower-class boys and girls will have university aspirations.

The relationship between voluntary organization participation and increased proportions of lower-class students with university aspirations holds for both boys and girls at each grade level. There is, however, some variation in the strength of the relationship between the grade cohorts. Membership in voluntary organizations more clearly distinguished lower-class boys and girls with university aspirations from those with no university aspirations in Grade 10 than in Grade 8 or Grade 12. However, the proportion of boys aspiring to university in Grade 10 is lower than in either Grade 12 or 8, in part because Grade 12 is a survival grade where if lower-class boys have persisted they are likely to have higher aspirations than those in Grade 10. The relationship between parental participation in voluntary organizations and students' university aspirations appears most clearly for lower-class students in the middle of their high school careers, Grade 10, which is a point at which many are revising their aspirations downward or considering leaving high school.

The Lower-Class Student and High Achievement

The schooling process has been described as "carrying" the bright students through the system despite their lower-class status.[18] Despite difficulties in obtaining information, Jackson and Marsden found that the successful lower-class boys and girls went on to college "because they had been carried along by the momentum of the educational process from certificate to certificate, rather than because they had made a series of informed and personal decisions."[19] Richard Hoggart, in his description of the lower-class scholarship boy, describes a similar process where the bright boy is recognized for his achievement and encouraged to continue on to grammar school.[20]

Kahl and Cohen note two important consequences of high early school performance. It is used by the parents for placing their children in school programs. Secondly, high school performance would lead to the development of a high self-concept which would encourage a student to have high educational aspirations.[21] A third consequence would be the establishment of a positive relationship between the lower-class child and school personnel. The studies by Jackson and Marsden and Hoggart suggest that lack of information about post-secondary opportunities and limited perceptions of its value are a general characteristic of the lower class, but this lack will be less detrimental for the lower-class high achievers because of increased interest by the school.

Very little data were presented in any of these studies showing the difference between middle- and lower-class high achievers. On the basis of the findings reported by Kahl, Cohen, Jackson and Marsden, and Hoggart, we could expect that a difference in the proportions aspiring to university between high achieving and low achieving students would be greater in the lower class than in the middle class. In other words, the additional advantage associated with high achievement would more clearly differentiate the aspiration levels of lower-class students than middle-class students, who have many other sources of educational reinforcement not usually available to the lower classes.

Table 12.11 shows that for the Grade 8 students, having high grades increased the probability of both lower- and middle-class students aspiring to university. However, contrary to the studies described above in which it is argued that high achievement is more important for the lower- than the middle-class student, in this study high school performance is more important for the middle-class than the lower-class student. Forty-two per cent more high achieving than low achieving middle-class boys aspired to university, while for lower-class boys the difference between high and low

Table 12.11
Percentage of Middle- and Lower-class Students Aspiring to University by School-reported Grades and Sex (Grade 8)

| | School-reported Grades | | | |
| | *Males* | | *Females* | |
Socio-economic Status	75+	–75	75+	–75
	(per cent)			
Middle	88 (59)*	46 (103)	61 (70)	27 (40)
Lower	65 (91)	31 (136)	41 (83)	22 (71)

*Numbers in brackets are those upon which percentages are based.

achievers is 34 per cent. This is true also of the Grade 8 girls, where in the middle class there are 34 percentage points difference in university aspirations between the high and low achievers but in the lower class a difference of only 19 percentage points.

As we explained in previous chapters, program in high school is itself a measure of school performance, since academic achievement in Grade 8 determines to some extent at least whether a student would be allocated to a five- or four-year program. The subject matter of the five-year program was more intellectually demanding than of the four-year program, and the teachers had greater expectations of their students.

To test the hypothesis that high achievement was more important for lower- than middle-class students in leading to high educational aspirations, then, it is necessary to separate the Grade 10 and Grade 12 students into five- and four-year programs. We might here remind the reader that, as we found in Chapter 10, program is related to social class. In Grades 10 and 12 about four-fifths of upper-middle-class students but only about half of the lower-class students were in the five-year program.

Since only students in the five-year program would be able to continue to Grade 13, get a Secondary School Honours Graduation Diploma and thus be eligible to attend university, we will look only at the aspirations of students in the five-year program to see whether high achievement had a greater effect on the aspirations of lower-class students than of students in higher classes.

The data show that there is no difference in the proportions of high achievers having university aspirations between middle- and lower-class students in Grades 10 and 12. Only upper-middle-class high achievers are more likely to have high educational aspirations. If a lower-class student is in the five-year program and performs very well academically, he is as likely as a middle-class student to want to go to university. However, both are less likely than the upper-middle-class student to have these aspirations. As for the effect of achievement on aspirations, the difference in the proportions with university aspirations between high and low achievers is much the same in each of the class levels in Grade 12. However, in Grade 10 achievement does seem to have a greater effect on the aspirations of lower-class students. There is a difference of 34 percentage points between high and low achievers aspiring to university in the lower class, but only 24 percentage points difference in the middle class. Many of the lower-class low achievers with low aspirations in Grade 10 would leave school before Grade 12, and that is very likely why there is no difference between the low and middle class in Grade 12 in the effect of achievement on aspirations.

The hypothesis that we advanced, based on previous studies that high achievement is more important in the formation of high educational aspirations for the lower than for the middle class, is borne out in our data only in the case of Grade 10 students. It is not supported by the findings for

Grade 12 students, and for Grade 8 students the reverse is in fact the case. The difference in aspirations between high and low achievers is greater for the middle than for the lower class.

Notes

1. This type of analysis has been called deviant case analysis by Kendall and Wolf (1949). They define deviant case analysis to include data not a part of the original study frame and possibly not originally collected. For this chapter some data not previously analysed will be used, but no new data has been collected. In our follow-up study of the Grade 8 students we specifically selected lower-class students for interviewing, thus expanding our capacity to analyse deviant cases.
2. Joseph A. Kahl, "Educational and Occupational Aspirations of 'Common Man' Boys," in *Harvard Educational Review* (Summer 1953), pp.186–203.
3. Brian Jackson and Denis Marsden, *Education and the Working Class* (London: Routledge and Kegan Paul, 1962).
4. Elizabeth G. Cohen, "Parental Factors in Educational Mobility," in *Sociology of Education* (38, Fall 1965), pp.404–425.
5. Irving Kraus, "Sources of Educational Aspirations among Working Class Youth," in *American Sociological Review* (Vol.29, No.6, December 1964), pp.867–879.
6. Jackson and Marsden, *op.cit.*
7. Cohen, *op.cit.*
8. Jackson and Marsden, *op.cit.*
9. Harold Wilensky and Hugh Edwards, "The Skidders: Ideological Adjustments of Downward Mobile Workers," in *American Sociological Review* (Vol.24, April 1959).
10. Kraus, *op.cit.*; Cohen, *op.cit.*
11. Kraus, *op.cit.*
12. Cohen, *op.cit.*
13. See Chapter 7 on Self-Concept of Ability.
14. Kraus, *op.cit.*
15. Wilensky and Edwards, *op.cit.*
16. Cohen, *op.cit.*
17. James Curtis, "Voluntary Association Joining: A Cross-National Comparative Note," in *American Sociological Review* (Vol.36, 1971), pp.872–880.
18. Christopher Jencks, *et al.*, *Inequality: A Reassessment of the Effect of Family and Schooling in America* (New York: Basic Books, 1972).
19. Jackson and Marsden, *op.cit.*
20. Richard Hoggart, *The Uses of Literacy* (New Jersey: Essential Books, 1957).
21. See the discussion in Chapter 7 on the development of a self-concept of ability.

13
The Franco-Ontarians

At the time of this survey of Ontario students there had been in existence for a few years, and for the first time, public secondary schools in which the language of instruction was French. It is extraordinary to consider that it was not until one hundred years after Confederation that consideration was given to establishing public French-speaking secondary schools. The reason was that the goal of all political parties in Ontario had been assimilation of the French-speaking population. Early in the century, as French-speaking families moved into Ontario, there was bitter controversy about whether there should be any instruction in French at all in the public schools. The controversy culminated in Regulation 17 in 1912, which required that,

> English was to become the sole language of instruction after the third year, and the study of French as a language was limited to one hour a day.
> ... Both provincial political parties officially supported this concept, although many critics wished to exclude French entirely from Ontario schools.[1]

Because of the bitter denunciations of the regulation by both Franco-Ontarians and French Canadians in Quebec, a compromise was eventually arrived at, and after 1927, while English was still the official language of instruction after the third grade, in practice French was often used in all elementary grades of the "bilingual schools."

Eventually, some concessions were made to French-speaking students in the English-speaking high schools. A more advanced course of *français* was introduced in 1961 for those whose mother tongue was French. The Department also gave permission to school boards to have Latin taught in French, and in 1966 this permission was extended to geography and history.

New legislation in 1969 called for French-language secondary schools, and required that a school board provide classes, or even a school, in French when a written request was received from ten or more Francophone parents and when there were enough students to justify it. The legislation was not implemented without conflict and bitterness in some communities.

There could be no doubt that educational opportunities for Franco-Ontarians had been grossly inadequate, and the Carnegie Study of Identification and Utilization of Talent in High School, which traced the secondary school careers of all children who had enrolled in 1959 in Grade 9 in Ontario, showed the consequence for the French. Thirteen per cent of Anglophone children who entered Grade 9 in 1959 completed Grade 13 after five years of schooling. The figure was 17 per cent for children from homes where neither English nor French was the principal language, but only 3 per cent of French-speaking children who entered Grade 9 in 1959 completed Grade 13 five years later.[2]

On standardized tests, too, which were administered as part of the Carnegie Study, the Francophone students had significantly lower scores than either Anglophone or "other language" children. While socio-economic factors undoubtedly played a part in this, the Royal Commission on Bilingualism and Biculturalism was convinced that a part of the explanation was that many of the French-speaking students were not able to be educated in their own language and had experienced a hostile and alien environment in the schools that was not conducive to learning.[3]

An important variable, therefore, in a study concerned with equality of educational opportunity in Ontario is language of instruction. Accordingly, in this survey it was decided to treat French and bilingual schools as a sub-domain in each of the three grades. Because the French-speaking school population is small relative to the English population, and in 1971 less than half the Francophone student population was in French-language schools, it was necessary to over-sample the French student population in French-language schools.[4] Thus a different sampling ratio was employed for the French-language than for the English-language schools. Even so, the numbers are small and conclusions from cross-classifications must be treated with a great deal of caution. Sample sizes for the French schools were 346, 249, and 162 for Grades 8, 10 and 12, representing response rates of 94, 93 and 87 per cent respectively.

In this analysis we will first draw a profile of the students in the French schools, comparing them with respect to some major characteristics with the students in the English schools. Since the Royal Commission on Bilingualism and Biculturalism (popularly known as the B & B Commission) felt that an important reason for the lower levels of educational attainment of Franco-Ontarians compared to other parts of the population was the fact that they did not have the opportunity to be educated in their own language, it should be illuminating to compare the students in the French-language schools with the Francophones in the English-language schools.

There are two ways of selecting Francophones in the English schools. One is by ethnicity using the responses to the question, "To what ethnic or cultural group did your ancestor (on the male side) belong on coming to this continent?" The other is by mother tongue using the question, "What language do your parents *mostly* speak when they are at home with the family?" It is tempting to use the ethnicity question because the numbers are greater. For example, in Grade 12 there were 178 in the Anglophone schools who would be considered ethnically French, but only 80 who would be classified as having a French mother tongue. No doubt that is a measure of the degree of assimilation of the Francophones in Ontario. However, since the question about ethnicity (which is the same as the question asked in the Canadian census) refers to the ancestor on the *male* side, a person could be classified as ethnically French whose mother, maternal grandparents and paternal grandmother were English speaking. In that case it would be a fiction to regard such a person as French speaking and likely to experience handicaps in being in an English-speaking school.

Though the numbers are small, for our purposes clearly French, defined according to the language mostly spoken at home, is a better indicator of the French-speaking population in the English-language schools who might, according to the views advanced in the Report of the Royal Commission on Bilingualism and Biculturalism, be expected to experience disadvantages because of language difficulties. Accordingly, we will now present a profile of the Franco-Ontarian students, comparing those in French schools with those in English schools, and comparing both with the total sample in the English schools.

Profile of the Franco-Ontarian Students

According to the 1971 census about 6 per cent of Ontario's population gave their mother tongue as French. An additional 10 per cent were ethnically French, as revealed by the question concerning their ethnic origin through their male ancestor. They came from four main regions in the province: Ottawa-Carleton, Sudbury–Sault Ste. Marie, Prescott–Russell–Renfrew, and Iroquois Falls–Kirkland Lake. Although the majority of the French, like all Ontarians, live in urban areas, they do live disproportionately in small urban areas (1,000-9,999) and rural non-farm areas. They also have a lower level of educational attainment. The tendency to leave school earlier than the general population was continuing until 1971, when of the 15-24 year olds more than two-thirds of those whose mother tongue was French were out of school compared to less than half of the rest of the population.

While the Royal Commission on Bilingualism and Biculturalism thought that the lower educational levels of the Franco-Ontarians and the fact that they were disproportionately in rural areas might be a factor in the greater attrition rate of students as reported by the Carnegie Study, they felt that beyond these factors were others for which they had no data, such as the fact that there was no public secondary education in French in the province. Since by the time of this study French secondary schools did exist, we should be able to see whether they were right in their view that providing educational experiences in French would improve the attitude to education of the Franco-Ontarians. Of course, it must be remembered that these schools had been in existence only a short time and that some of the students in our sample, at least the Grade 12 ones, might have started out in English-speaking schools. On the other hand, in Ottawa, which has the largest French-speaking population in the province, there had been French fee-paying secondary schools which many who were subsequently enrolled in the French-speaking public schools had attended.

With these factors in mind, we will now look at selected characteristics of the three categories of students that we mentioned earlier: the French-speaking students in the French schools, those with French mother tongue in the English schools, and the total sample in the English schools. Table 13.1 shows the proportions in Grades 10 and 12 in these three categories. Column I has the figures for the French schools, Column II for those in the English schools whose mother tongue was French, and Column III for the total sample in the English-language schools.

First, looking at the background characteristics, it is interesting to notice that, on the whole, the sub-sample in the Francophone schools was more like the total sample in the Anglophone schools than either was like the French in the Anglophone schools. For example, in Grade 12 the proportions in the lower social classes were 49 and 48 per cent respectively in the Francophone and Anglophone schools, but 58 per cent of French students in the English schools. And of those whose fathers had at least an educational level of high school graduation, the proportions were about 30 in the Francophone and Anglophone schools, but only 19 among the French in the Anglophone schools. In Grade 10 the similarity is not as great in the proportions with these characteristics in the Francophone and Anglophone schools. No doubt the similarity in Grade 12 can be explained, as we have noted before, by the fact that Grade 12 is a "survival grade," and those who survive in the French-language schools tend to be more like students in the English-language schools than do those who leave school early.

However, as far as family size is concerned, the two groups of French students were similar, with two-thirds in Grade 12 coming from families of four or more children, while this was true of less than half of the English school sample. The final category, urban residence, shows that 61 per cent of the students in French-language schools in Grade 12 lived in large cities, while this was so of only 31 per cent of the French in the English-language schools. This reflects the fact that the cities where Franco-Ontarians live, such as Sudbury and Ottawa, are more likely to have established French-language public high schools than the rural areas where Franco-Ontarians live.

In looking at family characteristics, we can see that in some respects the two groups of French speakers were more alike than either was to the

Table 13.1

Selected Characteristics of the Total Sample in Anglophone Schools, of Students with French Mother Tongue in the Anglophone Sample and of the French Sub-sample (Grades 10 and 12)

	I		II		III	
	Francophone Schools		French Mother Tongue in English Schools		Anglophone Schools (total sample)	
	Grade		Grade		Grade	
Characteristics	10	12	10	12	10	12
			(per cent)			
Background Characteristics						
Lower social class	61	49	70	58	51	48
Educational level of father (high school grad. or more)	19	29	16	19	28	31
More than 4 children in the family	80	66	72	67	52	48
Urban residence	41	61	34	31	52	49

Family Characteristics						
Religiosity (once a week or more to church)	77	53	66	66	43	37
Significant others—parents helping most in hopes	57	47	42	30	52	41
No one helping	16	20	34	35	30	33
Perceived mothers' LEA post-secondary	63	67	53	63	69	72
Very much parental influence	24	39	34	28	13	14
School Characteristics						
5-year program	64	75	43	54	62	64
Positive attitude towards schoolwork	28	42	30	50	20	35
School performance 75+	15	17	11	11	15	17
Personal Characteristics						
Aspirations to university	31	40	19	20	31	36
High occup. expectations	31	41	23	16	27	31
High SCA	27	28	11	9	21	25
High mental ability	23	17	23	11	36	30
N=	249	162	53	80	2,964	2,862

English sample. In other respects the sample in the French schools was more like the sample in the English schools than either was like the French group in the English schools. The most religious group in Grade 12 consisted of the French in the English schools, with two-thirds of them going to church once a week or more. Somewhat more than half of those in French-language schools went that frequently, but less than two-fifths of the English sample went that often. In Grade 10, however, the most religious group was in the French-language schools, with more than three-quarters reporting that they went to church at least once a week. The falling off in church attendance between the age groups in the Francophone schools is striking.

Another family characteristic that seemed relevant could be determined in the responses to the question, "Who helps you most in thinking about your future education?" As we showed in the chapter on significant others (Chapter 8), parents, either father or mother, or father and mother equally, were most likely to be the ones who helped most. Forty-one per cent of the Grade 12 English-speaking sample answered this way. The proportion was higher in the French-language schools (47 per cent). In contrast, only 30 per cent of the French in English-language schools answered that parents were helping most. In the chapter on significant others we were surprised at the large proportion that answered that no one helped them. This was true of one-third in the Anglophone schools. But the proportion in the French-language schools that said no one was helping them was much lower—only 20 per cent. A similar pattern prevails in Grade 10. The French generally, whether in French or English schools, seem more family oriented, as is revealed in the proportion who considered that their families had very much influence on them. Only 14 per cent of all students in the English schools in Grade 12 had this view, compared to 28 per cent of the French in the English schools and 39 per cent in the French schools.

As far as educational aspirations are concerned, the students' perception of their mothers' aspirations for them is important. Again the French in the English schools had the lowest proportions of the three groups who thought that their mothers would like them to take some form of post-secondary education.

Consistent with the pattern that is emerging in these figures and with the Royal Commission hypothesis—that the French in the English schools are most disadvantaged in their educational opportunities—is the fact that a much lower proportion of them were in a five-year program than either of the other two groups. And although we have shown that school performance figures are an unreliable measure of educational achievement since they mean different things in the five- and four-year programs and between different schools, these figures showing the proportions who had school-reported grades of over 75 per cent are again consistent with the picture of disadvantaged French students in English schools, with only 11 per cent having these grades compared with 17 per cent of the other two groups in Grade 12.

The one surprising finding among what we are calling school characteristics is the attitude towards schoolwork, where the highest proportion with a positive attitude are the French in the English schools. This is true of both Grades 10 and 12, which tends to add credence to the finding. This could perhaps be explained by the fact that a higher proportion of these students were in the four-year program where they might have found the subject matter of their practical courses more interesting and less difficult than students in the five-year program would find the subject matter of their academic courses.

Our major dependent variable in this study is educational aspirations, and so, of course, it is interesting to see how our three groups of students compare in this respect. As we see from the fourth part of Table 13.1, very similar proportions in the French- and English-language schools aspired to university. In Grade 10 the proportions were exactly the same (31 per cent), and in Grade 12 the proportion in the French schools who wanted to go to university was higher than in the English schools (40 to 36 per cent). But among the French in English schools the proportions who wanted to go to university were much lower in both grades. Only one-fifth had these aspirations. As would be expected, we find the same differences in the proportions with high occupational expectations between the French in French-language and in English-language schools. Forty-one per cent of the former, only 16 per cent of the latter, had high occupational expectations. The proportion in the English schools with such expectations was 31 per cent.

We have argued frequently in this text that a person's image of himself and of his ability is important in determining how well he performs and what he will see himself capable of doing in the future. In this table we are using the full Brookover scale of self-concept of academic ability, which includes the questions relating to how well a student rates himself within his classroom and school, as well as how well he thinks he is capable of doing at university. Not surprisingly, in view of our other findings, the proportions with a high self-concept of ability were much lower among the French in English schools than among our other two groups. The proportions in Grade 12 with a high self-concept in the Francophone and Anglophone schools were 28 and 25 per cent respectively, but only 9 per cent of the French in English schools rated themselves very highly.

Given the similarities between the students in the French schools and all the students in the English schools in terms of aspirations, it is very surprising and puzzling to observe the differences in the proportions of students with high mental ability scores. The IPAT culture fair test, which we have described in Chapter 4 and which was used to determine mental ability, does not contain verbal tests of intelligence. The test consists entirely of the ability to manipulate symbols logically. Furthermore, in the French-language schools instructions were given in French. The scores of the students in the English schools were divided roughly into thirds to create high, medium and low mental ability categories. Using exactly the same division points, we find that only 11 per cent of the French students in the English schools in Grade 12 had high mental ability, compared to 30 in the whole sample. (In Grade 10 the figures are 23 and 36 per cent.) This might be explained in part by the fact that these students received their instructions in English, in which, since they speak French at home, they are at a disadvantage. Also, we have already discussed the fact that in spite of it being a culture fair test, the results are related to social class, and we suggested that a reason for this might be that middle-class children are more oriented to trying hard in tests, especially when there are no rewards for doing well. Since there is a higher proportion of lower social class students among the French in the English schools than in the whole sample, this might also be a factor in these differences.

But what is very surprising is that differences in the proportions of students with high mental ability also exist between the Francophone students in the French schools and all the students in the English schools. Though the proportion of French students with high mental ability is not as low in the French schools as in the English schools (17 per cent in Grade 12 and 23 in Grade 10), they are still considerably lower than the proportion with high mental ability in the English schools. Yet as we have seen, the

Table 13.2
Percentage with University Aspirations by Socio-economic Status
of Ethnically French in Anglophone Schools and
Francophones in Francophone Schools (Grades 12 and 10)

Schools	Socio-economic Status of Franco-Ontarian Students		
	Upper-middle	Middle	Lower
	Grade 12		
	(per cent)		
Anglophone School	36 (11)*	33 (51)	20 (89)
Francophone School	78 (16)	50 (41)	32 (75)
	Grade 10		
	(per cent)		
Anglophone School	25 (9)	44 (41)	14 (92)
Francophone School	50 (15)	46 (6)	25 (151)

*Numbers in brackets are ones on which percentages are based.

social class composition of these students in the French schools is very similar to that of the students in the English schools. Can we conclude that French-speaking students are less intelligent or at least less able to perform the symbolic manipulations of the culture fair test? It seems very unlikely. Further research will have to be done to try to understand these findings.

Can we draw any conclusions from this profile about the importance of French-language schooling to the educational aspirations of Francophone students? Our comparison of the French in the French schools with the students in the English schools whose mother tongue is French should enable us to do so. But a problem is that these two groups are different in their background characteristics. The French in the English schools are more likely to come from a lower social class, have a father who had not graduated from high school, and to live in a rural area than the French in French-language schools. As we have demonstrated in Chapter 5, these characteristics—social class, educational level of the father and urban-rural residence—are all related to educational aspirations. Therefore, a difference in educational aspirations between these two groups might be attributed to the difference in the proportions with these relevant characteristics, rather than to a difference in the language of instruction.

Educational Aspirations by Social Class

The only way to determine whether the language of instruction makes a difference in aspirations is to compare the educational aspirations of the two groups, controlling for such important factors as social class. This we do in Table 13.2. The numbers are very small for such a cross-classification, particularly in the upper-middle class, and therefore cannot be considered totally reliable. In this case, in order to increase the number of French in the English schools, we have used ethnicity rather than mother tongue to identify the French. There is a possibility, as we suggested before, that in using this measure we are including some who are totally assimilated, but the effect of this would be to modify the picture of the French. The differences that we observe between the two groups of French are conservative differences. If we had used French mother tongue in the contingency table, the differences would have been greater. The table is striking, because in both Grades 12 and 10 at each social class level the proportions of French students aspiring to university are considerably higher in the French schools than in the English schools. This finding provides strong evidence that going to a French school enhances the probability of a Francophone student having high educational aspirations.

Francophone and Anglophone Aspirations:
Other Studies

We have been comparing the Franco-Ontarians in French-language and English-language schools, and we have been comparing both with the full sample in the English schools with respect to a number of characteristics. We have observed that there is no difference between the proportion with high educational aspirations in the French-language schools and in the total sample in the English-language schools.

This conclusion was also one reached by a group of researchers who compared the SOSA data with data generated through a survey of Quebec students conducted by Guy Rocher and Pierre Belanger in 1972.[5] François Beland, Louise Laforce and Guy Rocher were interested in testing a hypothesis of Pierre Belanger and E. Pedersen that in comparing educational and occupational aspirations of young French and English Canadians it is necessary to take into account regional differences. They argue that Canadian sociologists are guilty of a "universal fallacy" when they compare Francophones and Anglophones in the whole of Canada without taking into consideration the fact that the Francophones of Quebec, those of Ontario and those of New Brunswick constitute different regional groups belonging to socio-economic structures that are not the same, and that conclusions which are drawn from an analysis of all the Francophones in Canada are not necessarily valid for the Francophones of Ontario and New Brunswick, since they are much smaller in numbers than those of Quebec. Using a multivariate, hierarchical analysis they compared the educational aspirations of students in four samples, Anglophones and Francophones in Quebec and Anglophones and Francophones in Ontario. They identified as Anglophones the students attending English schools and as Francophones those in French schools. They concluded that there was no difference in the educational aspirations of Anglophones and Francophones in Ontario, but in Quebec the Anglophones had considerably higher educational aspirations than the Francophones.[6]

A survey of Franco-Ontarian senior high school students, "L'Avenir des Etudiants Franco-Ontarien de 12 et 13 années, 1974-75," commissioned by the Ministry of Colleges and Universities in 1976, reports similar findings.[7] Seventy-three per cent of the students attended French secondary schools, while the rest received their instruction in English secondary schools. The authors conclude that students from French secondary schools, even when academic achievement is controlled, are more likely to aspire to university than students from English-language schools. Also, with academic achievement controlled, students in French schools have higher academic self-conceptions than those in English schools.

However, for these Franco-Ontarian students, knowledge of English was also a factor in their aspirations. If their parents were able to speak English, they were more likely to want to go to university. Students from bilingual homes were more likely to have higher self-evaluations of their ability to do university work and to aspire to university than students from unilingual French homes. And students who were themselves fluent in English were more likely to want to attend university and have positive self-evaluations of their ability to do university work than students who were not fluent in English.

These two findings seem somewhat contradictory. On the one hand, students in French schools were more likely than French students in English schools to aspire to university. On the other hand, students who were fluent in English were more likely than those who were not to want to go to university. The contradiction arises, of course, from the fact that one would expect that the students in the English schools would be the ones most fluent in English.

Although the findings seem contradictory, they can be explained in terms of the minority position the Franco-Ontarians are in. The Franco-phones in the English schools are constantly aware of their minority status, feel inadequate compared to their English-speaking peers, have a low academic self-concept and do not feel themselves capable of doing univer-sity work. The Francophones in the French-language schools, on the other hand, can forget about their minority status in the province, since it does not infringe on the classroom. They can have a high academic self-concept in relation to their French-speaking peers, and they can feel themselves capable of doing university work. But without a knowledge of English, opportunities for students in the occupational world of Ontario are extremely limited. It is unlikely that a student who has not had the opportunity or the motivation to learn English would have the necessary ambition to consider a university education. It seems that a Franco-Ontarian student is most likely to aspire to university if he goes to a French-language secondary school and is able to speak English.

Raymond Breton in his 1965 study of Canadian students expected to find that the French would have lower educational aspirations than the English, but instead he found that they had what he called "unrealistically" high aspirations, which he explained as follows:

> It can be argued that membership in a disadvantaged group in society—a linguistic group—has a tendency to create feelings of inferiority and/or a fear of failure. These feelings, in turn, probably prompt the individual to form either very low or very high goals to avoid competition or to disassociate himself from a possible source of his sense of inadequacy.[8]

It should be pointed out that in their comparison of students in Quebec and Ontario, Beland, Laforce and Rocher[9] were extremely critical of Breton for not attempting to analyse students' aspirations by province, though he had collected his data in that way. In their analysis of the SOSA and ASOPE data, they show that while in Ontario Francophone students had relatively high aspirations—"unrealistically high," Breton would say—in Quebec the aspirations of the Francophone students were much lower than those of the Anglophone students.

The interesting question is whether, in fact, aspirations of the Franco-phones in the French schools were unrealistically high. As we will show in our description of the results of the follow-up studies that were conducted a few years later of the students in this survey, the aspirations of all students were unrealistically high. Of the students in the Grade 12 sample in 1971, 38 per cent wanted to go to university, and in fact only 28 per cent did. Only 19 per cent wanted to go to work immediately after leaving high school, and 44 per cent actually did. But were the aspirations of the Francophones more unrealistic than of the other students? If their actual educational attainment turned out to be lower than that of the students in the Anglophone sample, we would conclude that their aspirations were more unrealistic than those of the other students since, as we have seen, they were very similar. An indication of whether they were more unrealistic can be gained by looking at the results of a follow-up study of Grade 8 students conducted by Maria Barrados five years after the original data were collected. In the winter of 1976, the students who were in Grade 8 in 1971 were re-contacted and were asked to complete a short questionnaire on their school progress to that time and their future educational and occupational plans. Most of the students who were still in school in 1976 were in Grade 13, or Year 5 as it was by then called. If the students were already out of school, they were asked if they had had any training outside of high school, what type of work they were doing, and if they planned to take any further training.

Educational Attainment of Anglophone and Francophone Students

Barrados has compared the educational attainment of the Anglophone and Francophone students.[10] In her analysis she defined as Francophones those who were in French-language schools in Grade 8 and as Anglophones those who were in English-language schools at that time. They may or may not have attended French high schools. In fact, of the 76 per cent of the original French sample of 346 students that Barrados was able to contact, 44 per cent said that their language of instruction was predominately French, 17 per cent predominately English, and 39 per cent English and French. We cannot, therefore, draw conclusions from her analysis about the effect on educational attainment of Francophone students being entirely educated in French. But we can compare the overall educational attainment levels of Francophone and Anglophone students.

Eighty-one per cent of the students who were in the Grade 8 English sample and, as we mentioned, 76 per cent in the Grade 8 French sample in 1971 were successfully contacted in 1976.[11] Table 13.3 shows the completion rates of 100 sample students starting high school in the fall of 1971 when the original sample was surveyed. Some of the students who were contacted five years later were still in high school, most likely in Year 5 or Grade 13; and since these students were contacted relatively late in the school year (from February to June), and with few exceptions all expected to complete their course requirements, the figure for the number of students in Year 5 is felt to

Table 13.3
Completion Rates of Every 100 Sample Students Starting Grade 9
(Weighted Sample)*

	Year 1 Start	Year 1 Complete	Year 2	Year 3	Year 4	Year 5 In	N
		1972	1973	1974	1975	1976	
English	100	98	92	83	72	34	2,683
French	100	99	85	72	64	20	343

*See Note 11 for an explanation of the weighting.

be a reasonable estimate, possibly a little high, of the proportion of students actually completing Year 5.

The table shows that the French students were more likely than English-speaking students to leave school early, after Year 3, and were less likely to continue to Year 5. Both French and English were more likely to finish high school than was the case in the Carnegie Study that started in 1959, when only 13 per cent of Anglophone and 3 per cent of Francophone students completed Grade 13. The difference in the proportions of Francophone and Anglophone students completing Year 4 or Grade 12 was not as great as it had been in the early 1960s. Then, only 42 per cent of the English sample and 26 per cent of the French sample had completed grade 12, whereas in this study 72 per cent of the English and 64 per cent of the French completed Year 4. But there still was quite a large difference of 14 percentage points in the proportions of Anglophones and Francophones in Year 5. The drop in the proportion attending school between Year 4 and Year 5 was greater for the French than for the English.

It might seem that though, as we showed earlier, the aspirations of the Francophone students were similar to those of Anglophone students, they were more likely to leave school earlier. And therefore we might conclude that their aspirations were more unrealistic than those of the English-speaking students. But this would be an unwarranted conclusion because, as we pointed out, the Francophone students as they were defined in the follow-up study may or may not have taken their secondary schooling in French. The 17 per cent who said they took their courses in English would certainly fall in the category that we described in the early part of this chapter as having the lowest aspirations—the French speakers in English-language schools. And perhaps that would apply to at least some of the 39 per cent who said that their secondary school courses were in both English and French.

We have shown that the Francophones in the English-language high schools differed from those in the French-language high schools on a number of characteristics that would be related to their staying in school till

Year 5. They were less likely to be in a five-year program, to have academic grades over 75 per cent, to want to go to university, to perceive their mothers as wanting them to continue their education after high school, to have high occupational expectations and to have a high self-concept of ability.

Unfortunately, the coding that was employed in the follow-up study does not allow us to separate the Francophones who went to French-language high schools from those who went to English-language high schools. Clearly, then, we cannot use the results of the follow-up study to address the proposition that we have been examining in this chapter—the question of whether the lower educational attainment level of the Franco-Ontarians is due to the fact that they have not had the opportunity to continue their education after elementary school in French.

However, the analysis that we have made of the Grade 10 and 12 Francophones in French- and English-language schools shows that they differ in the variables that explain much of the variance in educational aspirations. Barrados, in her multivariate analysis of the follow-up sample, shows that these variables—academic achievement, school program, perceived parental aspirations, educational aspirations and self-concept of ability—also account for much of the variance in educational attainment (years spent in high school). Tentatively, we can say that our data support the hypothesis of the B & B Commission that lack of opportunity to take their secondary schooling in French accounts for the lower educational levels of the Franco-Ontarians.

Notes

1. *Report of the Royal Commission on Bilingualism and Biculturalism*, Vol. 2. (Ottawa: Queen's Printer, 1968). The historical information in this chapter can be found in Chapter III of the *Report*.
2. *Ibid.*, p.87.
3. *Ibid.*, p.91.
4. In 1970-71 there were 28,000 students enrolled in 20 French-language secondary schools compared to 574,520 students enrolled in the English-language secondary schools. *The Report of the Minister of Education, 1971*.
5. Guy Rocher and Pierre Belanger conducted a survey of 6,204 students who attended French-language schools and 2,568 who attended English-language schools in 1972. Their survey is known as ASOPE, Université de Montreal et Université Laval.
6. François Beland, Louise Laforce, Guy Rocher, "Les Aspirations Scolaires des Jeunes au Canada: Une Etude Comparative" (mimeo).
7. Gabriel Bordeleau and Louis M. Desjardins, "L'Avenir des Etudiants Franco-Ontarien de 12 et 13 Années, 1974-75" (Ministry of Colleges and Universities, Government of Ontario, 1976).
8. Raymond Breton, *Social and Academic Factors in the Career Decisions of Canadian Youth* (Ottawa: Information Canada, Department of Manpower and Immigration, 1972), p.152.
9. Beland, Laforce and Rocher, *op. cit.*

10. Maria Barrados, *A Study of Early School Leaving in Ontario*, Ph.D. thesis, Department of Sociology and Anthropology, Carleton University, Ottawa. See also John Porter, B.R. Blishen, Maria Barrados, *Survival of a Grade 8 Cohort* (Toronto: Ontario Government Bookstore) (microfiche).

11. An analysis of some of the characteristics of the follow-up respondents in comparison with the students who could not be contacted from the original sample showed that the sample of follow-up respondents was somewhat biased in favour of students who had a more positive orientation towards schooling. For example, the respondents were found to be more likely to have higher grades and higher educational expectations than non-respondents. A simple weighting scheme was devised that removed this bias.

14

The Follow-Up of Grade 8
and Grade 12 Students

Previous chapters have analysed the relationship between a range of social and psychological variables and educational and occupational aspirations and expectations of a sample of students in Grades 8, 10 and 12. We now turn to an examination of the extent to which these educational and work goals were actually realized by the samples of Grade 8 and Grade 12 students. These two cohorts were each the subject of a follow-up study on which the following summary analysis is based.[1] The Grade 8 cohort was contacted five years after the 1971 survey, as we explained in Chapter 13. These students were chosen for analysis because it was possible to determine what effect, if any, some of our social and psychological variables had on the realization of these goals. Some of them would have completed, or would have been in the process of completing, secondary school at the time of the follow-up study. The Grade 12 cohort was contacted in 1972, one year after the original survey. This cohort was chosen because it included students who had entered the labour force after completing their schooling, as well as others who had decided to continue their education.[2] In what follows, a summary of the main points of the Grade 8 follow-up study will be given first, followed by a summary of the highlights of the Grade 12 follow-up study.

The analysis in Chapter 13 focussed on the French student and was based on the sample of French students. In the Grade 8 follow-up study an attempt was made to compare the experience of French and English students, but unfortunately the number of French students made cross-tabular analysis using some of our independent variables impossible. We have indicated in Chapter 13 the difference in educational attainment of the two groups. As for the Grade 12 cohort, no distinction was made between English and French students. Furthermore, the analysis of this cohort was far less detailed than the one undertaken for the younger cohort. For these reasons comparison between the two cohorts is difficult. This should be kept in mind when reading the summary of the main points of these two studies.

The Grade 8 Student Cohort

The students in the Grade 8 cohort in 1976 were in one of three groups: not in school at all; taking some other form of schooling outside of high school; or still in high school. Nearly half of the English students and nearly two-thirds of the French students were taking no further schooling.[3] Sixteen per cent of French students were still in school, and this was less than half the 39 per cent of English students in this position.

Most of the respondents not taking any form of schooling were working (80 per cent of the English, 69 per cent of the French), many were looking for work or were unemployed (13 per cent of the English, 19 per cent of the French), some were housewives (7 per cent of the English, 10 per cent of the French) and a small proportion were either travelling or ill. Not only were the French students more likely to be out of school, but those that were in this situation were more likely to be unemployed. Of the students who were out of high school but taking some other form of training, the majority were taking courses at a community college (58 per cent of the English, 62 per cent of the French).

Inequality of Chances

We have already referred to the social and psychological variables that affect educational and occupational aspirations and expectations. The extensive literature in the sociology of education shows that many of these same variables influence the child's progress through school. We now turn to an analysis of the relationship between some of these variables and the likelihood of the student completing the various high school grades.

Two of the variables that we identified in Chapter 5 as affecting educational aspirations were social class and mental ability. Not surprisingly these two variables affected the number of years students stayed in school.

When we examine the influence of social class on the relationship between mental ability and years of secondary school attainment for these students, as shown in Table 14.1, it appears that upper-middle-class students were more likely to have more years of high school attainment than lower-class students, regardless of mental ability. The differences in the proportions of school attainment between those with low and those with high mental ability were substantial for all classes, particularly the middle group. However, the likelihood of students attaining the last year of high school was consistently higher for students with higher mental ability as well as higher class. Students with lower mental ability were less likely to attain Year 5, but those from the upper-middle class were still clearly at an advantage.

Table 14.1
Secondary School Attainment by Mental Ability Scores (1971)
Controlling for Social Class
(Weighted Sample)

Socio-economic Status	Years in Secondary School	Mental Ability		
		High	Medium	Low
			(per cent)	
Upper-middle	Grade 8 only	1	-	2
	Year 1	1	2	5
	Year 2	3	4	6
	Year 3	1	7	8
	Year 4	29	33	40
	Year 5	64	54	39
		99	100	100
	N=	216	193	103

$X^2 = 29.76$ $p > .001$
Conditional Gamma = .290

Middle	Grade 8 only	-	1	2
	Year 1	4	4	9
	Year 2	7	9	12
	Year 3	9	11	12
	Year 4	32	37	39
	Year 5	48	38	27
		100	100	101
	N =	258	324	258

$X^2 = 36.4$ $p > .001$
Conditional Gamma = .235

Lower	Grade 8 only	1	3	6
	Year 1	3	7	11
	Year 2	10	9	13
	Year 3	11	14	15
	Year 4	44	40	40
	Year 5	31	27	15
		100	101	100
	N =	297	465	406

$X^2 = 57.25$ $p > .001$
Conditional Gamma = .247

Summary Gammas Zero Order = .282
First Order Partial = .248

Another of our important variables is school performance. Class differences in school performance were found to be similar to mental ability differences, with 64 per cent of upper-class students, 55 per cent of middle-class, and 49 per cent of working-class students who had high scores in school performance.

Our data indicate that the relationship between sex of the student and high school attainment was negligible. Boys were somewhat more likely to leave school before Year 4 and stay to Year 5. Girls, on the other hand, were somewhat more likely to stay in school and complete Year 4 rather than stay to Year 5, but these relationships are not strong and not statistically significant.

Our data also indicate that the relationship between urban or rural residence and years spent in high school is very weak but statistically significant. Students living in urban areas had a greater likelihood of staying to Year 5. Forty-two per cent of the respondents living in Toronto and surrounding urban areas stayed in high school until Year 5, compared to 30 per cent of students living in rural areas. Respondents in rural and minor urban areas were more likely to leave school before completing Year 4 than students in the Toronto urban area and other Ontario major urban areas.

In addition to the cross-tabular analysis summarized thus far, our Grade 8 follow-up study also showed the extent to which the probabilities of educational decision-making were affected by the background variables already discussed.

Raymond Boudon[4] refers to the differences between the different social classes in school attainment along such "dimensions" as mental ability, rural-urban residence and the like as primary effects of stratification or social and economic inequality. Our findings bear out his general thesis that these differences set groups of students apart as being more or less advantaged. These primary stratification effects set the conditions for the development of the child's future plans and educational decision-making—such as the types of courses the individual will take, his program of studies and when he leaves school. These decisions become the secondary effects of stratification on the educational process, and all involve some estimation of costs and benefits. This decision-making is then conditioned by the advantages and disadvantages resulting from the primary effect, and so may be described in terms of conditional probabilities of the individual proceeding through the various choices presented by the school structure.

Probabilities of Secondary School Attainment
The probabilities of students reaching each of the attainment levels from Grade 8 to Year 5 in secondary school are presented in Table 14.2. High early achievers from upper-middle-class families had the highest probability of staying in secondary school to Year 5. When the influences of social

Table 14.2
Probabilities of Secondary School Attainment with Grade 7 School Performance and Social Class Controlled
(Weighted Sample)

Socio-economic Status	School Performance	Grade 8 Only	School Attainment					
			Year 1	Year 2	Year 3	Year 4	Year 5	N
Upper-middle	High	.006	.006	.02	.02	.28	.67	(305)
	Average	.02	.05	.04	.10	.37	.42	(152)
	Low	-	.05	.19	.12	.52	.13	(39)

$X^2 = 89.30$ Conditional Gamma = -.547

Middle	High	.007	.02	.04	.07	.32	.55	(420)
	Average	.006	.08	.12	.14	.43	.23	(306)
	Low	.03	.16	.22	.22	.30	.07	(95)

$X^2 = 168.8$ p .001 Conditional Gamma = -.565

Lower	High	.01	.03	.06	.11	.42	.38	(505)
	Average	.05	.07	.13	.17	.43	.16	(432)
	Low	.09	.21	.18	.18	.33	.02	(169)

$X^2 = 197.5$ p .001 Conditional Gamma = -.506
Zero order Gamma -.548
First order Gamma -.528

class and high academic achievement were examined separately, the probabilities of staying to Year 5 were high (.55 and .51 respectively). When early achievement and social class were considered together in Table 14.2, the probability of staying to Year 5 increased to .67. This table illustrates quite clearly that high achieving lower-class students were *less* likely to stay to Year 5 than high and average achieving upper-middle-class students and high achieving middle-class students. Low achieving students are least likely to stay to Year 5, but again marked social class distinctions are seen. Lower-class students with low achievement have a probability of only .02 of staying in school to Year 5, while the same probability for low achieving upper-middle-class students is .13.

Probabilities of Taking a Five-Year Program

As we have shown in previous chapters, family background and early school achievement further limited the educational opportunities of Ontario students by affecting the choice of high school courses and programs of study—whether they were directed to a secondary school graduation diploma at the end of four years of study or the honours diploma at the end of five years of study. At the time of the original study in 1971, students were asked what program of high school studies they planned to take. Thirty-six per cent planned to take a four-year program and 64 per cent planned to take a five-year program. By the time of the follow-up study, 47 per cent of the students described their course of studies as a four-year program and 53 per cent said they were taking a five-year program of studies. It would appear that before or some time during their high school career, a number of students had switched from longer to shorter programs, and *vice versa*. In fact, 24 per cent of the students who planned to take a four-year program actually took a five-year program, and a somewhat larger portion, 29 per cent, who planned to take a five-year program took a four-year program. Seventy-six per cent of the students who planned to take a four-year program were in the same program at the time of the follow-up, and 71 per cent of the students who planned to take the five-year program were in the same program at the time of the follow-up. When the changes from planned program to actual program are controlled for social class, a striking pattern of differentiation between the classes emerges, as shown in Table 14.3.

Upper-middle-class students had the highest probability of having planned to take and subsequently remaining in a five-year program of studies. If they changed their program, they most likely changed from the shorter to the longer program, by necessity relatively early in their secondary school career. Lower-class students, on the other hand, had the highest probability of having planned to take and subsequently remaining in a four-year program. If they changed their program they did so from the five-year to the shorter four-year program. Table 14.3 shows that these changes

Table 14.3

**Probability of Staying in the Expected Program of Studies
with Social Class Controlled (Weighted Sample)**

Socio-economic Status	Expected Program	
	5-Year Program[1] No Change	4-Year Program No Change
Upper-middle	.83 (378)[2]	.58 (103)
Middle	.71 (529)	.71 (262)
Low	.63 (611)	.82 (478)

1. Expected program of studies in 1971 compared with actual program of studies as reported in 1976.
2. Marginal totals, i.e. the total number of students of a particular SES group planning to take a particular program of studies, including those who actually took another program.

in intentions further increased the inequalities by social class. The decision to switch to the shorter program of studies reduced the alternatives open to the student and limited his choices of post-secondary education.

What were the probabilities of students taking the five-year program? Table 14.4 shows that students from upper-middle-class families were consistently more likely to have taken a five-year program of studies. At each class level the probability of having taken a five-year program dropped as the level of early achievement dropped. However, it is noteworthy that the probability of an upper-middle-class student with *low* achievement taking a five-year program was close to the same probability of average achieving middle- and lower-class students. Similarly, the *average* achieving upper-middle-class students had a similar probability of taking a five-year program as *high* achieving lower-class students.

Since we have shown that students from upper-middle-class families were more likely to have been enrolled in a five-year program, or if they had changed their intended program they were likely to have changed from a four-year to a five-year program, we could expect that upper-middle-class students in a five-year program would be less likely to leave school in Years 1 to 4. Table 14.5 shows that this was the case, although 25 per cent of these students did not complete the fifth year of studies. This table shows that, regardless of family background, young people were less likely to leave school from the five-year program in Years 2 to 4. Respondents from upper-middle-class backgrounds were the least likely to leave in these years, particularly if they were in the five-year program. While middle- and lower-class young people in a five-year program were more likely to leave secondary school during and at the end of the first year, they were also less likely to leave secondary school in contrast to other students of the same status groups but in the shorter programs.

We have shown the influence of a number of factors in a young person's background, as well as his place in a high school program, on his secondary school attainment. We now briefly examine how the student's Grade 8 educational expectations to complete high school were fulfilled.

Grade 8 Expectations and High School Studies

In Chapter 10 we showed that, regardless of family social status or level of achievement, if at the time of our original survey Grade 8 students had hoped to complete Year 5 or go to university they were much more likely to expect to take a five-year program in high school. In our follow-up study five years later, we found that if these students had expected to complete Year 5 or go to university they were, in fact, very likely to be in a five-year program. For example, 83 per cent of high achieving, middle-class students who expected to complete Year 5 were in a five-year program, while only 44 per cent of high achieving, middle-class students who did not expect to complete Year 5 were in this program. Similarly, 87 per cent of students of the same background and achievement level who had expected to go to

Table 14.4
Probabilities of Taking a Five-Year Program of Studies
with Grade 7 School Performance and Social Class Controlled
(Weighted Sample)

Socio-economic Status	School Performance	5-Year Program
Upper-middle	High	.87
	Average	.60
	Low	.31
		(370)

$X^2 = 82.1$ p .001 Conditional Gamma = −.688

Middle	High	.77
	Average	.37
	Low	.15
		(456)

$X^2 = 186.34$ p .001 Conditional Gamma = −.736

Lower	High	.63
	Average	.30
	Low	.07
		(462)

$X^2 = 196.3$ p .001 Conditional Gamma = −.687
Zero order Gamma = −.707
First order Gamma = −.704

Table 14.5
Probabilities of Secondary School Attainment with
Program of Studies and Social Class Controlled
(Weighted Sample)

Secondary School Attainment	Five-Year Program		
		Socio-economic Status	
	Upper-middle	Middle	Lower
Grade 8 only	-	.002	.01
Year 1	-	.02	.03
Year 2	.02	.04	.03
Year 3	.02	.04	.07
Year 4	.21	.21	.27
Year 5	.75 (372)	.69 (453)	.58 (477)

Secondary School Attainment	Four-Year Program		
		Socio-economic Status	
	Upper-middle	Middle	Lower
Grade 8 only	-	.01	.04
Year 1	.08	.10	.10
Year 2	.10	.15	.16
Year 3	.13	.19	.19
Year 4	.69	.54	.51
Year 5	.007 (133)	.01 (371)	.001 (668)

Zero order Gamma = .840
First order partial Gamma = .804

university in Grade 8 were in a five-year program, while 66 per cent who did not expect to go to university were in this program.

The pattern of relationships between the presence of either of the higher levels of educational expectations and choice of the five-year program is generally the same. The probabilities of taking a five-year program, depending on whether the student expected to complete Year 5 or go to university, were similar for upper-middle-class high achievers, but tended to be higher for the middle- and lower-class high achievers and the middle-level achievers in all classes if the student expected to go to university. Except for the select few upper-middle-class and high achieving students, the presence of expectations for university attendance in Grade 8, rather than only expectations to complete Year 5, increased the likelihood that the student would take the longer program in high school.

Upper-middle-class status and/or high achievement increased the probability that the student would be in the more advanced course, even though he had not expected to complete Year 5 studies in Grade 8. A combination of parental or school intervention probably influenced the student to re-define his course of high school studies or, in cases of uncertainty, influenced him on his choice of courses.

Grade 8 educational expectations are also found to be related to the years spent in school. If the Grade 8 student expected to stay in high school to Year 5, he had a much higher probability of staying in school longer, and also a lower probability of leaving school before Year 4. Of the students who expected to complete Year 5, 48 per cent reached Year 5 in contrast to students who did not expect to stay to that year, of whom only 9 per cent actually reached it. Of the students who did not expect to complete Year 5, the largest proportion—44 per cent—completed Year 4.

Table 14.6
Probability of Staying to Year 5 or Less by Expectation
in Grade 8 to Complete Year 5, Controlling for Social Class
(Weighted Sample)

| Socio-economic Status | Expectation to Complete Year 5 | | | |
	Stay to Year 4 or Less	Stay to Year 5	Total	N
Upper-middle	.37	.63	100	(407)
Middle	.50	.50	100	(575)
Lower	.62	.38	100	(636)

| | Expectation Not to Complete Year 5 | | | |
	Stay to Year 4 or Less	Stay to Year 5	Total	N
Upper-middle	.78	.22	100	(99)
Middle	.89	.11	100	(245)
Lower	.93	.07	100	(508)

Zero order Gamma = .793
First order partial Gamma = .778

To what extent was the actual attainment of those with high educational expectations affected by social class? Table 14.6 indicates that students from upper-middle-class families were the most likely to have their educational expectations matched with their educational attainment. Sixty-three per cent of upper-middle-class students who expected to complete Year 5 stayed that year, while only 38 per cent of lower-class students who expected to complete Year 5 stayed to the last year of high school.

Of the students who did not expect to complete high school, a greater proportion of upper-middle-class than lower-class students stayed to Year 5. Twenty-two per cent of upper-middle-class students, but only 7 per cent of lower-class students, who had not expected to stay to Year 5 actually stayed in high school that long.

Even lower-class students with university expectations in Grade 8 were less likely to stay to Year 5 than upper-middle-class students, as can be seen from Table 14.7. Of the upper-middle-class students with university expectations, 71 per cent stayed to Year 5, while only 53 per cent of lower-class students with expectations to go to university stayed that long. Of the students who had not expected to attend university, a larger proportion of

Table 14.7
Probability of Staying to Year 5 or Less
by Expectation in Grade 8 of University Attendance,
Controlling for Social Class (Weighted Sample)

Socio-economic Status	Expectation of University Attendance			
	Stay to Year 4 or Less	Stay to Year 5	Total	N
Upper-middle	.29	.71	100	(278)
Middle	.42	.58	100	(326)
Lower	.47	.53	100	(248)

Socio-economic Status	Expectation of Non-University Attendance			
	Stay to Year 4 or Less	Stay to Year 5	Total	N
Upper-middle	.65	.35	100	(231)
Middle	.76	.24	100	(500)
Lower	.84	.16	100	(907)

Zero order Gamma = .707
First order partial Gamma = .671

upper-middle-class students, 35 per cent, stayed to Year 5 than lower-class students, of whom only 16 per cent stayed to that year. The lower-class students appeared to be particularly disadvantaged by being less likely to have high educational expectations in elementary school, and even if they had them, they were less likely to realize them.

Beyond High School

At the time of the follow-up study, some respondents were still in high school, some were out of high school but taking another form of schooling, and others were out of high school but taking no further training. In what follows, the educational expectations of the respondents still in high school and of the respondents not taking any further schooling are combined with the educational goals of the respondents already taking some form of training outside of high school. Table 14.8 shows that upper-middle-class students were least likely to have no further educational expectations, least likely to expect to take other short courses or attend a community college, but most likely to expect to go to university. Middle-class students tended to fall midway between the upper-middle and lower-class students in terms of the expectation of taking no further training, other short courses, and university studies. Students in the middle-class were more likely than those in other classes to expect to attend community college. Conversely, lower-class students were the most likely to expect to take no further educational training and the least likely to expect to attend university. These findings of the pervasive and persistent effects of social class are consistent with what we might expect from the preceding analysis. The trends by sex of the student are somewhat different.

While the expectation to attend a community college (measured at the end of high school) tended to be higher for the two lower status groups, within these two groups there was also a small but significant difference between the sexes in the proportions who expected to attend this type of institution. For both the middle and lower classes, young women were somewhat more likely to expect to go to a community college, and young men were somewhat more likely to expect to take no further courses or other short courses.

The Grade 12 Follow-up Study

So far in this chapter, we have used data from a 1976 follow-up study of Grade 8 students to analyse the important factors in determining the educational destinations of these students five years after the original survey. The remainder of this chapter will show where the Grade 12 students in our sample actually ended up after leaving high school and reasons for the continuance or non-continuance of their education.

Table 14.8
Educational Expectations at Time of the Follow-up Study
by Sex of the Student Controlling for Social Class
(Weighted Sample)

Socio-economic Status	Educational Expectations	Male	Female
		(per cent)	
Upper-middle	No further educational expectations	27	26
	Other short courses	8	8
	Community College	20	21
	University	50	44
		100 (281)	99 (239)

$X^2 = 2.04$ $p > .56$ Gamma = $-.10$

	No further educational expectations	34	31
Middle	Other short courses	13	10
	Community College	25	33
	University	28	26
		100 (484)	100 (369)

$X^2 = 7.96$ $p > .05$ Gamma = $.04$

	No further educational expectations	48	43
Lower	Other short courses	15	13
	Community College	21	28
	University	16	16
		100 (594)	100 (590)

$X^2 = 8.83$ $p > .03$ Gamma = $.10$

The Gap: Aspirations and Reality

The Grade 12 follow-up study indicates that students had somewhat inflated aspirations for their level of attainment. Nearly 56 per cent would have liked to leave high school after Grade 13, but in fact about 54 per cent left after Grade 12; thus only 46 per cent continued to Grade 13. An examination of the relationship between aspirations and reality is shown in Table 14.9, which presents the cross-classification of students' aspirations

Table 14.9
Aspirations by Reality, Outflow Percentages from Aspirational
Levels to Post-Secondary Destinations

Aspirations After Leaving High School	Reality						
	In the Labour Force	Trade School Apprenticeship	Teachers' College or Nursing School	Community College	University	Other	Total
	(per cent)						
Enter the Labour Force	80	3	-	7	3	7	100
Trade School or Apprenticeship	62	14	-	15	1	8	100
Teachers' College or Nursing School	30	3	43	10	10	4	100
Community College	37	4	1	46	8	4	100
University	16	1	2	12	63	6	100
Other	45	4	3	13	12	23	100
Total	39	4	5	16	30	7	100

with what they did after they left high school percentaged by rows, that is, their actual destinations as a proportion of their aspirations.

Nearly 80 per cent of the students who wanted to work in fact ended up doing so, but of those who originally aspired to attend a trade school, business school, or to enter an apprenticeship, only 14 per cent did so, while over 60 per cent ended up working. An examination of the flows between teachers' colleges and nursing schools, community colleges and universities shows that universities were by far the most "stable" of the three in that 63 per cent of the students who aspired to attend university actually made it, compared with only 46 per cent for community colleges, and only 43 per cent for teachers' colleges and nursing schools. Regardless of aspiration, a sizeable minority of students who did not realize their aspirations ended up in the labour force. In the case of those who wished to go to a trade school or enter an apprenticeship, this became a majority.

Program determined to a large extent when students left school. Not unexpectedly, over 90 per cent of the students in the four-year program left high school at the end of Grade 12. Surprisingly, 7 per cent stated that they completed Grade 13, though only those in the five-year program were eligible to do so. On the other hand, the relationship between being in the five-year program and completing Grade 13 is less definite, with only just over two-thirds of the students in the five-year program having managed to complete Grade 13. Thus, being in the five-year program was a necessary but not sufficient condition for the completion of Grade 13.

In this follow-up study, other conditions related to this outcome were examined. Table 14.10, which presents the proportions of students in a five-year program who completed Grade 13 by mental ability and by social class, indicates the importance of social class to the completion of this grade. This is evident from an examination of the row and column effects in the table, which clearly shows that overall the effect of social class was somewhat stronger than the effect of mental ability.

The effect of social class when mental ability is held constant appears to be strongest in the high mental ability range, to decline substantially in the moderate range, and to be relatively small in the low mental ability range. When social class is held constant, it appears that for the lower class mental ability seems to make little if any difference at all in the proportion of students completing Grade 13. When we consider both effects together, it is clear that the effects of social class are much stronger than those of mental ability. In the proportions who completed Grade 13 there is a difference of 13 percentage points between the upper-middle and lower classes, but only a difference of 9 percentage points between those with high and with low mental ability.

The final stage for some of these Grade 12 students was enrolment in university. A striking fact which emerged from this follow-up study was that though 37 per cent of the students in Grade 12 had wanted to go to

Table 14.10
Percentage of Students in a Five-Year Program and Completing Grade 13,
by Socio-economic Status and Mental Ability

| Mental Ability | Socio-economic Status | | | |
	Upper-middle	Middle	Lower	Total
High	88 (107)	78 (122)	68 (136)	76 (365)
Medium	73 (71)	75 (137)	65 (133)	70 (341)
Low	71 (22)	66 (55)	67 (80)	67 (157)
Total	80	74	67	(863)

university, only 28 per cent actually did so: 45 per cent of the upper-middle class, 31 per cent of the middle class and 28 per cent of lower-class students.

Table 14.11 shows for the students in the follow-up study who had completed Grade 13 the proportions who were enrolled in university broken down jointly by social class and mental ability. Social class was a factor even for these well-qualified students. In the high mental ability group, social class effects were quite marked, with 74 per cent of the upper-middle-class students enrolled in university and only 59 per cent of the lower-class students going that far. For the students of medium mental ability, class had no effect at all. For those of low mental ability, class effects were evident, in that 52 per cent of the upper-middle class compared with 40 per cent of the lower class were enrolled in a university at the time of the follow-up study. Compared with the effects of class, the effects of mental ability on the probability of university enrolment were both relatively strong and consistent across all classes. However, since mental ability was an indicator of potential rather than actual achievement, in this follow-up study the effect

Table 14.11
Percentage of Students Who Had Completed Grade 13 and Were in University,
by Socio-economic Status and Mental Ability

| Mental Ability | Socio-economic Status | | | |
	Upper-middle	Middle	Lower	Total
High	74 (81)	62 (81)	59 (84)	64 (246)
Medium	52 (39)	52 (76)	53 (77)	51 (192)
Low	52 (12)	46 (30)	40 (36)	44 (78)
Total	64	55	52	(516)

of the students' school performance in Grade 13 on their going to university was examined.

Even though some social class effects remain among high performance students, with 90 per cent of upper-middle-class "A" students entering university compared with only three-quarters of the "A" students in the lower class, the effect of final grades on a student's chances of entering university were quite strong compared with the effects of either social class or mental ability.

Among the "A" students, who represent the prime candidates for university, it may be a source of some comfort that regardless of social class the institution manages to capture at least three-quarters of these students. What is surprising, however, is that 46 per cent of middle-class students in the 50-65 percentage range went to university.

Those Who Did Not Go On

In addition to an examination of students who went on after high school, and particularly with those who went on to university, the Grade 12 follow-up study undertook an analysis of the almost 50 per cent of students who did not go on.

Not all of the students who did not continue their education after the end of high school had terminated their education permanently. Many were unsure of what they wished to do, others felt they needed a rest before continuing their education, and others found it necessary to work for a few years in order to raise the financial resources to go on. Of the students who had not gone on at the time of the follow-up study, just over 23 per cent claimed they planned to return full-time, over 15 per cent planned to return part-time, 30 per cent were definitely not returning and the remainder did not know or gave no answer.

What is the effect of social class on students' plans to return? Both planning to return for further education and, given that decision, planning to do so at a university were clearly related to social class. However, the choice of institution appears to be more strongly related to class than was the decision simply to go back to school. This is evident in the difference between the upper-middle and lower classes with respect to the two decisions. Of the upper-middle-class students, 68 per cent planned to return to some type of further education, whereas only 40 per cent of the lower class expressed the same intention—a difference of 28 percentage points. In terms of intention to attend university, 56 per cent of the upper-middle-class students reported that they would do so, as opposed to only 24 per cent of the lower-class students—a difference of 32 percentage points.

One other factor which could be expected to affect a student's decision to return to university for further education would be the grades that the student received in his last year in high school. This was clearly the case, with a strong direct relation between grades and the decision to go to

Table 14.12
Percentage of Working Respondents Planning to Return to School,
and Percentage of Those Planning to Attend University,
by Grades in Last Year of High School*

	Grades			
	75%+	66%-74%	60%-65%	50%-59%
Planning to Return	40 (34)	47 (87)	49 (88)	64 (32)
Planning University	62 (21)	30 (27)	28 (25)	**

*Excluding no answers.
**Cell too small.

Note: In the case of those planning to return to university, neither program of study in high school nor grade at which the student left high school need be considered. This is due to the availability at all Ontario universities of mature student admission programs, and at some of special student programs which do not require full or, in the case of special students at Carleton, even partial matriculation from high school.

university (see Table 14.12). However, there was an inverse relationship between grades and the decision to return to some form of education. Unfortunately, the data did not permit further subdivision in order to examine this relationship further.

Notes

1. The analysis of the Grade 8 cohort that follows is a summary version of the detailed analysis that appears in John Porter, Bernard Blishen and Maria Barrados, *Survival of a Grade 8 Cohort: A Study of Early School Leaving in Ontario* (Ontario Department of Education, 1977). This study contains full details of sample design and weighting procedures, questionnaire design, types of response and non-response, and a factor analysis of items in the questionnaire.

2. For a detailed analysis of the Grade 12 cohort plus a description of the sample and questionnaire design, see Hugh A. McRoberts, *Follow-up of Grade 12 Students from the Blishen-Porter Study of Educational Aspirations* (Ottawa: Carleton University, 1974) (mimeo). This follow-up study was confined to students who had attended English-speaking schools, whereas the original study also included students attending French-speaking schools in Ontario.

3. The designations of English and French samples refer to the two samples drawn at different sampling ratios from students whose language of instruction was English and from students whose language of instruction was French.

4. See Chapter 4 for a discussion of Raymond Boudon's work and an explanation of why we are, here in the Grade 8 follow-up study, using the concept of probabilities rather than presenting the data as percentages as we have heretofore in this volume.

15

The Formation of Aspirations:
A Multivariate Analysis*

As we have seen from an extensive examination of cross-tabulations, the level of educational aspirations varies considerably by different characteristics of students. Among the most important, and very much as we anticipated, are: sex; socio-economic status or social class origin; mental ability; school program, inevitably because of the then existing restrictive four-year programs; school performance; self-concept of ability; parental level of education; and cultural enrichment. Less clearly linear are birth order, size of family and degree of urbanization (that is, for every addition of variable x—say, number of children in the family—there is an equivalent loss of educational aspirations). For birth order and size of family, it is not until the fourth ordinal position among siblings or until the fairly large families of four or more children that aspirations fall off substantially. As for urbanization, there is a relative uniformity of aspirations between the metropolitan Toronto area and the other major cities of the province. Aspirations are reduced, however, for smaller communities and rural areas.

Our task now is to sort out the relative effects of these variables when they are all considered together, and to determine how much of the variation in the level of educational aspirations might be attributed to them. Moreover, we would like to separate the direct and indirect effects and to trace the way in which the indirect effects of the different variables influence aspirations.

The method we have chosen—path analysis—requires that certain variables be dropped because they violate in some way the assumptions and restrictions of this analytical technique. All techniques have their price. The

---

*This chapter was originally published as an appendix to *Does Money Matter?* by Marion R. Porter, John Porter and Bernard R. Blishen (Toronto: Macmillan, 1979).

major constraints of path analysis are that the variables be measured on interval scales, that the relationships be linear—or reasonably so—and additive or lacking interactions; that is, that a particular variable affects another uniformly throughout its range.

Religion, ethnicity, immigrant status of parents and sex are clearly nominal variables. Moreover, our evidence so far suggests that leaving them out as early background variables would not seriously impair the multivariate model we develop. Sex might have been treated as a "dummy" variable by assigning a value of 1 to being male and 0 to being female, but then our cross-tabular analysis suggests some interaction between sex and socio-economic status in that the depressing effects on aspirations of being female are substantially greater the lower the social class. Our solution to this problem is to control for the effects of sex by treating our male and female students as separate populations. We also, of course, treat grades as separate populations. The models we construct, then, will be for each sex and the three grades.

Our first step was to develop a grand matrix in which all the variables that seemed in any way relevant were intercorrelated with each other. We then created a reduced matrix omitting variables that did not have significant correlations with our variables of major concern—aspirations, mental ability, school performance and socio-economic status. The reduced matrix based on listwise deletions is in Table 15.1. The variables are described in Chapter 4, but below is a brief indication of the measurements that were used of the variables that appear.

Table 15.1
Simple Correlations Between Variables Entering Into Path Model 1, Grade 10 Boys and Girls*

Variable		X_1	X_2	X_3	X_4	X_5	X_6	X_7
Popoc	X_1		.214	.239	.181	.224	.273	.301
MA	X_2	.112		.345	.338	.169	.255	.336
Prog	X_3	.222	.325		.333	.374	.489	.610
SP	X_4	.114	.326	.284		.187	.352	.411
Sigother	X_5	.167	.107	.305	.166		.405	.512
SCA-U	X_6	.181	.212	.438	.308	.387		.643
LEA	X_7	.285	.296	.625	.376	.483	.635	

*Boys above diagonal, girls below. Listwise deletion of missing data.

Defining the Variables

Socio-economic Status (X_1—Popoc) is measured by the Blishen scale. The full scale was used in this analysis.

Mental Ability (X_2—MA) is determined by the raw score values of the IPAT Culture Fair Test.

Program (X_3—Prog) is a dichotomous variable comprising the five-year and the four-year program.

School Performance (X_4—SP) School-reported grades are used. Values from 1 to 5 are assigned to categories ranging from 1 for under 50 per cent to 5 for over 75 per cent.

Influence of Significant Others (X_5—Sigother) The perceptions of parents' and friends' aspirations are combined in a scale ranging from 0 to 40. "Don't know" answers are scored as 0 since they indicate that either parents or friends have no influence.

Self Concept of Ability (X_6—SCA-U) The factor weighted scale that was developed using the questions pertaining to university is the one used here as the most appropriate measure.

Level of Educational Aspirations (X_7—LEA) A scale from 1 for wanting to leave school at Grade 10 to 10 for wanting to do graduate work was developed.

Ordering the Variables

Because path analysis provides a causal model, it is necessary to arrange the variables in a temporal sequence, as we have done in Figure 15.1. Thus, the antecedent variables have effects on the variables, which appear subsequent to them in the model. The entire process is unidirectional or recursive. The causal ordering depends upon commonsense, logic and theoretical sophistication. To take some obvious examples, we know that school program can in no way determine sex and so must come later than sex in a causal ordering. Similarly, we know that birth order cannot be determined by self-concept of ability, and so the former must precede the latter. For many of the variables, however, causal ordering requires rigorous argument, particularly when we consider such variables as self-concept of ability and school performance. Path models assume, when the paths of influence are unidirectional, that there are no feedbacks. Yet we know in reality that there can be feedback loops, such as, for example, when the achievement of high marks in school will heighten self-concept of ability, which in turn can react upon future school performance. Our present model building is limited to unidirectional cause, and hence requires even more rigorous

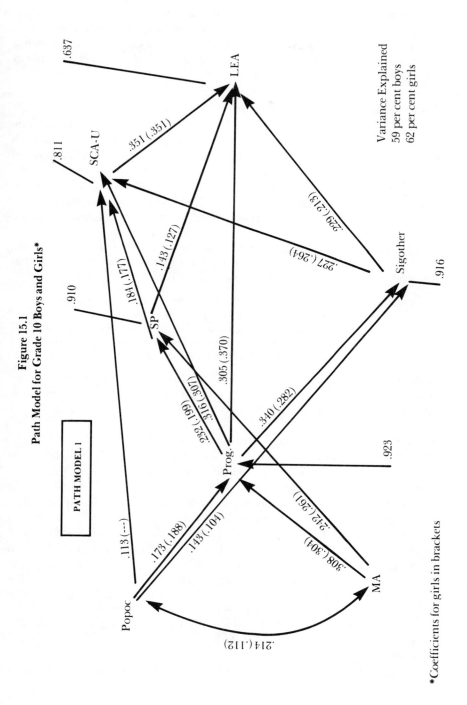

Figure 15.1
Path Model for Grade 10 Boys and Girls*

PATH MODEL 1

Variance Explained
59 per cent boys
62 per cent girls

*Coefficients for girls in brackets

consideration of the appropriate sequential ordering of variables in the model than would be the case if we could account for reciprocal causality.

It is now necessary to argue for this sequential ordering. In following the reasoning it might be helpful to look at Path Model 1 to get a picture of the sequential ordering in the path diagram.

Background Exogenous Variables

There are two early background variables: socio-economic status (Popoc), measured on the full Blishen scale, and mental ability (MA), measured with the full range of raw scores. Within a path model no causal explanation of these background or exogenous variables is undertaken; rather, it is their effects on the other variables in the model, the endogenous variables, on which a causal ordering can be imposed. The bidirectional arrows between the two exogenous variables represent the simple correlations between them.

Mental ability might have been considered as an endogenous variable, with some portion of its variance attributable to father's occupation. But as Hauser has noted in dealing with this difficult issue,

> the status of the family and the intelligence of the student have un-measured common causes. That is, parental abilities, attitudes and practices which facilitate the development of children's intelligence also contribute to the attainment of parental status, so the link between socio-economic background and intelligence is partly spurious.[1]

Although, as we have argued, our use of a culture fair test has to some extent reduced the effects of home environment on intelligence test performance, some common determinant of these two variables no doubt remains.

Intervening (Endogenous) Variables

The first endogenous variable, school program, has been referred to sufficiently so that its inclusion requires no further argumentation. However, its location in the model in relation to school performance is important. Since the allocation to programs was allegedly based on ability and elementary school performance, it would have been useful to have a measure of school performance in Grade 8 of the Grade 10 and Grade 12 students; we could have expected that to have a considerable effect on program allocation. Unfortunately, we do not have such Grade 8 data, and since our measure of school performance for Grade 10 students is for their Grade 9 year, when they most likely would already have been allocated to a program, it follows that school performance should follow rather than precede program in the model. We must now argue for the location of significant others' influence in relation to program, school performance and self-concept of ability.

If parents had been able to choose their child's program, and had our questions specifically related to the period when these Grade 10 students were in Grade 8, it would have been logical to place Sigother before Prog in the model. However, Breton presents evidence that school personnel are more important in the initial allocation to programs than are parents. Of the principals questioned in his study, only 9 per cent said parents' wishes were important, while 63 per cent said school marks were and 52 per cent said judgements of teachers and principals were important.[2] It seems likely, then, that the school would act as the gate-keeper to the superior five-year program, although students themselves could choose to go into four-year programs if they wished even though they might be eligible for the five-year programs. Parents' aspirations must then be influenced by the program the child is in, at least by the time he or she is in Grades 10 and 12. It seems plausible, too, to place Sigother after SP since parents are likely to be affected in their aspirations by the way their child performs in school. Since our Sigother variable includes educational aspirations of first and second friend, it seems likely that the program the child is in and the way he performs in school will determine his choice of friends.

As for self-concept of ability, it seems logical to place it after school performance since it is the way in which a student performs in school that gives him the idea that he can or cannot manage university. Some other measure of self-concept—say, measuring a person's self-concept relative to others—might tap a subjective state of self-confidence and so affect the way he performs in school; but since SCA-U is oriented to the ability to cope with higher education, it seems logical to put it in the model after SP.

Estimating the Effects: The Basic Model

The matrix of inter-correlations from which the path coefficients are estimated is presented in Table 15.1 for Grade 10, with the correlations for boys above the diagonal and for girls below. Path analysis is a method of decomposing the correlations between two variables in a set into direct and indirect causal effects and non-causal effects. The path coefficients are standardized partial regression coefficients. The indirect effects, as we will illustrate later, can be calculated from the path diagram following the basic theorem of path analysis.[3] Path Model 1, Figure 15.1, is our basic model of aspiration formation. Path Model 1 explains 59 per cent of the variance for boys and 62 per cent for girls.

The coefficient of fit measuring the capacity of the model as shown to reproduce the original matrix after the insignificant paths were removed was, for boys .938 and for girls .926. It will be noted that all of the influence of father's occupation is indirect, primarily through program but also through significant others and, in the case of boys, through SCA-U. The strongest paths are from self-concept of ability to educational aspirations (.351 for both boys and girls); from program to significant others (.340 for boys, .282 for girls); from program to self-concept of ability (.316 for boys,

.307 for girls); from program to LEA (.305 for boys, .370 for girls); and from mental ability to program (.308 for boys, .304 for girls).

The most influential path through the model, then, is from mental ability to program, to significant others' influence, to level of educational aspirations. Thus the slightly greater influence of mental ability than father's occupation on aspirations shown in the correlation matrix is reflected in the greater indirect influence of mental ability through program, which in turn has a strong effect on aspirations directly, but also indirectly through significant others' influence and on self-concept of ability. Another interesting observation to be made is the relatively insignificant effect of school performance on educational aspirations. It has a slight direct effect, no indirect effect through significant others, and much less through self-concept of ability than does program. Program has an effect on school performance, confirming our observation about the greater success five-year program students had than four-year program students in mastering their more difficult subject matter.

The model might be described as one which is balanced between meritocratic and ascriptive qualities in that mental ability comes through as strongly as social class origin, as measured by father's occupation. Full equality of educational opportunity in Ontario would, of course, depend on there being no influence of social class on aspirations. The major influence of father's occupation is indirect through program and through significant others, reflecting the fact that the higher the social class the more likely are students to be in five-year programs and the more likely are their significant others to influence their aspirations; but these indirect associations are not strong, a fact that is indicated by both the path coefficients and the original correlations. Thus all of the influence of social class (father's occupation) on aspirations represented by the correlation of .301 (boys) and .285 (girls) is indirect. Some portion of the indirect effects of father's occupation and mental ability is unique to each and the remainder shared with the other because of the unanalysed correlation between them (.214 boys). The unique and shared effects of both for boys can be seen in Table 15.2, which illustrates how the correlations can be decomposed. Once again, father's occupation is slightly weaker than mental ability. The unique indirect plus the shared indirect effects of both, that is, their total indirect effects, equal their correlation with LEA. The correlations shown in Table 15.2 are slightly lower than those in Table 15.1 because they are from the matrix reconstructed after insignificant paths were removed.

The remaining variables in Table 15.2 have direct and indirect effects on aspirations. Almost half of the effect of program is indirect through the other variables in the model. About one-quarter of the effect of significant others is indirect through the remaining variable in the model. SCA-U, self-concept, being the last variable in the model, can have no indirect effect on aspirations. The indirect non-causal "effects" shown in Table 15.2 represent the common antecedent causes that aspirations share with the other variables in the model. Logically, because of the sequential causal ordering, we cannot speak of indirect effects back through the antecedent variables. Hence the "effects" derived from the correlations are non-causal or spurious with respect to this explanatory model.

Two further observations might be made for the reader unfamiliar with this type of analysis. The first concerns the residual paths from outside the model to each of the intervening and the dependent variables. These represent the causal influences operating on each from factors outside the model, as well as measurement and other error. It will be noted that all the residuals are high. For example, the residual to SCA-U (Path Model 1, boys) is .811, which means that only 34 per cent of the variance (1-Res^2 x 100) in SCA-U is explained by the preceding variables in the model. Since we are not seeking to explain SCA-U with this model, the point is moot. The second and more important point, an assumption of path analysis, is that the residuals should not be intercorrelated themselves with antecedent variables in the model. The extent that they might be will raise questions about the explanatory power of the model. We feel fairly confident, however, from our cross-tabular analysis, the elimination of variables with low correlations, and the relatively weak influences of such background variables as religion and ethnicity, that we have minimized violation of this assumption. This is not to say, of course, that other variables may not be introduced to elaborate the basic model presented here.

Table 15.2
Decomposition of Intercorrelations* of
Exogeneous and Intervening Variables in Path Model 1
with Aspirations, Boys, Grade 10

Variable	Causal Effects			Indirect Non-Causal Effects
	Indirect	Direct	Total	
	Unique Shared			
Popoc	.184 + .048	—	.232	—
MA	.229 + .039	—	.268	—
Prog.	.267	.305	.572	.038
SP	.065	.143	.208	.182
Sigother	.080	.229	.309	.191
SCA-U	—	.351	.351	.287

*The intercorrelations decomposed are those of the reconstructed matrix after the deletion of insignificant paths as in Path Model 1. Where weak paths have been deleted, the correlations will be somewhat lower than those in the original matrix in Table 15.1.

The second explanation is for those who may not understand what the numbers in the intercorrelation matrices and the path models stand for. The correlation coefficient, say that between Popoc and LEA (Table 15.1) for boys, is: $r_{lea.popoc}$=.301, which means that for every unit change in father's occupation on the Blishen scale there is about a 30 per cent change, in gross terms, in the level of the aspirations scale as constructed. When all the other variables in the model are considered or controlled, however, the relationship disappears, and hence there is no direct path. Similarly, the correlation for boys between Popoc and Sigother: $r_{sigother.popoc}$=.224 indicates that a unit change in Popoc produces about a quarter of a unit change in significant others' influence in gross terms, but the path coefficient of .143 from Popoc to Sigother (Path Model 1) tells us that when all the other variables are controlled the influence is almost halved; that is, a unit change in Popoc produces little more than one-seventh of a unit change in Sigother, the rest being shared with the other variables because of their common determinants. When we speak of unit changes, of course, the reference is to statistically standardized units since our variables are measured with different metrics.

The Basic Model: A Comparison of Grades

We will now turn to comparisons between sexes and grades. To do so we need two sets of coefficients: the standardized or path coefficients which we have been discussing in Path Model 1 and the corresponding raw, unstandardized or metric coefficients. These can be found in the regression analysis in Table 15.3, which has the metric coefficients on the left-hand side and the path coefficients on the right for boys and girls in Grades 10 and 12. Table 15.3 is read from top to bottom in the same way as a path diagram is read from left to right. The first four lines show the effects of father's occupation and mental ability on program for each of the four subpopulations. In lines 5 to 8 are the effects of father's occupation, mental ability and program on school performance; lines 9 to 12, the effects of the antecedent variables on significant others; lines 13 to 16, on self-concept of ability; and lines 17 to 20, on level of educational aspirations.

The path coefficients are standardized in standard deviation units and so enable us to compare within a model variables that are measured in different units. For example, in Path Model 1 we can say that for Grade 10 boys the effect of SCA-U is somewhat greater than the effect of program on his LEA because the former is .351 standardized units and the latter .305. This can also be seen in line 17 of Table 15.3 on the right-hand side. If we had only the raw or metric coefficients, we would not be able to make this comparison, since program is a dichotomous variable and is treated as a dummy variable and SCA is derived from a scale developed from answers to questions about how well the student thought he would do at university.

As can be seen on the left-hand side of Table 15.3 in line 17, the corresponding metric coefficients for the effect of program and SCA-U on LEA are 1.04 and .557, and it would clearly make no sense to compare these figures. Standardized coefficients are therefore essential for comparing variables within a model; but if we wish to compare the effects of a particular variable on another between models—for example, the relative effect of mental ability on school performance for boys and girls in Grades 10 and 12—it is better to use the metric coefficients, because path coefficients, which are standardized in standard deviation units, may not reveal the true relationship of variables in different populations if their variability is different. Both standardized and metric coefficients are partial coefficients and indicate the effect of a particular variable on a dependent variable when all the others are held constant.

The most important general conclusion to be drawn from Table 15.3 is that the basic model of aspiration formation (Path Model 1) developed for Grade 10 boys applies also to the three other sub-populations. For all, program is strong, as is self-concept of ability. Both father's occupation and mental ability affect aspirations indirectly, there being no significant paths from them to aspirations (lines 17 to 20). Also, and somewhat surprisingly, school performance does not count for much in the formation of aspirations, and even disappears as a path for Grade 12 girls. If students do not derive aspirations from doing well in school, it was probably because high grades were not necessary for advancement into post-secondary education. If one could get by on low grades—as was possible—high school performance need no longer be necessary to high educational ambition.

Given the similarity in the pattern of aspiration formation for all four categories of students, we may be thought to be searching out trivial differences if we engage in a close comparison. However, we will point out some interesting differences revealed by the regression analysis. The way Table 15.3 is laid out enables us to take each of the variables in the model in turn as a dependent variable and to estimate the influence of the preceding variables in the model in each case. We can tell for each dependent variable, from the R^2 column, the amount of variance explained by the variables that precede it in the model. At first we examine the full model (lines 17 to 20) with level of educational aspirations as the dependent variable.

We see from the path coefficients (right-hand side of Table 15.3) how similar the pattern is for all four categories. In all four cases neither father's occupation nor mental ability has any direct effect. In all four cases program is very important. For Grade 10 boys, however, self-concept of ability is the most important. In all four cases self-concept of ability and significant others have some influence and school performance a minor direct influence. For Grade 12 girls school performance is very minor in that the path has disappeared.

The metric coefficients show that with all the other variables con-

Table 15.3
Parameters for the Basic Model of Aspiration Formation,
Males and Females, Grades 10 and 12

DEPENDENT VARIABLES	INDEPENDENT VARIABLES													
	Metric Coefficients**								Standardized Coefficient					
Program	Popoc	MA	Prog	SP	Sig. Other	SCA-U	R^2	Constant	Popoc	MA	Prog	SP	Sig. Other	SCA-U
1. Grade 10 Males	.006 (.001)	.030 (.003)					.147	.394	.173	.308				
2. Grade 10 Females	.006 (.001)	.031 (.004)					.141	.424	.188	.304				
3. Grade 12 Males	.007 (.001)	.031 (.003)					.152	.574	.198	.309				
4. Grade 12 Females	.006 (.001)	.031 (.003)					.160	.641	.173	.333				
School Performance														
5. Grade 10 Males	—	.447 (.063)	4.46 (.655)				.173	40.36	—	.242	.232			
6. Grade 10 Females	—	.532 (.076)	3.82 (.756)				.143	41.93	—	.261	.199			
7. Grade 12 Boys	—	.499 (.063)	.312* (.638)				.085	51.99	—	.290	—			
8. Grade 12 Females	—	.336 (.058)	2.30 (.622)				.093	54.23	—	.212	.146			

(continued)

Significant Others' Influence												
9. Grade 10 Males	.100 (.025)	—	6.51 (.719)	.055* (.037)		.162	6.41	.143	—	.340	—	
10. Grade 10 Females	.068 (.024)	—	5.33 (.790)	.086* (.039)		.109	8.46	.104	—	.282	—	
11. Grade 12 Males	.037* (.019)	—	6.75 (.586)	.153 (.032)		.199	6.92	—	—	.398	.149	
12. Grade 12 Females	.088 (.018)	—	5.42 (.539)	.040* (.030)		.191	10.36	.168	—	.364	—	
Self-Concept of Ability												
13. Grade 10 Males	.009 (.002)	—	.683 (.073)	.021 (.004)	.025 (.003)	.341	.96	.113	—	.316	.184	.227
14. Grade 10 Females	.004* (.002)	—	.620 (.077)	.018 (.004)	.027 (.004)	.294	1.32	—	—	.307	.177	.264
15. Grade 12 Males	.011 (.002)	—	.869 (.074)	.021 (.004)	.019 (.004)	.333	.56	.134	—	.394	.173	.143
16. Grade 12 Females	.004* (.002)	—	.515 (.071)	.022 (.004)	.021 (.004)	.219	1.22	—	—	.270	.195	.178

DEPENDENT VARIABLES	INDEPENDENT VARIABLES													
	Metric Coefficients**								Standardized Coefficient					
	Popoc	MA	Prog	SP	Sig. Other	SCA-U	R²	Con-stant	Popoc	MA	Prog	SP	Sig. Other	SCA-U
Level of Educational Aspirations														
17. Grade 10 Males	—	—	1.04 (.099)	.024 (.005)	.040 (.004)	.557 (.045)	.594	-.20	—	—	.305	.143	.229	.351
18. Grade 10 Females	—	—	1.28 (.102)	.021 (.005)	.038 (.005)	.596 (.048)	.615	-.72	—	—	.370	.127	.213	.351
19. Grade 12 Males	—	—	1.23 (.099)	.026 (.005)	.041 (.005)	.403 (.042)	.550	.77	—	—	.376	.142	.213	.284
20. Grade 12 Females	—	—	1.49 (.094)	.015* (.005)	.054 (.006)	.418 (.044)	.582	-.11	—	—	.434	—	.241	.249

*Insignificant paths retained for comparative reasons.
**Standard errors in brackets.

trolled, self-concept of ability is more important for girls than for boys and more important in Grade 10 than in Grade 12. This probably means that in Grade 10 students who think they can manage university work are more likely to want to go on to university than are those in Grade 12—because in Grade 12, when they are closer in time to making the decision, other factors may intervene, such as the need or desire to get a job, the reluctance to continue studying, and the costs. The difference between boys and girls in both grades, while not very great, may reflect the fact that boys are more likely than girls to have high educational aspirations whether or not they think they have the ability to do the work.

The only other difference that seems in any way significant is the effect of program on aspirations. In both Grades 10 and 12 it has stronger effects for girls than for boys, net of the influence of the other variables. No doubt this is because the four-year Commercial program that girls took was more closely related to the occupational world than the four-year program that most boys took, thus dampening their educational aspirations. Program also had stronger effects on girls in Grade 12 than in Grade 10 and for boys in Grade 12 than in Grade 10, again reflecting the fact that the closer they are to the time of decision about post-secondary education, the more likely their aspirations are to be modified by their programs.

From the R^2 column on the left side of the table, we see that 59 per cent of the variance is explained for Grade 10 boys and 62 per cent for Grade 10 girls, and somewhat less for Grade 12 students, 55 per cent for boys and 58 per cent for girls. Evidently, the closer they are to the time of decision, the more likely are other factors not in the model to influence their aspirations.

With self-concept of ability as the dependent variable (lines 13 to 16) we see from the path coefficients that in all four cases program has the most influence on whether a student thinks he can do well in university. For the Grade 10 students the next most important influence is significant others, while for Grade 12 students it is school performance. Older students are less likely than younger students to be influenced by their significant others in the development of their self-concept. It is interesting that in both grades there is a minor path for boys from father's occupation to self-concept of ability. Boys seem slightly more likely than girls to be influenced by their social class origin in their views of their ability.

The metric coefficients show one significant difference: with the other variables controlled, influence of program is greater on the boys' self-concept of ability than on girls'. This is particularly true in Grade 12 where the influence of program, net of the other variables, is 50 per cent greater for boys than for girls (lines 15 and 16, .869 for boys and .515 for girls). This is an interesting reversal from the effect of program on educational aspirations where, as we have seen, it had more influence for girls than for boys. Perhaps girls in the four-year program who were learning successfully a useful skill would estimate their ability to pursue other kinds of studies much as girls in five-year programs. Boys who were in the four-year program, however, were not as likely to succeed in mastering a marketable skill as were girls, and hence would have a lower estimate of their abilities than boys in five-year programs. The model explains less of the variance of girls' self-concept than boys'.

With Sigother as the dependent variable, we find once again from the path coefficients that for boys and girls in Grades 10 and 12 the program they were in had most effect on the influence of their significant others. There is one difference in the four models, however, in the variables affecting Sigother. For Grade 12 boys there is a path from school performance (line 11) and no path from father's occupation.

The metric coefficients show that though the differences are not great, the coefficient is larger for Grade 12 boys between school performance and Sigother than is the case for the other three categories, and it is smaller for Grade 12 boys than for the other three between father's occupation and significant others' influence. It is not surprising that father's occupation should have some effect on the level of influence of significant others, but it is hard to explain why it should be less important for Grade 12 boys. The explanation could be that Grade 10, when school is still compulsory, contains many potential drop-outs, particularly lower social class boys whose parents would not have high educational aspirations for them. By Grade 12, which we have referred to earlier as a survival grade, these lower social class potential drop-outs would have left. That could account for the higher coefficient between social class and the influence of significant others for boys in Grade 10 than in Grade 12. The effect of program is greater for boys than for girls in both grades; that is, when boys are in the five-year program their significant others are more likely to have high educational aspirations than they are for girls in the five-year program. This disadvantage experienced by girls is a reflection, of course, of the prevailing social values.

There are no direct paths to school performance from father's occupation in any of the categories (lines 5 to 8), and predictably there are direct paths in all of the categories from mental ability. The somewhat surprising path from program to school performance that we discussed earlier in our analysis of Path Model 1 (Grade 10 boys) exists also for Grades 10 and 12 girls, but not for Grade 12 boys. The metric coefficients show a much lower value for Grade 12 boys than for the three other categories (line 7, Grade 12 boys, .312; Grade 10 boys, 4.46; Grade 10 girls, 3.82; Grade 12 girls, 2.30). Again this may be because the potential drop-outs among the Grade 10 boys in the two- and five-year programs have left by Grade 12. Girls in Grade 10 convert their mental ability into higher school performance than do boys, but the reverse is so for Grade 12. By Grade 12 the three variables, Popoc, MA and Prog, explain less of the variance in school performance than in Grade 10.

Finally, the effects of father's occupation and mental ability on program are very similar in the four sub-populations. In all of them, mental ability is much more important than father's occupation. As we pointed out in our analysis of Path Model 1, full equality of opportunity would mean that there was no association between social class as measured by father's occupation and program, which at the time determined how far a student could pursue his education.

The main conclusion to be drawn from this comparison of sexes and grades is the great similarity in the four models. The differences we have pointed out are all minor ones. Social class, though it had no direct effect on educational aspirations for boys or girls in either Grades 10 or 12, did affect them all through its influence on the program they were in and its importance in the influence of significant others.

The Grade 8 Model

It was not possible to use the same model for Grade 8 as we used for Grades 10 and 12, because program, an important variable and a characteristic of high schools in Ontario at the time of the survey, did not exist in Grade 8. No doubt there were other forms of streaming, but they would have varied from school to school and it would not have been possible to obtain relevant data. Our grand matrix of zero order correlations showed that, for boys at least, correlations with family size were higher in Grade 8 than in Grades 10 and 12, and we therefore decided to include family size as one of the exogenous variables. Another change we made was to substitute the original self-concept of ability scale for Self-Concept of Ability-University. As we explained in Chapter 4, a factor analysis showed two dimensions in the original scale in the case of Grade 10 and 12 students. However, these two dimensions did not exist for the Grade 8 students, who were closer in age to the students that Brookover used in developing the scale.

The other variables were the same as used in Path Model 1 for the Grade 10 and 12 analysis: school performance, as reported by the school; Sigother; and the dependent variable, level of educational aspirations. Family size is an additional exogenous variable to mental ability and father's occupation.

Table 15.4 shows the metric coefficients for the Grade 8 model. Path coefficients for boys and girls are shown in Path Model 2 (Figure 15.2). The most striking feature of this model is that it explains much less of the variance than did the Grade 10 and 12 model: only 42 per cent for boys and 33 per cent for girls. We are, therefore, more limited in what we can say about aspiration formation among Grade 8 students. The strongest path is from school performance to self-concept of ability to LEA. The relatively strong path from mental ability to school performance makes this model fairly meritocratic. It is interesting that school performance comes through much more strongly than in the higher grades. Not only is the strongest path in the model from it to SCA (.572 for boys, .460 for girls), but there is also a direct path from SP to LEA and another indirect one through Sigother. No doubt performing well in Grade 8 is a fairly important determinant of whether a student feels he is capable of doing well academically and having high educational aspirations. In high school, students know that they do

Table 15.4
Metric Coefficients for Grade 8
Model of Aspiration Formation,
Males and Females**

DEPENDENT VARIABLES	Popoc	MA	Family Size	SP	Sig. Other	SCA	R²	Con-stant
School Performance								
Males	.085 (.024)	.438 (.067)	-.528 (.152)				.113	53.21
Females	.073 (.022)	.480 (.060)	-.279* (.145)				.126	55.64
Significant Others' Influence								
Males	.111 (.027)	—	-.478 (.174)	.193 (.043)			.084	10.90
Females	.085 (.029)	—	-.189* (.187)	.182 (.050)			.051	4.11
Self-Concept of Ability								
Males	.008 (.002)	—	—	.669 (.004)	.012 (.003)		.408	9.85
Females	.008 (.002)	—	—	.050 (.004)	.012 (.003)		.295	8.81
Level of Educational Aspirations								
Males	.012 (.004)	.015* (.011)	-.117 (.025)	.027 (.008)	.045 (.006)	.521 (.061)	.420	6.53
Females	.011 (.004)	.034 (.010)	-.049* (.023)	.021 (.007)	.040 (.005)	.448 (.061)	.339	5.97

*Insignificant paths retained for comparative purposes.
**Standard errors in brackets.

Figure 15.2
Path Model for Grade 8 Boys and Girls*

PATH MODEL 2

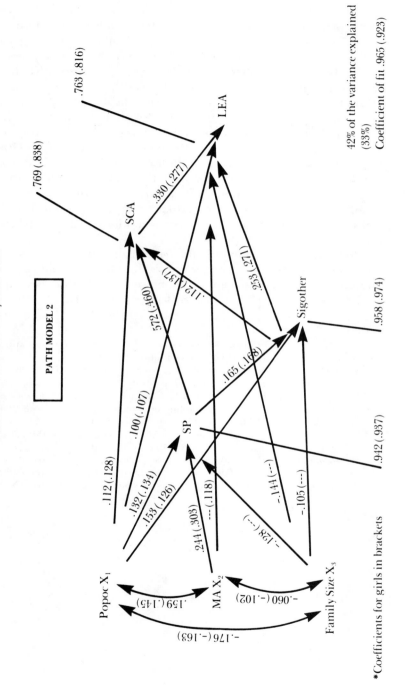

42% of the variance explained
(33%)
Coefficient of fit .965 (.923)

*Coefficients for girls in brackets

not have to perform very well to get into university, and as we have said, school performance is not very important in aspiration formation.

The addition of family size to the model tells us something about boys in Grade 8 and something about the differences between boys and girls. In the final path model, after the deletion of insignificant paths, there are no paths left from family size in the girl's model, but the paths in the boy's persist to school performance (-.128) to Sigother (-.105) and to LEA (-.144).

The metric coefficients in Table 15.4 show us that the influence of family size on all the endogenous variables is considerably stronger for boys than for girls. In fact, generally the model indicates that in Grade 8 the system is somewhat less meritocratic for boys than for girls. Not only is family size more important for boys than for girls, but so too is (very slightly) father's occupation in its influence on school performance and significant others. Boys are more likely than girls to translate their self-concept of ability into educational aspirations (.521 to .448 in metric coefficients).

While the factors entering into the formation of aspirations in the high school years combine in a similar fashion for Grades 10 and 12 and for boys and girls, it is clear that aspirations, however unrealistic they might be in the last year of elementary school, are formed differently.

Notes

1. Robert M. Hauser, *Socioeconomic Background and Educational Performance* (Washington, D.C.: The American Sociological Association, 1971).
2. Raymond Breton, *Social and Academic Factors in the Career Decisions of Canadian Youth* (Ottawa: Information Canada, 1972).
3. As we proceed with the path analysis below, we give from time to time some assistance to those who are unfamiliar with this technique. The tracing rules for path analysis are set out in Otis Dudley Duncan, "Path Analysis: Sociological Examples," in *American Journal of Sociology* (Vol.74, 1968), pp.119–137. In employing path analysis we have been guided by Kenneth C. Land, "Principles of Path Analysis," in Edgar F. Borgatta, ed., *Sociological Methodology* (San Francisco: Jossey-Bass, 1969); and Ronald S. Burt, *The Theory Construction Potential of Path Analysis: An Interdisciplinary Perspective* (Albany, N.Y.: International Center for Social Research, State University of New York).

16
Inequality of Opportunity

In analysing the complex factors that contribute to the formation of educational aspirations, a major concern throughout this report has been to determine the extent to which the policy of accessibility to post-secondary education for all who want it and can benefit from it—the stated goal of the government of Ontario—has been realized.

We have attempted to measure the success of this goal through a study of the aspirations of Ontario students in three crucial grades of their schooling: in Grade 8, where the choice has to be made of the courses that they will take in high school; at Grade 10, when many will reach the school leaving age and the option of dropping out exists; and at Grade 12, when the student must choose between leaving with an Ontario Secondary School Graduation Diploma or continuing to Grade 13 in order to get an Ontario Secondary School Honours Graduation Diploma, which would qualify him or her for university. Throughout the analysis the relationship of social class and of sex to aspirations stands out.

The full ramifications of the effects of class inequality on educational inequality would depend on a long and expensive longitudinal study that would take all the children entering elementary school in a given year, or a very large sample of them, and follow them through each successive year for, say, twenty-five years when those who made it would likely have completed their higher studies. Any study that seeks to measure the effects of social class differences based on senior high school years or those attending university will always under-estimate the effects of class inequality on education because of the disproportionate falling-out or grade retardation of lower-class children.

It was necessary, therefore, with our cross-sectional design to go into the school system, select appropriate grades and use educational aspirations as our dependent variable, since quite obviously we could not use educational attainment because the children were still in the educational process. Aspirations are not as concrete phenomena as "years of schooling completed," but by measuring them we have been able to show how social class, interrelated with many other factors, affects the perceptions of opportunity; at the same time, these aspirations stand as a surrogate measure of attainments.

In our chapter on the making of educational aspirations, we showed strikingly how the desire to graduate from university is related to both social class and sex with mental ability controlled. Of the Grade 12 students with high mental ability, 75 per cent of upper-middle-class boys but only 42 per cent of lower-class boys wanted to graduate from university. The equivalent percentages for girls were 61 and 36. Students' self-concept of ability affected their aspirations. Those with a high self-concept were much more likely to have high aspirations.

In examining the factors that were associated with self-concept of ability, we found that boys of all ages were more likely to have a high self-concept than girls, and with age this difference between the sexes increases. Self-concept of ability was closely associated with the students' school performance, with the degree of parental influence and with the educational aspirations that students thought their parents had for them. If students thought that either their fathers or their mothers wanted them to go to university, they were likely to have a high self-concept of ability. If they thought that their parents wanted them to go to work, they were much less likely to have a high self-concept of ability. And, in general, parental influence on educational plans and aspirations was more likely for students at the highest socio-economic levels than for those at the middle and lower levels. Thus, having a high self-concept of ability, which is associated with having high educational aspirations, is very much related to the perceived parental aspirations and to the degree of parental influence, which in turn are largely a function of social class.

However, we found that school performance was not strongly related to social class. In the five-year program there was a significant relationship only for Grade 10 males and Grade 12 females. And, in spite of the fact that girls were less likely to have a high self-concept than boys, girls out-performed boys in school in both Grades 10 and 12 in four- and five-year programs and at all mental ability levels.

At the time of the study, the four- and five-year programs that students found themselves in determined the legitimacy of their educational aspirations. In studying the Grade 8 students, we found a strong relationship between social class and program. Yet, on the surface the allocation to a program seemed to be based on universalistic criteria. Those who had high grades and high aspirations were very likely to be in a five-year program, regardless of their origin, and those who had lower aspirations and/or lower grades were less likely to be there. The explanation was that neither grades nor aspirations are independent of social class. Social class determined to a large extent what program a student would be in through its effect on the grades that he/she got in Grade 7 or in the high educational aspirations that he/she had.

Although social class origin influenced the educational aspirations of students in that those from the middle and higher socio-economic levels were more likely than those from lower levels to aspire to university, there was a deviant group from the lower socio-economic levels who had high aspirations. We found that a lower-class mother who had work experience at a middle or upper socio-economic level increased the likelihood that the student would have university aspirations. Where lower-class students had parents whose education was above the average for parents of that class, the likelihood of them having high educational aspirations was increased. When lower-class students came from homes with a high level of cultural enrichment, they were more likely than those from homes with a low level of cultural enrichment to aspire to a university education.

Finally, to try to determine the relative importance of the major variables on the making of educational aspirations, we developed a path model in which educational aspirations was the dependent variable, mental ability and father's occupation were exogenous variables, and intervening variables were program, school performance, significant others' influence and school performance. There were no direct effects of social class on educational aspirations for Grade 10 or 12 students, although there were minor direct paths in Grade 8. In Grades 10 and 12 the effects of social class were indirect through program, significant others' influence and self-concept of ability. The effects of mental ability were also indirect through program and school performance. And the paths from mental ability to program were, in all cases, stronger than the paths from fathers' occupation to program.

We can conclude from this analysis that the Ontario educational system is reasonably meritocratic. Yet, we cannot ignore the fact that social class also plays an important part in determining what opportunities a young person is likely to have. This is clearly not a deliberate policy on the part of the educational authorities. Both the analysis of programs and the path analysis show that the effects of class are indirect. Class has an influence on the program a student will be in, the perceived educational aspirations of his/her parents, and his/her self-concept of ability, all of which have an effect on the educational aspirations of the student. School performance, too, was related to social class, although not as much as we expected in Grades 10 and 12.

We have shown how social class interacts with other variables to produce educational aspirations. We are still left with the question of the extent to which this analysis is valid for an understanding of educational attainment, which is, of course, the concern of sociologists. In order to determine this we conducted the two follow-up studies described earlier in the text.

We were not surprised that our follow-up studies show that at the time of our survey in 1971 students' aspirations were somewhat unrealistic. Only 62 per cent of the Grade 12 students who aspired to university actually made it. And in the Grade 8 sample only 44 per cent of those who expected to go to university in 1971 when they were in Grade 8 still expected to go to university five years later. Those figures make it appear that aspirations or expectations at an early age are not a reliable indicator of what a student might eventually do.

However, there are two factors that must be taken into account. One is that the variables related to a student's aspirations, social class, sex, and so on, are still related in the case of the Grade 12 students to their actual attainment, and in the case of the Grade 8 students to their continued aspirations/expectations when they reach the higher levels of the secondary school. This indicates that the forces we have identified as operating on aspirations are operative on attainment, so that in using aspirations as a dependent variable we are not distorting class effects or the nature of inequality. It seems that students for a variety of reasons, not all of which by any means we were able to measure, are likely to lower their aspirations/expectations as they make their way through the secondary school system. It may be that they do not find the learning environment a hospitable one. It may be that they do not have the mental ability to master academic work easily. It may be the attraction of being independent. But, over-riding these tendencies that may apply to all is the inescapable fact that whether we are looking at educational aspirations or educational attainment, social class, in particular, plays a large part in the probability that an individual will make it to higher education.

The second major point to observe in the Grade 8 follow-up study is that social class is not simply an extraneous characteristic that affects a student's decision at the end of his high school career. As Barrados has shown, it is a characteristic that affects his/her decision at crucial points from the time he/she enters the secondary school system.

In the Grade 8 follow-up study, Barrados has shown that the probabilities of completing Year 5 are related to both social class and Grade 7 school performance. In Chapter 10 we showed that high academic performance in Grade 7 was strongly related to social class. However, with school performance controlled we still find that social class had great importance. From the upper-middle classes 67 per cent of those with high achievement in Grade 7 completed Year 5. In the lower classes the percentage of those with high achievement in Grade 7 who completed Year 5 was only 38.

To be eligible for university a student would have to take courses in the five-year program. Of the upper-middle classes 87 per cent of those who had high achievement in Grade 7 took courses in the five-year program. Of the lower classes the percentage was 63.

But, what is most interesting in the Grade 8 follow-up study is the importance of Grade 8 expectations on the choice of program in high school, on the probability of completing Year 5, and on the probability of still expecting to go to university at the end of a high school career. For example, 79 per cent of high achieving lower social class students who expected to go to university took five-year program courses, compared to 56 per cent of high achieving lower social class students who did not expect to go to university. Of those who expected to go to university in Grade 8, 61 per cent completed Year 5. Of those who did not expect to go to university, only 21 per cent did. Of those who expected to go to university in Grade 8, 44 per cent, as we said before, still expected to go at the time of the follow-up. Of those who did not expect to go to university in Grade 8, 11 per cent expected to do so five years later. Again social class enters the picture. Of those who expected to go to university in Grade 8, 57 per cent of the upper-middle class still expected to go five years later, but only 34 per cent of the lower classes still had these expectations.

What these data show, of course, is that the decision to embark on a path that will eventually lead to university is made very early. This decision may be modified, or the student may be bumped off the path, but it is more likely to be modified if a student is from a lower rather than an upper-middle-class background.

To understand the factors that account for educational attainment we cannot simply look through a cross-sectional, time slice design at those who attained a grade level. We must look at students early in their school years to try to understand what makes them follow the courses that they do, and eventually to make the decision to pursue or not to pursue their education. When we do this, we see—despite the gains that many of the less privileged children make—how the structure of educational inequality is being reproduced from generation to generation as those from different backgrounds are prepared for their "respective stations" and "prospective callings."

Future Action

Having analysed the ways in which educational aspirations were affected by social and psychological factors, we must now consider what can be done to lower the barriers to greater accessibility to post-secondary education in Ontario. That these barriers are still with us in 1981 is evident from the *Report of the Committee on the Future Role of the Universities in Ontario*,[1] which asserted that accessibility to education is unequally distributed across all socio-economic groups. The Report specifies particular groups for whom accessibility could be improved: Franco-Ontarians, women, residents of northern Ontario, native peoples, part-time students, the handicapped and those who live a long distance from any university. Accessibility for all is still a challenge to be met.

In our earlier volume *Does Money Matter?*[2], we grappled with this problem. We distinguished between the rights of young people as individuals to acquire a post-secondary education and the rights of parents to give their children an education. Ideally, we would have liked to be able to propose that young people be treated as individuals. That would mean parental resources would not be taken into consideration in determining the kind of financial assistance available to students.

But in our society, where income distribution is very unequal, and where higher income groups benefit disproportionately from a resource that all taxpayers support because of values and attitudes that they acquire in the home, we concluded that such a policy could not, on the grounds of fairness, be supported. Instead, we recommended that tuition fees should be higher than at present so that students would pay a higher proportion of the costs of their education than the approximately 15 per cent they now do.[3] However, we also recommended that there should be a greatly increased financial assistance program, of which the first and major component should be a non-repayable grant. A means test based on parental resources would determine a student's eligibility for a grant. For students who wished to be independent, there should be a loan scheme with a contingency repayment feature[4] for which parental income is irrelevant. These recommendations still seem to us to be the fairest way of promoting accessibility. A concern in 1981 is that governments in their efforts to reduce educational expenditures might be tempted to increase tuition fees, or to encourage universities to increase tuition fees without a concomitant increase in financial assistance. This would be a regressive social policy and contrary to the principle of accessibility.

But if tuition fees were increased, as long as financial assistance was available at a level that would prevent any person from being denied access for financial reasons, the system would be fairer because those who benefit most would pay more. Such a program would have the effect of transferring public funds from the universities to individuals. Such a transformation would require much thought to try to determine the consequences for institutions.[5]

Although such a policy of higher fees and greatly increased grants would be fairer than the present one, and although it would make post-secondary education accessible to students who were eligible to attend, providing it was widely publicized, it still would not enhance opportunity for those who were not eligible for university admission.

We have seen in this report that aspirations are formed very early, that in Grade 8 aspirations were related to social class, and that aspirations and achievement largely determined the program that a student would enter in Grade 9. The program that a student was in determined the educational aspirations that were realistic. And as our follow-up studies showed, educational aspirations were a reliable indicator of the educational level likely to be attained.

Although programs no longer exist in Ontario high schools, it is still necessary to take courses at the advanced rather than the general level in order to qualify for Grade 13 courses and university admission. Without careful guidance, streaming could take place in a more subtle way than it did when students were blatantly slotted into a program that would determine their educational future. Parents who understand the system, and these are likely to be the ones who are highly educated themselves, will do their best to ensure that their children will take the necessary courses if they are to have the opportunity to go on to university. Parents who do not understand the consequences of the courses that their children take in the early years of high school will very likely acquiesce when their children decide to take undemanding courses.

Guidance counsellors in the higher grades of the elementary schools could play a crucial role in making students aware of the importance of making choices that would maximize their opportunities. It is not enough to have guidance counsellors in the schools. They must see their task as providing a bridge between the family environment and the educational and occupational world. Social workers employed by school boards could also increase awareness of opportunities by going into lower-income homes, especially those whose children had high mental ability, and explaining to parents the opportunities that exist. Other possibilities are enrichment programs for lower-class children at an early age, introducing children while they are still in elementary school to the university and explaining its role and its value both for the individual and the society.

Although the vocational aspect of a university education is often stressed and used as a justification for attending, it is important to remember that the non-vocational rewards to the individual are great. It enlarges intellectual and cultural horizons, making it possible to live a fuller life. It provides the student with three or four years in which he or she can escape the demands of the marketplace, and during which he or she has the opportunity to enjoy intellectual stimulation, companionship and freedom from nine to five routines. And, of course, it does provide credentials that are useful in the occupational world.

Because of high unemployment levels in the 1970s and stories of university graduates driving taxicabs, some say it is misguided to encourage students to develop their intellectual potential and to pursue their education. However, throughout the 1970s the unemployment rate for all university graduates, even in the age group 15-24, was consistently lower than for those without university qualifications.[6] It is true that many university graduates were "under-employed." It is also true that many employers use university degrees as a screening device so that university graduates get jobs for which the academic requirements are high school graduation or less. One solution to this problem is to make discrimination on the grounds of unnecessary academic credentials illegal, as discrimination on account of sex or race is illegal. But even if credentials were not required for lower level jobs, they still would be for higher level jobs. Those who have them have the opportunity to receive the benefits associated with interesting, well-paid jobs. Young people, because of their social class background, should not be deprived of this opportunity.

There is another reason for encouraging the able, whatever their social class background, to pursue their education. In the high technology world we are moving into we are at the mercy of experts who increasingly monopolize the technical knowledge that could be used to control us. The best defence of democracy is an educated, informed citizenry.

We must not limit our concern for accessibility to high school students. For those who drop out there must be a second chance. The admission of mature students with minimum academic qualifications to the universities, academic credit for equivalent non-academic work, and the expansion of continuing education courses create opportunities for learning outside the traditional route. We cannot force people to become better educated, of course, however much we think they and the society would benefit. The most we can do is to encourage and provide opportunity. And we must not think that providing educational opportunity will solve the injustices in society. At the most, education can promote upward mobility. Other measures must be taken to alleviate the injustice that arises from the inequality of income distribution.

Further Research

We have demonstrated in this report that sex was as great a factor as social class in determining educational aspirations. And when sex and class interacted, as they did for lower social class girls, the situation was one of double jeopardy. Since this survey was undertaken the inequalities that women have experienced have become more visible. Following the *Report of the Royal Commission on the Status of Women*[7] a myriad of organizations have been established, governmental and non-governmental, whose goal is to improve the status of women. The participation of married women in the labour force has increased to 50 per cent, and though they are still a minute percentage of the total, women are appearing in more and more high places. It would be interesting to find out whether the discrepancy between boys' and girls' aspirations still exists. One would expect, after all the publicity on the issue, that that discrepancy would have disappeared. On the other hand, the women's movement may be largely a middle-class movement, and its effects may not be felt at lower levels of the class structure.

Another group that should be examined are the Franco-Ontarians. At the time of this survey publicly financed French secondary schools had been in existence only a short time. It was expected that with the opportunity to be educated in their own language at public expense the attainment levels of Francophone students would improve. In fact, in our chapter on the French-speaking students (Chapter 13) we showed that Franco-Ontarians in

French-speaking schools had as high educational aspirations as Anglophones and much higher aspirations than French-speaking students in English-speaking schools. However, the follow-up study of Grade 8 students indicated that Francophone students were likely to leave school earlier than Anglophone students. But the follow-up study did not distinguish between Francophone students in French-speaking schools and Francophone students in English-speaking schools. A study of Franco-Ontarians now would demonstrate whether or not the Royal Commission on Bilingualism and Biculturalism was right in its contention that the low educational level of Franco-Ontarians was due to the fact that there were no publicly financed French-speaking secondary schools.

Social change is slow and inequalities are hard to eradicate. A constant effort to expose the ones that exist is an important and necessary task before we can expect any change to take place. In this task social science plays a crucial role.

Notes

1. *Report of the Committee on the Future Role of the Universities in Ontario* (Ministry of Colleges and Universities, Ontario, 1981).
2. M.R. Porter, J. Porter and B.R. Blishen, *Does Money Matter?* (Toronto: Macmillan, Carleton Library, No. 110, 1979).
3. *Report of the Special Program Review* (Toronto, 1975). Arguments have been made, however, that students should not, through their tuition fees, be expected to contribute to the non-teaching functions of the university. John A. Buttrick, in *Educational Problems in Ontario and Some Policy Options* (Ontario Economic Council, 1977), recommended that the costs of teaching should be separated from the other functions of the university, such as research and public service, and that students should pay an increasing share of the former costs but that the community should pay fully for the latter costs.
4. The Contingency Repayment Assistance Program (CORSAP) is described in *Does Money Matter?*, p.20. Basically the plan is one in which the student would repay his loan over 20-30 years in annual payments that would be a percentage of the graduate's income.
5. Much higher tuition fees, even with a greatly increased financial assistance program, might make university revenues much less certain than when the largest part of their funding comes directly from government. Students who were not eligible for grants might be discouraged from attending, especially if financial returns after graduation were not assured. Individuals' perceptions about the value of the university to them would determine their decision about whether to use their time and money on education or something else. If the university's main source of funds were tuition fees, these decisions could have an enormous impact on their future and would make it difficult to plan for the future.
6. *Recent Trends in Degrees Awarded and Enrolments at Canadian Universities*, Ministry of State, Science and Technology, Canada (Ottawa: Ministry of Supply and Services, 1981).
7. *Report of the Royal Commission on the Status of Women* (Ottawa: Information Canada, 1971).

Bibliography

Socio-Cultural Climates

Bell, G.D. "Processes in the Formation of Adolescents' Aspirations." *Social Forces*, 42, December 1963, 179-186.

Boyle, Richard. "Community Influence on College Aspirations: An Empirical Evaluation of Explanatory Factors."*Rural Sociology*, 31, September 1966, 277-292.

Boyle, Richard. "On Neighbourhood Context and College Plans III." *American Sociological Review*, 31, October 1966, 706-707.

Burchinall, Lee G. "Differences in Educational and Occupational Aspirations of Farm–Small Town and City Boys." *Rural Sociology*, June 1961.

Duncan, Beverly. "Education and Social Background." *American Journal of Sociology*, 72, January 1967, 363-372.

Elder, S.H. "Achievement Orientations and Career Patterns of Rural Youth." *Sociology of Education*, 37, 1962, 30-58.

Greeley, Andrew M. "Influence of Religion on Career Plans and Occupational Values of College Graduates." *American Journal of Sociology*, May 1968.

Grigg, C.M. and R. Middleton. "Community of Orientation and Occupational Aspirations of Ninth Grade Students." *Social Forces*, 38, 1960, 303-308.

Haller, Archibald O. "The Occupational Achievement Process in Farm Reared Youth in Urban Industrial Society." *Rural Sociology*, September 1960.

Haller, Archibald O. and William H. Sewell. "Occupational Choices of Wisconsin Farm Boys." *Rural Sociology*, 32, March 1967, 37-55.

Hauser, Robert M. *Socio-economic Background and Educational Performance*. Washington: American Sociological Association, 1973.

Herriott, Robert E. "Some Social Determinants of Educational Aspiration." *Harvard Educational Review*, 33, 1962, 157-177.

Jackson, Brian and Dennis Marsden. *Education and the Working Class.* Harmondsworth: Penguin, 1966.

Kahl, A. "Some Measurements of Achievement Orientations." *American Journal of Sociology,* 70, 1965, 669-681.

Pike, Robert M. *Who Doesn't Go to University and Why: A Study on Accessibility to Higher Education in Canada.* Ottawa: Association of Universities and Colleges of Canada, 1970.

Sewell, William H., Archibald O. Haller and Murray A. Strauss. "Social Status, and Educational and Occupational Aspirations." *American Sociological Review,* 22, February 1957, 82-92.

Sewell, William H. "Community of Residence and College Plans." *American Sociological Review,* 29, February 1964, 24-38.

Sewell, William H. and Alan M. Ornstein. "Community of Residence and Occupational Choice." *American Journal of Sociology,* 70, March 1965, 551-563.

Sewell, William H. and Archibald O. Haller. "Educational and Occupational Perspectives of Farm and Rural Youth," in Lee G. Burchinal, ed., *Rural Youth in Crisis: Fact and Social Change.* Washington: U.S. Government Printing Office, 1965.

Sewell, William H. and J. Michael Armer. "Neighborhood Context and College Plans." *American Sociological Review,* 31, April 1966, 159-168.

Sewell, William H. and Vimal P. Shah. "Socio-economic Status, Intelligence, and the Attainment of Higher Education." *Sociology of Education,* 40, Winter 1967, 67-73.

Sewell, William H. and Vimal P. Shah. "Social Class, Parental Encouragement and Educational Aspirations." *American Journal of Sociology,* 73, March 1968, 559-572.

Sewell, William H. and Vimal P. Shah. "Parents', Education's and Children's Educational Aspirations and Achievements." *American Sociological Review,* 33, April 1968, 191-209.

Sewell, William H. and Vimal P. Shah. "The Educational and Early Occupational Attainment Process." *American Sociological Review,* 34, February 1969, 82-92.

Sewell, William H., Archibald O. Haller and George W. Ohlendorf. "The Educational and Early Occupational Status Attainment Process: Republication and Revision." *American Sociological Review,* 35, December 1970, 1014-1027.

Sewell, William H. "Inequality of Opportunity for Higher Education." *American Sociological Review,* 36, October 1971, 793-809.

Turner, Ralph H. "Some Family Determinants of Ambition." *Sociology and Social Research,* 46, 1962, 397-411.

Turner, Ralph H. "One Neighborhood Context and College Plans." *American Sociological Review,* 31, October 1966, 698-702.

Significant Others

Alexander, C. Norman and Earnest Q. Campbell. "Peer Influences on Adolescent Educational Aspirations and Attainments." *American Sociological Review*, 29, August 1964, 568-575.

Bell, Gerald D. "Processes in the Formation of Adolescents' Aspirations." *Social Forces*, 42, December 1963, 179-186.

Bordua, David J. "Educational Aspirations and Parental Stress on College." *Social Forces*, 38, March 1960, 262-269.

Duncan, Otis Dudley, Archibald O. Haller and Alejandro Portes. "Peers' Influences on Aspirations: A Reinterpretation." *American Journal of Sociology*, 74, September 1968, 119-137.

Ellis, Robert A. and W. Clayton Lane. "Structural Supports for Upward Mobility." *American Sociological Review*, 28, October 1963, 743-756.

Haller, A.O. and C.E. Butterworth. "Peer Influences on Levels of Occupational and Educational Aspiration." *Social Forces*, 38, May 1960, 289-295.

Kahl, Joseph H. "Educational and Occupational Aspirations of 'Common-Man' Boys." *Harvard Educational Review*, 23, Summer 1953, 186-203.

Pavalko, Ronald M. and David R. Bishop, "Peer Influences on the College Plans of Canadian High School Students." *Canadian Review of Sociology and Anthropology*, 3, November 1966, 191-200.

Rehberg, Richard A. and David L. Westby. "Parental Encouragement, Occupation, Education and Family Size: Artifactual Expectations?" *Social Forces*, 45, March 1967, 362-374.

Sewell, William H. and Vimal P. Shah. "Social Class, Parental Encouragement and Educational Aspirations." *American Journal of Sociology*, 73, March 1968, 559-570.

Sewell, William H. and Vimal P. Shah. "Parents' Education and Children's Educational Aspirations and Achievement." *American Sociological Review*, 33, April 1968, 191-209.

Siemens, Leonard B. *The Influence of Selected Family Factors on the Educational and Occupational Aspirations of High School-Aged Youth*. Winnipeg: Faculty of Agriculture and Home Economics, University of Manitoba, 1965.

Toomey, Derek M. "Home-Centred Working Class Parents' Attitudes Towards Their Sons' Education and Careers." *Sociology*, 3, September 1969, 299-320.

School Variables

Boyle, R.P. "The Effect of High School on Student Aspirations." *American Journal of Sociology*, 71, May 1966, 628-639.

Breton, Raymond and J.C. McDonald. *Career Decisions of Canadian Youth: A Compilation of Basic Data*. Ottawa: Queen's Printer, 1967.

Breton, Raymond. "Academic Stratification in Secondary Schools and the Educational Plans of Students." *The Canadian Review of Sociology and Anthropology*, 7, February 1970, 17-34.

Breton, Raymond. *Social and Academic Factors in the Career Decisions of Canadian Youth.* Ottawa: Queen's Printer, 1972.

Coleman, James S. *The Adolescent Society: The Social Life of the Teenager and its Importance on Education.* New York: Free Press, 1961.

Coleman, James, et. al. "Equality of Educational Opportunity." Washington: U.S. Superintendent of Documents, 1966.

Forcese, Dennis P. and Leonard B. Siemans. *School Related Factors and the Aspiration Levels of Manitoba Senior High School Students.* Winnipeg: Faculty of Agriculture and Home Economics, University of Manitoba, 1965.

Heyns, Barbara. "Social Selection and Stratification Within Schools." *American Journal of Sociology*, 79, May 1974.

Krauss, Irving. "Sources of Educational Aspirations Among Working Class Youth." *American Sociological Review*, 29, December 1964, 867-879.

McDill, E.L., *et al.* "Institutional Effect on the Academic Behaviour of High School Students." *Sociology of Education*, 40, 1967, 181-199.

McDill, E.L., *et al.* "Educational Climates in High Schools: Their Effects and Sources." *American Journal of Sociology*, 74, 1969, 657-686.

Wilson, Mary D. "The Vocational Preferences of Secondary Modern School Children." *British Journal of Educational Psychology*, November 1953.

Self-Concept of Ability and Attitudes and Values

Brookover, Wilber B. *Self-Concept of Ability and School Achievement.* Michigan: Educational Publication Services, College of Education, Michigan State University, 1962.

Brookover, Wilber B., Shailer Thomas and Ann Paterson. "Self-Concept of Ability and School Achievement." *Sociology of Education*, Spring, 1964, 271-278.

Hyman, Herbert H. "The Value Systems of Different Classes: A Social-Psychological Contribution to the Analysis of Stratification," in Reinhard Bendix and Seymour Martin Lipset, eds., *Class, Status and Power.* Glencoe: Free Press, 1953.

Kahl, Joseph A. *The Measurement of Modernism.* Austin and London: University of Texas Press, 1968.

Rosen, Bernard. "The Achievement Syndrome: A Psychocultural Dimension of Social Stratification." *American Sociological Review*, 21, April 1956, 203-211.

Rosen, Bernard. "Race, Ethnicity and the Achievement Syndrome." *American Sociological Review*, 1959.

Rosenberg, Morris. *Society and the Adolescent Self-Image.* Princeton, N.J.: Princeton University Press, 1965.

Sasson, Ruth M., Archibald O. Haller and William H. Sewell. *Attitudes and Facilitation in the Attainment of Status.* Washington: American Sociological Association, 1972.

Strodtbeck, Fred L. "Family Interaction Values and Achievement," in David McClelland, *et al., Talent and Society.* Princeton: Van Nostrand, 1958.

Woelfel, Joseph and Archibald O. Haller. "Significant Others, the Self-reflective Act and the Attitude Formation Process." *American Sociological Review,* Vol. 36, No. 1, February 1971, 74-87.

Index

Academic achievement, meaning of, 160; *see* school performance
Adelson, Joseph, 212, 235n
Alexander, Karl L., 209n
Aristotle, 1, 10n
Aspirations Scolaires et Orientations Professionelles des Etudiants, 52
Atkinson, A.G., 92n

Bardwick, Judith M., 235n
Barnes, K.J., 92n
Barrados, Maria, 53n, 270, 272n, 273n, 291n, 314
Beauvoir, Simone de, 234n
Beland, François, 268, 269, 272n
Belanger, Pierre, xii, 268, 272n
Blalock, Herbert M., 38n
Blau, Peter M., 38n
Blishen, Bernard 53n, 92n, 93n, 155n, 181n, 273n, 291n, 319n
Blishen Class Scale, 44, 45, 96, 100, 107, 232, 240, 246, 296, 300
Bogue, Donald J., 92n
Bohan, Janis S., 235n
Boocock, Sarane S., 167, 179, 181n
Bordeleau, Gabriel, 272n
Borgatta, Ronald S., 310
Boudon, Raymond, 40, 41, 53n, 277, 291n
Bourdieu, Pierre, 9, 11n, 180n
Bowles, Samuel, 9, 11n, 180n
Breton, Raymond, xii, 49, 50, 53n, 87, 93n, 114, 115n, 196, 209n, 272n, 310n
Brookover, Wilbur B., 47, 53n, 118, 119, 121, 135n
Burchinal, Lee G., 92n

Cameron, David M., 184, 209n
Canadian Conference on Education, *1958*, 21
Clark, Samuel D., 92n
Cohen, Elizabeth, 238, 239, 255, 257n
Coleman, James, xi, 7, 11n, 36, 38n, 50, 148, 155n, 159, 179, 181n, 212, 235n
Colleges of Applied Arts and Technology, 22, 43, 86, 54, 114, 209n

Collins, Randall, 9, 11n
Combs, A.W., 120, 121, 136n
Commission on Post-Secondary Education in Ontario, 6, 22, 181n
Community Colleges, 42; aspirations to, 62
Contingency Repayment Assistance Program, 319n
Cook, Martha, 209n
Cooley, Charles H., 38n, 117, 135n
Cross, Kathryn Patricia, 235n
Curtis, James, 253, 257n

Davis, K., 9
Davis, William, 41
Dawson, R. MacGregor, 11n
Desjardins, Louis M., 272n
Douglas, James W.B., 52n, 180n
Douvan, Elizabeth, 212, 235n
Duncan, O.D., 38n, 310n

Education: expansion of post-secondary, 22; financial barriers to, 22; free and compulsory introduced, 20; parental attitude to, 52; streaming, 9-10, 182
Educational aspirations, 28, 29, 30, 31, 34, 35, 39, 42, 60 **and:** gender, 211ff; occupational aspirations, 99-100; school performance, 87-88, 174-176; school program, 84-87, 186-187, 200, 201, 205; self-concept of ability, 88, 121; significant others' influence, 145ff; social class, 57ff, 236-237 **by:** attitude scale on adult feminine role, 231; cultural enrichment and SES, 90; frequency of church attendance and sex, 76; influence of parents, 144, 146, 148; influence of peers, 145, 147, 149; religious affiliation and sex, 73; separate school attendance, 77; socio-economic status and number of children in family, 85; socio-economic status and sex, 66; urban-rural

location and sex, 66;
differences between males and
females, 55ff, 214-215, 318;
divergence from reality, 270,
286-287, 314; effects of working
mother, 216-217, 244-245; of
Franco-Ontarians, 265, 268, by:
social class, 267; immigrants,
79ff; lower-class students by:
educational level of mother
and father, 247; employment
status of mother, 244; family
cultural enrichment, 252; level
of lower-class status, 238, 240,
241; occupational status of
father's first full-time job, 244;
parental participation in
voluntary organizations, 253;
post-secondary experiences of
frequent family visitors 251;
school-reported grades, 255;
social class of grandfather, 242;
social class level of mother's
occupation, 245; total family
income, 250; making of, 54-93;
measurement of 42; model of
formation of, 31, 34, 298ff; role
of achievement in, 160; to
community college, 62; to
return to school of those who
left after grade 13, 291; validity
of use as surrogate measure of
educational attainment, 313-
315
Educational attainment:
comparison of Ontario and
U.S., 15; of Anglophone and
Francophone students, 270-271;
percentage of students in five-
year program and completing
grade 13 by SES and mental
ability, 289; percentage of
students who had completed
grade 13 and were in university
by SES and mental ability, 289;
probability of, with program
and social class controlled, 282;
probability of staying to year 5
or less by expectations in grade
8, 283; probability of staying to
year 5 or less by expectations
in grade 8 of university, 284;
and sex, 277; validity of using

educational aspirations as
surrogate measure of, 313-315;
urban-rural differences, 277
Educational expectations: difference
from aspirations, 60; and
school program, 199-201, 205;
see also educational aspirations
Educational opportunity, xi, 1-11,
298; accessibility, xiii, 158, 316,
317, 318; equality of: and
Franco-Ontarians, 251; rural
youth, 65-66; school programs,
200
Edwards, Hugh, 238, 257n
Empey, La Mar T., 106, 115n
Equality: in Upper Canada and
Ontario, 12-24; income
distribution, 14; in education,
157
Equality of condition, 1-6
Equality of opportunity, 4-6;
education as a means to, 6-10;
in Upper Canada and Ontario,
13-21; of educational
opportunity, 25
Erickson, Edsel L., 135n
Ethnicity and aspirations, 82-84;
and school performance, 171,
173
Etzioni, Amitai, 235n

Firestone, Shulamith, 234n
Fleming, William G., 181n, 183,
209n
Ford, C.R., 183
Francophone students, 258ff;
attitude to schoolwork of, 270-
271; educational attainment of,
270-271; and educational
opportunity, 259; in English
schools 83; family size of, 261;
mental ability of, 265; self-
concept of ability, 265; social
class, 261

Gasson, Ruth M., 38n
Gerth, H.H., 92n
Gilbert, Sidney N., 209n
Gintis, H., 9, 11n, 180n
Ginzberg, Eli, 214, 235n
Glaser, Nathan, 92n
Gnemin, Lawrence, 23n

Gordon, Chad, 116, 135n, 179
Gornick, Vivian, 234n
Gottlieb, D., 119, 135n
Guidance counsellors, 138, 139, 317
Guillet, Edwin, 16, 23n

Hall-Dennis Report: *see* Report of
   the Provincial Committee on
   Aims and Objectives of
   Education in the Schools of
   Ontario
Haller, A.O., 11n, 92n, 95, 96, 115n
Hartley, Ruth E., 235n
Harvey, Edward B., 235n
Hauser, Robert M., 38n, 310n
Hawkins, Freda, 92n
Henshal, Marie, 235n
Hoggart, Richard, 254, 255, 257n
Homans, George C., 38n
Houston, Susan E., 23n

Immigrants and aspirations, 79ff;
   bipolar character of, 81-82
Inequality of condition, 13

Jackson, Brian, 38n, 53n, 237, 254,
   255, 257
Jackson, R.W.B., xii
Jacobson, Lenore, 135n, 209n
Jencks, Christopher, 38n, 257n

Kahl, Joseph A., 116, 135n, 181n,
   237, 238, 239, 255, 257n
Kammeyer, Kenneth, 235n
Katz, Michael, 17, 23n
Klein, Viola, 235n
Komarovsky, Mirra, 212, 235n
Kraus, Irving 238, 257n

LaForce, Louise, 268, 269, 272n
Lagacé, M.D., 235n
Land, Kenneth C., 310n
Lavin, David E., 167, 181n
Lecky, W.E.H., 10n
Lewin, Kurt, 92n
Lipset, Seymour M., 93n
Locke, John, 2, 10n
Lucas, Rex, 64, 92n

Maccoby, Eleanor E., 212, 235n
Macpherson, C.B., 10n, 12, 23n
Mann, Horace, 15
Marsden, Denis, 38n, 53n, 237, 254,
   255, 257n

Marsden, Lorna R., 235n
Marshall, T.H., 180n
Maslove, Allan M., 12, 14, 23n
Massey, Vincent, 19
McDill, Edward, 209n
McFarlane, Bruce A., 235n
McRoberts, Hugh A., 91n, 209n,
   291n
Mead, George Herbert, 118, 135n
Mental ability, 40, 313; and
   aspirations, 61ff; in a causal
   model, 296; and educational
   attainment, 275, 289; of
   Franco-Ontarians, 265; and
   occupational expectations, 109-
   111; and school performance,
   168-169; and school program,
   167, 189, 191, 204; and self-
   concept of ability, 126; and
   significant others' influence,
   144-149
Meritocracy, 156, 157, 158
Miller, Irwin, 95, 96, 115n
Millett, Kate, 235n
Mills, C. Wright, 92n
Moore, W.E., 9
Moran, Barbara K., 234n
Moynahan, Daniel P., 92n
Myrdal, Alva, 235n

Naegele, Kasper D., 93n
Niebuhr, H. Richard, 92n

Occupational aspirations and
   expectations, 95ff; difference
   between, 102-103; differences
   between sexes, 98-99, 106-107;
   and self-concept of ability, 112;
   and social class, 104ff; *see also*
   occupational expectations
Occupational expectations
   and: attitude to adult feminine
   role, 231-232, 234; school
   performance, 174-177
   by: mental ability, SES and sex,
   110, 112; program, SES and sex,
   113; self-concept of ability,
   mental ability and sex, 111-112;
   SES, 105, 108; *see also*
   occupational aspirations
Occupational mobility, 107, 109
Ontario Department of Education
   Circular H.S.I., *1967*, 53n

Ontario Educational Association, 16, 18
Ontario Report of the Minister of Education, *1971*, 91n, 92n
Ontario Student Awards Program (OSAP), 22
Ostry, S., 235n

Parsons, Talcott, 38n
Passerson, Jean-Claude, 180n
Path analysis, 292ff
Pedersen, E., 268
Peitchinis, Stephen, 9, 11n
Piaget, Jean, 38n
Pineo, Peter C., 92n
Porter John, 53n, 92n, 115n, 181n, 235n, 273n, 292n, 319n
Portes, Alejandro, 116, 122, 135n, 136n
Post-industrialism, 22, 26
Prentice, Alison, 16, 17, 23n
Putman, J.H., 23n

Questionnaire, 40; student, 42-50; parent, 50-52

Raimy, V.C., 118, 135n
Religion, 18, 45
    and: educational aspirations, 69ff; school program, 78; school performance, 171; SES, 72
Reorganized Program, 21, 49, 184
Report of the Committee on the Future Role of the Universities in Ontario, 315, 319n
Report of the Provincial Committee on Aims and Objectives of Education in the Schools of Ontario, 181n, 197, 209n
Report of the Royal Commission on Education in Ontario, *1950*, 21, 24n
Report of the Special Program Review, 319n
Richardson, Ellen, 92n
Richmond, Anthony H., 92n
Robarts Plan:
    see Reorganized Program
Rocher, Guy, xii, 268, 269, 272n
Rosen, Bernard, 167, 181n
Rosenthal, Robert, 135n, 209n
Ross, Jean M., 180n

Royal Commission on Bilingualism and Biculturalism, 92n, 93n, 259, 260, 264, 272, 272n
Royal Commission on the Status of Women in Canada, 234n, 318
Russell, Bertrand, 10n
Ryerson, Egerton, 1, 15, 16, 17, 18, 23n

Sample survey, 39-42, 259
Scharr, John H., 4, 8, 11n
School performance, 156ff, 312
    and: aspirations, 87-88, 160, 174-176, 255; attitude to schoolwork, 178; ethnicity, 171; mental ability, 163; occupational expectations 174-177; parental influence, 178-180; programs, 161-162, 166, 281; religion, 171; school attainment, 275; self-concept of ability, 125, 178
    by: mental ability and sex, 164, 165, 168, 169; personal attitudes, 174, 175; selected background characteristics, 172-173; in causal model, 297ff; differences between boys and girls, 162-163, 227; measurement of, 49-50, 160, 161
School programs, 32, 40, 49-50, 182ff, 312; abandonment of, 158; allocation to, 196-198
    and: educational aspirations, 84-87, 186-187, 200; educational expectations, 199-201, 205; educational opportunity, 186, 200; father's education, 194; mental ability, 167, 189, 191, 204; occupational expectations, 114; probabilities of school attainment, 278; school performance, 161-162, 166, 202-203; self-concept of ability, 123, 124; SES, 190-193, 203; sex, 187; significant others' influence, 150, 151, 152
    by: aspirations, 201; father's education, 194; grade, aspirations, branch and sex, 186, 188, 205; grades in quartiles, 202; highest grade which respondent expects to

complete in high school, 199;
mental ability, 190, 191, 204;
SES, 192, 193, 203; criteria in
assigning students to, 197; five-
year Arts and Sciences vs. all
others, 195; probabilities of
taking five-year program with
school performance and social
class controlled, 279-281;
selection by SES, 206, 207, 208

Schoolwork, attitudes to: of Franco-
Ontarians, 265; of girls, 227;
measurement of, 48; rural-
urban differences, 69

Self-concept of ability, 27, 116ff
and: achievement in school,
159, 178; educational
aspirations, 88, 121; learning,
118-120; occupational
aspirations, 112; significant
others' influence, 130-133
by: effect of complaints, 134;
help from significant others,
132; mental ability, programs
and sex, 126; parental
influence, 127; perceived
father's aspirations, 131;
perceived mother's aspirations,
130; program, 123, 124; school
performance, 125; teacher's
influence, 129; in a causal
model, 297ff, 312; difference
between males and females,
116ff, 213-214; of Franco-
Ontarians, 265; of girls, 225-
227; measurement of, 47-48

Sewell, W.H., 11n, 50, 53n, 92n,
181n

Sex, 210ff; aspirations of girls *by*:
mother's level of education,
218-219; parental educational
aspirations, 220-223; attitudes
to adult feminine role, 48-49,
52, 55, 223-224, 228-230; and
educational aspirations, 230-
231; and occupational
expectations, 231-232, 234; sex
differences *in*: educational
aspirations by correlations with
mother's educational
aspirations, 222; by mother's
level of education, 219; by size
of family, 221; formation of

aspirations, 98-99, 106-107;
school attainment, 277; school
performance, 162-163, 227; self-
concept of ability, 116ff, 226-
227

Shah, Vimal R., 53n

Shauss, M.A., 11n

Significant others' influence, 32, 36,
37, 137ff, 312
and: educational aspirations,
145-149; program, 151-152; self-
concept of ability, 130-133;
social class, 138-142; in a causal
model, 297ff; degree of
influence, 142-147; on school
performance, 178-180; source of
family assistance by SES, 150,
151

Silberman, Charles, 6, 11n

Simpson, Howard R., 180n

Skinner, B.F., 38n

Smith, Adam, 2, 10n

Snygg, D., 120, 121, 136n

Social class, advantages of middle-
class children over working-
class children in schools, 9
and: cultural enrichment, 88-
90, 253; educational
aspirations, 57ff, 236-237;
educational inequality, 311;
occupational ambitions, 104ff;
school attainment, 275-276,
282; significant others'
influence, 138-142; barriers for
lower-class children, 19;
educational class system, 17;
lower-class students with high
educational aspirations, 236ff;
measurement of, 44; *see also*
socio-economic status

Socialization, 25-28, 117, 154;
differences between boys and
girls, 211-213; of girls, 211

Socio-cultural climates, 32

Socio-economic status (SES) 312,
313
and: cultural enrichment, 90;
educational aspirations, 21,
58ff; mental ability, 47;
occupational expectations, 105,
108; program selection, 206,
207, 208; religion, 72; school
performance, 167-171; school

program, 21, 190-193, 203, 205;
significant others' influence,
140-150; *see also* social class
Strodbeck, Fred, L., 38n
Sutherland, Neil, 23n
Symbolic interaction theory, 25-28,
117, 125, 160

Titmuss, Richard, 6, 38n
Tocqueville Alexis de, 2, 10n
Turner, Ralph, 107, 115n, 167, 235n

Universal Declaration of Human
Rights, 3, 6
Urbanization and attitudes to
schoolwork, 69; and
educational aspirations, 64ff;
and school attainment, 277;
measurement of, 45; urban-
rural differences, 69

Variables, dependent and
independent, 30-36; attitudinal,
47-49; demographic, 46-47;
dependent, 42-44; independent,
44-46, school, 49-50; significant
others, 47

Warren, Bruce L., 92n
Weber, Max, 92n
Whyte, Donald, 64, 92n
Wilensky, Harold, 238, 243, 257n
Wilson, Alan B., 116, 122, 135n,
136n
Wilson, Donald, 23n
Women: changing role, 27; adult
feminine role, 27; *see also* sex
Wylie, Ruth C., 135n

Young, Michael, 5, 11n, 180n